Laws in the Bible
and in Early Rabbinic Collections

Laws in the Bible
and in Early Rabbinic Collections

The Legal Legacy of the Ancient Near East

SAMUEL GREENGUS

CASCADE *Books* · Eugene, Oregon

LAWS IN THE BIBLE AND IN EARLY RABBINIC COLLECTIONS
The Legal Legacy of the Ancient Near East

Cascade Books
An Imprint of Wipf and Stock Publishers
199 W. 8th Ave., Suite 3
Eugene, OR 97401

www.wipfandstock.com

ISBN 13: 978-1-60899-946-0

Cataloging-in-Publication data:

Greengus, Samuel.

   Laws in the Bible and in early rabbinic collections : the legal legacy of the ancient Near East / Samuel Greengus.

   xx + 334 pp.; 25.4 cm.—Includes bibliographical references and indexes.

   ISBN 13: 978-1-60899-946-0

   1. Bible. O.T.—Criticism, interpretation, etc. 2. Law (Theology)—Biblical teaching. 3. Jewish law—History. 4. Law, Ancient. 5. Comparative law. I. Title.

BS1199 L3 G7 2011

Manufactured in the USA.

For Lesha

Contents

Contents

Preface

HAVING TAUGHT IN A seminary for many decades, I fully appreciate that the Bible will most often be read in terms of what it says to contemporary readers. Today's readings will claim a place, alongside of the many centuries of previous biblical study by rabbis, preachers, priests, pastors, and scholars. Yet I firmly believe that it is also meaningful to think about how the words of the Bible might have been heard and understood by the ancient Israelites, to whom they were originally addressed. I believe that consideration of this "ancient setting" is valuable in reading the text even today, as one searches for new inspiration and contemporary meanings.

In order to recover and reanimate the ancient environment, I join with other scholars and have devoted years of study to the literatures of the ancient Near East that were written during biblical and pre-biblical times. My particular focus has been on the study of the social institutions, as illustrated by the ancient laws and related legal materials of the ancient Near East that were written during those times. I have of course also continued my study of the Bible and of post-biblical Jewish writings, which interpret the Hebrew Bible and Jewish law. Through these studies, I am better able to visualize the spectrum of laws, legal practices, and attitudes on law and ethical conduct that existed in biblical and non-biblical societies during those centuries.

In this book I focus upon an important group of biblical and early rabbinic laws within the ancient spectrum. I look at biblical laws for which there are laws on the same themes preserved in the ancient Near Eastern "law codes." I also examine an important group of early rabbinic laws for which there are likewise laws in the ancient Near Eastern "law codes" on the same themes. Although these rabbinic laws are not found in the Bible, these rabbinic laws are nevertheless very old and clearly go back to pre-biblical times. One does in fact find evidence of their themes and content within the Bible, outside of the formal law statements.

I tried to write this book in a style and format that will be accessible to non-specialists, as well as to students and scholars. The presentation and discussion is designed to allow all readers to experience the ancient sources in as direct a fashion as possible. I strongly believe in the primacy of using original sources; and I have championed and practiced this mode of teaching throughout my entire career. To my mind, original sources supply the most reliable basis for independent analysis and interpretation—whether by scholars or by laymen. I have endeavored to put my readers in a position to do this.

All key ancient texts are given in translations that look to reflect the original wording or as closely as possible, within the framework of proper English usage. References to original languages are kept to an absolute minimum, restricted to passages where problems impact our ability to translate. (Scholarly readers will be able to access the original sources on their own if they need to do so.) I have also added footnotes. Their purpose is to provide reference data and links to supporting data, or they will point to discussions by other scholars that I believe may be important or useful to those who might want or need "to know more." The notes are generally short and are not intended to interrupt the main discourse.

A Historical Timeline and Appendix supply additional background for non-specialist readers on the historical periods and the ancient literatures, which are discussed in this book. The bibliography reflects my goal of using accessible materials, e.g., dictionary and encyclopedia articles by respected scholars, giving preference to reference works in English where possible.

I try to write in a non-polemical fashion. From time to time, mostly in footnotes, I do mention biblical or other references, as well as the writings of scholars. This is done both to indicate support for what I have written, and sometimes to note problematic data or differing opinions. However, this book is not intended to be a summary of everything that has been said before. I have used it as a vehicle to present my own best interpretations of the laws. Many of the ideas have in fact not been presented before by me or, to the best of my knowledge, by others. The larger goal of this book is to promote consideration of the ancient Near Eastern comparative evidence into the exegetical study of Christians, Jews, and others who are interested in close study of the Bible text and who are ready to think about how biblical—and certain rabbinic—laws emerged out of the ancient environments, which created them.

Acknowledgments

MY WORK ON THIS book has benefitted from the help and encouragement of many persons. Foremost among them is my wife, Lesha B. Greengus, to whom this book is dedicated. For years she has urged me to write a serious book, based on cherished research that, at the same time, could be read and understood by nonspecialists. I have tried in this book to meet that goal. As the manuscript developed, I received invaluable input from my daughter, Rachel E. G. Schultz, who, as a physician and student of literature, read it carefully and critically. She constantly challenged me to write better and more clearly if I hoped to reach out to nonspecialists like her as well as to more learned readers. I also gained from having parts of the manuscript read by my longtime friend, Norman Kantor and his wife Donna Steele—also non-specialists, students of English literature, who have had long careers in advertising.

There are a number of established scholars who assisted me by reading through all or parts of the manuscript. I turned to them because of their expertise in fields of study and research that are included in the book, especially Bible, rabbinic literature, Roman law, and history of law. I am deeply grateful to David H. Aaron, Richard S. Sarason, Archie J. Christopherson, and Gordon A. Christenson. They are of course not to be held in any way responsible for errors and oversights that may have remained in my manuscript.

I have benefited from many published resources in the writing of this book and have been thankful to have them. I have regularly consulted respected translations of the Hebrew Bible, notably the NRSV and the NJPS. I have indicated all verbatim quotations from these editions; and any explanatory words that I have added are given in square brackets. In all other Hebrew and Aramaic passages, biblical, targumic, and rabbinic, etc., I have supplied my own translations. I have worked from the best editions of these original works. English translations are available for some of the rabbinic works cited; a few are mentioned within the book and in my bibliography. For the Septuagint, I have relied upon *A New English Translation of the Septuagint and Other Greek Translations Traditionally Included Under That Title*, edited by Albert Pietersma and Benjamin G. Wright. For Sumerian and Akkadian laws I have regularly consulted Martha Roth, *Law Collections from Mesopotamia and Asia Minor*. I have generally relied upon the transliterations given there, except where indicated. However, the English translations of all Sumerian and Akkadian texts are my own. For Hittite, I have fully relied upon Harry A. Hoffner, Jr. *The Laws of the Hittites: A Critical Edition*; any departures from Hoffner's edition are described in the footnotes.

Abbreviations

A.	Sigla for cuneiform tablet in various museum collections
AB	Anchor Bible
AbB	*Altbabylonische Briefe in Umschrift und Übersetzung.* Edited by F. R. Kraus. Leiden: Brill, 1964–
ABD	*The Anchor Bible Dictionary.* Edited by David Noel Freedman. 6 vols. New York: Doubleday, 1992
ADD	*Assyrian Deeds and Documents.* Edited by C. H. W. Johns. 4 vols. Cambridge: Deighton, Bell, 1898–1923
AfO	*Archive für Orientforschung*
AHw	*Akkadisches Handwörterbuch.* Edited by Wolfram von Soden. 3 vols. Wiesbaden: Harrassowitz, 1965–1981
AnOr	Analecta Orientalia
Ant.	*Jewish Antiquities*
AOAT	Alter Orient und Altes Testament
AOS	American Oriental Society
ARM	Archives royales de Mari
AMT	R. Campbell Thompson, *Assyrian Medical Texts from Originals in the British Museum.* London: Oxford University Press, 1923
ANET	*Ancient Near Eastern Texts Relating to the Old Testament.* 3rd ed. Edited by James B. Pritchard. Princeton: Princeton University, 1969
Arakh.	*Arakhin*
AS	Assyriological Studies
B.	*Bava*
b.	*Babylonian Talmud*
BaghM	*Baghdader Mitteilungen*
B. Bat.	*Bava Batra*
BBSt	*Babylonian Boundary-Stones and Memorial Tablets.* 2 vols. (with portfolio of plates). London: Sold at the British Museum, etc., 1912
BE	The Babylonian Expedition of the University of Pennsylvania. Series A: Cuneiform Texts
Bekh.	*Bekhorot*

Bekhor Shor	(Joseph ben Isaac) *Commentary of Rabbi Joseph Bekhor Shor on the Torah*. Edited by Yehoshafat Nebo. Jerusalem: Mosad Harav Kook, 1994 [Hebrew]
Ber.	*Berakhot*
BIN	*Babylonian Inscriptions in the Collection of James B. Nies*
B. Metz.	*Bava Metzi'a*
CAD	*The Assyrian Dictionary of the Oriental Institute of the University of Chicago*. Chicago, 1956–2010.
CANE	*Civilizations of the Ancient Near East*. Edited by Jack M. Sasson. 4 vols. New York: Scribner, 1995
CT	*Cuneiform Texts from Tablets in the British Museum*
D	*The Digest of Justinian*. Translated and edited by Alan Watson. 2 vols. Rev. ed. Philadelphia: University of Pennsylvania Press, 1998
Der. Er. Rab.	*Derekh Eretz Rabbah*
Ed.	*Eduyoth*
EncJud	*Encylopedia Judaica*. Edited by Cecil Roth et. al. 16 vols. Jerusalem: Keter, 1972
ERE	*Encyclopedia of Religion and Ethics*. Edited by James Hastings et al. 13 vols. New York: Scribner, 1908–1927
ErIsr	*Eretz Israel*
FLP	Free Library of Philadelphia
Gaius, *Inst.*	*The Institutes of Gaius*. Part I: *Text with Critical Notes and Translation*, by Francis De Zulueta. Oxford: Clarendon, 1946
Git.	*Gittin*
H.	Hatra
HALOT	Ludwig Koehler, Walter Baumgartner, and J. J. Stamm, *The Hebrew and Aramaic Lexicon of the Old Testament*. Translated and edited under the supervision of M. E. J. Richardson. 4 vols. Leiden: Brill, 1994–1999
Hazzequni	*Commentary on the Torah of Hezekiah ben Manoah*. Edited by H. D. Chavel. Jerusalem: Mosad Harav Kook, 1981 [Hebrew]
HSCP	*Harvard Studies in Classical Philology*
HUCA	*Hebrew Union College Annual*
Hul.	*Hullin*
Ibn Ezra	*Commentary on the Torah of Abraham Ibn Ezra*. Edited by Asher Vaizer. 3 vols. Jerusalem: Mosad Harav Kook, 1976 [Hebrew]
Ibn Kaspi, Joseph.	*Mishna Kesef*. Edited by Isaac Halevy Last. 2 vols. 1905/6. Reprinted. Jerusalem: Sifrit Mekorot, 1969 [Hebrew]
ICC	International Critical Commentary
IOS	*Israel Oriental Society*

IM	Iraq Museum
j.	*Jerusalem (i.e., Palestinian) Talmud*
JAOS	*Journal of the American Oriental Society*
Jastrow, Dictionary	Marcus Jastrow, *Dictionary of Talmud Babli, Yerushalmi, Midrashic Literature and Targumim.* 2 vols. 1903. Reprint, New York: Pardes, 1950
JCS	*Journal of Cuneiform Studies*
JE	*The Jewish Encyclopedia.* Edited by Isidore Singer. 12 vols. New York: Funk & Wagnalls, 1907
JEN	Joint Expedition with the Iraq Museum at Nuzi
JENu	Joint Expedition with the Iraq Museum at Nuzi, unpublished
JEOL	*Jaarbericht van het Vooraziatisch-Egyptisch Gezelschap (Genoot-schap) Ex oriente lux*
JESHO	*Journal of the Economic and Social History of the Orient*
JJP	*Journal of Juristic Papyrology*
JJS	*Journal of Jewish Studies*
JNSL	*Journal of Northwest Semitic Languages*
Josephus, *Ant.*	*Jewish Antiquities*
JSOT	*Journal for the Study of the Old Testament*
JSOTSup	Journal for the Study of the Old Testament Supplement Series
JSS	*Journal of Semitic Studies*
K	Tablets in the Kouyunjik collection of the British Museum
KAJ	*Keilschrifttexte aus Assur Juristischen Inhalts,* copied and edited by Erich Ebeling. Wissenschaftliche Veröffenlichung der Deutschen Orient-Gesellschaft 50. Leipzig: Hinrichs, 1927
KBo	*Keilschrifttexte aus Boghazköi.* Wissenschaftliche Veröfflichungen der deutschen Orientgesellschaft 30, 36, 68–70, 72–73, 77–80, 82–86, 89–90. Leipzig: Harrassowitz, 1916–
Ker.	*Keritot*
Ket.	*Ketubbot*
Kil.	*Kil'ayim*
KJV	King James Version
LCL	Loeb Classical Library
Lieberman	*Tosefta.* Edited by Saul Lieberman. New York: Jewish Theological Seminary of America, 1955–83 [Hebrew]
LXX	Septuagint
m.	*Mishnah*
Maimonides, Guide	Maimonides, Moses. *The Guide of the Perplexed.* Translated and with Notes by Shlomo Pines. 2 vols. Chicago: University of Chicago Press, 1963

Makk.	*Makkot*
Maksh.	*Makshirin*
MARI	*Mari: Annales de recherches interdisciplinaires*
Meg.	*Megillah*
Meʿil.	*Meʿilah*
Mekhilta	*Mekhilta of Rabbi Ishmael.* Edited by S. H. Horovitz and, after his death by Abraham Rabin. Frankfurt: Kauffmann, 1970. Reprinted, Jerusalem: Sifre Vahrman, 1970 [Hebrew]
Metz.	*Metziʿa*
MHET	Mesopotamian History and Environment. Texts
MSL	*Materialen zum sumerischen Lexikon.* Edited by Benno Landsberger et al. Rome: Pontifical Biblical Institute, 1937–
MT	Massoretic Text (i.e., the traditional, received Hebrew text of the Bible)
Nahmanides	[Moses ben Nahman] *Commentary on the Torah.* Edited by H. D. Chavel, 2 vols. Jerusalem: Mosad Harav Kook, 1962–1963 [Hebrew]
Ned.	*Nedarim*
Nid.	*Niddah*
NJPS	*Tanakh: The Holy Scriptures: the New JPS Translation according to the Traditional Hebrew Text*
NRSV	New Revised Standard Version
NSG	Adam Falkenstein, *Die neusumerische Gerichtsurkunden.* 2 vols. Abhandlungen der Bayerische Akademie der Wissenschaften n.s. vols. 39–40. Munich: Bayerischen Akademie, 1956
NT	New Testament
OED	*Oxford English Dictionary.* 2nd ed. 20 vols. Oxford: Oxford University Press, 1989
PAAJR	*Proceedings of the American Academy of Jewish Research*
PBS	Publications of the Babylonian Section, University Museum, University of Pennsylavania
PSD	*The Sumerian Dictionary of the University Museum of the University of Pennsylvania.* Edited by Åke Sjöberg, with the Collaboration of Hermann Behrens et al. Philadelphia: Babylonian Section of the University Museum, 1984–
Q	Qumran Document
Qam.	*Qamma*
Qidd.	*Qiddushin*

Qimhi	*Commentary on the Torah of David Qimhi*, edited by Mordekhai L. Katsenelenbogen. In *Torat Hayim. Pentatueuch. Aleppo Codex*. Edited by Mordecai Breuer, Joseph Kafaḥ, Mordekhai L. Katsenelenbogen. 6 vols. Jerusalem: Mosad Harav Kook, 1986 [Hebrew]
R.	Rabbi
R	British Museum. *The Cuneiform Inscriptions of Western Asia*. Prepared for publication by H. C. Rawlinson et al. 5 vols. London: Lithographed by R. E. Bowler, 1861–1884
RA	*Revue d'assyriologie et d' archéologie orientale*
Rashbam	(Rabbi Samuel ben Meir) *Commentary of the Rashbam on the Torah*. Edited by A. I. Bromberg based upon ms. published by David Rosin 1881 in Breslau. Tel Aviv: Sifriyati, 1964 [Hebrew]
Rashi	(Rabbi Solomon ben Isaac) *Commentary on the Torah*. Rev. ed. Edited by H. D. Chavel. Jerusalem: Mosad Harav Kook, 1982 [Hebrew]
RB	*Revue Biblique*
RIDA	*Revue internationale des droits de l'antiquité*
RlA	*Reallexicon der Assyriologie*. Edited by Erich Ebeling et al. Berlin, 1928–
Rm.	Rassam, Tablets in the Collection of the British Museum
RS	Ras Shamra
Saadia	(Saadia ben Joseph) *Commentary of R. Saadia Gaon on the Torah*. Edited by Yosef Kapaḥ. Jerusalem: Mosad Harav Kook, 1963 [Hebrew]
SAAS	State Archives of Assyria Studies
Sanh.	*Sanhedrin*
SBAW	Sitzungenberichte der bayerischen Akademie der Wissenschaften
SBL	Society of Biblical Literature
SBLRBS	Society of Biblical Literature Resources for Biblical Study
SBLWAWS	Society of Biblical Literature Writings from the Ancient World Series
Septuagint	*A New English Translation of the Septuagint and Other Greek Translations Traditionally Included under that Title*. Edited by Albert Pietersma and Benjamin G. Wright. Translated by Albert Pietersma, Benjamin G. Wright et al. Oxford: Oxford University Press, 2007
Shabb.	*Shabbat*
Shev.	*Shevi'it*
Shevu.	*Shevu'ot*
Sifra	*Commentar zu Leviticus*. Edited by Isaac Hirsch Weiss. Vienna: Jacob Schlossberg, 1862 [Hebrew]

Sifre D	*Sifre on Deuteronomy.* Edited by Louis Finkelstein incorporating contributions of H. S. Horovitz. New York: Jewish Theological Seminary of America, 1969. First published 1939 in Berlin by Gesellschaft zur Förderung der Wissenschaft des Judentums [Hebrew]
Sifre N	*Sifre.* Numbers. Schriften herausgegeben von der Gesellschaft zur Förderung der Wissenschaft des Judentums. Edited by H. S. Horovitz. 1917. Reprinted, Jerusalem: Sifre Vahrman, 1966 [Hebrew]
Sforno	(Obadiah ben Jacob Sforno) *Commentary of R .Obadiah Sforno on the Torah.* Edited by Avraham Darom and Wolf Gottlieb, Jerusalem: Mosad Harav Kook, 1980 [Hebrew]
Spec. Laws	*Special Laws*
t.	*Tosefta*
Ta'an.	*Ta'anit*
TCL	Textes cunéiforms, Musée du Louvre
Theodosian Code	Clyde Pharr, Theresa Sherrer Davidson, and Mary Brown Pharr. *The Theodosian Code and Novels and the Sirmondian Constitutions.* 1952. Reprinted, Union, NJ: Lawbook Exchange, 2001
Tem.	*Temurah*
Ter.	*Terumot*
TIM	Texts in the Iraq Museum
UCP	University of California Publications in Semitic Philology
UET	Ur Excavation Text
UM	Tablets in the collections of the University Museum of the University of Pennsylvania, Philadelphia
USDA ERS	United States Department of Agriculture Economic Research Service
VAB	Vorderasiatische Bibliothek
VTSup	Vetus Testamentum Supplements
W	Tablet, Warka Excavations
XII Tab.	*The Twelve Tables*
Yad.	*Yadayim*
Yebam.	*Yebamot*
YOS	Yale Oriental Series, Texts
ZA	*Zeitschrift für Assyriologie*
ZAR	*Zeitschrift für altorientalische und biblische Rechtsgeschichte*
ZAW	*Zeitschrift für alttestamentliche Wissenschaft*
Zuckermandel	*Tosephta.* Based on Erfuhrt and Vienna Codices. Edited by M.S. Zuckermandel with "Supplement to the Tosephta" by Saul Lieberman. 2nd ed. Jerusalem: Bamberger & Wahrmann, 1937 [Hebrew]

Introduction

WHAT I HOPE TO accomplish in this study is to focus attention on the historical relationship that existed between the biblical, rabbinic, and ancient Near Eastern law collections. I believe that exploring this relationship should play a primary role in the study and interpretation of the biblical laws as well as of certain early rabbinic laws, enabling us to achieve a perspective on their fundamental level of meaning, closest to what the ancient peoples themselves may have understood these laws to say in their own time and setting. This study, in some places, will also provide a glimpse of how the biblical writers and later rabbis reshaped older laws in ways that, to their understanding, would more adequately reflect divine will and expectations for moral and ethical human conduct. It is my hope that this study will be of value to the larger exploration and reconstruction of the biblical, rabbinic, and ancient Near Eastern legal systems.

In the Hebrew Bible, laws are framed as divine commands, whose observance is required for the progress of human life and society. Already at the beginning of human history, Adam and Eve, Noah, and Abraham received divine instructions and commands; and, as a climax, Moses receives larger bodies of formal laws in the wilderness after the Exodus.[1]

Although the biblical laws are said to be of divine origin, they were not considered so extraordinary as to be beyond human comprehension and attainment; Deut 30:11–14 therefore states:

> Surely, this instruction, which I enjoin upon you this day, is not too baffling for you, nor is it beyond reach. It is not in the heavens, that you should say, "Who among us can go up to the heavens and get it for us and impart it to us, that we may observe it?" Neither is it beyond the sea, that you should say, "Who among us can cross to the other side of the sea and get it for us and impart it to us, that we may observe it?" No, the thing is very close to you, in your mouth and in your heart, to observe it. (NJPS)

In other words: the divinely endorsed laws were related to human history and experience; and, as such, a good deal of what they mandated was already familiar to the ancient Israelites. This is because a substantial part of biblical law was based upon pre-existing Near Eastern laws.[2]

26:2–5. Moses receives the law in many places; major biblical collections connected to Moses are: "the Book of the Covenant" (Exod 20:23—23:19) following the Decalogue (Exod 20:1–17//Deut 5:6–21); the so-called "Cultic Decalogue" (Exod 34:10–27); the "Holiness Code" (Lev 17–26); and the Deuteronomic laws (Deut 12–26).

2. The pre-existing heritage of laws was intuited by the medieval rabbis; Rashbam—followed by

1. See Adam and Eve in Gen 1:28–30 and 2:16–17; Noah in Gen 9:1–7; and Abraham in Gen

1

There are ancient Near Eastern laws that bear remarkable resemblance to biblical laws contained in the Hebrew Scriptures and, to a lesser extent, to a number of early rabbinic laws. These rabbinic laws are not found in the Hebrew Bible, but are contained in the so called "Oral Law," the Mishnah and Tosefta, which were codified later than the Hebrew Scriptures, as well as in the *baraitot* (sg. *baraita),* which survive only in scattered citations mentioned in the Talmud.[3] These "ancient" rabbinic laws, which resemble the ancient Near Eastern laws, were evidently carried over from biblical times even though they were formally codified at a much later time. Their absence from the Hebrew Bible is not in itself a problem, since in every one of these literatures we are dealing with excerpts or perhaps even "fragments" out of a much larger body of material that once existed in these ancient societies.[4] The extensive similarities that are now evident to us from the surviving ancient writings—biblical, early rabbinic, and Near Eastern—make this present study both possible and necessary, and provide us with valuable insights into what the ancient law systems were all about.[5]

For many centuries, the ancient Near Eastern laws were unknown because all formal knowledge and study of ancient Near Eastern laws disappeared with the abandonment of cuneiform writing sometime after the first century CE. The ancient Near Eastern laws were forgotten. But during the past century, archaeological excavations uncovered documents recording many ancient Near Eastern laws. The most important of these discoveries are collections of laws, which were anciently written down at the behest of rulers who were sovereign over the ancient lands of Sumer, Babylonia, Assyria, and Hatti (the homeland of the Hittites).

Biblical laws, on the other hand, continued to be taught and interpreted in postbiblical epochs as part of rabbinic Jewish law, which continued through Roman and medieval times, even up to the present day. The present study, however, is centered on the biblical period and seeks to create perspective on how our focus group of biblical—and certain early rabbinic laws—might have instructed Jews in ancient times, before later authorities and exegetes re-read and further interpreted them. In order to recover the "voices" of the ancient Near Eastern world, we must attempt to "peel away" the layers of

---

Hazzequni, Qimhi and Nahmanides—in his commentary to Gen 26:5 noted the existence of "well-accepted laws, like theft, adultery, covetousness, civil laws, and hospitality for guests, all of which were observed before the giving of the Torah but were repeated and elaborated to the Israelites [at Sinai where] they entered a covenant to fulfill them." See Lockshin, *Rabbi Samuel ben Meir's Commentary on Genesis,* 141–42.

3. The term "Mishnah" denotes "repetition," apparently of orally transmitted teachings. "Tosefta" denotes "supplement," usually understood to be supplementary legal material not found in the Mishnah; the term *baraita* (pl. *baraitot*) refers to "external," i.e., law formulations not included in the Mishnah, although at times these laws are mirrored in the Tosefta. See Strack and Stemberger, *Introduction,* 35–49, 171–77.

4. This point is elaborated upon in Greengus, "Law," 243–44. Westbrook, "Codification and Canonization," notes a tendency to look at law collections as if they were exhaustive in nature.

5. At this point it may prove useful to the reader to peruse the Appendix and Historical Timeline while proceeding further in this Introduction. The Appendix and Timeline may also be useful to the reader while reading other parts of this book. A list of the major ancient Near Eastern laws appears in the Timeline; for more details see Preface. The paucity of legal materials from Egypt and my use of available sources are discussed in the Appendix.

interpretation that come from later centuries, which at times changed or obscured the "original" meanings. This is a critical necessity when reading biblical and "ancient" rabbinic texts, which have been subject to continuing religious reinterpretation since they were written down, over two thousand or more years ago.

Exegetes of many faiths have extensively studied the biblical laws and commented upon them. But in Judaism particularly we see an extraordinarily strong focus upon the written laws and a deeply felt need to bring the older texts in line with evolving postbiblical life and practice. To achieve conceptual harmony, the rabbis presented their interpretations in a seamless interface with the ancient biblical texts. For them, law was religiously definitive, the basis of their covenant with God, unlike, e.g., in Christianity, where the "Old Testament" could be more easily or overtly set aside, superseded by newer teachings or interpretations.

This endeavor will not ignore all later exegesis. However, in reading the laws of the Hebrew Scriptures, we can only base our understanding upon what the rabbis long ago termed the "plain meaning" or *peshat* of Scriptures. This "original" understanding, at times, may differ from authoritative rabbinic (or other) legal readings that later developed. Even the rabbis themselves have long recognized the existence of such differences.[6] One

may cite here as an example the statement of Rashbam (Rabbi Samuel ben Meir c. 1050 CE) where he states his goal of expressing the plain meaning of the text, while at the same time bowing to the religious authority of the rabbis who may have ignored or overridden this very content: "I will explain the laws and rules [of the Torah] in a manner that conforms to the [natural] way of the world. Nevertheless, it is the halakhic level of interpretation that is the most essential one, as the rabbis said (*b. Sotah* 16a) 'Halakhah uproots [the plain meaning of] the biblical text.'"[7] Halakhah denotes "the way" or "the path" that Jews should follow and observe. Rashbam here acknowledges that the rabbis at times super-imposed upon the biblical laws their own authoritative interpretations, which were intended to support instruction in Halakhah or religious conduct.

For the purpose of this study, there are places where enormous benefit can be gained from consulting the works of the rabbis when they read the text in a straightforward way that relates to its context—in other words, its *peshat* or plain meaning. For the rabbis—notably in medieval times—were careful and close readers of the biblical Hebrew texts, because they were vitally interested in matters of legal practice and interpretation. Their *peshat* readings can thus be a valuable resource to help establish meaning and interpretation. They will therefore be used in our study alongside of what other

---

6. Some classic examples are given in Weiss Halivni, *Peshat and Derash*, 4–5. These include e.g., changing the literal interpretation of "eye for eye" in Exod 21:24 (and Deut 19:19–21); making the living brother the legal father of the child born from levirate marriage in Deut 25:6; and ignoring the obvious distinction between animate and inanimate deposits in Exod 22:6–12, using the case instead to distinguish between a "gratuitous bailee"

and "a bailee for hire." We will revisit these changes in secs. 1.1.2; 5.1; 5.3, when we come to look at the biblical laws in these cases.

7. Citation is taken from Lockshin, *Rashbam's Commentary on Exodus*, 225–26, at the beginning of his commentary on Exodus 21.

commentators and scholars—ancient and modern—may contribute to our overall understanding of biblical laws in their ancient, pre-rabbinic setting. In addition, I will at times also note rabbinic interpretations, which diverge from the plain meaning. Their divergent readings can occasionally help bring into relief the "original" content of the laws in biblical times, over against the interpretations later given to these laws by the rabbis. My primary goal in this work is to present biblical laws in their "proto-halakhic" understanding, as they might have been read and understood closer in time to when they were first written down. We are not studying halakhah in its post-biblical development (although this is an endeavor that is important and valuable in its own right).

The primary purpose is to compare biblical and early rabbinic laws with similar laws from the contiguous, Near Eastern cultures of ancient times. Some scholars hesitate to make such cultural comparisons, worrying that this method pays insufficient attention to the integrity and unique character of the individual cultures that are being compared. Each culture, they argue, must first be studied in terms of its own particular context. I, too, certainly agree on the importance of context; but one must also ask, particularly when looking at these ancient laws: How narrowly is context to be defined? To judge from the similarities found between both biblical and ancient Near Eastern law collections, it would appear that these are areas of shared cultural experience that framed them on a large stage. These shared cultural experiences grew out of economic, political, and other interactions that went beyond the conventional borders of language and religion and

which "leaped over" as it were, the unstable and shifting political borders of city and nation states.

Differences in language are overstated as a cultural barrier. Sumerians, Akkadians, Assyrians, Amorites, Arameans, Hebrews (or Canaanites), and speakers of other languages like Eblaite, Ugaritic, Hurrian, and Hittite clearly were shareholders in a common civilization that continued for over two thousand years, touching even upon Egypt, Iran, Anatolia, and the Aegean. They shared common writing systems and there was regular communication, trade, and extensive movements of population through their territories. Bilingualism was not unknown. The cuneiform language and system of writing became widely used in Palestine and Syria during the second millennium BCE when Amorite kings conquered and ruled both in the West and in the East. The use of cuneiform continued during the first millennium BCE during times when there was political conquest and centuries of rule over Israel by Assyrians, Babylonians, and Persians. The Hebrew language is linguistically closely related with Phoenician, Aramaic, and Amorite; we know for a fact that speakers of those languages were for centuries economically and culturally connected to Mesopotamia.

During the first millennium BCE, there was also a linguistic tide that went from West to East; the Aramaic language became widely used and was both written and spoken in Assyria and Babylonia. Not surprisingly, Aramaic penetrated into the Bible itself, as one sees in the books of Ezra and Daniel. Aramaic continued to be the main spoken and commercial language in Palestine during late biblical, i.e., Second Temple times and continued in a dominant position until the rise of Islam. For these reasons, we cannot assume that the Israelites were uniquely insulated and separated from their neighbors. While the Israelites considered themselves "chosen" out of those very peoples and nations, it is clear that they, at the same time, also had to struggle mightily in order to separate themselves from the religious ideas and cultures of these same, neighboring nations.[8]

The cultural context of our ancient laws must include the entire region of the "Fertile Crescent" from East to West. For the ancient laws, perhaps because of trade, commerce, conquest, migration, etc., somehow transcended the conventional boundaries of ethnicity, nationhood, and language.[9] The comparative study undertaken in this book is in response to striking evidence of similarities. These commonalities cannot be ignored even in the face of theoretical or other presuppositions about the nature, separateness, or independence of ancient (or modern) cultures. The similarities between the laws

require study and explanation; these ancient law collections should be investigated and discussed together.

One cannot, however, overlook the fact that the Israelites also lived as a people with an identity separate from their ancient Near Eastern neighbors and the biblical laws were not always identical with the laws of their neighbors. Thus, we will look at differences as well as similarities; we will also need to ponder carefully what these differences might mean and how they came about. In this way, comparisons between the ancient laws may teach us more about biblical laws than we could ever know from reading just the Bible itself.[10]

The existence of a "cultural dialogue" with surrounding cultures is reflected in biblical passages, which attest to Jews possessing awareness about their own laws, juxtaposed with the laws of the peoples around them. Consider Deut 4:6–8:

> You must observe them diligently, for this will show your wisdom and discernment to the peoples, who, when they hear all these statutes, will say, "Surely this great nation is a wise and discerning people!" For what other great nation has a god so near to it as the LORD our God is whenever we call to him? And what other great nation has statutes and ordinances as just as this entire law that I am setting before you today? (NRSV)

Another such passage is Ps 147:19–20: "He declares his word to Jacob, his statutes and ordinances to Israel. He has not dealt thus

---

8. Consider, e.g., passages like Ezek 16:3: "Thus said the Lord GOD to Jerusalem: By origin and birth you are from the land of the Canaanites—your father was an Amorite and your mother a Hittite" (NJPS); similarly, Ezek 16:45. Cf. also 1 Kgs 9:20–21, which speaks about the native populations who continued to live alongside of the Israelites; and the rebuke in Ezra 9:1 "The people of Israel and the priests and Levites have not separated themselves from the peoples of the land whose abhorrent practices are like those of the Canaanites, the Hittites, the Perizzites, the Jebusites, the Ammonites, the Moabites, the Egyptians, and the Amorites" (NJPS).

9. Some scholars see this interaction extending into the eastern Mediterranean, having noted striking similarities with the laws of early Rome and Greece. See Smith, "East Mediterranean Law Codes"; Westbrook, "Nature and Origin of the XII Tables," and "Trial Scene in the *Iliad*." See further below in secs. 1.5.2 and 5.6.1.

10. Examining the ancient Near Eastern context enhances the study of many aspects of biblical religion, literature, and culture, not just the laws. Cf. Hallo, "Compare and Contrast"; and Younger, "The Contextual Method."

with any other nation; they do not know his ordinances. Praise the LORD" (NRSV). In Ezek 5:7, we see both awareness of gentile laws and of their moral standards: "Assuredly, thus said the LORD God: Because you have outdone the nations that are round about you—you have not obeyed My laws or followed My rules, nor have you observed the rules of the nations round about you" (NRSV). Such biblical statements confirm that ancient Israel was indeed cognizant of the laws and cultures of neighboring nations. Consideration of the similarities and differences between the ancient Near Eastern and biblical laws gives us important perspectives on the shaping and formation of ancient biblical and early post biblical law in Israel during the second half of the first millennium BCE and the first two centuries CE.

This study uses the ancient Near Eastern laws, which were largely written down centuries earlier than the Bible, as a kind of cultural "base-line," reflecting a familiar "customary law" or "law of the nations" tradition, which continued into biblical and even rabbinic times. There is therefore no need to look for personal contact between the writers of the Bible and the scribes who wrote or copied the legal composition from the ancient Near East currently in our possession.[11] The extant ancient Near Eastern laws were themselves a part of the larger law tradition and therefore they can serve as the basis of our commentary on the background behind the later biblical laws. Coming from diverse neighboring countries, they

give us a way to reconstruct what laws and practices existed among the Israelites—and perhaps also among their Canaanite neighbors—prior to the emergence or development of our present biblical laws. Otherwise there is little knowledge of these apart from certain statements in the Bible. We will see evidence that the "cultural dialogue" taking place between the Israelites and their neighbors was not always negative or oppositional, since many of the ancient Near Eastern "customary laws" continued unchanged even into rabbinic times. As for those biblical laws, which do substantially differ from the older ancient Near Eastern "customary laws", one may consider the possibility that the corresponding ancient Near Eastern laws were known but were then consciously modified or perhaps even rejected by the early biblical writers. Such differences may very well illuminate the development of Israel's emerging unique religious identity.

This process of Israel's cultural transformation is very complex and has been linked, by tradition and scholarship, to events associated with the lives of biblical figures like Moses, Joshua, prophets like Jeremiah and Ezekiel, kings like Jehoshaphat, Hezekiah and Josiah, and leaders like Nehemiah, and Ezra the scribe. These figures represent a span of some eight to ten centuries. But no absolute certainty is possible as long as scholars remain unable to verify the actual dates of our biblical writings by external means, such as through dated manuscripts from archaeological find spots. It therefore remains difficult to prove, to the satisfaction of all, any connection between specific formulations of laws to a particular leader or epoch.

---

11. For theories of more direct contact and dependence see, e.g., Müller, *Die Gesetze Hammurabis*, who argues for the patriarchal period; Wright, *Inventing God's Law,* for the late monarchy; and Van Seters, *A Law Book for the Diaspora,* for the exilic period.

The scholarly literature on dating biblical writings is vast and varied and it is not the purpose in this present work to enter into dispute with any of these theories. I do however work with some general assumptions, namely, that the written texts of the biblical law collections as we now have them were written down between the eighth and fifth centuries BCE. But it would not be a problem for my analysis if this range of dates were extended a century or two earlier or, for that matter, later. The dating of the early rabbinic law collections is not known with certainty. Conventionally, they are assumed to have been written down during the late second or early third centuries CE; but clearly older material is preserved.

In addition, I assume that the knowledge and transmission of all ancient laws was not dependent upon writing, although professional scribes and their writing may have played an important role both in preservation and dissemination of legal formulations and content. I believe that the ancient written records were used in support of a more widespread, oral process that continued to be used for commerce, administration, learning and teaching.[12] One sees additional evidence for the roles played by "schools" and scribes in the topical arrangement of laws within the ancient law collections. Thus, for example, laws on torts and personal injury are still found grouped together in the Bible much as they were in ancient Near Eastern law collections.[13]

I also recognize that there were active parties or "interest groups" within ancient Israel who may have left their impress upon the biblical law collections. The activity of such interest groups is perhaps most clearly suggested when we encounter reformulations of older laws within the Bible itself.[14] These influences may be due to kings, prophets, priests, and possibly others, aligned according to economic, clan, or ideological interests. I will refer to these "interest groups" from time to time as we look at individual laws within the biblical collections. But I do not, *a priori*, assign an entire collection of laws solely to any one party. The approach that I have used is unit driven; but the unit, for the purpose of this study, remains each individual law statement, not the literary structure into which the law is embedded. The reconstruction of the laws within larger literary structures is certainly a valid undertaking, but remains outside of our scope here. In a similar fashion, I have not attempted to analyze and group law statements on the basis of stylistic variation in their formulations.

This study will not be looking at the entire corpus of biblical laws; we will be considering only those biblical laws for which there exists comparative material from the ancient Near Eastern collections. These laws are obviously of great

12. Cf. the comments of Civil, *Materials for the Sumerian Lexicon*, 14, 7–15, 168, on the relationship between writing and memorization in the long history of Mesopotamian scribal schools. See also Lambert, "The Laws of Hammurabi" for a late Assyrian commentary explaining some of the (at that time) archaic legal terms used in the Laws of Hammurapi, which were being re-copied and evidently still being studied. For a general overview, cf. Baines, "Literacy (ANE)."

13. See Otto, "Die rechtshistorische Entwicklung" 1–31; Wright, *Inventing God's Law*, 1–50, tables 1.1—1.3 on p. 9, and additional literature cited 366 n. 18. Interdependence among the Old Babylonian law collections is discussed in Eichler, "Examples of Restatement."

14. See for example, the repeated laws on debt slavery, discussed in sec. 2.

antiquity, with roots going back into pre-biblical times. In general, law within the Bible contains two components: an ethical program regulating relationships between humans, and a ritual program creating relationships between humans and God. The former invariably are laws that deal with civil matters rather than with ritual or cultic concerns. The latter are not the subject of this study inasmuch as ritual matters are only rarely addressed in the ancient Near Eastern law collections.

My use of pertinent rabbinic laws will be even more selective; rabbinic laws that restate biblical laws will be generally excluded unless they add something new to what we already find in the Bible; the primary focus is, after all, the earlier, i.e., the biblical level. Rabbinic legal materials are included when they demonstrate continuities with ancient Near Eastern laws that are absent or "missing" in the biblical law collections or when they reveal significant discontinuities between the plain meaning of biblical laws and rabbinic interpretations. It is then necessary to bring their separate and differing identities into focus. The presentation will do this through citations of actual laws rather than rely only upon summary statements about the laws; I will thus attempt to allow the laws to speak for themselves. Through this overall comparative study, one hopes to reveal the meanings of the biblical laws in their ancient time and setting.

It is also important to remember that all written laws may be more part of a world of "ought" than of "is." In other words, the laws project social ideals and expectations. They do not automatically tell us what people were actually doing "on the ground." Performance, i.e., compliance, always depends upon the powers of government as well as upon the will and internalized values of the population. In the case of some biblical laws, for example, we do have evidence of discontinuities in the rebuke of prophets who sharply criticized their fellow Israelites for their failure to live up to standards of conduct that we also find being demanded of them in the written laws. We also find variances in the biblical narratives, in stories that reveal legal practices different from what is presented in the formal law collections.

Similarly, when reading rabbinic laws—whether reinterpretations of biblical laws or laws known only from rabbinic legal collections—we likewise need to keep in mind that we may be dealing with scholastic tradition rather than with depiction of operative law. Thus, for example, rabbinic Jewish laws—especially those dealing with criminal matters—should be viewed as projections of social and ethical ideals, not necessarily realizable in everyday life.

The Jews, already in biblical times, experienced diminution or outright loss of their political sovereignty; and the entire development of rabbinic Jewish law took place under gentile rule. It is my view that foreign rulers had no reason to eradicate all aspects of the local legal systems operating within their subject populations. At the same time, it is equally likely that they would not at any time hesitate to express their own sovereign will and policies. The exact balance between local and royal law is not yet fully known; this would be true for Judea under Assyrian, Babylonian, Persian, Greek, as well as under Roman rule. I tend to believe that adherence to Jewish law was more strongly promoted from within the community by internal motivations—religious and social—rather than being imposed by external state controls.[15]

With respect to the ancient Near Eastern laws, there is likewise a problem of knowing how close the stated laws stand with actual legal practices. To some extent, we are able to test this relationship when we have additional ancient legal records of contemporary court proceedings and transactions. But this is not possible in every instance, so here, too, we are often left with knowing the "ought" but wondering about the "is." This study will attempt to work with the materials and sources that we have been able to identify; but evidence will inevitably fall short of full symmetry and completeness in every case.

As for arrangement of laws in their ancient collections, it is widely acknowledged that we do not know what principles, if any, may lie behind the selection and order of the laws cited. They appear random, although there are "pockets of association" visible here and there among laws within some groupings. However these do not point to any overall structure in the individual collections.[16] This random quality is true not only for the ancient Near Eastern "codes" but for the Bible as well. This fact was long ago observed by the medieval Jewish exegete Ibn Ezra: "I will tell you a general rule before I begin to explain (the verses to follow) because (regarding) each law or commandment—every one stands on its own."[17] Writing

in the first century CE, Josephus made a similar observation, noting the absence of order within the pentateuchal laws given by Moses: "For they were by him [Moses] left in writing as they were accidentally scattered in their delivery, and as he upon inquiry had learned them of God."[18]

I have not been able to add any new wisdom to these ancient observations. The ordering of legal topics and laws in this book moves generally from laws dealing with relationships between persons and family members to those involving property; and concludes with laws on larger social structures. I make no claims for the superiority of this arrangement, and so must invite my readers' indulgence and patience.

There may be other lapses in my presentation that are due to my own failures. I ask the reader to overlook these shortcomings and to focus instead on what I have collected and attempted to present in this study. Readers may seek additional information in the works cited in the bibliography and in consulting other writings of these same authors. This book is intended to be introductory in nature, and to stimulate further interest in the subject, not only among students of these disciplines but also among a wider audience of interested, non-specialist readers.

---

15. For more discussion see Blenkinsopp, "Was the Pentateuch."

16. Cf. VerSteeg, *Early Mesopotamian Law,* 5–7, who also cites earlier literature.

17. This statement appears at the beginning of his commentary to the "Covenant Code" in Exod 21:2. He does try however to demonstrate how some of the initial laws in the "Code" echo

the ten commandments, which are presented in the previous chapter, as later does Nahmanides; cf. Greengus, "Some Issues." For the influence of the Decalogue on the arrangement of laws in Deuteronomy, see discussions and literature cited in Crüsemann, *The Torah,* 204–7; and Neusner, *Vitality,* 85–103.

18. Josephus, *Ant.* 4.196, Thackeray.

1

Laws Pertaining to Family Relations
and Sexual Behavior

1.1 MARRIAGE RULES AND INCEST

1.1.1 Incest Prohibitions between Parents, Children, and Siblings

RULES ON MARRIAGE AND incest regulate aspects of family life affecting sexual rights and access, paternity, and inheritance; they are especially important when several branches and generations of a family reside or work together in proximity. Families primarily consisted of free persons, related by ties of blood and marriage; the family households of wealthy individuals might also include non-free persons, i.e., slaves. The family structure of ancient Israel was generally patriarchal and patrilocal, i.e., the women who entered the family through marriage typically came to live in their husband's home. The rules governing incest become more understandable when we consider them from the vantage point of women; however in the Bible the rules themselves are usually addressed to actions taken by the males in a family group or prohibited to them. This was perhaps the case not only because females were physically weaker and could be coerced, but also because their freedom of action was more

curtailed, since women lived either under the legal authority of the lead male(s) in their natal or, when married, in their husband's family.

The biblical writings cover a long period of history during which there were changes in marriage rules. The older biblical practices are primarily preserved in narratives; and the newer rules in the Prophets and in the law collections found in the Torah or Pentateuch. The older rules are more limited in scope and prohibited a smaller range of relationships than the later rules, which expanded the definition of incest. The Bible does not state reasons for the expansion but shows some recognition of their novelty by the presence of statements condemning especially those relationships that were formerly permitted. The older rules are closer in content to norms that are attested in the ancient Near Eastern laws. The reason for this, that I would propose, is that they were part of a commonly accepted social foundation which prohibited a woman, within her natal family, from sexual relations with her father and brother; and, if she were married, with her husband's father, brother, and son. Most

11

of these same prohibitions remain with us in present day life; such laws are still needed because, even today, they are occasionally breached, as we discover when we read stories in the news about incidents of intra-familial sexual abuse and transgression.

A prohibition against sexual relations between a son and his mother appears in Lev 18:7, addressed to the son rather than to his mother: "Your father's nakedness and the nakedness of your mother, you shall not uncover; she is your mother—you shall not uncover her nakedness" (NJPS). One is surprised, in the Bible, by the absence of a stated prohibition against sexual relations between father and daughter; but the ancient existence of this prohibition can be inferred from Lev 18:10, which deals with grandfather and granddaughter: "The nakedness of your son's daughter, or of your daughter's daughter—do not uncover their nakedness; for their nakedness is yours" (NJPS).[1] Many commentators have labored to explain why a statement of prohibition between father and daughter is not found in the biblical text because, as will be shown, it is explicitly stated in ancient Near Eastern law collections, as we shall presently see. Its absence in the Bible may simply be due to an ancient textual omission, for the biblical law collections, like all other ancient law collections, made no claims for containing all of the known laws of their times.[2] I see no impediment

to assuming that the prohibition relating to father and daughter was also an Israelite societal norm since it is already present in the non-biblical ancient Near Eastern laws; and, as we shall see, the range of biblical taboos later came to exceed what is found among Israel's neighbors.

With respect to sexual relations between a brother and sister, there was, for Israel, change over time. Sexual relations and marriageability were earlier restricted only between a brother and sister who were born of the same mother. We see this clearly in the narratives; when Abraham passed off his wife Sarah as his sister, he later defends his deception pleading in Gen 20:11–12:

> "I thought" said Abraham "surely there is no fear of God in this place, and they will kill me because of my wife. And besides, she is in truth my sister, my father's daughter though not my mother's; and she became my wife." (NJPS)

The permissibility of a union between a half-sister and half-brother is seen again in the words of Tamar, a daughter of King David, who sought to defend herself against her half-brother Amnon's sexual advances by pleading:

> But she said to him, "Don't, brother. Don't force me. Such things are not done in Israel! Don't do such a vile thing! Where will I carry my shame? And you, you will be like any of the scoundrels in Israel! Please, speak to the king; he will not refuse me to you." (2 Sam 13:12–13, NJPS)

In other words, Tamar pleads to Amnon that coerced sex was neither necessary nor appropriate; they could, after all, be married since they were born to King

---

1. This inference is put forward in *b. Sanh.* 76a but is set aside for legal reasons in favor of a less transparent hermeneutical word play "linking" Lev 18:10 with Lev 18:17.

2. For discussion of various theories offered to explain the omission of a biblical prohibition regarding a daughter, see Milgrom, *Leviticus*, 1527–38.

David by different mothers.[3] There are scholars who claim that King David himself married his half-sister, Abigail. Abigail is the name of his sister in 1 Chr 2:13–16 and it is also the name of one of his wives, who was previously married to Nabal in 1 Sam 25:40–42. But there are some difficulties with taking these two women as the same person. David's sister Abigail's father's name is given as Nahash in 2 Sam 17:25 while David's father is known to be Jesse. Some Greek manuscripts do in fact have Jesse in place of Nahash. Some have therefore argued that Nahash is an error of the ancient scribe who may have mistakenly copied the name from 2 Sam 17:27 where a different Nahash is given as the father of David's ally Shobi; if so, then Abigail could have indeed been David's half-sister. Another possibility is that Abigail's mother, who is unnamed, married Jesse, father of David, at a time when both David and Abigail were already born; accordingly she could have been his step-sister by marriage.[4]

The ancient distinction between maternal and paternal half sisters was later rejected. Ezekiel 22:11 singles the latter relationship out for special scorn, grouping it with other undisputed sins of adultery and incest:

> They have committed abhorrent acts with other men's wives; in their depravity they have defiled their own daughters-in-law; in [i.e., among] you they have ravished their own sisters, daughters of their fathers. (NJPS)

The earlier permissibility of marriage between paternal half-siblings is likewise repeatedly attacked in pentateuchal laws, which, similarly, must come from a time later than the events depicted in the narratives. Leviticus 18:9, 11 states:

> The nakedness of your sister—your father's daughter or your mother's, whether born into the household or outside—do not uncover their nakedness . . . The nakedness of your father's wife's daughter, who was born into your father's household—she is your sister: do not uncover her nakedness. (NJPS)

The fact that this same prohibition is repeated yet again in Lev 20:17 and in Deut 27:22 supports the idea that it was a "newer" measure, needing repeated teaching and reinforcement. Leviticus 20:17 states:

> If a man marries his sister, the daughter of either his father or his mother, so that he sees her nakedness and she sees his nakedness, it is a disgrace; they shall be excommunicated [lit. cut off] in the sight of their kinsfolk. He has uncovered the nakedness of his sister, he shall bear his guilt. (NJPS)

Deuteronomy 27:22 appears in a litany of supportive, conditional curses: "Cursed be he who lies with his sister, whether daughter of his father or of his mother—And all the people shall say, Amen" (NJPS).

We find incest prohibitions in the ancient Near Eastern laws that are similar to the earlier biblical ones. I spoke earlier above about a common social foundation which restricts a woman, within her natal family, from engaging in sexual relations with her father and brother; and, if she is married, with her husband's father,

---

3. Their different parentage is reported in 2 Sam 3:2–3 and 13:1.

4. For discussion of this view and other explanations see Shearing, "Abigail."

brother, and son. This is reflected in the ancient Near Eastern laws.

Incest between a daughter and her father is prohibited in Hammurapi Laws §154:

> If a man should carnally know his daughter, they shall banish that man from his city.

The prohibition appears likewise in the third part of Hittite Laws §189:

> If a man sins (sexually) with (his) daughter, it is an unpermitted sexual pairing.

We know about incest prohibitions from non-legal sources as well. An ancient literary text proclaims that the empire ruled by Akkad was destroyed because its citizens practiced incest with daughter, mother, sister, and wife's mother. (From a female perspective: father, son, brother, and daughter's husband.) These last three incestuous relationships are also mentioned in a Neo-Assyrian ritual text dealing with neutralizing the "message" of disturbing omens, including frightening dreams depicting incestuous actions by the dreamer.[5] The prohibition of sex between a woman and her brother is also the background of an ominous entry found in a treatise on medicine from Neo-Assyrian times (but reflecting older practices):

> If he (the patient) is afflicted in his perineum (?) (it means that) he has (sexually) approached his sister; he

will have a protracted illness and die.[6]

Hammurapi Laws §157 severely punishes incest between a mother and her son:

> If a man, after his father's death, should lie with his mother, they shall burn them both.

We find another explicit prohibition against a man having sexual relations with his mother in the first part of Hittite Laws §189:

> If a man sins (sexually) with his own mother, it is an unpermitted sexual pairing.[7]

1.1.2 Restrictions Arising through Marriage

For a married woman, there were incest prohibitions with respect to her husband's father and to his brother. The husband's father is addressed in Lev 18:15:

> Do not uncover the nakedness of your daughter-in-law: she is your son's wife; you shall not uncover her nakedness. (NJPS)

This taboo is repeated in Lev 20:12:

> If a man lies with his daughter-in-law, both of them shall be put to death; they have committed perversion—their blood [guilt] is upon them. (NRSV)

5. For references and discussion see Petschow, "Inzest." On p. 149 Petschow cites passages dealing with the incestuous relationships described above in *CT* 29 48:14 (Rm. 155) and in K 2315+:85–86, also cited by Oppenheim, *Interpretation of Dreams*, 227–28 and subsequently more fully published in Oppenheim, "A New Prayer," 282–301. Cf. also for incest with a sister, Oppenheim, "Interpretation of Dreams," 291 (K 6768:8').

6. Labat, *Traité Akkadien*, 108 iv, 17 (cited in *CAD* A/1, 172).

7. Among the Hittites, there are rituals designed to purify a sinner who committed incest with his daughter, sister, or mother. It is not clear whether the offender suffered the death penalty or if he was banished. See Hoffner, "Incest, Sodomy, and Bestiality," 89, who notes that this ritual also mentions a man's sister, about which no law of prohibition has survived in our present evidence.

This prohibition is one of four highlighted in Ezek 22:11 cited above. The husband's brother is addressed in Lev 18:16:

> Do not uncover the nakedness of your brother's wife; it is the nakedness of your brother. (NJPS)

Again in Lev 20:21:

> If a man takes his brother's wife, it is impurity; he has uncovered his brother's nakedness; they shall be childless. (NRSV)

This prohibition, in addition to the one dealing with a husband's father, were, however, only in force as long the husband was alive. The rules were relaxed for a woman whose husband died, leaving her a widow in her new family, especially if she had no children who could look after her in old age. For a widow, childless or not, was viewed as part of the dead man's estate; the bond between the dead man and his widow survived his death and was passed as a kind of inheritance to his closest male relatives. Such customs, by our standards, appear both harsh and backward; yet, at the same time, we must also be aware that in these ancient patriarchal societies, a woman, once she was married, normally did not ever expect to go back and live with her parents or with siblings of her natal family. It was expected that she would become part of her husband's family and that they would in some way provide for her for the rest of her life, even in widowhood. This practice of retaining a widow in the husband's family is called levirate marriage; and the custom is found, in various forms, in many parts of the ancient world.[8]

8. Westermarck, *History of Marriage*, 3:208–22; Weisberg, *Levirate Marriage*, 1–22.

Levirate marriage is a key part of the story of Ruth, where we learn that customary law gave kinsmen of Ruth's deceased husband the right to take Ruth in levirate marriage. With this marriage, the kinsman would also acquire the right to the deceased husband's property, which he would later pass on to the sons born of the levirate marriage. In the story, one kinsman wanted to marry Ruth; but there was an impediment for him in that the property of the deceased was encumbered by debt and needed also to be redeemed; the kinsman (whose name is not given) was initially interested in the property but then realized that this enterprise would prove too costly for him and would adversely impact his total wealth and the future estate of his own children if he had also to take Ruth in levirate marriage. He therefore yielded his rights in favor of Boaz, a more distant kinsman, who wanted very much to marry Ruth and who also stood ready to redeem the encumbered family property. This is the background behind Ruth 3:9—4:12 (cited here in part):

> And she replied, "I am your handmaid Ruth. Spread your robe over your handmaid, for you are a redeeming kinsman." He [Boaz] exclaimed, "Be blessed of the LORD, daughter! . . . I will do in your behalf whatever you ask, for all the elders of my town know what a fine woman you are. But while it is true I am a redeeming kinsman, there is another redeemer closer than I." . . . Then [Boaz] took ten elders of the town and said, "Be seated here"; and they sat down. He said to the redeemer, "Naomi, now returned from the country of Moab, must sell the piece of land which belonged to our kinsman Elimelech.

I thought I should disclose the matter to you and say: Acquire it in the presence of those seated here and in the presence of the elders of my people. If you are willing to redeem it, redeem! But if you will not redeem, tell me, that I may know. For there is no one to redeem but you, and I come after you." "I am willing to redeem it," he replied. Boaz continued, "When you acquire the property from Naomi and from Ruth the Moabite, you must also acquire the wife of the deceased, so as to perpetuate the name of the deceased upon his estate." The redeemer replied, "Then I cannot redeem it for myself, lest I impair my own estate. You may take over my right of redemption, for I am unable to exercise it." (NJPS)

The right of levirate came first to the nearest relative of the deceased husband, usually his brother or father. We see this in the story of Judah and Tamar, told in Genesis 38. Judah had married a Canaanite woman who bore him three sons, the eldest of which was Er, whom he married to Tamar. When Er died, he gave her to his second son Onan who, the Bible tells us, married her but was unwilling to allow her to conceive a child who would belong legally to Er, his dead brother. God killed him for having this evil intent. Judah was now obliged to marry Tamar to his third son Shelah but, unaware of God's will, was worried that she might bring him to the same fate as his brothers; so he sent her off to her parents, promising to marry her to his third son when he was a bit older. Judah procrastinated for some years. So Tamar decided to take matters into her own hands; and disguising herself as a veiled harlot enticed Judah himself and became pregnant by him but then

also disappeared from the scene leaving him unable even to pay her what he had promised to give for her payment. Some months later, when learning that she was pregnant, Judah blamed Tamar for committing what he thought was an act of adultery with a man outside of the family, since she was technically still a "married woman" waiting to be united with her husband's next-of-kin.[9] Tamar, threatened with death by burning, was exonerated after she confronted Judah with personal items of his that he had left with her during his tryst as security for his undelivered payment. In this story of Judah we thus see a progression of levirate rights moving from husband's brother to husband's father; while in the story of Ruth, we see the levirate rights moving even further on to other close male relatives.

The Bible, however, later attempted to restrict the progression of levirate rights; perhaps because it permitted the relaxation of prohibitions formerly in place, before the death of the deceased brother. For Deuteronomy, moreover, there was to be only one opportunity for levirate marriage; and that was to be offered to the nearest relative, who would typically be a brother of the dead husband. This newer law may also have had the intent to restrict the levirate to brothers only as we shall presently see. But in any case, if the brother refused to marry the widow, then she would be set free from her husband's family rather than being passed on to the next available kinsman like was done for Ruth. An added restriction limited levirate marriage to childless women only. Thus in Deut 25:5–10:

9. Adultery is more fully discussed in sec. 1.3.1 below.

When brothers dwell together and one of them dies and leaves no son, the wife of the deceased shall not be married to a stranger, outside the family. Her husband's brother[10] shall unite with her: he shall take her as his wife and perform the levir's duty. The first son that she bears shall be accounted to the dead brother that his name may not be blotted out in Israel.[11] But if the man does not want to marry his brother's widow, his brother's widow shall appear before the elders in the gate and declare, "My husband's brother refuses to establish a name in Israel for his brother; he will not perform the duty of a levir." The elders of his town shall then summon him and talk to him. If he insists, saying, "I do not want to marry her," his brother's widow shall go up to him in the presence of the elders, pull the sandal off his foot, spit in his face, and make this declaration: Thus shall be done to the man who will not build up his brother's house! And he shall go in Israel by the name of "the family of the unsandaled one." (NJPS)

The rejected widow was then free to marry outside of the family.

10. The term "levirate" is in fact derived from Latin *levir* "brother-in-law," who is one of the more typical candidates for this relationship; the term may in fact be derived from Deut 25:5–10 where this is the case. Scholars however now apply the term in a more general fashion to any eligible kinsman.

11. It is not clear what exactly is meant by this provision as well as by the phrase "establish a name in Israel for his brother" or "build up his brother's house" in the verses following. These may relate to an obligation to venerate the memory of the deceased, legal paternity, or inheritance. The rabbis in *b. Yebam.* 24a refuse to read it literally (as mentioned in the Introduction). For a thoughtful discussion of possibilities cf. Tigay, *Deuteronomy,* 482–83; see also Driver, *Deuteronomy,* 283–85.

At the same time, if he decided to marry his brother's widow and he himself then died before giving her a child, apparently she would be passed on to the next brother as was the case with Tamar. We see this same understanding in the story told in the New Testament about a confrontation between Jesus and a group of Sadducees:

The same day some Sadducees came to him, saying there is no resurrection; and they asked him a question, saying, "Teacher, Moses said, 'If a man dies childless, his brother shall marry the widow, and raise up children for his brother.' Now there were seven brothers among us; the first married, and died childless, leaving the widow to his brother. The second did the same, so also the third, down to the seventh. Last of all, the woman herself died. In the resurrection, then, whose wife of the seven will she be? For all of them had married her." Jesus answered them, "You are wrong, because you know neither the Scriptures nor the power of God. For in the resurrection they neither marry nor are given in marriage, but are like angels in heaven. (Matt 22:23–30, NRSV)[12]

From the response given by Jesus it is clear that, even as late as in his day, the institution of the levirate conformed to what is described in Deut 25:5–10; the levirate succession itself was not a matter for theological dispute for the Sadducees.

Another limitation on the levirate came about through a prohibition which prevented a widow—whether childless or not—from marrying her stepson. For in early Israel, while sexual relations

12. Cf. also Mark 12:18–25; Luke 20:27–35.

between a woman and her husband's son was forbidden during the father's lifetime, it was not so after the father's death. This can be seen from Adonijah's request of Abishag after David's death in 1 Kgs 2:22–25; in Absalom's publicly taking his father's ten concubines in 2 Sam 16:21–22; and in Reuben taking his father's wife in Gen 35:22. Adonijah's request for Abishag was seen as appropriate by David's wife Bathsheba, since David had died; but the request was threatening to his brother Solomon because of its implication that Adonijah, his elder brother, in marrying his father's wife, would thereby be proclaiming that he had a better claim to the throne of David than did Solomon himself. Solomon thereupon had Adonijah assassinated.[13] Absalom's public act was premature in that his father David was still alive; but it boldly demonstrated that Absalom was ready to take his father's place; henceforth—as far as his son Absalom and his followers in rebellion were concerned—David was as good as dead and irrelevant. This is clearly stated in the advice given by Ahitophel to Absalom:

> And Ahithophel said to Absalom, "Have intercourse with your father's concubines, whom he left to mind the palace; and when all Israel hears that you have dared the wrath of your father, all who support you will be encouraged." So they pitched a tent for Absalom on the roof, and Absalom lay with

his father's concubines with the full knowledge of all Israel. (2 Sam 16:21–22, NJPS)[14]

Reuben's action was also premature; he was the eldest son but his father Jacob, although old, was still alive. For his impatience and disrespect, Reuben was later rebuked by his father in his deathbed blessings and deprived of his birthright, as described in Gen 49:3–4. This is more clearly stated in 1 Chr 5:1:

> The sons of Reuben the firstborn of Israel. He was [indeed] the firstborn, but because he defiled his father's bed, his birthright was given to the sons of Joseph son of Israel, so that he is not enrolled in the genealogy according to the birthright. (NRSV)

From these narratives it is clear that, earlier on, there was no barrier to sexual relations between a man and his father's wife (not his own mother) after the father's death. There is also no indication from these narratives that the father's widow would have to be childless as in Deut 25:5–10. This could explain why it was necessary to repeat the later prohibition concerning a father's wife repeated five times! Thus, Lev 18:8:

> Do not uncover the nakedness of your father's wife; it is the nakedness of your father. (NJPS)

Again in Lev 20:11:

> If a man lies with his father's wife, it is the nakedness of his father that he has uncovered; the two shall be put to death—their bloodguilt is upon them. (NJPS)

13. 1 Kgs 1:4 adds the comment that King David had not had sexual relations with Abishag; but I take this to be an ancient editor's gloss (see discussion following below); for normally a woman was prohibited to other men from the time of espousal even without consummation having taken place. This is the entire point of the situation described in Deut 22:23–27 (discussed below in sec. 1.3.)

14. 2 Sam 20:3 relates that David left ten of his concubines behind when he fled Jerusalem.

Similarly the statement in Ezek 22:10:

> Among you they have uncovered their fathers' nakedness; they violate women during their menstrual impurity.

A two-fold repetition of this prohibition occurs in Deuteronomy; Deut 23:1: "No man shall marry his father's wife, so as to uncover his father's garment"; and in Deut 27:20: "Cursed be he who lies with his father's wife, for he has uncovered his father's garment—and all the people shall say, Amen." This frequent repetition leads one to believe that these statements reflect a "reformist" movement to make this prohibition an absolute one, without relaxation or exception for levirate marriage inasmuch as these passages do not acknowledge any distinction between a father's lifetime or after his death. The law in Deut 25:5–10 may likewise reflect this movement, in restricting levirate eligibility to brothers of the deceased man only and not mentioning the eligibility of the father or sons of the deceased, as was formerly practiced.

In this connection we must look at an interesting comment that appears in Gen 38:26: a statement that Judah did not subsequently continue conjugal relations with Tamar after she became pregnant: "And he was not intimate with her again" (NJPS). It appears to be an ancient scribal gloss bringing Judah's behavior in line with later, limiting views, which desired to exclude the dead husband's father from levirate eligibility. This more restrictive view thus condemned Judah's role; this is clearly reflected in the Pseudepigrapha in the *Testaments of the Twelve Patriarchs* where Judah himself is presented saying:

> But I did not go into her [Tamar] again until the end of my life because I had done this thing which was revolting in all Israel . . . because before the eyes of all I turned aside to Tamar and committed a great sin.[15]

In view of the repeated and clear biblical taboo, the rabbis in general had also to agree; however they found a problem here. The line of King David and of the royal house of Judah descended from Perez, the firstborn of Tamar and Judah. The medieval rabbinic scholar Hazzequni thus adds an insightful comment:

> And if you may ask: how did the Holy One Blessed be He allow that all the kings of Judah should descend from Perez who himself was born of Tamar who became pregnant illicitly? One can answer . . . that she did not became pregnant illicitly since (in the times) before the Torah was given all near relatives were eligible to undertake the levirate marriage—even the father of the dead husband. So when Shelah did not undertake the levirate, it fell upon Judah to do so. And when the Torah was given, a new law was promulgated (Deut 25:5–10) that only brothers of the deceased sharing his paternal line should undertake the levirate. Nevertheless, if there were no brothers, other near relatives of the husband who were otherwise not forbidden to her could do so; and thus Tamar acted appropriately in the same fashion as in the case of Boaz with Ruth even after the Torah was given.

15. Kee, *Testaments*, 798–99; citations are from the section, *Testament of Judah* 12:8 and 14:5.

Therefore, states Hazzequni, if Judah did stop having sex with Tamar, it was not because she was forbidden to him; rather (as intimated in Gen 38:11), it was because he thought she was a 'black widow' (having 'dispatched' two previous husbands).[16] The comment of Hazzequni is interesting in that it reveals awareness of the historical development, which I have described in connection with the stated biblical prohibitions later limiting the earlier levirate marriage practices. The rabbis supported a policy making the levirate more attractive to the husband's kin by having the levir become the legal parent of the widow's children and allowing him to absorb the dead husband's property as his own property.[17]

Nevertheless, over time, we see further evidence of ancient Jewish sentiment against any form of levirate marriage. One cause was the view that a man should not take more than one wife at a time under any circumstances. This was the opinion of the ancient Essenes, whose writings in the Dead Sea Scrolls in the so-called Covenant of Damascus (CD 4:20—5:1) states that there are three traps of Belial in which Israel is caught, one of which is:

> . . . fornication by taking two wives in their lifetimes, although the principle of creation is "male and

female He created them (Gen 1:27) and those who went into the ark "went two by two" (Gen 7:9).[18]

Philo, who did not share this restrictive view on monogamy, nevertheless explicitly eliminates the possibility of levirate marriage when he says:

> But such careful precautions has our law taken in these matters that it has not even permitted the son of a first marriage to marry his stepmother after the death of his father, both on account of the honour due to his father . . . On this principle he [Moses] prohibits many other unions, not allowing marriage with a son's daughter or a daughter's daughter, nor with an aunt whether paternal or maternal, nor with one who has been wife to an uncle or son or brother, nor again with a stepdaughter whether widow or unmarried . . .[19]

The rabbis in the Mishnah later effectively eliminated the levirate altogether by making the marriage option of Deut 25:5–10 a "dead letter" in the Torah; this is stated in the Mishnah, *m. Bekh.* 1:7:

> Originally, the duty of levirate marriage takes precedence over the duty of "removing the sandal" because then they were intent on fulfilling [it as] a religious duty; but nowadays when they are not intent

16. Hazzequni on Gen 38:13, 26; cf. also Bekhor Shor on this same verse and on Gen 38:26; Nahmanides makes similar observations at Gen 38:8. Ibn Ezra, in his comments on Deut 25:5 allows that even in this passage, which deals with "two brothers," one cannot be certain from the text that the "brothers" are actually siblings and not simply "close relatives."

17. Weisberg, *Levirate Marriage,* 110–11, 123. Already in biblical times, we see that Boaz is already considered to be the father of Obed, the son born to Ruth, in the "official genealogies" given in Ruth 4:21 and 1 Chr 2:12.

18. Wise et al., *Dead Sea Scrolls*, 55–56. Belial is a Satan-like figure in postbilical Jewish writings; in the NT, 2 Cor 6:15, he is an "Anti-Christ" figure. In the Bible he is equated with Death in Ps 18:5 and identified with evildoing e.g., in Prov 6:12; 16:27.

19. Philo, *Spec. Laws* 3.20, 26, Colson. Driver and Miles, *Assyrian Laws,* 249 n. 4, suggest that the penalty of childlessness in Lev 20:21 may imply an even earlier polemic for total prohibition of the levirate, whose purpose would be defeated if God were to punish the couple by rendering their marriage infertile.

on religious duty, [the rabbis enjoined that] the duty of "removing the sandal" comes before the duty of levirate marriage.

But this view was reversed in the Babylonian Talmud; and the possibility of levirate marriage was thus maintained by Jews living in polygamous Islamic societies but was then abandoned by Jews living in monogamous Christian countries; there only the ceremony of removing the sandal was permitted; levirate marriage itself was no longer a possibility.[20]

In the ancient Near East, we likewise find incest prohibitions governing relationships arising through marriage. Hammurapi Laws §§155–156 deals with the prohibition between a woman and her father-in-law:

> If a man has chosen a bride for his son and his son has carnally known her, and [afterwards] he himself lies in her bosom and they catch him [doing so], they shall bind that man and throw him into the [river] water. If a man chose a bride for his son but his son has not yet carnally known her, and he himself lies in her bosom, he shall pay her one half mina sliver and restore to her whatever she brought in from her father's house; and a man of her choice may marry her.

These laws are strict in that a father-in-law, actual or perspective, is prohibited from having any degree of sexual relationship with a woman chosen, i.e., betrothed, to be his daughter-in-law.

However, in the ancient Near Eastern laws, as in ancient Israel, the normal prohibition against sexual relations between

20. Cf. *b. Yebam.* 39b; for later rabbinic development see Rabinowitz, "Levirate Marriage and Halitza," 122–31.

a woman and her husband's brother was relaxed if she became a widow: thus Hittite Laws §192 states "If a man's wife dies, [he may take her] sister [as his wife.] It is not an offense." Moreover, as in the case of Boaz and his kinsman, there was an order of eligibility rights for the levirate. The order: husband's brother, father, and uncle is given in Hittite Laws §193:

> If a man has a wife, and the man dies, his brother shall take his widow as wife. (If the brother dies,) his father shall take her. When afterwards his father dies, his (i.e., the father's) brother shall take the woman whom he had. There is no offense.

We are not informed in this law paragraph about the place of the son's succession rights with respect to the order given. But we know that the son was not forbidden to play this role. The relationship of a widow to her husband's son appears in Hittite Laws §190: "If a man sins (sexually) with his stepmother, it is not an offense. But if his father is (still) living, it is an unpermitted sexual pairing."

We have more information about levirate succession rights from Assyria. According to Middle Assyrian Laws §A 43, a woman, even if only betrothed, already belonged to her "new family." A 43, in addition, maintains a right of the husband's family to retain the woman for levirate even if her husband ran off and did not die:

> If a man has poured oil upon the head (of an intended bride) or has brought the (customary) betrothal gifts (for the ceremonial betrothal meal], (and then) the son for whom he has assigned the wife either dies or runs away, he may give

(the bride) unto (one of) his remaining sons—to anyone he wishes—from the eldest to the youngest who is (at least) ten years of age. If (her) father (–in law) is dead and the son for whom he had assigned the wife is dead, a son of the (dead) son who is (at least) ten years of age shall marry her. If the sons of the (dead) son are less than ten years old, then if the father of the daughter wishes, he may give his daughter (nevertheless); or if he prefers, he may institute an equal return (of the marriage gifts given). If there is no son (to marry her then) as much as he received (for her), precious stones or anything that is not edible [i.e., perishable] he shall return in full value; but (the value of) what is edible, he need not return.

In this law, the succession rights passed first to the brothers and then presumably to his father—had he not died—before passing on to the dead husband's sons. There is no mention of the dead husband's uncle here at all like in the Hittite Laws cited above. This Assyrian law paragraph also informs us about the age of eligibility for levirate marriage; a closely similar rule is in fact preserved in later rabbinic writings, which set levirate eligibility at nine years and one day.[21] Rabbinic law likewise affirms the obligation of levirate marriage for a woman whose husband died after betrothal but before the marriage took place.[22]

21. Cf. *m. Yebam.* 7:4; 10:6–9; *m. Nid.* 5:5.

22. This is not a matter of dispute among the rabbis; what they do argue about, however, is the degree of control over other aspects of her life during the time while she awaits levirate marriage. Thus, for example, *m. Ned.* 10:5, 6 contains a debate on the levir's legal right to cancel her vows during that period of time.

The position of the dead husband's father in levirate succession is again and more clearly stated in Middle Assyrian Laws §A 33; part of the ancient text is missing in the document that has survived; but enough remains to show what is taking place. The paragraph begins with a situation where the widowed bride is a woman who already had children of her own; and she was still living in her own father's house. Presumably, as already seen, her children would support her. The end of the paragraph, emerging after a lacuna of some lines, describes a second situation where both the widow and her dead husband had no sons. In this case the woman's father apparently may institute a return of marriage gifts as in §A 43 or else:

> . . . if he (her father) wishes, he shall give her in marriage to her father-in-law. If her husband and her father-in-law are (both) dead and she has no son (of her own), then she is a (legally unfettered) widow; she is free to go wherever she wishes.

It appears from this law that the father-in-law's right of succession was not automatic but subject to the consent of the woman's father; if he were too old, infirm, or deemed otherwise unsuitable, the marriage could be terminated if there were no brothers or sons of the dead husband.

Middle Assyrian Laws §A 46 deals with levirate marriage for women who became widowed under circumstances different from the women in §§A 43 and 33. Here we see that a widow who had given birth to sons was not expected to marry any other member of her dead husband's family. However, if she were the dead husband's second wife, she could be taken by

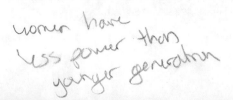
women have less power than younger generation

one of her stepsons in marriage even if she had sons of her own.

Choice

If a woman whose husband is dead, does not (choose to) move from his house after (his) death, (and) if her (late) husband did not write over any (assets) to her, she shall live in a house of her sons wherever she chooses. (All of) her husband's sons shall sustain her; they shall covenant together to supply her with food and drink as for a daughter-in-law whom they love. If she is a second wife (and) has no sons (of her own), she shall live with one (of her husband's sons) and they shall all together sustain her. (But) if there are sons (of her own) and the sons of the first wife are unwilling to sustain her, then she shall live in a house belonging to (one of) her own sons wherever she wishes. Her own sons will sustain her and she will do work for them. And if there is one among her husband's sons who will marry her, [he alone shall provide for her; her other sons need] not sustain her.

reciprocity

It appears that there are two determinations: first, whether a wife had borne sons; and second, whether she was a first or second wife. A man's first wife who bore sons was entitled to generous lifetime support by them after the death of her husband; she is not subject to levirate marriage. So, too, is a second or later wife that the husband married—presumably after the death of the first wife—who also had borne sons; the second wife is obligated to do housework in return for her support; but she may also be taken in marriage by one of her stepsons. The second wife, therefore, even with sons, remained subject to levirate marriage. The second wife who had borne sons was, however, of higher status

than a concubine, whose sons born to the husband would not inherit from their father unless he had formally raised her status to that of a full wife; the only exception to this was if the father had no other sons born to him by ranking wives.[23]

In Babylonia, we also find a distinction between widows according to their rank and their having born sons; according to Hammurapi Laws §158:

> If a man after his father (died) is seized [lying] in the bosom of his (father's) principal wife who has borne children [i.e., sons], that man shall be disinherited from (his) father's estate.

The woman could not to be taken in marriage by her stepson. But she could of course marry other persons, including her dead husband's brother and relatives. Otherwise we have no reference to a law on right of levirate succession in Babylonia.[24]

The Near Eastern practices invite us to take another look at our biblical cases and lead us to ask: To what extent was childlessness a precondition for levirate marriage? Was there consideration to be given to wife's rank or position within the family? And finally, was there a fixed order of priority among the male relatives of the deceased husband? As for

23. The status of the concubine and her children are delineated in Middle Assyrian Laws §A 41 (not cited here). The husband could however raise the status of his concubine to that of a "full" wife.

24. A possible exception may be present in a royal decree of a king of Ugarit (in northern Syria). The king pronounces a curse upon anyone other than his brother who would marry his widowed queen after his death. This document is RS 16.144, discussed by Tsevat, "Marriage and Monarchical Legitimacy in Ugarit and Israel"; and Cardascia, "Adoption matrimoniale et lévirat dans le droit d'Ugarit."

childlessness as a precondition, this is certainly the position taken in Deut 25:5–10. Tamar and Ruth had no children prior to their levirate marriages. Nor had Abishag who was wanted by Adonijah. But Bilhah, who was sexually approached by Reuben, had born two sons to Jacob (Gen 30:4–8). Although she is described as a concubine, her sons had been accepted into the family; this would have raised her status as well; and this view of her status may then have figured in Jacob's postponed, deathbed retaliation against Reuben, removing him from his position as first born son; Reuben's penalty would thus conform to what is found in Hammurapi Laws §158. Jacob may have postponed his retaliation because Reuben's act was taken at the time when Jacob had determined to raise the status of Bilhah and her sons; Reuben's action may have been an attempt to block Jacob from doing so, preferring that Bilhah be seen as a concubine and that her children not be recognized as his full brothers. A motive of this sort is suggested by Nahmanides, in his commentary to Gen 35:22 and 49:4. He ascribes to Reuben an economic motive, pointing to his act being juxtaposed to a statement in Gen 35:22 that the "sons of Jacob were twelve," and following Gen 35:19–20 which relate the death of Rachel. He suggests that Reuben, the first born and having the expectation of receiving a double portion of inheritance as in Deut 21:17 (sec. 1.5.1), was worried lest his father have more sons through Bilhah, who, Nahmanides surmised, had replaced Rachel as his father's favorite wife and who, Nahmanides further suggests, might have been a younger woman still able to bear children. Reuben's act of violation would render her less desirable in the eyes of Jacob;

for indeed Jacob, after Reuben's action, sired no sons beyond the twelve that he already had at that time.[25] But Jacob did, apparently, raise Bilhah's status and that of her sons. Bilhah (and her co-concubine Zilpah) are called "maidservants" in Gen 33:2 but "wives of Jacob" in Gen 37:2. The sons of the concubines are also explicitly numbered among the twelve sons of Jacob in Gen 35:23–26 and again, e.g., in Gen 46:8–27 and in Exod 1:1–4.

What we have discovered about levirate succession rights in the ancient Near Eastern laws can also supply us with insight into the action taken by Tamar with Judah, her dead husband's father. Tamar was dutifully waiting to be taken by Shelah, her dead husband's surviving brother; but when he did not do so, then Judah, her father-in-law, was next in line. This factor would explain Tamar going after Judah. Judah admits as much when he declares (Gen 38:26): "She is more in the right than I, inasmuch as I did not give her to my son Shelah" (NJPS).

As for priority of rights among male relatives, Hittite Law §193 specifically first extends levirate succession rights to the dead husband's uncle. We in fact do have a parallel to a widow marrying the uncle of her husband in the Bible, in the story told in 2 Sam 3:6–11 concerning Abner, who was the brother of Saul's father Kish (1 Sam 14:50; 1 Chr 9:36); Abner took Rizpah the concubine of Saul after Saul and Jonathan had died in battle.[26] Rizpah thus

25. The medieval commentator Qimhi on Gen 35:22 suggests that Jacob henceforth gave up all pursuit of sexual relations; this would conform to David's abandonment of sexual relations with his concubines, who were violated by Absalom, as recounted in 2 Sam 20:3.

26. In the view of the rabbis, a marriage between a man and his brother's son's widow could

24

married her husband's uncle. But Ishbaal, Saul's son, who had become king after his father's death, was angry with Abner for taking her (2 Sam 3:7):

> Now Saul had a concubine named Rizpah, daughter of Aiah; and [Ishbosheth] said to Abner, "Why have you lain with my father's concubine?" (NJPS)

Ishbaal (here called Ishbosheth—to suppress the name of Baal) had to yield because Abner was so powerful and important to him politically and militarily. The Bible does not reveal the reason for Ishbaal's wrath. But now, based upon what we have seen in the ancient Near Eastern sources, I can suggest two possibilities to consider. One possibility may be that this was an argument over levirate succession rights: did Ishbaal's right as a son precede that of his uncle Abner's? Our evidence from the Assyrian laws mentions the son but not the uncle. The Hittite laws attest to the eligibility of both the son and the uncle, but their relative order in precedence is not clear from the sources preserved. In the Bible, as one can see from the cases of Reuben, Absalom, and Adonijah, the son's rights were clearly present. The right of the uncle in levirate succession is not discussed; but I would think it should follow from the right of the father-in-law, i.e., his being a brother of the dead husband's father.

Another possibility relates to Rizpah's status. Could Ishbaal's complaint perhaps have been based on her not being subject to levirate marriage because of her status? Rizpah is described as Saul's concubine;

but she had born him two sons who were later handed over by David to the Gibeonites for execution (2 Sam 21:8–9). Was her situation then like that of Bilhah in that Saul had accepted her sons as full heirs? This is certainly not implied in the genealogy of Saul given in 1 Chr 9:39 where her sons are not named together alongside of Jonathan. According to this view, it seems that David just collected whatever children and grandchildren of Saul had survived and, without consideration of their status, gave them to the Gibeonites. For in 2 Sam 21:1 we are told that their death came about because:

> There was a famine during the reign of David, year after year for three years. David inquired of the LORD, and the LORD replied, "It is because of the bloodguilt of Saul and his house, for he put some Gibeonites to death." (NJPS)

The Bible further tells us in 2 Sam 21:7–9:

> The king spared Mephibosheth son of Jonathan son of Saul, because of the oath before the LORD between the two, between David and Jonathan son of Saul. Instead, the king took Armoni and Mephibosheth, the two sons that Rizpah daughter of Aiah bore to Saul, and the five sons that Merab daughter of Saul bore to Adriel son of Barzillai the Meholathite, and he handed them over to the Gibeonites. They impaled them on the mountain before the LORD; all seven of them perished at the same time. They were put to death in the first days of the harvest, the beginning of the barley harvest. (NJPS)

Abner in his reply to Ishbaal (2 Sam 3:8) was unwilling or unable to defend his

---

not be considered as incest; cf. *m. Yebam.* 11:4. Permissibility of this union is more clearly stated in *j. Yebam.* 2d and 12a.

action; rather, he attacks his nephew for troubling him over a woman:

> Am I a dog's head from Judah? Here I have been loyally serving the House of your father Saul and his kinsfolk and friends, and I have not betrayed you into the hands of David; yet this day you reproach me over a woman! (NJPS)

Abner does not dispute the correctness of Ishbaal's charge; and based upon the evidence we have, Abner, the uncle, was, most likely also an eligible candidate for a levirate union. But perhaps, taking advantage of his power, he may have pushed himself ahead in line of succession, overriding what may have been the more legitimate, i.e., prior right of Ishbaal, Saul's son.[27]

This dispute between Ishbaal and Abner also contains political overtones and points to the possibility of treason. Abner's comment about non-betrayal leads us to imagine that Ishbaal was also worried that Abner, by exercising priority in the levirate, might also be reaching for kingship. The tension between them would thus be reminiscent of the tension between Solomon and Adonijah over his wanting to marry Abishag. Our proposed interpretation of the quarrel between Ishbaal and Abner therefore is that it involved levirate marriage, the order of succession within the levirate, and, possibly also—by implication—who would be seen as the rightful heir to the throne of King Saul.[28]

1.1.3 Prohibited Intergenerational Unions

Later changes in the biblical marriage rules eliminated the possibility of marriage between a man and his aunt. Earlier, as the Pentateuch relates, Amram, the father of Moses, Aaron, and Miram, had in fact married his father's sister. Amram was the grandson of Levi. We read thus in Exod 6:20:

> Amram married Jochebed his father's sister and she bore him Aaron and Moses . . . (NRSV)

Also in Num 26:59:

> The name of Amram's wife was Jochebed daughter of Levi, who was born to Levi in Egypt; she bore to Amram Aaron and Moses and their sister Miriam. (NRSV)[29]

The possibility of this intergenerational marriage was later forbidden as we read in Lev 18:12–14:

---

27. According to the genealogies cited above (1 Sam 14:50 and 1 Chr 9:36), Abner 's father Ner was a brother to Kish, who, in turn, was the father of Saul and grandfather of Ishbaal. In 1 Sam 14:51, the MT as preserved literally states: "Kish the father of Saul and Ner the father of Abner the son of Abiel" (NJPS). NJPS interprets this verse by translating "Kish, Saul's father, and Ner the father of Abner were (both) sons of Abiel." This is attractive since in 1 Sam 9:1 Kish, father of Saul, is also given as a "son of Abiel"; I have followed these traditions here. But the Greek to 1 Sam 14:51 read an entirely different text: "and Ner the father of Abenner, was the son of Iamin, son of Abiel." The Greek text, by adding an intervening generation, would make Abner the nephew of Kish and cousin to Saul! In 1 Chr 8:33, Ner is again recorded as the father of Kish and grandfather of Saul; this would support our seeing Abner as Saul's uncle.

28. The interpretation of this conflict given above was earlier presented in Greengus, "The Quarrel Between Ishboshet and Abner,"

29. The Septuagint to Exod 6:20 reads "the daughter of the brother of his father" i.e., making Jochebed into Amram's first cousin; but the MT passage in Num 26:59 makes the relationship clear—at least in the tradition preserved there. She is also called "daughter of Levi" in Exod 2:1; NJPS hides the plain meaning by translating "a Levite woman."

Do not uncover the nakedness of your father's sister; she is your father's flesh. Do not uncover the nakedness of your mother's sister; for she is your mother's flesh. Do not uncover the nakedness of your father's brother: do not approach his wife; she is your aunt. (NJPS)

It is important to note, however, that the possibility of an intergenerational marriage between a woman and her uncle, i.e., the brother of her father or mother, was not forbidden in the Bible. According to one biblical genealogy, Othniel, the younger brother of Caleb, married his niece Achsah, Caleb's daughter; this story is told in Josh 15:13–17 and again in Judg 1:12–13.[30] One of the Dead Sea documents entitled "The Visions of Amram," preserves a tradition that Miriam, daughter of Amram, married her uncle Uzziel.[31] But the Essenes, living at the end of the biblical period, came to see this union of niece and uncle as sinful. They believed that what applied to a male, i.e., a man and his aunts, should also apply to females,

30. Othniel is again identified as the son of Kenaz and younger brother of Caleb in Jud 3:9–11. There is, however, another tradition in the Bible about the family of Caleb, where he is recorded as son of Jephunah (e.g., Num 13:6; Deut 1:36) and sometimes also adding that he was a Kenizzite (e.g., Josh 14:6, 14). The Talmud in *b. Sotah* 11b suggests that Jephunah became the father of Caleb after marrying the widow of Kenaz, Othniel's father. Thus Othniel son of Kenaz could have been a half-brother to Caleb. Qimhi on Josh 15:17 takes Kenaz to be be a more distant ancestor, common to both sides of the family. NJPS follows a similar path by translating "Othniel the Kenizzite" for "Othniel son of Kenaz" and "younger kinsman of Caleb" for "younger brother." For a concise discussion on the problem, cf. Barton and Ginzberg, "Caleb."

31. Uzziel is identified as brother of Amram in Exod 6:16–18. The "Vision of Amram" is preserved in 4Q543–48; cf. Wise, et al., *Dead Sea Scrolls*, 434.

i.e., a woman and her uncles; accordingly all such intergenerational unions should be forbidden. We find their more strict view emphatically expressed in another of the Dead Sea Scrolls; the "Covenant of Damascus" CD 5:8–10 states:

> Furthermore they marry each man the daughter of his brothers and the daughter of his sister, although Moses said 'Unto the sister of your mother you shall not draw near; she is the flesh of your mother' (Lev 18:13). But the law of forbidden relations is written for males and females alike, so if the brother's daughter uncovers the nakedness of the brother of her father, she is in fact that (same) flesh.[32]

The Essene view is supported by Philo who in the passage cited above (in sec. 1.1.2), adds: "No man shall marry . . . his niece nor his aunt."[33] Later rabbinic practice however did not follow this view; on the contrary, the rabbis praise the marriage of uncle and niece as desirable and blessed.[34] While the reasons for their view are not stated, it may perhaps relate to reduction of economic costs, with bride-price and dowry rendered unnecessary or at least balanced through exchanges between close relatives, whose affairs were often closely entwined. Moreover, we have evidence that Philo's view was not shared by all Jews of his own times; for when

32. Wise, et al., *Dead Sea Scrolls*, 56. This injunction is also found in the Temple Scroll (11Q19) 66:15–17 (ibid., 632), and in the biblical commentary 4Q251 frag. 17 (ibid., 351).

33. Philo, *Spec. Laws* 3.20, 26, Colson.

34. Positive statements praising these marriages are found in *Der. Er. Rab.* 2; *b. Yebam.* 62b; *t. Qidd.* 1:4, Lieberman. But the Samaritans, Falashas, and Karaites supported the view that this union was forbidden. See Levinson, "Textual Criticism," 232 n. 59.

Antipas, son of Herod the Great, married Herodias, daughter of his brother Aristobulus in 31 CE, their marriage was not criticized over this kinship relationship. Some people, however, criticized Antipas because Herodias had formerly been the wife of Antipas's half- brother Herod Phillip, who was still living. But there was no apparent objection to a marriage relationship between uncle and niece.[35]

1.1.4 Restrictions Affecting Wife's Sister, Daughter, or Mother

An incest prohibition affected the relationship between a man and his wife's sister. (From a female perspective: between a woman and her sister's husband.) But this was not an absolute rule; it applied only as long as both sisters were living. Thus Lev 18:18:

> Do not marry a woman as a rival to her sister and uncover her nakedness in the other's lifetime. (NJPS)

However, marriages involving two living sisters earlier did occur, as told in the Gen 29:16–30 narrative where Jacob married two sisters, Leah and Rachel. Even more interesting—and possibly attesting to the late survival of this practice—is the parable told in Ezekiel 23 where God is depicted as being married to two sisters, Oholah and Ohalibah, who represent the sister nations of Judea and Samaria! This is an allegory; but Ezekiel's ancient Israelite audience was apparently able to receive the parable without its message being

seriously compromised by the inclusion of a potentially conflicting norm. The same image was used in Jer 3:6–13, where God divorces one faithless woman (Israel) and then marries her sister (Judea) who proves even more faithless; God—imagined as the husband—then expresses his desire to have the first wife return. This suggests that Lev 18:18 was either a late addition to the list of prohibitions or was not universally accepted until much later on. It is clearly present, however, in the writings of Philo, who discusses the prohibition in more detail beyond what is given in Lev 18:18, making the point that the restriction of "in the other's lifetime" will apply in all cases, even if the man had divorced the first sister. He also offers a reason for the law: "avoidance of jealousy between the two women whose relationship to one another should otherwise be close."[36]

Another prohibition considers a man's relationship to his wife's daughter. (From a female perspective: between a woman and her stepfather.) In Lev 18:17 we read:

> Do not uncover the nakedness of a woman and her daughter; nor shall you marry [lit. take] her son's daughter or her daughter's daughter and uncover her nakedness: they are kindred; it is depravity. (NJPS)

Related in turn to this rule is the prohibition against a man engaging in sexual relations with his wife's mother. It is not mentioned in the Leviticus list but the act is condemned among the curses in Deut 27:23:

---

35. Furor over this marriage, because Herodias had previously been the wife of Phillip, Antipas's brother, is recounted in the New Testament Gospels (Matt 14:3–4; Mark 6:17–18; Luke 3:19). However, the account of Josephus, *Ant.* 18.109–19 gives quite different reasons for the unpopularity of Antipas, which are unrelated to family kinship issues.

36. Philo, *Spec. Laws* 3.27, Colson.

> Cursed be he who lies with his mother-in-law.—And all the people shall say, Amen. (NJPS)

The prophet Amos 2:7 condemns as unseemly a girl having sex with a father and son at the same time:

> Father and son go to the same girl, and thereby profane My holy name. (NJPS)

The pentateuchal statements, i.e., Lev 18:17 and Deut 27:23, describe situations where a man is married to one of the women involved. But it is less clear that some previous marriage was involved in Amos 2:7.[37] The position taken by the rabbis is that while this sexual liaison was lewd and unseemly, it would not legally rise to be considered as a punishable act of incest. This is stated in *m. Yebam.* 11:1: "A man may marry a woman who was violated or seduced by his son." The Mishnah goes on to relate that R. Judah argued against permitting this marriage. However, his view, while respected, was not taken as binding. A similar statement regarding a man with his woman's mother, daughter, or sister is given in the Tosefta, *t. Yebam.* 4:15, Lieberman:

> A man suspected (or accused) of having sexual relations with a woman should not marry her mother, daughter, or sister; (but) if he did marry (one of these relations) he does not have to divorce her.

Thus, the position taken in the Talmud and in later rabbinical law was that marriage needed to be present in order to trigger legal action against incest.[38]

In the ancient Near East we also find prohibitions against a man engaging in sexual relations with female relatives of his wife: her mother, her daughter, and her sister. In an Old Babylonian record from Mari in a trial for adultery, a man's wife was required to swear that she did not "pleasure father and son (together)."[39] There were likewise very strict prohibitions among the Hittites. Relations with mother and daughter are prohibited in Hittite Laws §195b:

> If a (free) man has a free woman (in marriage) and approaches her daughter (sexually), it is an unpermitted sexual pairing.

Hittite Laws §195c add an additional prohibition on a wife's sister:

> If he has the daughter (in marriage) and approaches her mother or her sister (sexually), it is an unpermitted pairing.

But, as in Lev 18:18, the wife's sister was permitted after the death of the wife; thus Hittite Laws §192:

> If a man's wife dies, [he may take her] sister [as his wife.] It is not an offense.

The Hittites were even stricter on the prohibition against a wife's sister than was the case in biblical Israel for they extended the prohibition even to the wife's female cousins who were classified as "sisters." We find this stated in a document from the fourteenth century BCE where the Hittite king Suppululiuma made a

---

Maimonides, *Mishnah Torah, Hilkhot Issurey Bi'ah* 2:11, 13.

37. Cf. e.g., Rashi, who says the girl was betrothed, while Qimhi assumes her to be unmarried.

38. Cf. the discussion in *b. Yebam.* 97a; cf.

39. ARM 26 488 (A.267). This document is treated in Lackenbacher, "Lettres de Buqâqum," 423–24.

treaty with Huqqana of Hayasa (located in modern day Armenia); their alliance was cemented by the Hittite king giving his daughter in marriage to Huqqana. In their treaty document the Hittite king included a provision instructing his barbarian vassal as follows:

> Furthermore, this sister whom I, My Majesty, have given to you as your wife has many sisters from her own family as well as from her extended family. They belong to your extended family because you have taken their sister. But for Hatti it is an important custom that a brother does not take his sister or female cousin (sexually). It is not permitted. In Hatti whoever commits such an act does not remain alive but is put to death here. Because your land is barbaric, it is *in* conflict(?). (There) one quite regularly takes his (wife's) sister or female cousin. But in Hatti it is not permitted. And if on occasion a sister of your wife, or the wife of a brother, or a female cousin comes to you, give her something to eat and drink. Both of you eat, drink, and make merry! But you shall not desire to take her (sexually). It is not permitted, and people are put to death as a result of that act.[40]

The Neo-Assyrian literary and religious passages mentioned above (sec. 1.1.1) likewise imply a prohibition concerning a man's wife and her mother. But we also see that these strict prohibitions might be relaxed for sex with slave women and other unfree persons; they could also be relaxed if the parties were not married. This is true for a woman's mother and her daughter, as well as a brother's or a father's sexual partner. This is seen in Hittite Laws

40. Beckman, *Hittite Diplomatic Texts*, 27–28.

§194 and §200a. The law in §194 reads as follows:

> If a free man has intercourse with slave women, sisters who have the same mother, and also with their mother, it is not an offense. If brothers sleep with (the same) free woman, it is not an offense. If father and son sleep with the same female slave or prostitute, it is not an offense.

Again in §200a:

> If anyone is regularly cohabiting with an *arnuwlaš*–woman and has intercourse with her mother and her sister, it is not an offense.[41]

The legal position taken here is essential agreement with what the later rabbis said (cited above) about there being no legal consequences attached to such liaisons when they involved unmarried women.

The situation in Babylonia was apparently not as strict as among the Hittites with respect to sexual connection between a married man and the sisters of his wife. We know of one instance, where Zimrilim, king of Mari gave two of his daughters in marriage to the same neighboring king. The two women were apparently half-siblings to one another; and the situation seems to be one in which the second sister was given after her eldest sister proved to be childless. There was friction between the sisters; and when later, the eldest did have children, the younger sister became very unhappy; she was subsequently divorced and returned home to Mari.[42]

41. This is the second part of §200a; the first part is treated in sec. 1.8. Hoffner, *Laws of the Hittites*, 273 notes that scholars have taken the *arnuwalaš*–woman to be a female captive, taken in battle.

42. For the documents describing the married lives of the two sisters see Sasson, "Biogaphical

Childbearing was apparently also a key consideration in a number of marriage contracts involving sisters from the Old Babylonian period where a senior wife—apparently childless—took another woman into her home to be a second wife to her husband. In these marriages, the second woman was of inferior rank to the first and was required to do domestic service for the first wife; sometimes it is clear that the second wife was a slave woman. The second wife was however at times designated as a "sister" to the first; the relationship was an adoptive one, designed to maintain solidarity with the senior wife; their husband could not divorce one without the other also leaving him. One may understand this relationship as a means of creating a measure of protection against internal rivalry between the two women and protecting the senior wife against the consequences of change in affection between the husband and his first wife; this is in fact explicitly stated in many of the marriage contracts involving sisters.[43] Many, if not most of the senior wives were priestesses; and it has been suggested that these were unions without the expectation of normal sexual relations between the senior wife and her husband. The second wife provided sexual companionship and the possibility of offspring.[44]

We find another depiction of one man marrying two sisters in the Sumerian version of the Epic of Gilgamesh, in the encounter between Gilgamesh and the monster Huwawa who guards the Cedar Mountain. Gilgamesh promises him two of his sisters in marriage in exchange for surrendering one of his protective auras:

> Let me send you my big sister Enmebaragesi to be your wife on the mountain . . . let me send you my little sister Peshtur, to be your secondary wife on the mountain. Give me one of your auras of terror and I will become your kinsman.[45]

The relationship between the eldest and youngest of the two sisters mirrors resembles what we see in the later sisterhood adoptions by senior priestess wives, where the second or younger wife is subordinate to the first or eldest. Because the element *En,* which can mean "high priestess" occurs in the personal name of the elder sister, it has been suggested that the elder sister of Gilgamesh was, in fact, a priestess.[46] If this is so, then the pattern here would correspond to what is seen in the Old Babylonian records involving the marriages of priestesses. I should also mention here three cases where the main priestess wife came into her husband's home with her dowry plus a secondary wife, who is described as already being a sister of the priestess. There is no evidence in these records to suggest that the relationship between the sisters was not a natal one—although, to be sure, "adoption" may have occurred at or just before the marriage took place.[47]

Notes," A more recent and complete study is that of Durand, "Trois etudes"; see also the comments in Charpin, "Les Représentants," 43–46.

43. Greengus, "Sisterhood Adoption," 13–15 and documents cited there. Cf. also Wilcke. "*CT* 45 119."

44. Marriages involving childless *nadītu* priestesses, who either gave their husbands a second wife or allowed him to take one, are discussed in Hammurapi Laws §§144–147 (not cited here); these laws also show the inferior status of these wives. Cf. further, for life of chastity, Harris, "Hierodulen."

45. George, *Epic of Gilgamesh,* 116, lines 140–44.

46. Shaffer, "Gilgamesh and Huwawa," 307–13.

47. The marriage records are BE 6/1 84, *CT*

We see a relaxation of the prohibition against a man marrying a woman and her daughter at Emar in northern Syria, during the last half of the second millennium BCE, In one contract, the primary wife, a *qadištu* priestess, gives her daughter in marriage to her husband and pledges if that daughter dies, she will give him another of her daughters in marriage; and, if the second daughter dies, a third daughter![48] Marriage with the priestess herself may have been a union without sexual relations, like what I have surmised in dual marriages involving priestesses and their sisters. In another document, a man marries a woman and declares that, at the same time, her daughter is also designated as his wife. The husband in this contract also gives his own daughter to the woman's son, whom he adopts as his own son, while, at the same time disinheriting his own natural son.[49] The relationship between the two families was thus meant to be very close; and the wife's daughter appears to have been kept as a potential wife "in reserve" in case her mother died. In any event, at Emar, we see that the prohibition against a man marrying his wife's daughter was not an absolute taboo.

1.1.5 Reflections on the Incest Rules

If one considers the ancient Near Eastern prohibitions and compares them with the prohibitions found in the biblical laws, it seems that they are really not so far apart. Accordingly, the condemnation in Lev 18:27–30, "for all those abhorrent things were done by the people who were in the land before you, and the land became defiled" (NJPS), appears to be excessive, at least with respect to all incest rules, since we find that most of the earlier biblical prohibitions were widely known if not also observed in non-Israelite societies. The condemnation in Lev 18:27–30 could therefore only apply to later, stricter prohibitions, which were not generally known or practiced outside of Israel.[50] There is, moreover, some evidence that the practices similar to the early biblical ones were also known in the wider ancient world. Philo, for example, in his defense of the later standards in Judaism, states that among the Greeks, Solon allowed two sisters who were not of the same mother to be married to the same husband; and that the Lacedaemonians permitted a man to marry his paternal half-sister (as Abraham did anciently); however, states Philo, the Egyptians allowed full siblings to marry each other.[51] His last statement about Egypt must, however, be qualified; prior to Roman times, there was marriage of full siblings in the royal family but among ordinary Egyptians, such unions were rare and mostly involved half-siblings. However, during Roman times—the time of Philo and later—such unions were permitted among Egyptians, although remaining as a forbidden union for Roman citizens.[52]

---

8 2a, and *CT* 45 119; see discussion in Greengus, "Sisterhood Adoption," and Wilcke. "*CT* 45 119."

48. Arnaud, *Emar*, 124.

49. This document is published and discussed in Hallo, "Love and Marriage at Ashtata."

50. Ibn Ezra in his commentary to Lev 18:18 thus offers the opinion that the condemnation in Lev 18:27–30 is a general statement; it was meant to imply only that the gentiles had committed a large part but necessarily not all of the listed offenses.

51. Philo, *Spec. Laws* 3.22–24.

52. Jasnow, "Egypt: New Kingdom," 324; Manning, "Egypt: Demotic Law." 835. Evidence for Egyptian marriages during Roman times is given in Middleton, "Brother–Sister."

In at least one instance, the incest rules among the gentiles could be stricter than those of the Jews; this was true in regard to marriage between an uncle and his niece. Roman law absolutely forbade a Roman citizen to marry his sister's daughter; marriage between a man and his brother's daughter was apparently also frowned upon, although it was later permitted by action of the emperor Claudius. Imperial Rome also tolerated different marriage rules for her subjects who were not Roman.[53]

Thus when one compares the marriage rules found in ancient Near Eastern sources with those found in the Bible, one finds that, with few exceptions, they are similar to the older biblical incest rules. The Bible does not tell us convincingly why it was necessary or desirable for Israel to extend the range of incest prohibitions beyond those which were practiced in earlier times both among the Israelites and among the gentiles of the ancient world. One can therefore only speculate on possible reasons. One possible reason, as already mentioned, may be a reluctance to relax barriers to relationships that were once in place; this would explain the restrictions that developed to limit the possibility of once permitted unions like levirate marriages and barring sons "inheriting" their father's concubines. Maimonides suggests that the enhanced prohibitions were enacted to prevent sexual contact between males and females who, because of being close kin, would come into easy contact with one another.[54] Some of the newer biblical rules were simply generational ex-

tensions of existing ones, e.g., extending the prohibition regarding a man's daughter to his granddaughter (Lev 18:10) or step-granddaughter (Lev18:17). Similarly, the prohibition against sisters of a man's mother or father who, like his own sisters, were now also to be forbidden (Lev 18:12–13; 20:19). The newer biblical rules appear to favor exogamy over endogamy; I will have more to say about this in my conclusions (sec. 9).

We should observe that many of the biblical prohibitions are stated without penalty; it appears, therefore, that when the Bible expanded the range of incest, it did not, at the same time, explicitly expand the range of penalties that were to be imposed upon those who violated these newer rules. I believe that these omissions were due to the circumstance that when the full, expanded body of incest rules was written down in Leviticus, the Jews were then living under Persian rule. The local Judean courts were perhaps limited in their power to impose the most serious kinds of punishment—especially capital punishments—beyond that which were customary and in place for longstanding and widely held incest violations. The Bible therefore stresses that the Israelites should observe these rules because they were divine commandments; and indeed we find statements of divine authority preceding the lists of incest rules in Lev 18:4–5 and 20:7–8:

> My rules alone shall you observe, and faithfully follow My laws: I the LORD am your God. You shall keep My laws and My rules, by the pursuit of which man shall live: I am the LORD. (Lev 18:4–5; NJPS)

> You shall sanctify yourselves and be holy, for I the LORD am your

---

53. Treggiari, *Roman Marriage,* 37–39 citing Gaius, *Inst.*1.62. Cf. also 1 Cor 5:1.

54. *Guide* 3.49 in Maimonides, *Guide,* 2:606–7.

God. You shall faithfully observe My laws: I the LORD make you holy. (Lev 20:7–8 NJPS)

The observance of the incest rules thus became part of each person's religious duty; every Jew was obligated to observe the divine commandments. Acts of incest that violated prohibitions held in common by both Judean and Persian customs, however, might still be severely punished by the courts. For such offenses, even the death penalty could be imposed. Thus we find sexual relations between a man and his wife's mother are punished by death in Leviticus 20:14 which conforms to the practice found in Hittite Laws §195b and §195c (cited above). Sexual relations between and man and his son's wife are punished by death both in Lev 20:12 as in Hammurapi Laws §155 (cited above). Sexual relations between a man and his father's wife were clearly forbidden (as we have seen above) in Hittite Laws §190 and Hammurapi Laws §158 (although, as we have also seen, this restriction could be relaxed to varying degrees after the father's death). Lev 20:11 therefore could assign the death penalty for this offense. We unfortunately possess no real information on the exact incest rules followed under the Persians; but it seems likely that they would have be in line with the older Near Eastern norms.

But for violation of newer prohibitions that were unique to the Judeans, no judicial punishments are stated. As divine commandments, however, there was a theological expectation that their violation would be subject to punishments of divine origin. Thus, a man who engages in sexual relations with his mother's or father's sister in Lev 20:19 will have to "bear his sin"; and sexual relations between a

man and his brother's wife or his father's brother's wife are both punished by childlessness in Lev 20:20–21. The Bible also uses the rubric of divine punishment to yoke together a newer prohibition against marriage with a paternal half-sister with the ancient, longstanding prohibition against marriage with a maternal sister. In Lev 20:17 one who violates either prohibition is subject to "being cut off" by Heaven.[55]

There are still other prohibitions for which no penalties of any kind are stated; these include sexual relations between a man and his granddaughters (Lev 18:10), his wife's daughter or granddaughter (Lev 18:17), and his wife's sister (Lev 18:18). Were these left to be unpunished? Not according to R. Isaac in a *baraita* cited by the Babylonian Talmud (*b. Meg.* 7b, *Makk.* 23b) where he states that all incest offenses were included in the "umbrella" statement of Lev 18:29: "All who do any of those abhorrent things—such persons shall be cut off from their people" (NJPS). Therefore these, too, were subject to divine punishment even if a punishment was not explicitly stated in the biblical laws. Other rabbis, however, were unable to stand by and leave matters to Heaven, at least in cases where offenders were caught and clearly guilty. In such cases they argued that rabbinical courts should flog the offenders even if they were subject to divine punishment. Flogging, they believed, could actually benefit the offenders—at least ones who repented of their sin; the offenders would thereby be forgiven and

55. Jewish tradition has consistently taken the punishment of being "cut off" as due to divine action. Milgrom, *Leviticus,* 1:457–60 presents views on this punishment, and argues for understanding it as divine action rather than as social ostracism or "excommunication" as others have argued.

the penitent would be spared further, divine punishment.[56] These rabbinic statements may reflect the social reality that I have already mentioned, namely, the limited authority of Jewish courts to impose more, severe corporal punishment not only during Roman times, but also during the earlier centuries of Babylonian, Persian, Ptolemaic, and Seleucid rule. Moreover, it is probable that if the local Jewish courts of those times could ever impose the death penalty—and we do not know if they could—it would likely have been for offenses that were similarly treated by the laws of their rulers. Local Jewish courts may however have been given authority to flog, which in those days was a socially accepted—and nonfatal—penalty.

1.2 DISSOLUTION OF MARRIAGE

1.2.1 Divorce

There are no formal laws in the Bible that deal with the customary solemnities involved in the formation of marriage, although there are some references to betrothal, brideprice, dowry, and the celebration of nuptials.[57] These customary elements, however, are mentioned in biblical laws dealing with the dissolution of marriage, especially in divorce, which often generated conflicts over property and assets. Deuteronomy 24:1–4 describes the dissolution of marriage through divorce and goes on to prohibit a man from remarrying his divorced wife if she had

married another husband in the intervening time:

> If a man takes a wife and (sexually) possesses her and it happens that she fails to please him because he finds something objectionable about her, and he writes her a bill of divorcement, hands it to her, and sends her away from his house and she leaves his household and becomes the wife of another man; then this latter man hates (i.e., rejects) her, writes her a bill of divorcement, hands it to her, and sends her away from his house; or if he—the man who married her subsequently—dies. Then the first husband who (previously) divorced her shall not take her to be his wife again, since she has been defiled—for that would be abhorrent to the Lord. You must not bring sin upon the land that the Lord your God is giving you as a heritage.

A sentiment against remarriage, similar to what is stated in Deut 24:1–4, is presented in Jer 3:1:

> [The word of the LORD came to me] as follows: If a man divorces his wife, and she leaves him and marries another man, can he ever go back to her? Would not such a land be defiled? Now you have whored with many lovers: can you return to Me?—says the LORD. (NJPS)

A prohibition against this type of remarriage was not part of the general list of marriage prohibitions in Leviticus 18 and 20. It appears to be a newer innovation, because elsewhere in biblical narratives we find that husbands might indeed take back their wives who had been married to other men. This was done by David who, after Saul's death, claimed back his

---

56. Cf. *m. Makk.* 3:1; *m. Ker.* 1:1; *b. Sanh.* 10a; *b. Makk.* 13b.

57. Betrothal is mentioned in Deut 20:7; brideprice in Gen 34:12; Exod 22:16; and 1 Sam 18:25; brideprice is implied in Jacob's service for Laban in Gen 29:18, 27. A royal dowry is described in 1 Kgs 9:16. A customary week of wedding celebration is mentioned in Gen 29:27–28.

wife Michal, who (in 1 Sam 25:44) had been given to Palti son of Laish; in 2 Sam 3:14–16 it is told:

> And David also sent messengers to Ishbosheth, the son of Saul, saying, "Give me my wife Michal, whom I had espoused to me (by paying a brideprice) of one hundred Philistine foreskins." So Ishbosheth sent and took her away from [her present] husband [i.e.,] from Paltiel son of Laish. And her husband went with her, walking and weeping after her up to Bahurim; then Abner said to him: "Turn back," and he went back.

Writing much later during the first century CE, Philo, in a long comment on the law of Deut 24:1–4, sharply criticized any husband who might not choose to observe this law but instead take back his wife after she had married another man:

> And if a man is willing to contract himself with such a woman, he must be saddled with a character for degeneracy and loss of manhood. He has eliminated from his soul the hatred of evil, that emotion by which our life is so well served and the affairs of houses and cities are conducted as they should be, and has lightly taken upon him the stamp of two heinous crimes, adultery and pandering. For such subsequent reconciliations are proofs of both. The proper punishment for him is death and for the woman also.[58]

Philo's lengthy rationalization may suggest that the prohibition against remarriage contained in this law was not practiced among non-Judeans living in his time. I find no parallel to this prohibition in the ancient Near Eastern collections; this prohibition—as far as I know—is biblical only. Philo in his interpretation however also introduces additional descriptive elements—adultery and pandering. These ideas go back to the phrase "because he finds something objectionable about her" which can more literally to be translated "because he found in her a matter of sexual shame." The Septuagint and *Targum Onqelos* in fact anciently translated: "shameful thing, a matter of transgression." There is, moreover, a long tradition of rabbinic interpretation, which like Philo, takes the literal reading and understands the husband in Deut 24:1–4 to have divorced his wife because of her questionable behavior or loose conduct, perhaps lacking actionable proof upon which to convict her of adultery.[59] Taking her back after being the sexual partner of another man—even if she was legally married to the second man, was for Philo akin to pandering, i.e., the willful sharing of a wife with another man. For Philo, this behavior is comparable to that of adulterers, who deserve the death penalty (as in sec. 1.3.1).

The writing of a bill of divorcement in Deut 24:1–4 can be linked to other biblical references, which describe a document of divorce being written in the context of a wife's alleged immoral conduct:

> Jer 3:8 . . . because faithless Israel had committed adultery, I sent her away and gave her a document of divorce; yet her sister, treacherous Judah, had no fear and she too went and was a whore.

---

58. Philo, *Spec. Laws* 3.30–31, Colson.

59. This idea is repeated numerous times in rabbinic literature; cf. e.g., *m. Sotah* 6:3; *m. Git.* 9:10; *b. Ber.* 25b; *b. Shabb.* 150a; *b. B. Metz.* 114b; *j. Sotah* 17b, cf. also *m. Ket.* 7:6, which is discussed in sec. 1.2.4 below.

Isa 50:1 Thus said the Lord: Where is the document of divorce belonging to your mother whom I sent away? And (to) which of my creditors did I sell you (in slavery)? Indeed, you were sold because of your sins and for your transgressions was your mother sent away.[60]

The writing of a formal record of divorce may thus have been a means of creating a clear and public break in a marital relationship, which fell under the cloud of adultery, so that this husband will not be tempted to take back a wife whom he divorced because of such suspicions. This scenario would fit in with the interpretation given by Philo, associating Deut 24:1–4 with pandering and adultery. Matthew 5:31–32 appears, like Philo, similarly to link a husband's divorcing his wife with his suspicions about her sexual conduct:

> It was also said, "Whoever divorces his wife, let him give her a certificate of divorce." But I say to you that anyone who divorces his wife, except on the ground of unchastity, causes her to commit adultery . . . (NRSV).[61]

This same sentiment is preserved in the Mishnah, *m. Git.* 9:10, where an influential group of scholars argued:

> (The followers of) the House of Shammai declare (that) a man may only divorce his wife if he has found in her (some) shameful

matter, as it is written (in Scripture) "because he found something of sexual shame about her."

But the majority of scholars disagreed and instead chose to interpret the verse in the broadest possible way, allowing the husband an unlimited right to divorce his wife upon any grounds. It has, however, also been suggested that the time and expense involved in preparing and writing of a formal divorce document was as a means to delay a divorce being rashly instituted by a husband on frivolous grounds.[62]

Such reasoning may have led the rabbis to require the writing of a written record of divorce for every divorce, even in cases where there was no suspicion of adultery or loose conduct. The rabbis further legislated, on the basis of Deut 24:1–4, that only husbands had the legal authority to issue a divorce document.[63] However, it is clear that a written document was apparently not seen as always necessary during earlier, biblical times, where one finds that divorce, initiated by either spouse on unspecified grounds, might normally be accomplished by a formal, oral declaration presented before an assembly or congregation. This in fact was the practice of the Jewish community living in Egypt at Elephantine during the fifth century BCE.[64] Their practice of divorce and

60. The prophet here omits the expected parallel "her transgressions" and his stating "your transgressions" instead moves directly to address the guilty nation, whose behavior is the real object of his criticism.

61. Cf. also Matt 19:9 (where a document is not mentioned) and Matt 1:19, where Joseph was planning to divorce Mary because she was pregnant before marriage took place.

62. This is suggested in Driver, *Deuteronomy,* 270–73.

63. Josephus, *Ant.* 15.259 appears to agree with the later rabbinic view, when he criticizes Salome for divorcing her husband and sending him a document of divorce. But Mark 10:11–12 is aware of a wife initiating divorce, and condemns a wife as well as a husband for doing so.

64. The cited passages, Cowley Papyrus 15, Kraeling Papyrus 7, and 2 have been fully republished in Porten and Yardeni, *Textbook of Aramaic Documents,* 60–63, 78–83, 139–40.

assigning an associated penalty are the same in each case; but the stated financial consequences could vary, reflecting each party's wealth and specific prenuptial agreements between the couples. The written documents at Elephantine in fact record a variety of prenuptial agreements. Let us first consider the Elephantine document, Kraeling 2:7–11, where the provisions are the same for husband and wife:

> Tomorrow or a later day, if Anani will stand up in an assembly and say: "I hate Tamut my wife," divorce (lit. hatred) money is on his head; he will give to Tamut 7 shekels (and) 2 quarters; and all that she brought in (to their home) she will remove–from straw to string. Tomorrow or a later day, if Tamut will stand up and declare: "I hate my husband Anani," divorce money is on her head. She will give to Anani 7 shekels (and) 2 quarters; and all that she brought in on her part she will remove—from straw to string.

The same bilateral process of declaration but with variation in divorce penalties is described in Cowley 15:22–31:

> Tomorrow or a later day, if Mibtahiah will stand up in an assembly and declare: "I hate Eshor my husband, divorce money is on her head. She will sit by the scales and weigh out to Eshor 7 shekels (and) 2 quarters; and all that she brought in (to their home) she will take out—from straw to string—and she may go wherever she likes; and there is (to be) no suit or process against her. Tomorrow or a later day, if Eshor will stand up in an assembly and say "I hate my wife Mibtahiah, the brideprice (he paid for) her is forfeit and all that she brought in her hand she shall take

out—from straw to string—in one day in one stroke; and she shall go wherever she likes; and there is (to be) no suit or process.

Yet another description of declaration and divorce money, with more complex personal property arrangements, is found in Kraeling 7:21–28:

> Tomorrow or a later day, if Ananiah will stand up in an assembly and declare: "I hate my wife Yehoyishma, she will not be a wife to me," divorce money is on his head. All that she brought in to his house he will give her—her money and her garments valued at 7 shekels and 8 hallurs and the rest of her goods, which are recorded (above). He shall give (these) to her in one day in one stroke and she shall go wherever she wishes. And if Yehoyishma will hate her husband Ananiah and declare: "I hate you, I will not be a wife unto you," divorce money is on her head. She will (also) forfeit her brideprice; she will sit by the scale and give to her husband Ananiah 7 shekels (and) 2 quarters; and she will go out from him with the rest of her money and her goods and her property valued at 6 karsh 8 shekels and 5 hallur and also the rest of her goods recorded (above). He shall give (these) to her in one day and in one stroke; and she can go to her father's house.

These three documents were written at the time of marriage because of a need to record property items belonging to the wife, which she and her family were interested to recovering in case of divorce; these documents thus also include other prenuptial provisions that the couple agreed to at the time of marriage and did not wish to see later disputed. Otherwise, there was no need to write a document to record the existence of either a marriage or a divorce. Change in legal status, obligation, and similar transactions were created by witnessed public ceremonies involving oral declarations and symbolic acts. What we see at Elephantine was also true in the larger ancient Near Eastern world; documents were written only as an evidentiary measure to further secure and bear witness to changes in property, rights, or status.[65]

I therefore tend to regard the writing of a document in Deut 24:1–4 as supplementary to the divorce action; it could there have served to underscore the rejected status of a woman who was divorced by her husband because of loose conduct or suspected adultery. The delivery of a document may have offered a substitute, less public procedure, avoiding the potential embarrassment of having the husband "standing up in the assembly" and needing to "explain" why this divorce was happening. The wife, too, was similarly spared public embarrassment for a divorce unsupported by evidence of her wrongdoing; but there could be no uncertainty about her divorced status when a document to that effect was in her possession. The later rabbis may have favored this more private method of divorce and therefore adopted it as a universal practice.

Moreover, by rabbinic times, perhaps aided by the influence of Roman practice, the understanding of written records had changed. Documents signed by the parties or their representatives were seen as the vehicle effecting the legal transactions they recorded, rather than merely as witness to them. Yet, interestingly, even into rabbinic times, the legal documents that were written e.g., for manumission, marriage and divorce, still preserved the earlier, customary oral declarations between the parties. This is clearly evident in the Mishnah, *m. Git.* 9:3:

> The essential language for a divorce document is "Behold, you are permitted to (i.e., allowed to marry) any (other) man." . . . The essential language for a manumission document is "Behold you are a free woman, you belong to yourself."[66]

Divorce documents are therefore, not surprisingly, rare in the ancient Near East. When they do occur, they appear to have been written to record the payment and receipt of divorce penalties, similar to those mentioned in the Elephantine documents above. In early Babylonia, we also find formal oral declarations of divorce and sometimes also a formal ceremony of severance; the divorcing party—in our examples the husband—cuts the hem of his wife's garment as a symbolic gesture of separation.[67] The declarations uttered are straightforward: "You are not my wife" or "You are not my husband." Similar

---

65. On the essentially oral character of ancient Near Eastern contracts, including marriage, divorce, adoption, see Greengus, "Redefining 'Inchoate Marriage,'" 134–36; and Greengus, "Old Babylonian Marriage Contract," 512–24—for Old Babylonian, Middle Babylonian, and Late Babylonian contexts. Cf. also for Neo-Assyrian times the statements in Postgate, "Assyrian Ladies," 99, and Radner, *Neuassyrischen Privaturkunden,* 157–58. Wilcke, *Early Ancient Near Eastern Law,* 76 maintains that this oral process is already the practice in the earliest periods from which we have records.

66. For additional discussion of early rabbinic divorce documents cf. Brewer, "Deuteronomy . . . Origin of the Jewish Divorce Certificate," 236–43. For an oral declaration in connection with *prosbul* (discussed below in sec. 2.4) cf. *m. Shev.* 10:4.

67. For cutting the hem as a rite of divorce cf. *CAD* S, 322 sub *sissiktu*.

negative statements were also used to repudiate adoption, e.g., "You are not my son" or "You are not my father/mother."[68]

The Bible in fact also preserves traces of such oral declarations; in Hos 2:4, we find:

> Upbraid your mother, upbraid her! For she is not my wife and I am not her husband. And let her put away her harlotries from her face And her adulteries from between her breasts.

Hosea here appears to use a poetic paraphrase of the direct second person address that we saw in the Elephantine documents: "You are not my wife" or "You are not my husband." We also find a literary echo of the symbolic cutting the hem of a garment in 1 Sam 15:27–28, in a scene where Saul desperately seeks to keep the prophet Samuel from abandoning him:

> And Samuel turned to go off and Saul seized the corner of his robe, and it tore. And Samuel said to him, "The Lord this (very) day has ripped away the kingship of Israel from you and has given it to your neighbor, (who is) better than you.[69]

One is able to assume, therefore, that Biblical society was familiar with divorce or separation ceremonies accomplished through the use of oral declarations and possibly also with symbolic actions or gestures like cutting the hem. The required or recommended use of the divorce document (as in Deut 24:1–4; Jer 3:8; and Isa 50:1) appears to be a biblical innovation, perhaps introduced for the special situation of private, but unproven, suspicion that has been described. Specially written divorce documents are absent at Elephantine; and in non-Israelite ancient Near Eastern practice, divorce records, when they rarely do occur, generally seem to be written in order to record payments of penalties or distribution of financial assets.[70] Both wife and husband, at least in theory, seem to have had equivalent legal power to divorce the other partner, although (as we shall see in sections 1.2.3–1.2.4 below) measures were anciently often instituted to suppress the ability of wives to divorce their husbands.

1.2.2 Marriage Cancellation

There are additional laws relating to the dissolution of marriage found in rabbinic sources, which do not appear in the Bible. Similarity between these rabbinic laws and laws found in ancient Near Eastern traditions indicate that these laws were part of a larger stream of legal traditions going back over many centuries. One can therefore regard these rabbinic laws as preserving ancient content that was "omitted" by the Biblical writers who, after all, nowhere claim that the laws written in the Torah encompassed the totality of the ancient legal traditions of their time. Later rabbis could thus with some justification represent these and other laws "omitted" from the Bible as part of an oral or unwritten tradition which, in their view of history, went back to the time of Moses or

---

68. For examples, see references in my previous comments above on the oral character of contracts.

69. In Mesopotamia, in Old Assyrian documents, we also find "to hold the hem" used to describe detaining someone in order to settle a legal claim. Cf. *CAD* S, 255 sub *sikku*.

70. Cf. Greengus, "Old Babylonian Marriage Contract," 518 n. 62; Westbrook, *Old Babylonian Marriage Law,* 69–71; Westbrook, "The Character of Ancient Near Eastern Law," 48–49.

even earlier—among the "Noahide laws," which were given at the dawn of civilization (see, for discussion, Introduction and sec. 9. Final Thoughts).

There is a law, found both in the Mishnah and in the Tosefta, that deals with the disposition of the groom's prenuptial gifts when the wedding was cancelled because either the bride or groom had died. In the Mishnah (*m. B. Bat.* 9:5) we read:

> (In the case of) a man who sent prenuptial gifts to his (prospective) father-in-law's house—(if) he sent there (gifts worth) one hundred minas (i.e., 1000 dinars) and he ate there (with her family) even one dinar's worth of (food) at (his— i.e., the groom's prenuptial) feast (and afterwards he/she died), these (gifts) may not (then) be reclaimed. If he did not eat there, these (gifts) may be reclaimed. If (however) he sent copious prenuptial gifts (with the intention) that (some of these) would come back with her (after the wedding) to her husband's house, these (additional items) may be reclaimed. (However in the case of) less abundant betrothal gifts (where one expected) that they be used (up) in her father's house, these may not be reclaimed.

The Tosefta (*t. B. Bat.* 10:10, Lieberman) also addresses this case:

> (In the case where) a man sent prenuptial gifts to (his prospective) father-in-law's house and he ate there (some of his foodstuffs that were then used) for the celebrations for the birth of sons or (for) other purposes, whatever they all ate, they ate; but the (remainder of the) prenuptial (food) gifts remain

in their place (to be later consumed for the prenuptial feasts). (In the case where) one sent prenuptial gifts (and then he i.e., the groom died) things that would have been consumed in the house of her (the prospective bride's) father-in-law's house, she (the bride) is not required to return out of her hand; but she is required to return out of her hand items which would not customarily be consumed in the father-in-law's house. If she (i.e., the bride) died, her father is not required to return those items which would have customarily used up had she lived; but her father is required to return those items which would not ordinarily have been used up during her lifetime.

The principle embodied in these laws is summed up and more succinctly restated in the Gemara which comments upon the Mishnah (*b. B. Bat.* 146a):

> Prenuptial gifts that were expected to be used up may not be reclaimed; those that were not expected to be used up may be reclaimed.

The background for these laws was the custom, either following the making of a betrothal or "engagement" agreement or as part of the extended celebration prior to the wedding, for a groom to bring or send to the home of his future bride gifts of foodstuffs and non-consumables like clothing, jewelry, and the like. The groom, often accompanied by friends and members of his family, would there share a feast of celebration in honor of his future bride, her family, and friends before the wedding and later conducting the bride to his own home.

The customary gift of the groom was a traditional feature of marriage already in ancient times; and the problem of how to dispose of its assets is also treated in the ancient Near Eastern law collections. In Eshnunna Laws 17–18 we read:

> If the son of a (free) man brought the groom's gift[71] to the house of (his) father-in-law and if (afterwards) one of the two (i.e., future bride or groom) died, the silver (i.e., the value of the goods) returns to its owner. If he (the groom) married her and she entered his house (and then) either the groom or the bride died, he (i.e., the groom or his heir) may not take out all that he brought; only what is left over may he take back.

These Eshnunna Laws articulate a principle similar to that found in the rabbinic sources, namely that the groom (or his family) is entitled to recover the value of the gifts, but not any perishables or foodstuffs that might already have been consumed. We see this same principle again articulated in Middle Assyrian Laws §A 43, which was discussed above (sec. 1.1.2). That law describes a situation where groom disappeared or died after the betrothal gifts were delivered to the home of the bride. If no other relative of the groom can "fill in" taking the bride in levirate marriage, then the bride's father will return the betrothal gifts; however, "precious stones or anything that is not edible [i.e., perishable] he shall return in full value; but (the value of) what is edible,

he need not return." There seems to have been little change in applying this principle over the centuries, except that the Mishnah limits the right of the groom's family to recover the value of foodstuffs if the groom ate at the pre-nuptial feast before he (or the bride) died. The Tosefta goes further and precludes the recovery of the value of foodstuffs even if some of the groom's foodstuffs were "borrowed" and consumed at any another family celebration, taking place at the bride's home.[72]

1.2.3 Dissolution Because of Illness

We find another ancient "oral law" in the Mishnah and Tosefta, dealing with a husband whose wife was chronically ill; the husband should support her but he had the legal right to divorce her without blame. In the Mishnah, *m. Ket.* 4:9, we read:

> If she (his wife) has been smitten (with a chronic ailment), he is obligated for her healing. If he (however) says "here is her document of divorce and her marriage settlement, let her heal herself" he has the right to do so.

The nature of the wife's illness is not defined; the laws focus, rather, on the extent of financial responsibility that must be borne by the husband when chronic illness occurs. Although this is not stated, it is likely that the wife's illness had impaired

---

71. The ancient Babylonian sources employ a variety of terms to describe the groom's gifts. The Eshnunna Laws use the term *tirhatum;* in other places one also finds *biblum, zubullûm;* the latter term is cognate to Hebrew *sivlonot,* which is the term used in the rabbinic sources. The terms all literally denote "gifts carried in by the groom." Cf. *CAD* Z, 152–53, and Greengus, "Bridewealth in Sumerian Sources," 84–85.

72. Driver and Miles, *Assyrian Laws,* 186, recognized and noted the similarity with the rabbinic sources cited in the discussion above. The custom of bringing "betrothal gifts" is also attested in Sumerian sources and continued into the Middle Ages and beyond. See Greengus, "Bridewealth in Sumerian Sources," and 76 n. 210 there for later rabbinic citations.

the possibility for the couple to pursue a normal family life.

A variant of this law provision appears in the Tosefta (*t. Ket.* 4:5, Lieberman):

> If she (a widow married to her levir) was being maintained through her husband's assets and needed healing, that is considered as part of (her customary) maintenance. Rabbi Simeon ben Gamaliel said: if it is healing, which has a limit, it may be charged against her marriage settlement; if it is without limit, it is considered like maintenance (which would have been a continuing obligation upon a husband.) If it was during years of famine and he (the levir) said "take whatever property is yours and your marriage settlement (and) leave and take care of yourself (on your own), he has this right (to divorce her on these terms).

According the Tosefta, the obligation of supporting a sick wife passed on to her levir, who married her after her husband's death. However, according to R. Simeon ben Gamaliel, he had the option to transfer this responsibility to her personally if, at the same time, he relinquished to her possession whatever assets were her own or had been set aside for her by the deceased husband.[73]

Physical impairment as a basis for divorce is found in Hammurapi Laws §§148–149:

> If a man married a woman and then a skin(?) disease has taken hold of her (and) he decides to marry a second wife, he may marry; the wife upon whom the skin(?) disease has taken hold—he may not divorce her; she shall dwell in the household they fashioned (for themselves) and he shall continue maintaining her as long as she lives. If that woman does not wish to dwell in the house of her husband, he shall make good to her the dowry she brought from her father's house and she shall go off (on her own).

Physical impairment is also the basis of divorce in the Laws of Lipit-Ishtar §28:

> If a man's chosen wife (is ill to a degree that) her eye is affected(?) and her arm is disabled, she shall not leave home. Her husband may take an additional wife; the second wife must (help) support the chosen (i.e., the first) wife.[74]

The diseases mentioned are evidently chronic ones, not subject to healing; they are thus of the type characterized by R. Gamaliel as "without limit." The woman's physical impairment would explain why the laws permit the husband to take a second wife, although by doing so he may create an environment in which the sick wife no longer wishes to remain under the same roof with the husband and his new wife; the sick wife may then initiate a divorce, as described in Hammurapi Laws §148. Otherwise—at least according to what is stated in the ancient Near Eastern laws—the husband's obligation

---

73. This provision is discussed by Maimonides, *Mishnah Torah, Hilkhot Ishut* 18:5. In *Hilkhot Ishut* 14:17 he notes that while the first husband also possessed the legal power to divorce his wife in order to avoid the financial burden, Maimonides viewed the exercise of such right as a breach of decency.

74. A variant text has: "the husband who has taken a (second) able (bodied) wife must support (both) the second wife (and) the chosen (i.e. first) wife." See Civil, "New Sumerian Law Fragments," 2–3.

for continuing maintenance seems to be unlimited. There is no suggestion in the laws that he could divorce a sick wife who wished to remain in their home. Ancient documents demonstrate that these laws were generally operative as described but also reveal that divorce could sometimes happen. In one court case from Babylonia occurring sixteen years after the death of Hammurapi, a husband seeks to clarify that his former stepson is not his heir after he had divorced his mother because she had been "seized by a god." We have no information on why this husband had been allowed to divorce his sick wife; she had, however, been married previously and had a son from her first marriage. Evidently it was now the son's obligation to support his mother. In another court case written over a century earlier, the practice conforms more closely to Hammurapi Laws §148: a woman "smitten by a demon" allowed her husband to take a second wife as long as he continued to support her.[75]

There was, generally, no restriction against marrying a second wife under biblical and rabbinic laws, where polygyny was more freely permitted, although, to be sure, some husbands might be prevented from doing so by custom or prenuptial agreements. The rabbinic laws therefore did not need to focus upon the possibility of the husband taking a second wife. For the rabbis, the issue was, rather, divorce, since there normally was no restriction upon a husband's right to divorce his wife as is stated in the Mishnah cited above. Rabbi Gamaliel's rulings seem to focus

upon bringing the responsibilities and rights of a levir in line with those of the deceased husband; but perhaps he was also looking to limit rejection of the ill wife to situations of economic hardship.

In a kind of "trade-off," the Mishnah, in another law, also gave wives a limited right to divorce husbands on the grounds of certain physical ailments or occupations that tainted his person and rendered intimacy distasteful. In the Mishnah, *m. Ket.* 7:10, we read:

> And these are they that may be compelled to divorce (their wives): one who is afflicted with boils, who has a *polypus*,[76] who collects (dog excrement), a copper smelter, a tanner—whether these defects arose before they married or developed afterwards. And of all of these Rabbi Meir said (that) although the husband may have made it a condition with her (to marry him despite these defects), she may (later) declare: "I thought I could accept (them) but now I cannot." (But) the Sages rule (that) she must accept (these conditions) against her will, with the exception of one who is afflicted with boils, because she can worsen his (condition thereby).

The Sages, i.e., a majority of rabbis, made an exception for boils only because of a prevailing medical theory—as further described in *b. Ket.* 77b—that this condition could be worsened by sexual activity. This Mishnaic passage further reveals a move by the Sages to curtail earlier liberality with respect to woman's rights of divorce. Yet the historical principal that

---

75. The two cases are BE 6/1 59 and *NSG* 2 6. For discussion and suggestions about the possible identities of the ancient diseases see Stol, *Epilepsy*, 143.

76. This term describes a polyp or fleshy growth in a man's nose. *OED* records this same term and usage in medieval English. The Gemara in *b. Ket.* 77a explains it as causing an offensive nasal smell or offensive breath.

illness could affect the continuity of a marriage remained as a clearly recognized tradition. However, I have not found any parallel to *m. Ket.* 7:10 in the ancient Near Eastern sources.

1.2.4 The "Rebellious Wife"

Rabbinic sources preserve a law dealing with the dissolution of marriage by women in the case of a wife who wished to divorce her husband on personal grounds. In the Mishnah, *m. Ket.* 5:7, we read:

> (If) a woman "rebels" against her husband (by refusing him sexually), they (the court) may order a deduction from her marriage settlement[77] of seven dinars per week. Rabbi Judah says: seven tropaics (i.e., half-dinars per week). For how long does one deduct? (For a time period) corresponding to (the full value of) her marriage settlement. Rabbi Jose says: one always continues to reduce (her assets) to the point that even if an inheritance falls to her from another source, he (the husband) may also collect that (as part of the penalty due) from her. And similarly, if a husband "rebels" against his wife, they (the court) will add to her marriage settlement three dinars per week. Rabbi Judah says: three tropaics.[78]

77. Hebrew *ketubbah*; this is a written prenuptial contract required of all husbands, by which the husband pledges a certain sum of money as a stipend for his wife in the event of widowhood or divorce. This requirement was said to be instituted in the first century BCE by R. Simeon b. Shetah; cf. *t. Ket.* 12:1, Lieberman; *b. Ket.* 82b; *j. Ket.* 32b. For inheritance rights of the wife's children, see below in sec. 1.5.

78. The rabbis, to their credit, found scriptural foundation for securing the conjugal rights of wives in Exod 21:11, which deals with a husband's (minimal) obligations to his wife. This passage is discussed in section 2.1.

This law does not take the reader to the point of divorce; but the Gemara (*b. Ket.* 63b), in its comments on this Mishnah, recognizes that divorce must follow but seeks to make certain that it is due to irreconcilable differences:

> How does the case of the "rebellious wife" manifest itself? Amemar said: she said "I want him but I (am refusing him so as to) cause him distress." However, if she said: "he is repulsive to me," one shall not press her (to remain as his wife).

Another law dealing with women who wish to dissolve their marriages appears in the Mishnah, *m. Ned.* 11:12:

> Formerly, they (the Rabbis) used to teach: there are three women who must be divorced and receive their marriage settlement: one who says: "I am unclean to you," or "Heaven (alone knows what transpires sexually) between me and you" or "I am (bound by my vow to be) removed from (sexual relations with all) Jews (including my husband)." They (i.e., the Rabbis later) revised (their teaching) so that a woman would not be casting her gaze upon another man and act (in a way to) "spoil" herself for her husband. (Now) rather one who declares: "I am unclean to you", must bring proof (of her unchaste behavior); (for one who says:)"Heaven is between you and me," the court) must investigate the matter (to determine whether her husband is impotent); and (where she says:) "I am (bound by my vow to be) removed from (all) Jews," he (her husband) may annul that part of the vow which pertains to him so that she may again minister to him (as a wife) but she may

maintain her vow (in the future) against other Jewish men.

Women here again could not exercise the power of divorce as freely as did men; this right was frequently curtailed; and when it was (hesitantly) given, the woman might also have the burden of proving that her action was not due to her being involved in an adulterous liaison with another man. Rabbinic authorities over succeeding centuries continued to vacillate in their readiness to allow female initiated divorce; medieval opinions were at time, surprisingly, more accommodating than those given in more recent times.[79] We have also noted above the earlier existence of bilateral divorce provisions in the Elephantine papyri (sec. 1.2.1). Despite their general hesitation about female initiated divorce, the rabbis, too, made allowance for bilateral divorce without prejudice if such provisions were written into the marriage contract:

> Rabbi Jose said: those who write (clauses into the marriage contract): "If he "hates" (i.e., wishes to divorce), if she "hates", this is a financial stipulation and the stipulations are valid. And the rabbis have sustained this (practice).[80]

The ancient Near Eastern laws provide a forerunner to the rabbinic laws and likewise demonstrate a long history of ambivalence about female initiated divorce, as well as a requirement that the wife's chastity should not be in question. In Hammurapi Laws §§142–143 we read:

> If a woman "hated" her husband and (has said to him) "You shall

not have me (sexually," her past (conduct) in her district shall be investigated; and if she has behaved chastely and has no fault while (at the same time) her husband as been wont to go out and has greatly belittled her, that woman shall suffer no penalty. She may take her dowry and go back to her father's house. If (however) she has not behaved chastely and has been wont to go out (and) she has squandered her household goods (and) belittled her husband, they shall throw that woman into the water.

A wife whose chastity and conduct were without reproach is able to reject and divorce her husband; but this right is lost for a wife who has neglected her domestic duties and conducted herself in a loose manner.[81] This woman appears to fall under the unstated suspicion of having a lover and is therefore penalized. Jumping or being thrown into the river is a repeated motif in actual or suspected adultery cases (more fully discussed in secs. 1.3.1 and 1.3.2 following). The river ordeal procedure is mandated for a wife suspected of adultery in Hammurapi Laws §132:

> If a man's wife should have an (accusatory) finger pointed at her regarding (infidelity with) another man but she has not been caught lying with another man, she must undergo judgment by the river-god for (the sake of) her husband.

The river ordeal is even more fully described in diplomatic letters from the epoch of Hammurapi found at Mari. It took

---

79. For a wide-ranging presentation and discussion see Riskin, *Women and Jewish Divorce.*

80. See *j. B. Bat.* 16c, *j. Ket.* 30b.

81. We find the topos of a wife's wastefulness and thieving conduct anciently associated with her committing adultery and even murder in late Sumerian and Old Babylonian legal documents. See Greengus, "Old Babylonian Marriage Contract," 39.

place at a cataract of the Euphrates where the river formed rapids; the person undergoing the ordeal first took a solemn oath by the river-god invoking a judgment of death by drowning if not telling the truth; then had to leap into the river. If he or she survived, their innocence was proven; if he or she died, it was understood to be the judgment of the river-god.[82]

What then happened to the "rebellious wife" in Hammurapi Laws §142–143? There are scholars who believe that she was summarily thrown into the river and drowned without being given an opportunity to prove her innocence through the river ordeal.[83] If this were true, then she would be more severely treated than the wife actually accused of infidelity in Hammurapi Laws §132. Furthermore, in Hammurapi Laws §141, we see that the death penalty was not automatically given for a poorly behaved wife who wished to divorce her husband:

> If a man's wife who lives in that man's house makes up her mind to leave him; and she diverted goods, squandered her household goods, belittled her husband, and if her husband then affirms her leaving, he shall divorce her. No travel costs or divorce money shall be given to her at all. If (on the other hand) her husband does not affirm her divorce, he may take a second wife;

she (the first wife) shall dwell as a slave in the house of her husband.

While the wife's poor conduct was a critical issue and led to her being degraded to slavery, it was not sufficient grounds for a death penalty. Moreover, from Hammurapi Laws §§142–143, we see that sexual rejection by the wife was not in itself a wrongful act. For all of these reasons, I would argue that in Hammurapi Laws §§142–143, the wife with poor conduct and reputation was subjected to the river ordeal rather than summarily drowned.[84] What is clearly beyond question, however, is that the Hammurapi Laws give husbands the upper hand in matters of divorce. We find even more tyrannical expressions of this repressive tendency in clauses written into some marriage contracts of the period, where wives are severely penalized if they initiate a divorce, even if they were innocent of any improper conduct. These clauses state that wives seeking divorce could be sold into slavery, hurled from a watchtower, or tied up and thrown into the river.[85] Such repressive clauses, if indeed they were literally intended, may emerge from there being a significant degree of social or economic disparity between the contracting parties. The clauses may also have been designed to terrorize wives into submission to their husbands; and the husbands in the contracts, like

---

82. For details cf. Durand, "L'ordalie," A much later description of the river ordeal survives in *CT* 46 45 treated by Lambert, "Nebuchadnezzar, King of Justice." It is also attested in Middle Assyrian Laws §A 17, which is discussed in sec. 1.3.2.

83. Cf. Driver and Miles, *Babylonian Laws,* 1:299–303, where this interpretation is argued. There is no uncertainty about outright drowning, however, in Hammurapi Laws §129 (sec. 1.3.1) where known adulterers are bound and thrown into the river.

84. Lafont, *Femmes, Droit et Justice,* 51–55 comes to a similar conclusion; she sees the wife's statement in Hammurapi Laws §143 as a formal declaration of divorce.

85. For examples of such penalty clauses inserted into marriage documents from the Old Babylonian period, see Westbrook, *Old Babylonian Marriage Law,* 83 n. 99 and 112–38. For further discussion on the woman's right to divorce see Greengus, "Filling Gaps," 167–68 and Westbrook, "Character of Ancient Near Eastern Law," 48–49.

those in the laws, may very well have had discretion to withhold having these penalties actually imposed. We see this power of discretion very clearly in Hammurapi Laws §129 (sec. 1.3.1) below, where a husband may choose to spare his adulterous wife, who was caught in the arms of her paramour.

Typical signs of a wife's unchaste and improper conduct, similar to those enumerated in Hammurapi Laws §141–143, are also given in the Mishnah *m. Ket.* 7:6. The rabbis there find grounds for a husband to divorce his wife without paying her customary marriage settlement if:

> She goes out (of the house) with uncovered head, does her spinning (sitting outside) in the street, or speaks freely with all (strange) men . . . also who curses his parents to his face, and who speaks loudly . . . in her house so that her neighbors hear her voice. [86]

This woman will lose her marriage settlement, which originally came from her husband's assets; but she would retain her own dowry and similar assets that originally belonged to her.

1.3 ADULTERY

1.3.1 Proven Adultery

A marriage normally would come to an end if adultery took place because adultery, when unambiguously proven, was

---

86. For the symbolism of an uncovered head see further in connection with Hittite Laws §198 (1.3.1) below.

See further *j. Sotah* 16b on the behavior described in the Mishnah serving as the basis for a husband divorcing a wife that he suspected of infidelity. Unchaste conduct may also be in the background in the law of Deut 24:1–4, discussed in sec. 1.2.1.

---

considered to be an offense worthy of the death penalty both for the man and the married woman involved with him. Death is the consequence of a "guilty verdict" in the River ordeal described above (sec. 1.2.4) and is also the penalty meted out in Deut 22:22:

> If a man is found lying with another man's wife, both of them shall die, the man who lay with the woman as well as the woman. Thus you will purge the evil from Israel. (NRSV)

A punishment of death is again prescribed in Lev 20:10:

> A man who commits adultery with a married woman (i.e.,) who commits adultery with another man's wife, the adulterer and the adulteress shall be put to death.

The biblical laws here are uncompromisingly strict. But customary practice in ancient Israel recognized a range of possible responses, ranging from the death to lesser punishments, even forgiveness and reconciliation. We find these other responses in non-legal biblical passages, which reveal this wider range; and these are similar, as we shall see, to the range of responses found in our ancient Near Eastern sources. In a poetic passage, Ezekiel 16:38–41 compares Judea and her practices of idolatry to a faithless woman who has been proven to be unfaithful to her husband; his vision contains images of a transgressing wife being killed by an angry mob, conflated with brief flashes (identified here in italics) describing the destruction of her idolatrous shrines and cities by invading enemies. God, representing the betrayed husband, is the speaker:

> I will inflict upon you the punishment for women who commit

adultery and murder, and I will bring upon you blood of wrath and jealousy. I will deliver you into their hands, *and they shall tear down your eminence and smash your high places*; and they shall strip you of your clothing and take away your things of beauty, and leave you naked and bare. They shall raise up a public mob against you to pelt you with stones *and hack you with their swords*. They shall *burn your houses and* execute judgments upon you in the sight of many women; thus I will put a stop to your being a harlot, and you shall pay out no more payments (of inducement to your lovers.)[87]

The non-italicized text, as we shall further see, represents typical actions of social, i.e., community retaliation against adultery. However, Ezekiel then also depicts this husband relenting and taking back his unfaithful wife; this act is also depicted later in Ezekiel 16, where the prophet portrays God as ready to take back Israel, who is compared to a whoring wife. A description of their reconciliation appears in Ezek 16:60–63:

> Nevertheless, I will remember the covenant I made with you in the days of your youth, and I will establish it with you as an everlasting covenant ... I will establish My covenant with you, and you shall know that I am the LORD. Thus you shall remember and feel shame, and you shall be too abashed to open your

mouth again, when I have forgiven you for all that you did—declares the Lord GOD. (NJPS)[88]

The possibility of reconciliation was apparently not unknown in biblical times; we find another reference to it—albeit condemning—in the Greek translation of Prov 18:22. The Greek version adds a passage, 18:22a, not found in our extant Hebrew text:

> 18:22 He who finds a good wife has found favors and has received cheerfulness from God.[89] 18:22a He who rejects a good wife, rejects the good, but he who keeps an adulteress is foolish and impious.

Evidence of mutilation as a punishment for adultery is found in another complaint against Israel's unfaithfulness given in Ezek 23:25-26: here, again, descriptions of war and exile (which I have put in italics) are interwoven with punishments for adultery:

> I will direct My passion against you, and they shall deal with you in fury: they shall cut off your nose and ears. *The last of you shall fall by the sword; they shall take away your sons and daughters, and your remnant shall be devoured by fire.* They shall strip you of your clothing and take away your dazzling jewels. (NJPS)[90]

---

87. Cf. earlier, in Ezek 16:32–34, where the faithless wife brazenly gives gifts to her lovers rather than receiving gifts from them. Payment of harlots is, however, also used a term to disparage gifts made in support of idolatry; cf. Deut 23:19 and Mic 1:7. If this is the sense of the passage, then one might translate: "*and you shall pay out no more (idolatrous) gifts.*"

88. A similar sentiment is found in Jer 3:1–14 where God—despite the sentiment expressed in Jer 3:1 (see sec. 1.2.1)—seeks the return of his "first faithless wife," who represents the northern kingdom of Israel or Samaria. Similarly in Hos 2:4–25, where God promises to restore Israel, pictured as an unfaithful wife.

89. The translation given here is from the Greek text; the Hebrew text of Prov 18:22 varies slightly: "He who finds a wife finds a good thing, and obtains favor from the LORD" (NRSV).

90. The custom of mutilation as a penalty for

Mutilations—and financial penalty—as we shall see below, are also known to be penalties for adultery in ancient Near Eastern sources.

The Bible also preserves evidence of yet other, less severe responses to adultery, namely, the payment of compensation to the husband. Such compensation is described in Prov 6:32–37 which, however, also warns that it may not be accepted by the husband:

> But he who commits adultery has no sense; he who does it destroys himself. He will get wounds and dishonor, and his disgrace will not be wiped away. For jealousy arouses a husband's fury, and he shows no restraint when he takes revenge. He will accept no compensation, and refuses a bribe no matter how great. (NRSV)

We perhaps find another echo of the practice of compensation in the story of Sarah's "abduction" by Abimelech who thought she was Abraham's sister and not his wife. In Gen 20:3–7, God appeared to Abimelech, revealed Sarah's true identity, and threatened him with death if he dared to take her sexually. Abimelech of course, refrains and later remonstrates with Abraham for having misled him in the first place. But in the end, Abimelech offers a gift in a gesture of apology; Gen 20:16 records Abimelech's statement:

> And to Sarah he [Abimelech] said, "I herewith give your 'brother' [i.e., Abraham] a thousand pieces of silver; this will serve you as 'covering of the eyes' before all who are with you, and you are vindicated before all."

Abimelech's gift to Abraham looks a bit like the "ransom" offered in Prov 6:32–37; payment may have been considered appropriate even for an intended, even if unconsummated, sexual transgression.[91] Otherwise, there were no other legal consequences for infidelity—as long as a man was not involved with another man's wife. This view is in keeping with a husband's legal right to marry more than one wife. The Bible thus viewed adultery fundamentally like an act of "trespass," invading a married man's sexual domain.

As can already be seen from the story of Sarah and Abimelech, a wife's adultery was widely recognized as a serious offense in Near Eastern societies; however, as Ezek 16:60–63 indicates, her punishment could be mitigated if her husband wished to forgive her. Thus in Hammurapi Laws §129 we read:

> If a man's wife is seized lying together with another male, they shall bind them and throw them into the waters. If the wife's husband would allow his wife to live, then the king will (also) allow his "slave" (i.e., other man) to live.

The punishment for adultery is drowning, just as we have earlier seen in the case of the River ordeal in Hammurapi Laws §132 discussed above (sec. 1.2.4); only this time the wife, whose guilt is beyond question, is tied up so she cannot swim and thereby escape being drowned. The husband may decide not to have his wife killed but then,

adultery in ancient Israel is not widely discussed; see however Paul, "Biblical Analogues to Middle Assyrian Law," 342–46.

91. In Middle Assyrian Laws §22, a man (forcibly?) recruited a woman to join his mercantile trading venture but she was subsequently discovered to be married. In addition to paying compensation, he must also swear that he did not know she was married and that they had no sexual relations. For literature and discussion, see Lafont, *Femmes, Droit et Justice*, 386–91.

the king, representing court and justice system, will also free her paramour, the "king's subject" or "slave." This pattern of a balanced penalty for wife and paramour is also found in Middle Assyrian Laws §A 15 where we read:

> If a man has seized (another) man with his wife (and) they (formally) charged (and) convicted him; they shall kill both of them. (If the husband slew him,) there is no blame for him (i.e., the husband). If he has seized (that man and) either brought him before the king or before judges (and) they (formally) charged (and) convicted him, if (then) the husband of the woman would kill his wife, then he must (likewise) kill the (other) man. Or, if he would cut off the nose of his wife, he shall turn the (other) man into a eunuch and they shall (also) lacerate his face. Or, if he frees his wife (from punishment), he must then (also) free the (other) man.

The Assyrian laws show a range of possibilities: death, disfigurement, or no punishment at all. But the principle of parity for wife and paramour is maintained throughout. The same principle of parity appears in Hittite Laws §198, which is a situation where the husband has caught his wife with another man:

> If he [the husband] brings them to the palace gate [for judgment] and says: "let my wife not be put to death" and [so] spares his wife, he must also spare the lover. He [the husband] may [then] cover her head. But if he says, "let both of them be put to death," then they shall "roll the wheel." The king [however] may have them killed or spare them.

Covering the head has been interpreted as a symbolic act taken by the husband, signifying that she is now (again) a married woman and his wife.[92] The "rolling of the wheel" is obscure; it may describe a mode of punishment. It is interesting that in the Hittite tradition, the husband's wishes may be over-ruled by the king; but the principle of parity is maintained. Based upon the near Eastern evidence one can now understand the reason for similar statements of parity in Lev 20:10 and Deut 22:22 cited above. They mean to say that if one of the pair is put to death, the same punishment applies to the other person as well.[93] These biblical laws do not entertain the possibility of punishments other than death; but we have now seen that other, lesser punishments or no punishment at all were also possibilities in early biblical times. For the later rabbis, however, only the passages in the law collections of the Torah were authoritative; and they understood these laws to mean that death was the only punishment for adultery; in their system, other possibilities were eliminated.[94]

92. Hoffner, *Laws of the Hittites*, 226. My translation of §198 follows Hoffner's more literal rendering there.

93. This principle is recognized by Nahmanides on Deut 22:22, who states that the plain meaning of the biblical text "both of them" is that we do not seek to apportion degrees of blame between the adulterers, inasmuch as they both willingly participated in the act.

94. In his commentary on Gen 38:24, Nahmanides noted that, when the community asked Judah to pass judgment upon his wayward daughter-in-law Tamar, it appeared to reflect a custom in that community of leaving the severity of the punishment for adultery to the judgment of the woman's guardian or husband. Judah at this point opted for the death penalty. Nahmanides was unaware of the ancient Near Eastern evidence we now know today; he based his insight upon similar customs

Lesser punishment of an adulterous woman—by facial mutilation, public humiliation, and financial penalty—is described in a Sumerian legal case that was preserved as part of the ancient scribal curriculum. A woman is described as having been stealing from her husband's storeroom and concealing her theft. This woman, lying with her paramour, was found by her husband, who tied them up and brought them to the local council for judgment and punishment.[95] But, as we see in the laws, punishment of adultery by death was far more typical. In addition to drowning, we also know of impalement and a number of Neo-Babylonian marriage documents include the provision that if the woman after being married "should be seized with another man, she shall die by the iron dagger."[96]

Middle Assyrian Laws §A 14 introduces another nuance into the laws on adultery, namely, whether the paramour knew that the woman was married:

> If the wife of a man—a man should fornicate with her either in an inn or in the street (and) he knew that she was a man's wife, (then) as he (i.e., the husband) declares his wife to be treated, they shall treat the fornicator. (But) if he did not know she was a man's wife and he fornicated with her, he is (in the) clear; the man (i.e., the husband) shall (formally) charge his wife (and) treat her as is his wish.

This principle is also appears in Middle Assyrian Laws §A 13:

> If the wife of a man should go out of her own house and go to the house of another man where he lives (and) he fornicates with her (there and he) knew that she was the wife of another man, they shall kill that man and that wife.

According to these laws, parity would only apply when the fornicator knew that the woman was married; but if she concealed that fact, then he was clear of blame. Middle Assyrian Laws §A 16 adds enticement to this scenario of concealment:

> If a man [should fornicate with] the wife of another man because of [the crafty words] of her mouth, there is no punishment for that man. The man (i.e., the husband) shall punish his wife as he wishes. If (however) he should fornicate with her by force, (and) they prove (the charge against) him (and) convict him, his punishment will be the same as the man's wife.

The nuance of female enticement has a long history in the law and it is suggested already in Urnamma Laws §7 whose formulation is not so precise as Middle Assyrian Laws §A 13:

> If the wife of a young man on her own follows another man around and he lies in her bosom, one (var. the man) shall kill that woman (but) that fellow—one shall set him free.

The fact that the other man is set free indicates that his behavior was found not to be at fault.

The Bible does not address enticement in the laws but it is spoken of and vividly described in Prov 7:6–27, which

---

allowing alternative punishments, which he observed among his medieval Iberian neighbors.

95. For discussion of this text, IM 28051, see Greengus, "A Textbook Case of Adultery."

96. For discussion of impalement and death by the dagger, see Roth, "Die by the Iron Dagger." The case of impalement, UET 5 203, is from the Old Babylonian period (ibid., 196–97).

describes how a "lad, void of sense" is taken in by a woman bent upon adultery. He might escape legal punishment here because the woman's husband is far away but morally it is wrong and thus verses Prov 7:21–27 reminds him:

> She sways him with her eloquence, Turns him aside with her smooth talk. Thoughtlessly he follows her, like an ox going to the slaughter, Like a fool to the stocks for punishment—Until the arrow pierces his liver. He is like a bird rushing into a trap, not knowing his life is at stake. Now, sons, listen to me; Pay attention to my words; Let your mind not wander down her ways; Do not stray onto her paths. For many are those she has struck dead, And numerous are her victims. Her house is a highway to Sheol Leading down to Death's inner chambers. (NJPS)

1.3.2. Accusations of Adultery

A charge of adultery was a serious matter and required proof. In the cases we have looked at so far, the matter was beyond dispute. But what if a husband only suspected his wife or was jealous? Under such circumstances, a woman was obliged to clear herself; an ordeal to be administered for suspicion of adultery is found in the Bible, similar in purpose to the divine River Ordeal discussed above (sec. 1.2.4) in connection with Hammurapi Laws §132 but not as perilous. It is described in Num 5:12–31:

> If a man's wife has gone astray and committed an act of unfaithfulness against him (in that) a man had sexual intercourse with her, and this was concealed from the eyes of her husband, and she keeps it

> hidden that she has defiled herself, and there is no witness against her, and she had not been caught. Then a spirit of jealousy comes over him and he feels jealousy about his wife and she had defiled herself; (or) a spirit of jealousy came over him and he is feels jealousy about his wife but she has not defiled herself—the man shall bring his wife to the priest . . .

The verses following go on to describe the ritual for her ordeal: first the husband presents a cereal offering for God, evidently a feature of his petition for divine justice and action. The suspected wife, with her head uncovered (some translate: "disheveled")[97] by the priest, must stand before him holding the offering while the priest recites a solemn oath for her invoking punishment upon herself if she had committed adultery; and she must in response say "Amen, Amen." The priest then writes out the words of the oath in a document. The priest prepares a draft for the woman to drink consisting of holy water into which he mixes dust from the floor of the sanctuary and the ink scratched off from the document containing the oath and its curse. The priest places the offering on the altar and the woman drinks the prepared draft. Then (Num 5:27–31),

> And (after) he has made her drink the water, then it shall come to pass, if she has defiled herself and

---

97. The text speaks of "head" and not "hair." Nevertheless the Mishnah in *m. Sotah* 1:5 interprets it as "loosens her hair"; and this understanding is followed e.g., by Rashi. However, Ibn Ezra on Num 5:18 (and in a similar passage in Lev 10:6) favors "uncover" as does LXX. The Mishnah, in *m. Ket.* 7:6, again speaks about a woman who goes about publicly with her hair in this same manner; but here again, the Gemara (*b. Ket.* 72b) understands it as "uncovered."

committed an act of unfaithfulness against her husband, then the curse–inducing water shall enter into her to bring on bitter (pains), so that her belly shall swell and her loin shall fall; and the woman shall become a curse among her people. But if she had not defiled herself and is pure, she shall be free (of injury) and may be "sown with seed." This is the law for cases of jealousy, when a woman goes astray under (the bond of marriage to) her husband and defiles herself, or when a spirit of jealousy comes over a man and he becomes jealous over his wife: and he shall have the woman stand before the Lord and the priest shall do to her (what is commanded in) all of this law.

It may be noted that this biblical ordeal, relying upon a solemn oath pronounced over the offering and in the drinking of the sacred potion, subjects the woman to a peril that is more psychological rather than physical in character.[98] The biblical ordeal may also contain the promise of a blessing for being innocent; LXX and Philo,[99] followed by some medieval rabbinic commentators e.g., Ibn Ezra, understood "being sown with seed" to mean that an innocent wife, being subjected to this (unnecessary) ordeal, will be blessed with seed i.e., offspring. But for other commentators, e.g., like Hazzequni, it simply states that the woman, now legally cleared, may resume normal conjugal life with her husband. This interpretation

98. Psychological effects, however, should not be minimized; similar ordeals involving ingestion of earth from the sanctuary or ink scraped off from written texts or even the texts themselves were once widely practiced among African peoples. See Gaster, *Myth Legend and Custom,* 283, 289.

99. Philo, *Spec. Laws* 3.62. This interpretation is also given in *b. Ber.* 31b.

reflects the rabbinic position taken in Mishnah *m. Sotah* 5:1, which declares that the wife whom the drinking ordeal found to be guilty should henceforth become forbidden both to her husband as well as her paramour:

> Rabbi said: "Twice in the section of Scripture (Num 5:13, 29) is it written 'and she defiled herself'—once for the husband and once for the paramour."

I have noted that the biblical ordeal for the wife of a jealous husband is not as severe or perilous as the River Ordeal of Hammurapi Laws §132 (cited in sec 1.2.4) The reason for a milder procedure is perhaps because a distinction was anciently made between the more serious situation where an accusation against her came from the outside—i.e., the pointing of an "(accusatory) finger"—and a situation where an accusation is made (without proof) by the wife's suspicious or jealous husband. In such a case, Hammurapi Laws §131 does not require the river ordeal but only an oath:

> If the wife of a man—her husband accuses her but she had not been taken lying with another male, she shall swear an oath by a god and may return to her home.

The principle here is that a wife may clear herself from her husband's suspicions by taking the solemn oath, which invoked divine punishment if she were not telling the truth. While the Babylonian laws do not describe the procedure in detail, we do know from other sources that the taking of an oath was, generally, a solemn affair. The oath-taker was required to go to the temple and to take hold of and lift the sacred emblem of a god while uttering the oath; and lawsuit records sometimes declare that a litigating party "shrank from the oath" and abandoned the lawsuit rather than take the risk of pronouncing the conditional self-curse required of an oath-taker in support of his claim. There is also evidence for the custom of the oath-taker uncovering his head when taking an oath; this is not unlike the priest uncovering the head of the woman prior to her taking the oath in Num 5:18.[100] But the taking of an oath is not the same as an ordeal, where the implementation of the consequences invoked by the self-curse expressed in the oath are transferred to a specific modality of judgment. This occurs in Hammurapi Laws §132, with the rushing waters of the divine River God, or in Num 5:18–19, with the drink containing the "curse-inducing waters that bring on the bitter (pains)." The biblical law, in requiring submission to an ordeal for a husband's suspicion, appears to be demanding more of the wife than does Hammurapi Laws §131, where her oath is sufficient. Perhaps the following reasons may be given. First, the prohibition against non-priests touching, let alone holding the sacra of the tabernacle or temple made it impossible to bring the Israelite oath-taker into the same degree of ominous contact with divinity as could be achieved in Mesopotamia, where oath-taker could herself grasp the divine symbol. Moreover, the absence of the most important sacred symbols during the second Temple made this possibility even more remote.[101] The procedure in

Num 5:15–28 created an alternative way: to bring the wife into the Temple, without her having to come into physical contact with the sacra. Second, submission to this kind of ordeal may have enabled a wife completely to exonerate herself from any lingering suspicions held by her accusing husband, which taking an oath by itself without this additional ceremony might not have fully accomplished.[102]

Deuteronomy 22:13–21 describes a situation where a husband accuses his wife of sexual misconduct prior to marriage. Her husband, who evidently wishes to become rid of her, charges her with having lost her virginity, presumably to another man, before their marriage during the time while they were betrothed. The husband seeks to establish this charge by claiming that, when they married, he did not find her to be a virgin when he was first intimate with her:

> If a man takes a wife and cohabits with her but then "hates" her and makes up charges against her based upon (his) statement (only) and defames her reputation, saying, "I married this woman; but when I approached her (sexually), I found that she possessed no signs of virginity." Then the young girl's father and mother shall produce the evidence of the damsel's virginity before the elders of the town at the gate. And the young girl's father shall say to the elders, "I gave this man my daughter to wife, but he "hates" her; now he has

---

100. For references cf. *CAD* M/1, 192, N/2, 83–84, Q, 103.

101. Num 4:15 and 2 Sam 6:6–7 relate that the punishment for touching the ark and other sacred objects was death. The absence of the ark in the second Temple is related in 2 Macc 2:4–8 and can be linked with the statement in Jer 3:16.

102. Cf. the comments of Brichto, "The Case of the *Śōṭā*," who argued that the procedure for testing the suspected wife—who was presumed innocent until proven guilty—was intrinsically benign and designed primarily to protect her and to shift the entire burden of proof to her "insanely jealous husband."

made up charges based upon (his) statement (only), saying, 'I did not find evidence of your daughter' virginity' But here is the evidence of my daughter's virginity!" And they shall spread out the (blood-stained) sheet before the elders of the town. The elders of that town shall then take the man and flog him, and they shall fine him a hundred shekels of silver and give it to the young girl's father, for the man has defamed a virgin in Israel. Moreover, she shall remain as his wife; he shall not have the right to divorce her (for) as long as he lives. But if the charge was true—the girl was found not to have had evidence of virginity, then the young girl shall be brought out to the entrance of her father's house, and the men of her town shall stone her to death; for she committed an outrageous deed in Israel, committing fornication in her father's house. Thus you will purge the evil from your midst.

The account of the husband's complaint suggests that her father—or perhaps the woman herself—had represented to him that his young wife was virgin at the time of betrothal; and since her husband found this not to be the case, it could be alleged that she had engaged in illicit sex with another man during the interval of time between betrothal and marriage while she was yet living in her parents' home. During that time she was considered as a married woman with respect to other men. We are not told as to how much time had elapsed between the time of marriage and the husband's accusation. But it would not matter, as long as the woman's parents could produce the blood stained bed sheet on which the couple had lain when they first consummated their

union, apparently in the bride's home, at the time of the wedding.[103]

This case is disquieting for a number of reasons. First is the basis of the accusation, which is based upon what could not be seen nor found. A second reason is the outcome where the husband can never divorce his defamed wife; this implies that it was "better" for the rejected and defamed wife to live with and be supported by a hateful husband rather than be separated from him. A third reason is that the way the "story is told" suggests that every woman who married for the first time was expected to be a virgin, even if not betrothed.[104] The later rabbis tried to address this disquietedness. They evidently felt uneasy about how to determine the veracity of the kind of accusation made by the husband in Deut 22:13–21; they note the complexity of female physiological development, her husband's possible sexual inexperience, her husband's negative bias, and the fact that the life of the woman depended upon the ability of the court to establish the truth of the matter in response to a charge based on circumstantial evidence. So the rabbis in effect rendered this law essentially inoperative through an overlay of hermeneutics and various hedgings. They further noted the repeated designation of the wife in this case as a "young girl." For the rabbis, this narrowed the scope of such complaints to girls older than twelve. At the same

103. The custom is described by Rashbam on Deut 22:15, citing *b. Ket.* 46a. Similar customs were practiced among other peoples in the Semitic and Mediterranean world. Cf. the references cited by Tigay, *Deuteronomy*, 384 n. 47; and by Driver, *Deuteronomy*, 255.

104. Berlin, "Sex and the Single Girl," takes this to in fact be the underlying social ethic underlying Deut 22:13–19.

time, the rabbis also added restrictions as to the extent to which they would accept such complaints for any girl who were older than twelve and a half who, according to their definitions, was no longer "a girl." They also allow the accused wife an unchallenged right to explain her lack of apparent virginity on the basis of physical injury or rape prior to betrothal. They also deprive the husband of any right to bring his complaint if during the betrothal period he and his future wife were left alone un-chaperoned at any time. The rabbis also add a requirement for witnesses to support the husband's assumption of her infidelity; otherwise there could be no death penalty imposed on the woman even if it could not be proved that she had been a virgin when they wed. As for the wife remaining with her hateful husband, the husband would be allowed to divorce his wife even after bringing a failed accusation, as long as he paid her the appropriate marriage settlement.[105] The rabbis thus created a more fair and reasonable version of the biblical case; but in doing so they had traveled far from the ancient biblical context!

One must note that in Deut 22:13–21, the husband did not suffer the full penalty of his having lied. While his wife, if proven guilty, could have been executed, he is punished only with a fine and the loss of his right to divorce the wife he unjustly defamed. He is also flogged; but he does not suffer the full measure of what would befall an unfaithful wife. The disparity between the husband and his new wife is even more evident in another version of this law found among the Dead Sea Scrolls, which omits flogging the husband:

> If a man brings an accusation against a virgin of Israel, if [it is at the time] he marries her, let him speak and they shall investigate her trustworthiness.[106] If he has not lied about her, she shall be put to death, but if he has testified f[alse]ly against her, he shall be fined two minas [and] he may [not] divorce her all of his life.[107]

The Dead Sea Scroll community also promulgated rules designed to prevent this kind of situation from happening in the first place—at least for members of the sect. A prospective wife's father was required to divulge information on any premarital sexual experience and a virgin woman was subject to physical examination prior to their being married; this applied even to a non-virgin about whom there were rumors of sexual misconduct:

> And if [a man betroths his daughter to another ma]n, he should tell him about all her defects, lest he bring upon himself the judgment of [the curse, which sa]ys "Cursed is he who leads the blind astray" (Deut 27:18). Moreover, he shall not give her to one who is unfit for her, for [this is a case of "forbidden mixtures," like plowing with an o]x and an ass [together or [wearing] clothing made of wool and linen together.[108] Let no man bring

---

105. Cf. the discussion in *b. Ket.* 36a–b cited by Ibn Ezra in his comments to Deut 22:19. See further *b. Ket.* 9b–12b; *j. Ket.* 25a (on *m. Ket.* 1:1–9); *j. Ket.* 28c (on *m. Ket.* 4:3); and Maimonides in *Mishnah Torah, Hilkhot Ishut* 11:12–17.

106. Others restore here: "trustworthy [women] shall examine her." Cf. Shemesh, "A Key to Sectarian Matrimonial Law," 254.

107. 4Q159 frags. 2–4:8–10 as translated in Wise et al., *Dead Sea Scrolls*, 232.

108. Cf. Deut 22:11 and 25:4 where these prohibitions appear.

[a woman into the covenant of holi]ness who knew to do "the deed" for a trifle or whom he knew [to "do the deed" in the house of] her father; or a widow who had intercourse after she became a widow, or any [woman who has a] bad [repu]tation while a virgin in the house of her father. Let no man marry such a one unless [she is examined by] dependable and knowledgeable [women] who are selected at the command of the Overseer who is over he [general membership; the]n he may marry her, but when he marries her let him do according to the re[gul]ation[and not] tell others about [her . . .].[109]

Comparison with ancient Near Eastern law reveals that all accusations of adultery required investigative response. However, persons who made false accusations of adultery were indeed not at all punished to the same degree of severity that would befall a wife who was so accused and found guilty. This disparity is ancient and clearly present in the earliest laws. One such case is Urnamma Laws §14:

If a man accuses the wife of a young man of having lain with another man (and) the river-god has cleared her (of guilt), the man who accused her shall p[ay] one-third m[ina silver].

The situation here involves a woman who was required to submit to the River Ordeal either to clear herself or to show herself guilty, by drowning. Yet her accuser gets off with a monetary penalty

just like the accusing husband in Deut 22:13–21. This same policy continues in the Middle Assyrian Laws §A 17:

If a man says to (another) man: "they (i.e., other men) are regularly copulating with your wife but there are no witnesses," they will set the terms and they will proceed to the River God.

In this case the court will determine the terms of the oath process, i.e., the content of the oath that must be sworn by the woman before she plunges into the river, and perhaps also the penalty to be paid by the informant if the woman proves to be innocent, as seen in Urnamma Laws §14.[110] Middle Assyrian Laws then adds another case, §A 18, where the accuser also claims to be able to prove the accusation himself.

If a man says to his neighbor, either in a private (aside) or in a quarrel: "they (i.e., other men) are regularly copulating with your wife—I can prove it to you" (but) he is not able to prove (the charge); that man— they shall smite him 50 times with canes; he must do the king's labor for one month of days; they will cut off his hair; and he must pay one talent of lead.

This accuser here creates more impact than the informant in Middle Assyrian Laws §A 17. The parties do not proceed to the River Ordeal but rather directly to a trial where the accuser promised to present his evidence. He is punished more

109. 4Q271 frag. 3 as translated in Wise et al., *Dead Sea Scrolls*, 67. Cf. also Shemesh, "A Key to Sectarian Matrimonial Law."

110. The subjects of the plural verbs are not clearly indicated in the text. My interpretation follows what we know about the River Ordeal in other situations: the accuser, the husband, and wife proceed to the River God; but only the wife undergoes the actual ordeal. Cf. Driver and Miles, *Assyrian Laws*, 101–2.

severely than the informant; he has trifled with his neighbor, his neighbor's wife, and made a mockery of the court. A similar fate befell the accuser in Hammurapi Laws §127:

> If a man caused a finger to be pointed at a *priestess* or at a man's wife but has not proven (the charge), they shall flog that man before the judges and shave off half his hair (as a sign of public disgrace).

Yet while these punishments are severe, the accusers do not suffer the death penalty that would have befallen his neighbor's allegedly adulterous wife. The husband in Deut 22:13–21 creates a similar situation; he makes the accusation and claims to be able to prove it, as well. In similar fashion, the husband suffers financial, corporal, and social punishment—in not being able to divorce his wife; for he, too, has troubled the court and community.

I am led from these comparisons to the conclusion that in biblical Israel, as in the ancient Near East, there was conscious social support given to those who could help uncover the sin of adultery in their communities. Perhaps for this reason, the informers or accusers were not subject to a full measure of retaliation if their charges or information proved to be false. Moreover, the burden of proof fell upon the wife, not upon the accuser, unless he clearly stated at the outset that he already possessed sufficient evidence to prove his accusation. To be sure, accusations of adultery were not to be made frivolously; but the penalties laid upon the false accuser were much lighter than the penalty of death for the accused woman.

Before leaving this subject one must mention Lipit-Ishtar Laws §33:

> If a man claimed that another man's virgin daughter had sexual relations (and) one can prove that she had no sexual relations, he shall pay 10 shekels silver.

Important details are lacking; there is a gap in the ancient tablet upon which this law is written; what came before and is now missing would, no doubt, have supplied the information we seek. But as the text now stands, it is not clear who brings the accusation: a future husband or an outsider. Whereas in Deut 22:13–21, the claim is that she had "committed fornication in her father's house," we here are not told where the young woman was residing at the time of the accusation; nor are we told that she was preparing to marry—although this would make sense if the situation were like Deut 22:13–21. We also are not told how her virgin status was proved nor, for that matter, what punishment would befall her if the accusation were found to be true. That indeed may have been the subject of the preceding paragraphs unfortunately now destroyed and missing. In the ancient Near East as in the Bible, a betrothed wife whose marriage was not yet consummated was considered married with respect to other men; and there was the expectation that she would behave chastely after betrothal. We do not otherwise encounter any legal requirement for virginity prior to marriage; and the absence of virginity could not have been an issue after marriage. Yet enough information is preserved to confirm to us that the practice of financial punishment for the accuser was clearly operative here, just as in Deut 22:13–21 and in the Near Eastern parallel cases that have been cited above.

1.4 RAPE AND SEDUCTION

1.4.1 Rape of a Betrothed or Married Woman

The ancients recognized that a woman who was raped was not an adulteress. The perpetrator certainly deserved punishment; nevertheless, the woman's own behavior during the encounter became a subject of scrutiny, especially if she was betrothed or married. In Deut 22:23–27 we read:

> If there is a virgin girl who is betrothed to a man and a(nother) man finds her in a town and lies with her, you shall take the two of them out to the gate of that town and stone them with stones so that they die: the girl because she did not cry out in the town, and the man because he violated the wife of his neighbor; and you will (thus) remove the evil from your midst. But if a man encounters the betrothed girl in the field, and the man seizes her and lies with her, then only the man who lay with her shall die. And you shall do nothing to the girl; the girl has (committed) no sin (deserving the) death (penalty), for this matter is like that of a man arising against his neighbor and murdering him. Because he came upon her in the field; the betrothed girl (surely) cried out, but there was no one to save her.

The case is carefully constructed to remove mitigation for the offender; it doesn't help him that the girl was only betrothed or that she was a virgin; in the eyes of the law, as we have already seen, a betrothed woman was considered as a married woman with respect to any man other than her husband. The woman, on the other hand, carried a responsibility to demonstrate through her behavior that she was not complicit to this sexual encounter. She was required to cry out and seek help; if the attack took place in the town, her outcry would presumably have been heard; but, isolated in the countryside, it is assumed that no one could come to her assistance and that she did, in fact, resist and cry out. The rabbis in their later exegesis, found reason to criticize the girl for venturing out of her house—evidently alone and unaccompanied. Rashi, paraphrasing *Sifre D* 243.23 on Deut 22:23, states: "A breach (in the wall) is an invitation to a thief; if she had stayed at home, this would not have happened to her." But other rabbis, in a less condemning fashion, restructure this case in order to ease the burden it placed upon the woman and also to erase the rigid distinction between city and field. Thus *Sifre D* 243.27 on Deut 22:27 argues that the matter should turn not on her outcry but on whether or not help was available nearby. Nahmanides, in his commentary, goes even further and argues more sympathetically that one must allow for other ways of female resistance, whether audible or not.

The rabbinic efforts to restate the biblical case certainly lead to a more just outcome and perhaps the ancient courts would also have been open to consider all attendant circumstances. Yet comparison with ancient Near Eastern laws reveals that features found in the biblical case were in fact well-established "guidelines," rooted in a long legal history that one finds in the ancient Near Eastern law collections. There are a number of laws to consider. We find the theme of a betrothed, virgin wife already in the second millennium BCE in Urnamma Laws §6: "If a man acted forcibly (and) deflowered the virgin wife of a young man, one shall kill that man." A similar case occurs in Eshnunna Laws §26; it includes the same situation of the betrothed, virgin wife but adds another factor–the consent of her parents, which was necessary for a marriage to be legally valid:

> If a man brought the groom's gift for a man's daughter and another person, without asking her father and mother, takes her forcibly and deflowers her, it is a capital offense; he shall die.

Hammurapi Laws §130 again states this same, basic law, adding that the victim is not to be blamed:

> If a man has overpowered a(nother) man's wife who did not (yet) know a male, and who was still living in her father's house and he lay with her and they catch him, that man shall be put to death (but) that woman goes free.

These early law cases clearly indicate that the female was taken by force but do not discuss her response to the attacker or the location in which it took place. However, an approximation of Deuteronomy's distinction between town and field does appear in Hittite Laws §197:

> If a man seizes a woman in the mountain(s) (and rapes her), it is the man's offense, and he shall be put to death, but if he seizes her in (her) house, it is the woman's offense; the woman shall be put to death. If the (woman's) husband (lit. the man) finds them (in the act), and kills them, he has committed no offense.

The Hittite Laws seem to be more discriminating than Deut 22:23–27 in that the contrast is between house and field

rather than between town and field. The woman, after all, might be bereft of help even in town if no one was nearby, as *Sifre D* points out. However, the biblical case in Deuteronomy helps us understand the thinking behind Hittite Laws §197, which does not state the reason why a woman in the mountains should be treated differently than one in the house. The Hittite Law also considers a situation where the husband surprises the couple at home in the act and, "taking the law into his own hands." kills them both in his rage. The more normal course was, of course, to seek redress through the courts. There is no parallel to this action by a husband in the Bible; but it is reminiscent of the act of Phineas described in Num 25:1–15 where he slew a man and a woman during their sexual act. The situation there was one of public indecency in connection with idolatry; Phineas was highly praised for his action, which may perhaps have been modeled on the more familiar extra-juridical response to adultery on the part of an outraged husband. The right—for any onlooker—to slay one who attacks and attempts to rape a betrothed maiden is supported by the rabbis in a *baraita* cited in *b. Sanh.* 73a):

> A betrothed maiden, whether at home or in the field, one may "save him" (i.e., the man who is attacking her) from committing this transgression even) at the cost of (taking) his (i.e., the attacker's) life . . . however, after the transgression has been committed, one does not save her by taking his (i.e., the attacker's) life.[111]

111. The Talmud here is commenting upon a more abbreviated version of this law in *m. Sanh.* 8:7. The *baraita* text closely resembles what appears in *t. Sanh.* 11:11, Zuckermandel; but that text is less clear.

Middle Assyrian Laws §A 12 describes a case where the woman was walking in the town; she resisted her attacker but, as in *Sifre D* on Deut 22:27 cited above, there was no one to come to her aid:

> If the wife of a man walked in the street (and another) man seized her and) has said: "I would copulate with you" (and) she does not agree and has (otherwise) always been chaste (and) he took her by force (and) copulated with her, whether they surprise him upon the man's wife or whether witnesses prove that he has copulated with the woman, they shall kill that man; there is no (punishable) offense for the woman.

This law does not blame the woman for walking in the street; nor does it require her to cry out as in Deut 22:23–27. However, her refusal of sexual connection must be evident in order for her to be free from any accusation of complicity; and her previous record of conduct is also a factor, namely, that her prior reputation was one of chastity.

Middle Assyrian Laws §A 23 reveals another required feature of female response to rape: the need for her not to conceal what had happened to her; otherwise she might be accused of complicity. In §A 23, a married woman was tricked into a compromising situation by another woman; the woman invited her into her house, where the other man was waiting for her. The married woman is not blamed even if the encounter took place inside of a house, but she was then expected to speak up and reveal the attack upon leaving the scene of her 'abduction':

> . . . But if the man's wife did not know and the woman who took her into her house brought the man to her by *trickery* and he copulated with her, then if upon her leaving the house she declares that she was sexually compromised, they shall release the woman, she is cleared (of blame). They shall kill the fornicator and the procuress. But if the woman should not speak up (upon leaving), the man (i.e., the husband) shall put whatever punishment he sees fit upon his wife (and) they shall kill the fornicator and the procuress.

The need of the victim to call attention to what happened to her is also seen in the tale of Potiphar's wife, whose overtures were rejected by Joseph. She felt it necessary to fabricate a story about Joseph attempting to sexually assault her and she thus wanted to be "on record" of having cried out to rebuff his advances; thus in Gen 39:11–18:

> One such day, he came into the house to do his work. None of the household being there inside, she caught hold of him by his garment and said, "Lie with me!" But he left his garment in her hand and got away and fled outside. When she saw that he had left it in her hand and had fled outside, she called out to her servants and said to them, "Look, he had to bring us a Hebrew to dally with us! This one came to lie with me; but I screamed loud. And when he heard me screaming at the top of my voice, he left his garment with me and got away and fled outside." She kept his garment beside her, until his master came home. Then she told him the same story, saying, "The Hebrew slave whom you brought into our house came to me to dally with me; but

when I screamed at the top of my voice, he left his garment with me and fled outside." (NJPS)

There was evidently a widely held social expectation for women who were sexually assaulted to show their resistance by making public outcry. We will see additional illustrations of this practice in the following sec. 1.4.2.

1.4.2 Rape of an Unmarried Woman

An unmarried woman who was sexually assaulted was also expected to make a public outcry. This is what Tamar did upon leaving the house of Amnon in 2 Sam 13:19. This episode has been mentioned earlier (sec. 1.1.1) Tamar was an unmarried virgin and had come to Amnon's house having been told that he was ill and needed nursing. Tamar was willing to stay with him and allow Amnon to "repair" his rape by marrying her (see below); but he was finished with her and threw her out of his house. It was in the street that she then cried out (2 Sam 13:19): "Tamar put dust on her head and rent the ornamented tunic she was wearing; she put her hands on her head, and walked away, screaming loudly as she went (NJPS). Her behavior finds an echo in the Mesopotamian composition known as "The Instructions of Shuruppak," where a Sumerian proverb, declares: "Do not commit rape upon a man's daughter; she will announce it in the courtyard."[112]

The biblical laws treat the case of rape of an unmarried woman in Deut 22:28–29:

> If a man finds a virgin girl who is not betrothed and he seizes her

and lies with her, and they are discovered, the man who lay with her shall pay the girl's father fifty shekels of silver, and she shall be his wife; because he oppressed her;[113] he shall not have the right to divorce her (for) all (of) his days.

The "solution" to the rape was to have the rapist marry the girl and pay a penalty for his action. This is what Tamar proposed to Amnon in 2 Sam 13:16:

> She pleaded with him, "Please don't commit this wrong; to send me away would be even worse than the first wrong you committed against me." But he would not listen to her. (NJPS)

One can find an echo of this same "remedy" or "repair" in the story about the rape of Dinah in Genesis 34, where Shechem, the rapist, offers conciliation to Jacob and his sons. In Gen 34:11–12 he states:

> Shechem (also) said to her father and to her brothers, "Let me find favor in your eyes, and whatever you say to me I will give. Set high the amount of brideprice and marriage gift, and I will give whatever you ask me; only give me the girl for (my) wife."

Dinah's brothers presented themselves as being ready to accept this offer, provided that Shechem underwent circumcision. He, the entire royal family, and following their example, all the males in the city were circumcised. Two of the brothers,

---

112. Alster, *The Instruction of* Šuruppak, 22–23, 38–39.

113. Alternatively translated "he degraded her." See Berlin, "Sex and the Single Girl," 104–5; and Sperling, "Dinah," for more extensive discussion of this Hebrew verb when used in sexual situations. KJV in similar fashion translated "humbled her" in this passage and also in the rape of a betrothed woman in Deut 22:23–27 (sec. 1.4.1).

Simeon and Levi, taking advantage of this incapacitation, came against the city, slew all of the adult males, and subjected their women and children and their possessions to pillage and plunder. Jacob (Gen 34:30) rebuked them for doing so; and on his deathbed, cursed their violent actions (Gen 49:7). But despite the treachery and this negative outcome, one can see that the offer of marriage made by Shechem conformed to a widely known practice, and he thus had every expectation that he and the Israelites had reached a satisfactory settlement.

The later rabbis, in their interpretation of Deut 22:28–29, adjusted this law of compensation so as to give the girl or her father the right to accept the payment without consenting to the marriage—but not to the rapist, who could not, on his own, refuse to marry his victim.[114] This is not stated in the text but the rabbis reasoned by analogy from the case of seduction found in Exod 22:15–16 (see below in sec. 1.4.3) where the father is explicitly given this right of refusal. The rabbis were not far off the mark in wishing to insert the judgment of the woman's father into the settlement of rape. We see this right present in Middle Assyrian Law §A 55:

> [If a m]an forcibly seized and raped a young woman [who was living in her] father's house, who was not betrothed [lit. asked for][115], whose "womb" had not been "opened," who has not been taken (sexually), and has no claim (concerning her marital status) against her father's house—if that man (acted) either inside the city or in the field, or at night, whether in the street or in a

barn, or during a city festival, the father of the young girl shall take the wife of that fornicator (who raped) the young woman (and) hand her over to be raped. He (the father) shall not return her to her husband; he shall keep her and the father shall give his own, violated daughter to the fornicator in marriage. If he (the rapist) has no wife, he shall pay her father three times the (normal bride)price for a young woman; her rapist shall marry her; he cannot reject(?) her. If (her) father is unwilling (to give her) he may accept the threefold money of a young woman (and) he may give his daughter (in marriage) to someone that he chooses.

The Assyrian laws here add a measure of "vicarious" retaliation against the rapist's wife that we do not find in the Bible. But otherwise we find familiar features: substantial monetary penalty and the requirement for the rapist to marry his victim—provided the father agrees.

There are some additional, earlier laws dealing with rape found in a Sumerian school text, which are of interest, because they invite us to look back to the story about the rape of Dinah by Shechem in Genesis 34 discussed above, and the offer of marriage as settlement. The first law is as follows:

> If he raped a man's daughter in the street (and) her father and mother did not know him (but) he (the rapist comes forward and) says to her father and mother: 'I would take her (in marriage),' then her father and mother shall give her to him (in marriage).[116]

---

114. Cf. b. Ket. 39b.

115. Reading follows AHw 1433b.

116. The document is YOS 1 28 v 3–25 and my reading follows Finkelstein, "Sex Offenses in Sumerian Laws." This law is treated in Roth, Law Collections, 44.

This law may be interpreted to describe a situation where the rapist himself brings the news and facts of the rape to the parents' attention and then also declares that he is ready to marry their daughter. In other words, he takes the initiative to inform them and to offer marriage as closure. The encounter between Shechem, who is also represented by his own father Hamor, with Jacob and Dinah's brothers, as related in Gen 34:4–8 looks like a very similar negotiation:

> (4) And Shechem said to his father Hamor, "Get me this girl for a wife."
>
> (5) Then Jacob heard that he had defiled his daughter Dinah; but his sons were with his cattle in the field, and (so) Jacob kept silent until they came home.
>
> (6) And Hamor, Shechem's father, came out to Jacob to speak to him.
>
> (7) And Jacob's sons came in from the field; when the men heard they were deeply hurt and very angry, because he had committed an outrage in Israel by lying with Jacob's daughter; and such a thing should not to be done.
>
> (8) And Hamor spoke with them, saying, "My son Shechem longs for your daughter. Please give her to him in marriage.

Verse 5 appears to be "out of order" in the story, which reads better as if it were placed after verse 6 rather than before it. According to Gen 34:26, Dinah remained in Shechem this entire time and in fact only returned after her brothers attacked and sacked the city; so she could not have told her family what had happened. So the plausible sequence was as follows: both Shechem and his father Hamor came to

Jacob to tell him about the rape and at the same time to offer matrimony; Jacob said nothing in negotiation since his sons were out in the field; he sent for them and waited until they returned home. At that point Hamor again presented the offer of marriage with all of them present.[117] The Sumerian law supports the understanding that this act of Shechem and his father— coming forward to inform Jacob, making a "clean breast of it," and offering to marry Dinah— would, in the ancient world of biblical times, have been the appropriate way to negotiate a settlement offer. Hamor and Shechem could only have left the meeting assuming that they had in fact reached a settlement.[118]

The second Sumerian law comes after the first case but goes in a different direction from what we have so far seen:

> If he raped the daughter of a man *in* the street (and) her father and mother did know (him, but) the (alleged) rapist denies that he knew (anything about the attack), he must [. . .] take an oath at the temple gate.

The second Sumerian law seems to describe a situation where the parents go

---

117. A somewhat similar understanding is implied by Sarna, *Genesis,* 234 who states: "Apparently, Hamor arrives before the brothers and is left cooling his heels until they came home."

118. Interestingly, Nahmanides, in his comment on Gen 34:13, recognizes that the gentiles, in the "Covenant of Noah," were also commanded to render justice in cases of rape and seduction; he faults Hamor, the king, for failing to punish his son Shechem for rape. But Nahmanides was not aware that Hamor's offer—subject of course to Jacob's approval—was in fact in keeping with ancient laws and customs. It is therefore also interesting that in the biblical account, Jacob's agreement is implied but not stated, perhaps because it was later overturned by the treachery of his sons.

after the man whom they believe or were told is the rapist; he did not come forward but, once accused by them, is required to take an oath to clear himself. His denial is not otherwise accepted. In this Sumerian case, it is not clear what happens after the (alleged) rapist took the oath; he seems to get off without any penalty. Is he able to do so because no one was able to prove otherwise? He thus would not be convicted of the rape even if he did commit the act. This is a disquieting conclusion and one is left to wonder whether the student scribe who wrote this tablet of laws left out some additional details.[119]

This second Sumerian case makes us think back again to the rape of Tamar by Amnon; why was he not punished by King David? Of course we are told the story through the eyes of a narrator so we "know" what really happened—but not everything. In 2 Sam 13:20–21 we read:

> Her brother Absalom said to her, "Has Amnon your brother been with you? Be quiet for now, my sister; he is your brother; do not take this to heart." So Tamar remained, a desolate woman, in her brother Absalom's house. When King David heard of all these things, he became very angry. (NRSV)

Had Amnon possibly sworn a false oath of denial and no other witnesses came forward? Or was the matter dropped or "hushed up" because this crime was intra-familial? Had David refused to have Amnon marry Tamar? For earlier in 2 Sam 13:15 we are told that after the rape: "Then Amnon felt a very great loathing for her; indeed, his loathing for her was greater than the passion he had felt for her" (NJPS). The Greek version of 2 Sam 13:21 adds another piece to the story: "he [David] did not grieve the spirit of his son Amnon, for he kept loving him, for he was his firstborn."[120] Had David surrendered to Amnon's churlishness and therefore did not force Amnon, the rapist, to marry his victim Tamar? Because no action of closure or correction was taken, two years later, Amnon later suffered a more violent punishment when Tamar's brother Absalom, took a private vengeance and had Amnon murdered at a family feast. We will look at this part of the story, when I discuss the laws of homicide (sec. 4.8).

1.4.3 Seduction of an Unmarried Woman

A case of seduction found in Exod 22:15–16:

> If a man seduces a virgin who was not betrothed, and lies with her, he must make her his wife by paying a bride-price. If her father absolutely refuses to give her to him, he must still weigh out silver (in the amount of the (customary) bride-price for virgins.

In the Bible, the "remedy" for seduction, like in the case of rape, is also for the man and woman to marry; the father has the right of refusal but nothing is said about the husband being denied any future right of divorce. However, in a version of this case found in the "Temple Scroll" of the Essenes, the seducer is not allowed to divorce his wife:

---

119. This law has been subject to other interpretations, depending upon how one understands the parents' "knowledge." It has been suggested that the man's relationship with their daughter was in some way condoned by her parents. For discussion cf. Lafont, *Femmes, Droit et Justice*, 105–21.

120. The Greek is supported by the Hebrew in 4Q51 (Sam^a); cf. *Dead Sea Scrolls Bible*, 247.

> If a man seduce a young virgin girl who is not betrothed one who by statute is a possible marriage partner for him and he has intercourse with her and is discovered, then the man must give woman's father fifty shekels of silver, and she will become his wife. Since he violated her, he cannot divorce her as long as he lives.[121]

The case in the Temple Scroll appears to contain some of the language and features found in the rape case of Deut 22:28–29 above (sec. 1.4.2). It has been suggested that, in the view of the Essenes, sexual relations even in the absence of marriage created a "marriage like" bond, which in their view should be permanent and lasting for a lifetime.[122] The biblical laws do not say anything about the woman's right of refusal but the rabbis defended their adjustment for this feature by appealing to the doubled verbal construction in Exod 22:16: "if her father absolutely refuses." The doubled verbal construction—while idiomatic—in their hermeneutic was used to support a "reading" of two refusals: that of the father and the (unstated) right of his daughter.

A law dealing with seduction is appended to Middle Assyrian Laws §A 55, the law cited above in sec. 1.4.2, which deals with rape. Middle Assyrian Laws §A 56 adds:

> If the young (unmarried) woman of her own will has given herself to the man, the man shall take an oath (to that effect) and they shall not approach his wife (for retaliation). The fornicator shall (however) pay threefold the (bride)price of a young woman. The father will do (with) his daughter as he wishes.

The Assyrian laws require the man to swear an oath that the encounter was consensual. He is not physically punished but must pay a substantial monetary penalty. There is no requirement for marriage, evidently because he already has a wife; and because the encounter was consensual, no retaliation is taken against his wife, as was the case of the rapist in Middle Assyrian Laws §A 55.

In the ancient Near Eastern laws, like in the Bible, one can see that the consent of a young woman's parents was needed in order for any marriage to be valid. We see this again in Eshnunna Laws §27, which deals with elopement:

> If a man took the daughter of another man without asking her father and mother and did not arrange a (marriage) contract and the (ceremonial) libation for her father and mother, even if she lives a year in his house, she is not a (lawful) wife.

The idea here is that cohabitation over time will not confer legitimacy upon the union, because a young unmarried woman was not legally empowered to marry on her own. One sees this clearly by comparing this law with one from Assyria dealing with a widow; a widow's union became legally recognized through cohabitation and passage of time. The widow, unlike the young unmarried woman, enjoyed full legal power to live as she wished. The law is Middle Assyrian Laws §A 34:

---

121. 11Q19 66:8–11; cf. Wise, Abegg, and Cook, *Dead Sea Scrolls*, 631; parentheses added there for line 9 are removed in the translation given here, since this line is present in the Temple Scroll, even if absent in MT.

122. Shemesh, "A Key to Sectarian Matrimonial Law," 247–49.

If a man took a widow without any formal marriage contract being made (and) she lives for two years in his house, she is a wife; she shall not leave.

We are not informed as to whether (and when) an unmarried woman might achieve legal independence and be married on her own.

1.4.4 Sexual Offenses against Slaves

There are separate laws dealing with sexual offenses against slave women; such actions were considered wrongs but the punishments given were different from those involving an attack on free women. The Bible presents one such case in Lev 19:20–22:

> If a man has sexual relations with a woman who is a slave, designated for another man but not ransomed or given her freedom, an inquiry shall be held. They shall not be put to death, since she has not been freed; but he shall bring a guilt offering for himself to the LORD, at the entrance of the tent of meeting, a ram as guilt offering. And the priest shall make atonement for him with the ram of guilt offering before the LORD for his sin that he committed; and the sin he committed shall be forgiven him. (NRSV)

It is noteworthy that the parties who participated in the sexual act are not punished. The slave woman is not punished most likely because as a slave she lacked full legal rights. As a slave, she may also not have been able to refuse the man who took her. But what can one say about the man? He can be viewed as having trespassed upon the rights of the other man, i.e., the "husband" to whom the slave woman was designated, but this would be so only if the other man was free. He could also be seen as having trespassed upon the property rights of the slave woman's owner; this would certainly be the case if the designated man or "husband" were himself another of the owner's slaves. The holding of an inquiry or investigation was apparently necessary to sort all of this out. Monetary compensation might need to be paid, perhaps even some corporal punishment like flogging? But the writer of Leviticus is not concerned with discussing these matters, as important as they might have been to the parties themselves. Leviticus focuses rather on the trespasser being a sinner to God. It may be that the writer of Leviticus was troubled by the legal disparity that existed between free persons and slaves; for had the woman been free and betrothed to a free man, both she together with her paramour, rapist, or seducer could have been given the death penalty. Leviticus therefore uses neutral language to describe the sexual encounter because, for a slave woman, these distinctions were not legally relevant. Nevertheless, a sin against the "spirit" of the prohibition against adultery had been committed; and the perpetrator, i.e., the free man who had sexual relations with the slave woman, owed a guilt offering to God to atone for what Leviticus considers, at the very least, a grievous private sin that the legal system did not embrace. Only with this offering could the matter be brought to a close in the eyes of God, even if all other aspects, e.g., property rights of the owner, were settled in the earthly court.[123]

123. The analysis given here, in essential details, follows Milgrom, *Leviticus,* 3:1665–77. Milgrom also discusses the opinions of various scholars who hope to locate within the term "inquiry"—which

The ancient Near Eastern laws focus solely on human legal rights and societal justice. They do therefore give us a glimpse of what kinds of financial settlements might have been required of the offender in Lev 19:20–22, beyond the required sacrifice. In Urnamma Laws §8 we read:

> If a man acts in an overpowering manner and deflowered another man's virgin slave woman, he shall pay 5 shekels silver.

A similar case appears in Eshnunna Laws §31:

> If a man has deflowered another man's slave woman, he shall pay one-third mina silver but the slave woman remains the property of her master.

The money paid is a penalty and does not purchase any rights in the slave woman. This comment is added because the amount of penalty is high—equivalent to 20 shekels or four times what is imposed in Urnamma Laws §8. It could be enough to purchase a slave! But penalties could actually go even higher. In the Sumerian legal literature there is preserved the record of an ancient trial that involved the same offense: a man had seized a slave woman belonging to another person, dragged her into a nearby commercial building, and deflowered her there. Her owner brought suit; the man denied the charge but the owner had witnesses that confirmed what had happened. The offender was sentenced to pay one half-mina silver, i.e., 30 shekels.[124] Evidently, there were

many factors to be considered in setting the penalties which would be determined, as probably also in Lev 19:20–22, by investigation in connection with a trial or settlement. One of the factors seems to have been the virgin status of the slave woman, which apparently rendered her more valuable in the marketplace. Loss of virginity thus appears in the Sumerian laws cited above. But it is also possible that in the case given in Lev 19:20–22, the slave woman was not a virgin; however a sacrifice was still required.

The rabbis pondered about the nature of the sin that had been committed in this encounter. It was at the very least a kind of "quasi-adultery" especially for the woman. One is able to infer this understanding from the Tosefta, where the investigation needs to ascertain whether the slave woman was complicit or not in the sexual encounter. If she had been willing, then the rabbis proscribed flogging for her. But for the man there was no additional punishment other than his needing to bring an expiatory sacrifice.[125] But there was some additional "carry over" for the man; because the rabbis also ruled that if a slave woman with whom a free man had sexual relations is later freed and that man marries her, then he cannot ever divorce her, like the case of the unmarried woman who is raped in Deut 22:28–29 and the seduced woman in the Temple Scroll version of Exod 22:15–16

appears only once in the Bible—a more specific obligation for the rapist to indemnify the owner of the slave-woman; thus, for, example, NJPS translates the term as "indemnity."

124. The case is published in Finkelstein, "Sex Offenses in Sumerian Laws," 359–60.

125. Cf. *t. Ker.* 1:16, Lieberman; and Maimonides *Mishnah Torah, Hilkhot Shegagot* 9:1. But as Maimonides notes in *Mishnah Torah, Hilkot Issurei Biah* 12:13–14, some ancient authorities evidently felt that the man was also worthy of flogging. One can see this idea reflected in *Targum Onqelos* on Deut 23:18b, which Onqelos rather freely interprets as prohibiting a free Israelite having sexual union with a slave woman!

(secs. 1.4.3 and 1.3.2). We read this in *t. Yeb.* 4:6, Lieberman:

> An Israelite who had sex with a slave woman or with gentile women, if at a later time that slave woman is freed or that gentile woman is converted (to Judaism), he should not marry her; but if he did marry her, he can never divorce (her).

The rabbis' initial hesitancy against the man marrying her is based upon their view that any woman who had a history of prior sexual promiscuity outside of wedlock was not a "proper" woman; some went so far to put her into the category of a fornicator or harlot.[126]

1.5 INHERITANCE

1.5.1. Inheritance by Sons

In biblical society, the inheritance rights of heirs seems ideally to have followed birth order, with male children taking precedence over female children. The first-born male was accorded special status and was entitled to a greater share in the father's estate than his siblings. The right of the male first born is treated in Deut 21:15–17:

> If a man has two wives, one loved and the other hated, and (both) the loved and the hated wives have borne him sons, and the first-born is the son of the hated one, when he apportions his property to his sons, he may not rank as first-born the son of the loved one over the son of the hated one, (who was) the first-born. Because he must acknowledge the first-born, the son of the hated one, giving him a double portion of all he possesses; since he is the first (product) of his sexual

power; the right of the first-born belongs to him.

The Bible elsewhere tells of wives who were hated or despised by their husbands; it is said of Jacob's wife Leah in Gen 29:31 "The Lord saw that Leah was hated and he opened her womb; but Rachel was barren." It is also said of a husband who "hated" his wife to the point of divorcing her as may have occurred in Deut 24:3 cited above (sec. 1.2.1). Indeed, we find this term "hate" used to describe the occurrence of divorce and its economic implications in the Aramaic marriage documents used by Jewish couples living at Elephantine in upper Egypt during the fifth century BCE (sec. 1.2.1). It is therefore possible that the "hated wife" described in Deut 21:15–17 was in fact his former wife now divorced. Nevertheless, Deut 21:15–17 maintains that personal feelings cannot interfere in the order of inheritance.

Yet it is clear that the customary "birthright" of the first-born was not always maintained. Jacob deposed Reuben, his first-born son, on his deathbed in Gen 49:3–4: "Reuben, you are my first-born, My might and first fruit of my vigor, exceeding in rank And exceeding in honor. Unstable as water, you shall excel no longer . . . "(NJPS). Jacob again reversed rank in preferring his grandson Ephraim over Manasseh in Gen 48:17–19:

> When Joseph saw that his father was placing his right hand on Ephraim's head, he thought it wrong; so he took hold of his father's hand to move it from Ephraim's head to Manasseh's. "Not so, Father," Joseph said to his father, "for the other is the first-born; place your right hand on his head." But his father objected, saying, "I

---

126. *Sifra Emor* 1.7 (on Lev 21:14); *m. Yebam.* 7:5.

know, my son, I know. He too shall become a people, and he too shall be great. Yet his younger brother shall be greater than he, and his offspring shall be plentiful enough for nations." (NJPS)

In 1 Chr 26:10, it is related about a prominent Levitical family, " Hosah of the Merarites had sons: Shimri the chief—although he was not the first-born, but his father made him chief." The "normal" succession is described as having taken place between king Jehoshaphat and his son Jehoram; evidently its "normalcy" was worthy of comment (2 Chr 21:1–3):

> . . . Jehoram succeeded him as king. He had brothers, sons of Jehoshaphat: Azariah, Jehiel, Zechariah, Azariahu, Michael, and Shephatiah; all these were sons of King Jehoshaphat of Israel. Their father gave them many gifts of silver, gold, and [other] presents, as well as fortified towns in Judah, but he gave the kingdom to Jehoram because he was the first-born. (NJPS)

A father, as head of the family, had the legal right to give away family property as he wished. Such gifts were given away while the father was still alive; the Bible knows nothing about wills, i.e., provisions that take legal effect after the death of the father. The customary rights of the first-born could thus only be circumvented or avoided by a father's actions during his lifetime. The Bible offers another illustration of this practice in connection with Abraham and his third wife Keturah (Gen 25:5–6):

> Abraham gave all he had to Isaac. But to the sons of his concubines Abraham gave gifts, while he was

still living, and he sent them away from his son Isaac, eastward to the east country. (NRSV)

We find that the giving away of family wealth outside of the line of inheritance was viewed negatively in Ezek 46:16–17:

> Thus said the Lord GOD: If the prince makes a gift to any of his sons, it shall become the latter's inheritance; it shall pass on to his sons; it is their holding by inheritance. But if he makes a gift from his inheritance to any of his servants, it shall only belong to the latter until the year of release. Then it shall revert to the prince; his inheritance must by all means pass on to his sons. (NJPS)

According to Ezekiel, sons have an inherent right to their father's property, which renders his gifts to outsiders as temporary. The outside recipients have possession but not true ownership. As for when a year of release might occur, I discuss this further below (sec. 2.4) in connection with debt slavery.

The custom of a parent making gifts during their lifetime is attested in ancient Babylonia, as we can see from Lipit-Ishtar Laws §31:

> If a father, during his lifetime, gives a son whom he favors a gift (and) writes for him a sealed document, after the father has died, the heirs shall divide the (remainder of the) paternal estate; they shall not contest the share that was allotted, they shall not contest their father's word.

In Babylonia there was evidently no mandated preferential share for any son; but a father was able to make gifts during his lifetime. This law does not consider gifts to persons outside of the line of succession; and one may wonder whether there is there a gap in our evidence or, as in Ezek 46:16–17, was there a bias against gifts to persons outside of family members, who were expected to inherit? This practice of preferential gifts to heirs is again described some centuries later in Hammurapi Laws §165:

> If a man gifted unto an heir of his whom he favored a field, orchard, or building (and) wrote out for him a sealed document (for that gift), then after the father has gone to his fate (i.e., died), when the brothers divide (his estate) he (i.e., the favored heir) shall have the gift he (the father) gave him but in addition, they will equally divide the father's estate.

As in Deut 21:15–17, sons from different mothers were not to be denied their rightful shares in the paternal estate. This principal is stated in Lipit-Ishtar Laws §24:

> If the second wife whom he married bore him a son, the dowry, which she brought from the house of her father, belongs to her son. (However) the son of the first chosen wife and the son of the second wife shall equally divide the property of their father.

We see the same idea in Hammurapi Laws §167:

> If a man married a wife and she bore him sons (but) that woman went to her fate (i.e., died). After her (death) he then married a second woman and she (also) has born him sons. After the father has gone to his fate, the children will not divide according to their mothers. (While) they shall (separately)

take the dowries of their (respective) mothers, they shall divide the property of the father's estate equally.

There is, however, evidence for giving the eldest son a preferential share in the later, Neo-Babylonian period; this distinction is sometimes applied even to daughters. The evidence for this practice comes from actual contracts dealing with inheritance, frequently also in situations of adoption.[127] On the other hand, the Neo-Babylonian laws—unfortunately not all preserved—assign greater privilege and status to the sons born to a man's first wife as a group, but do not deal with the privileges given to a first born son as an individual. Neo-Babylonian Laws 15 states:

> (In the case of) a man who married a wife and she bore him sons and (then) fate carried off his wife (i.e., she died) and he married a second wife and she bore him sons, after the father has gone to his fate, the sons of the first wife shall take a double portion and the sons of the later wife (the remaining) one-third share in the property of the father's estate. Their sisters who (still) reside in the father's house [. . .]

The end of this law is unfortunately broken away; it possibly required the brothers from each mother to provide dowries for their unmarried sisters, to be taken out of the shares they received from their father's estate. (There is more discussion about dowries and the rights of daughters below in sec. 1.5.2))

---

127. Cf. *CAD* T, 226–27 *sub. tardennu* "younger son (in rank)"; *CAD* R, 30 (*rabû*), "eldest (son)."

In Assyria the practice was to give a double portion to the eldest son. Middle Assyrian Laws §B 1 relates how a group of brothers were to go about dividing their father's estate:

> [If brothers divide their father's estate—orch]ards, [and wells in] the field(s), the eld[est son as his share] will choose (and) take two portions and afterwards his brothers shall choose (and) take in equal portions. (However,) for (every) field, the youngest son shall prepare (equivalent) lots (to be chosen from) whatever there are of indentured (?) laborers and equipment; the eldest son shall (first) choose one portion, but for his second portion he shall cast lots (together) with his brothers.[128]

We can see here the preferential rights of the first born to take a double portion and a right to select his first portion before any other distributions. But we also see some adjustments for fairness for his brothers, in letting the youngest son assemble the groupings of personnel and equipment to be "attached" to each land parcel. The casting of lots acknowledges intrinsic equal rights; after the eldest son took his the first group, the selection of rest was left to chance, which, as it was believed, was guided by higher powers. We see glimpses of this same practice in the Bible, i.e., the casting of lots for the dividing of land and offices.[129] But the Bible gives us no information on how the parcels were

divided and prepared prior to the casting of lots. The custom of giving a preferential share to the first-born son was known in other parts of the ancient Near East, e.g., in northern Syria (Emar, Alalakh, Ugarit) and Nuzi. The practice of favoring the first-born son was also maintained in rabbinic times.[130]

1.5.2 Inheritance by Daughters

Daughters did not have the same rights of inheritance as sons. When daughters married, however, it was customary to send them forth with a dowry; this was a widely practiced custom. The Bible records no law on this—only a fleeting reference in 1 Kgs 9:16, to Pharaoh conquering the city of Gezer and giving it along with his daughter to Solomon: "Pharaoh king of Egypt had come up and captured Gezer and he destroyed it by fire, killed the Canaanites who lived in the town, and gave it as dowry to his daughter, Solomon's wife" (NJPS).[131] Yet daughters could at times also be heirs alongside of their brothers. Job 42:15 relates: "Nowhere in the land were women as beautiful as Job's daughters to be found. Their father gave them estates together with their brothers" (NJPS). The Bible apparently adds this detail to the story in order to illustrate the magnitude of Job's wealth after his restoration; there was more than enough for all

128. The missing beginning of the law paragraph is restored from Middle Assyrian Laws §O 3, which begins in similar fashion but then breaks off. The law paragraphs on tablets B and O may have been duplicates of each other.

129. Cf. Neh 11:1; 1 Chr 6:46–50; 25:8; 26:13–16.

130. For the ancient Near East, cf. Westbrook, "Anatolia and the Levant: Emar and Vicinity," 678, 729–30; Zaccagnini, "Mesopotamia. Nuzi," 600–601; *CAD* Z, 140–41. For rabbinic times, cf. Shilo, "Wills."

131. In Josh 15:19 and Judg 1:15 Achsah mentions the dowry that her father Caleb gave to her and asks him to augment it with sources of water; but the term "dowry" does not appear; she refers to it only as "the Negev land you gave to me." The marriage of Achsah is discussed in sec. 1.1.3.

73

of his children. The more typical practice is reflected the story told about the daughters of Zelophehad, whose father died leaving no sons. Moses, acting through a divine oracle, awarded them their father's property and announced the following rules in Num 27:8–11:

> . . . If a man dies without leaving a son, you shall transfer his property to his daughter. If he has no daughter, you shall assign his property to his brothers. If he has no brothers, you shall assign his property to his father's brothers. If his father had no brothers, you shall assign his property to his nearest relative in his own clan, and he shall inherit it. This shall be the law of procedure for the Israelites, in accordance with the LORD's command to Moses. (NJPS)

The patriarchal family structure is clearly evident in these laws; with the exception of daughters, succession stays with males in the paternal family. In Num 36:6–9 we are told that this right of female succession underwent a further modification in order to make it more favorable to the interests of the paternal relatives of the deceased:

> This is what the LORD has commanded concerning the daughters of Zelophehad: They may marry anyone they wish, provided they marry into a clan of their father's tribe. No inheritance of the Israelites may pass over from one tribe to another, but the Israelites must remain bound each to the ancestral portion of his tribe. Every daughter among the Israelite tribes who inherits a share must marry someone from a clan of her father's tribe, in order that every Israelite may keep his ancestral share. Thus no

> inheritance shall pass over from one tribe to another, but the Israelite tribes shall remain bound each to its portion. (NJPS)

The daughters of Zelophehad closely followed the intent of this law; and so in Num 36:10–12, we are told that they dutifully married their first cousins, whose interests in their father's property were understandably most keen, standing as they did so near in the rights of succession:

> The daughters of Zelophehad did as the LORD had commanded Moses: Mahlah, Tirzah, Hoglah, Milcah, and Noah, Zelophehad's daughters, were married to sons of their uncles, marrying into clans of descendants of Manasseh son of Joseph; and so their share remained in the tribe of their father's clan. (NJPS)

This revised law of inheritance and its apparent reception in practice is reflected in the Book of Tobit, which scholars generally date to the late Persian or early Hellenistic period. In Tobit 6:11–13 we read:

> Then [the angel] Raphael said to him [i.e., to Tobias], "We must stay this night in the home of Raguel. He is your relative, and he has a daughter named Sarah. He has no male heir and no daughter except Sarah only, and you, as next of kin to her, have before all other men a hereditary claim on her. Also it is right for you to inherit her father's possessions. Moreover, the girl is sensible, brave, and very beautiful, and her father is a good man." He continued, "You have every right to take her in marriage. So listen to me, brother; tonight I will speak to her father about the girl, so that we may take her to be your bride.

When we return from Rages we will celebrate her marriage. For I know that Raguel can by no means keep her from you or promise her to another man without incurring the penalty of death according to the decree of the book of Moses. Indeed he knows that you, rather than any other man, are entitled to marry his daughter. (NRSV)

This same understanding of the law is given by Raguel the father of Sarah in his own speech to Tobias:

> But Raguel overheard it and said to the lad, "Eat and drink, and be merry tonight. For no one except you, brother, has the right to marry my daughter Sarah. Likewise I am not at liberty to give her to any other man than yourself, because you are my nearest relative. (Tobit 7:10 NRSV)

In this story, the claim of the male relatives is even more powerfully expressed than in Num 36:6–9 for it adds "the penalty of death according to the decree of the book of Moses" for those who fail to maintain their rights. But there is no mention of a death penalty in our text of Num 36:6–9; and I cannot say how or when it came to be added. Some biblical scholars see Num 36:6–9 as a late insertion into the biblical story, because of its place at the end of the Book of Numbers and the new limitations it seeks to impose. It may be of interest to note that in Greece, the Laws of Gortyn (c. 450 BCE) mandated a similar requirement that female heiresses marry their paternal uncles or cousins.[132] In the time of the Talmud, we are told that

this ancient requirement of heiresses to marry their close relatives was no longer operative.[133] But the precedence of sons over daughters was maintained and this was extended even to property belonging to their mother. The Talmud recalls that some groups, like the Sadducees, had once been more lenient in this regard, but later authorities subordinated the rights of daughters to sons.[134]

The rabbis further subordinated the inheritance rights of a woman's children to that of her husband. Thus, when a woman died, her husband became the first heir of her property; and only if he were already deceased, would her property pass to her sons and daughters. The earlier, biblical practice, however, was probably similar to what we see described in Hammurapi Laws §167 above (sec. 1.5.1), namely that a woman's property was to be inherited, not by her husband, but only by her own sons and daughters.[135] If a woman who was married died without offspring, her

132. Willetts, *Law Code of Gortyn*, vii 15—ix 2; this similarity is noted by Smith, "Early Mediterranean Law Codes," and by Westbrook, *Property and Family in Biblical Law*, 164.

133. This position is presented *in b. B. Bat.* 120a; *b. Ta'an.* 30b.

134. Cf. *j. B. Bat.* 16a; *b. B. Bat.* 111a, 115b; *t. Yad.* 2:20, Lieberman; and *m. B. Bat.* 8:2. But, earlier, in *t. B. Bat.* 7:10, Lieberman, the more lenient position is partially still maintained.

135. The *Sifre N Pinhas* 134 (on Num. 27:7) attempts to argue that the husband's right to inherit his wife's property is really based on Scripture; but the argument is recognized as faulty in *b. B. Bat.* 111b. Maimonides, *Mishnah Torah, Hilkhot Nahalot* 1:8 thus declares it to have been a social change introduced by post-scriptural rabbinic legislation. Reasons are not given; but one may suggest that it was, at least in part, an economic offset offered to husbands when the rabbis introduced the requirement for every husband to promise his wife a substantial prenuptial settlement (*ketubbah*) that would be collected from his property at the time of divorce or at his death. Cf. *t. Ket.* 12:1, Lieberman; and *b. Ket.* 82b. For the history of the *ketubbah* see sec. 1.2.4.

assets would revert to her natal family. This is stated in Neo-Babylonian Laws 10:

> A man who gave a dowry to his daughter and she has no son or daughter and fate carried her off [i.e., she died], her dowry shall return to her father's house.

The reversion of dowry to the family of a childless woman was still possible in later Jewish law, but only if this was formally agreed upon at the time of her marriage. We find this in the Palestinian Talmud, *j. Ket.* 33a:

> Rabbi Jose said: those who write (into their marriage contracts) "if she dies without children, let everything belonging to her revert to her father's house"—this is a financial stipulation and (such) a stipulation is valid.[136]

When we look at the ancient Near Eastern laws, we find additional evidence for female rights of inheritance. Fragments belonging to the Laws of Lipit-Ishtar[137] state:

> If a man died and had no male child, his (eldest?) daughter who has not taken a husband shall be his heir. If [a man died and] his (eldest?) daughter [was married], a younger (unmarried?) sister (of hers) [. . .] the paternal property.

Despite the fragmentary state of the text, enough context is present to confirm for us that, in the absence of sons, a daughter would inherit only if she were unmarried. The married daughter had presumably already received a dowry from her father; but her younger sister, who was still single, living at home, had not yet received any dowry; this law therefore protected her interest. It is also possible that, just as with sons, the birth order of daughters conferred priority in inheritance; but we have no further details on this possibility. In comparison, it is interesting to note that the daughters of Zelophehad were likewise unmarried; neither the Bible nor Lipit-Ishtar tells us what would have happened to the inheritance if all the daughters had already married and received their dowries at the time of their father's death. One could imagine that the inheritance would pass to the children of the married daughter.[138] But perhaps this path of succession was contested in biblical time and this is why in the later law about the daughters of Zelophehad in Num 36:6–9, unmarried daughters were directed to marry within their father's extended family. The Laws of Lipit-Ishtar do not mention any requirement for the daughter who became an heiress to marry within her father's family. The general practice of female inheritance described in Lipit-Ishtar is also found in a statement made by Gudea, who ruled the city of Lagash over a century earlier. In an inscription on his statue (B vii, 44–45) he proclaims that "(when) a household had no male heir, he (Gudea) had the daughter enter into it as its heir."[139]

---

136. The similarity of this statement with Neo-Babylonian Laws 10 was noted by Rabinowitz, "Neo-Babylonian Documents and Jewish Law," 191.

137. Roth, *Law Collections,* 26–27 b-c. Some scholars assign these fragments to the Laws of Ur-namma; cf. Lafont and Westbrook, "Mesopotamia: Neo-Sumerian Period (Ur III)," 183 n. 3, 206 n. 94; so, too, Wilcke, "Der Kodex Urnamma," 322.

138. In rabbinic law, a married daughter and her descendants take precedence over her father's family; cf. *m. B. Bat.* 8:2.

139. A similar statement appears in Gudea, Cylinder B xviii, 8–9.

1.5.3 Social Rank by Mothers

The social rank of the wives could affect the rights of children, especially if their mother was unfree. In the Bible we see this possibility in the conflict between Sarah and Hagar described in Gen 21:9–13:

> And Sarah saw the son of Hagar the Egyptian, whom she had borne to Abraham, playing with her son Isaac.[140] So she said to Abraham, "Cast out this slave woman with her son; for the son of this slave woman shall not inherit along with my son Isaac." The matter was very distressing to Abraham on account of his son. But God said to Abraham, "Do not be distressed because of the boy and because of your slave woman; whatever Sarah says to you, do as she tells you, for it is through Isaac that offspring shall be named for you. As for the son of the slave woman, I will make a nation of him also, because he is your offspring." (NRSV)

Abraham was distressed because Sarah (previously called Sarai) herself had given Hagar to him as a wife; she was originally a slave but now she had become his wife and had bore him a son. This history and the longstanding conflict between the wives is related in Gen 16:1–6:

> Now Sarai, Abram's wife, bore him no children. She had an Egyptian slave-girl whose name was Hagar, and Sarai said to Abram, "You see that the LORD has prevented me from bearing children; go in to my slave-girl; it may be that I shall obtain children by her." And Abram listened to the voice of Sarai. So, after Abram had lived ten years in the land of Canaan, Sarai, Abram's

> wife, took Hagar the Egyptian, her slave-girl, and gave her to her husband Abram as a wife. He went in to Hagar, and she conceived; and when she saw that she had conceived, she looked with contempt on her mistress. Then Sarai said to Abram, "May the wrong done to me be on you! I gave my slave-girl to your embrace, and when she saw that she had conceived, she looked on me with contempt. May the LORD judge between you and me!" But Abram said to Sarai, "Your slave-girl is in your power; do to her as you please." Then Sarai dealt harshly with her, and she ran away from her. (NRSV)

The biblical situation can be understood more clearly by considering a series of provisions recorded in the ancient Near Eastern laws. First is Lipit-Ishtar Laws §§25–26:

> If a man married a wife (and) she bore him a son and that son lived; and a slave woman (also) bore him a son, (and) the father established the free status of the slave woman and her children, the son of the slave woman is not to divide (the estate) with the son of the master. If (however) his first chosen wife died and he (then) married a slave woman after the wife (died), the son of the first chosen wife will be his heir. The son that the slave woman bore to her master will be considered like a free person's son; he (the heir) shall treat (him) well (in) his house.[141]

A similar situation is addressed in Hammurapi Laws §§170–171:

---

140. The words "with her son Isaac" are added from the LXX; they are not present in the MT.

141. This line is obscure. Roth, *Law Collections*, 31 translates "they shall make good his (share of the) estate."

If a man's first chosen wife bore him sons and his slave woman (also) bore him sons (and if) the father during his lifetime has declared to the sons whom the slave woman bore him: "(You are) my sons" (and thereby) he has counted them alongside the sons of the first chosen wife, after the father has gone to (his) fate (i.e., died), the sons of the slave woman and the sons of the first chosen wife shall equally divide the property of the father's estate. (However) a firstborn heir (who is) the son of the first chosen wife may select and take (his) share (first).

But if the father during his lifetime unto the sons whom the slave woman bore him has not declared "(You are) my sons," then after the father has gone to (his) fate, the sons of the slave woman shall not share with the sons of the first chosen wife. (But) freedom shall be instituted (for) the slave woman and her sons; the sons of the first chosen wife shall not raise any claim of slavery against the sons of the (former) slave woman. The first chosen wife shall take possession of her own dowry and any settlement which her husband gave her (and for) which he had written a legal record and as long as she lives may enjoy their use (and income) in the home of her husband. She may not sell (these assets); her estate will belong to her sons.

The slave woman in these laws was apparently the property of the father. But what if the slave woman belonged to the first wife? Hammurapi Laws §§146–147 addresses this situation and describes a case reminiscent of the conflict between Sarah and Hagar:

If a man married a priestess and she gave a slave woman to her husband and she (the slave woman) has born children [lit. sons]; (but) afterwards that slave woman has considered herself equal to her mistress, since she has born children, her mistress may not sell her; she may (however) place upon her (i.e., cause her to wear) a slave's hair-dress and consider her among her slaves women. (But) if she (the slave woman) has not born children, her mistress may sell her.

These cases establish the principles that a son of a slave woman could become a member of his father's family or an heir to the father's estate in two ways. One was if he was formally "legitimized" by the father even if his mother was not ranked as a wife; the second was if his father took his mother in marriage. The son would minimally be treated as a free person after the death of the father; and some degree of inheritance rights would follow. But if the main wife herself owned the slave woman, this gave her the option of treating the slave woman harshly if the slave woman, after giving birth, was no longer subservient; this is very much like what Sarah did to Hagar in Gen 16:1–6. Sarah's legal powers, however, did not extend to Ishmael whom Abraham earlier had apparently been ready to accept as his sole legal heir; there is evidence for this in Abraham's response to God's promise of Sarah bearing him a son in old age; in Gen 17:18 we read: "And Abraham said to God, "O that Ishmael might live before you (as my son)." However, while Abraham may indeed have been ready to consider Ishmael as his son, Sarah developed strong regrets about how the overall relationship had worked out. First there was Hagar's lack of subservience and then the birth of her own son, Isaac. Sarah did not want Ishmael to share the inheritance together with Isaac. She retained authority over Hagar but not over Ishmael. By requiring Abraham to send both Hagar and Ishmael away, Sarah in effect thereby agreed to relinquish her ownership rights and give Hagar her freedom. There was benefit for Hagar in this act, for perhaps custom would not have allowed Sarah to sell Hagar after Ishmael was born, as we see in Hammurapi Laws §§146–147. Hagar's expulsion would accomplish Sarah's wish that "the son of this slave woman shall not inherit along with my son Isaac." If Ishmael was Abraham's legitimatized son, then with God's promise, Abraham was enabled to fulfill the obligation described in Hammurapi Laws §170 and Lipit-Ishtar §26. Ishmael, as a legitimized son, would now one day receive an inheritance given by God to replace the one that would be due in the future from Abraham his father. Abraham seems only to have been persuaded to expel Ishmael together with Hagar because God had assured him that Ishmael would have a noble future, albeit a separate one from that promised to Isaac. In this story, the addition of God's promise to Ishmael softens the unhappy consequences of Sarah's attitude and Abraham's reluctant compliance to Sarah's harsh wishes.[142]

142. For textual and historical comments see Friedberg, "Hagar." For responses to this story by a variety of ancient and modern commentators, see Halevy, "Hagar in the Aggadah"; Liptzin, "Princess Hagar"; and Sarna, *Genesis*, 146–47, 361, upon whose discussion I build in my own presentation here.

1.6 ADOPTION

Every family hoped to have an heir who was capable of receiving and managing the family assets in the future. We have already noted how polygyny, i.e., a man taking a second wife, was one way of accomplishing this objective. Adoption was also a possibility, although not well attested for ancient Israel, perhaps because kinship networks continued to be so strong and close. There are no laws on adoption but traces of this practice are visible in narrative and in literary passages. Perhaps the clearest case is found in 1 Chr 2:34–35:

> And Sheshan had no sons, only daughters; Sheshan had an Egyptian slave, whose name was Jarha. And so Sheshan gave his daughter as wife to Jarha his slave; and she bore him Attai.

There is also recognition of the necessity of sometimes adopting one's slave in Prov 17:2: "A capable servant will rule over a son, who makes one ashamed, and share inheritance with the brothers (in the family)."[143] One can also mention Moses, who was adopted by Pharaoh's daughter when she pulled him out of the Nile; Exod 2:10 states:

> When the child grew up, she brought him to Pharaoh's daughter, who made him her son. She named him Moses, explaining, "I drew him out of the water." (NJPS)

In Ps 2:7–8, we have a passage that may contains the echo of a solemn declaration, publicly recited in order to inaugurate a formal adoption relationship:

143. Adoption of a young boy, apparently originally a slave, is attested in the Jewish-Aramaic papyus, Kraeling 8 from 416 BCE; see Porten and Yardeni, *Textbook of Aramaic Documents*, 84–85.

Let me tell of the decree: the LORD said to me, "You are My son, I have fathered you this day. Ask it of Me, and I will make the nations your domain; your estate, the limits of the earth." (NJPS)[144]

One may perhaps also mention Ezekiel 16, which records a vision where God, acting in the fashion of a human, took in a foundling girl who represents Israel. However, in this allegory, she is not called "daughter" and when grown, becomes his wife.[145]

Adoption is better attested in ancient Near Eastern sources. We have already mentioned (in sec. 1.5.3) the formula recited by a father to legitimize his slave-born offspring in Hammurapi Laws §171; similar formulas were apparently used to institute the adoptive relationship with children born to strangers. But—at least in some parts of Babylonia— there seems to have been a longstanding customary law against a man, who had a natural son adopting a slave; this was evidently to protect the interests of sons.[146] But we

also know of exceptions to this custom.[147] The adoption of a foundling child is the subject of Lipit-Ishtar Laws §20, unfortunately only partly preserved: "If a man rescues a child from a well, he shall [make a record of] his footprint . . ." The impression of the child foot was apparently put on a clay tablet, in which was inscribed the names of witnesses, who could testify to the circumstances of the adoption and the child's origins.[148] The practice of Sheshan, i.e., a man without sons freeing and adopting his slave as well as giving him his daughter in marriage is attested in legal documents found in northern Syria, at Emar; adoption of one's son-in-law is also found at Nuzi, in northeast Iraq.[149] The practice of adoption is often linked with old-age support because we find more adoption transaction involving adults than young children.[150]

1.7 HOMOSEXUALITY

The Bible condemns homosexual behavior between males in two laws. The first is Lev 18:22: "And with a male, do not lie as one lies with a woman; it is an abomination." The second law is Lev 20:13:

> And if a man lies with a male as one lies with a woman, the two of them have committed an abomination;

144. For a discussion of these and some other passages that have been linked with adoption see Paul, "Leshonot 'imutz," and "Adoption Formulae: A Study of Cuneiform and Biblical Legal Clauses"; see also Tigay, "Adoption." I accept Tigay's argument that adoption was not favored because of polygyny and the persistence of strong kinship bonds with extended family. Adoption was evidently not at all practiced in post-biblical Jewish law but has been "revived" in the modern State of Israel; see Schereschewsky, "Adoption: Later Jewish Law."

145. Malul, "Adoption of Foundlings in the Bible," sees evidence of formal adoption procedure reflected in some of the language appearing in Ezekiel's narrative.

146. See Greengus, "Some Issues," 81 with n. 52 on the Old Babylonian letter TCL 18 153 from Larsa, which has been republished in Veenhof, *Letters in the Louvre,* 188–89. The letter states: "Such an [act] has never occurred in Larsa. A father with sons does not adopt his slave as son."

147. Obermark, "Adoption," 90 n. 17 lists five such texts, including one from Larsa!

148. See Roth, *Law Collections,* 20, 35 n. 5 for other literature.

149. Westbrook, "Anatolia and the Levant. Emar and Vicinity," 667, and Zaccagnini, "Mesopotamia. Nuzi," 589.

150. This was clearly the practice going back to the Old Babylonian period, for which evidence has been collected and studied in Obermark, "Adoption in the Old Babylonian Period." For the Neo-Babylonian period, cf. Wunsch, "Findelkinder und Adoption."

they shall be put to death—their bloodguilt is upon themselves.

It would appear, however, that earlier, there were others within ancient Israel who had not regarded homosexual sex as sinful under all circumstances. The Bible makes reference to the institution of male cult prostitutes, which many modern scholars—as did also the ancient rabbis—understand as being available for homosexual acts.[151] Thus, for example Deut 23:18–19:

> None of the daughters of Israel shall be a temple prostitute; none of the sons of Israel shall be a temple prostitute. You shall not bring the fee of a prostitute or the wages of a male prostitute into the house of the LORD your God in payment for any vow, for both of these are abhorrent to the LORD your God. (NRSV)

Nahmanides points out that Lev 18:22 does not contain within it a clear statement on the guilt of the passive party, as some commentators have maintained.[152] The level of his guilt would therefore be less than that of the active party. The rabbis, in their interpretation of homosexual conduct, further sought to modify the harsh penalty imposed in the biblical laws by exempting a coerced victim from blame.[153] Furthermore, a *baraita* cited in the Talmud, *b. Sanh.* 54b–55a, states that guilt cannot attach to minors who are younger than nine years and a day.[154] In this same vein, rabbis assert that, under the biblical laws, punishment is not merited unless the sexual contact involves penetration with an erect penis; and thus fondling would also be exempted from the scope of the biblical laws.[155] The rabbinic modifications may take us beyond the biblical view; but their insights can perhaps help explain why the Bible contains no corresponding law against lesbianism; apparently because this activity neither produces offspring nor involves penetration by a male. In rabbinic law, lesbianism is considered unseemly but falls outside of halakhic purview.[156] Ibn Ezra comments that acts of homosexuality exist in nature but came to be prohibited to Israelite males in the name of achieving holiness. Nahmanides also attempts to rationalize the severe prohibition by the observation that it is forbidden because it does not lead to the reproduction of the species.[157]

---

course could point to Deut 22:26, where in the case of coercion and rape (cf. sec. 1.4), it states: "You shall do nothing to the girl; the girl has (committed) no sin (deserving the) death (penalty)."

154. Cf. Maimonides, *Mishnah Torah, Hilkhot Issurei Bi'ah* 1:14.

155. Cf. comments of Hazzequni to Lev 20:13 and the discussion in *b. Shevu.* 18a which is summarized in Maimonides, *Mishnah Torah, Hilkhot Issurei Bi'ah* 1:11, 4:11. The rabbinic viewpoint on partial penetration is given in *m. Yebam.* 6:1.

156. Cf. *t. Sotah* 5:6-7, Lieberman; *b. Yebam.* 76a–b.

157. Cf. the comments of Ibn Ezra and Nahmanides on Lev 18:22. Maimonides, *Guide,* 2:606, from a slightly different angle condemns bestiality (and also homosexuality) because the act has no natural purpose other than the pursuit of pleasure.

151. Measures to eliminate the practice of male cult prostitutes are described in 1 Kgs 15:12 and 2 Kgs 23:7. For rabbinic understandings cf. *b. Sanh.* 54b.

152. Nahmanides restates his argument in his commentary to Deut 23:18; in *b. Sanh.* 54b, we see that his reading of the laws follows other ancient authorities.

153. Cf. Ibn Ezra on Lev 20:13 on coercion; this principle is fully presented in Maimonides, *Mishnah Torah, Hilkhot Issurei Bi'ah* 1:9. The rabbis of

A negative view of homosexual conduct, in some respects similar to that of the Bible, is found in the Middle Assyrian Laws §A 19–20:

> §19 If a man in a furtive manner makes statements about his fellow saying: "They regularly sodomize him" (or) in a quarrel before other persons he declares to him: "They regularly sodomize you, I can prove (this against) you." (But) he is unable to prove it (and thus) has not proven (the accusation), that man—they shall smite him 50 blows with rods; one month he shall do the king's labor; they shall shave off his hair and he must pay one talent of lead (as a penalty.)
> §20 If a man has sodomized his fellow (and) they have proven him (guilty) and convicted him, they shall sodomize him (and) then shall turn him into a eunuch.

The verb "sodomize" is the same verb that is used to describe sexual connection between male and female. We may thus well wonder if considerations relating to penetration, similar to those mentioned by the rabbis, would also have applied in ancient Assyria. There is evidence for this very understanding in a fragmentary document from the Old Babylonian period, which records what appears to be the testimony of a man accused of a sexual violation. The man testifies as follows: "I did not have sexual connection *with* Shat-Askur; my penis did not enter into her vagina . . ."[158]

The Middle Assyrian laws do not clearly indicate that punishment would be given to both partners in sodomy. In §A 19, the law seems to imply that the accused person has been a willing and frequent partner, yielding to sodomy by others; evidently that is at the heart of the accusation there. In §A 20, where an act of sodomy actually took place, only one person is punished—evidently the active party; but nothing is said about his fellow. The punishment in §A 20, however, seems strange in requiring others to do the very act for which the offender is being punished. If the social purpose of the law was to prohibit all homosexual behavior, then adding this feature of punishment—a kind of male "gang rape"—is puzzling. It may, therefore, be preferable to interpret these laws in a more narrow fashion. The term "fellow" in §20 may actually indicate a situation of social parity between the parties; it has therefore been suggested that status may in fact have aggravated the offense; and that homosexual relations between persons of differing social status would not have been punished in the same way.[159] In §19, we can see that, in sodomy, the passive party was looked upon with contempt. At the same time, in the "gang rape" and castration, taking place in §20, we find sanctioned acts of violence, inflicting injury, pain, and social degradation. Homosexual activity was thus looked upon with equivocation. A Babylonian omen announces: "If a man sexually approaches the anus of his social peer, that man will be foremost among his brothers and associates."[160]

In this context, we should here also note the scenarios of "gang rape" depicted in the Bible, directed against vulnerable

158. This passage is cited in *CAD* E, 267; it is PBS 5 156: 1'–6'.

159. Cf. Driver and Miles, *Assyrian Laws*, 71; and Cardascia, *Les Lois Assyriennes*, 134–35.

160. *CT* 39 44:13; this omen (partly cited in *CAD* Q, 255b) has been noted in discussions on homosexuality in Mesopotamia. Cf. Nissinen, "Are There Homosexuals in Mesopotamian Literature?"

male travelers in Gen 19:4–8 (the angels staying with Lot) and in Judg 19:22–24 (the Levite lodging at Gibeah). One therefore has good reason to question the existence of an absolute prohibition against all forms of homosexual activity. What is more, just like in ancient Israel, we also find evidence for the existence of male and female temple prostitutes in ancient Babylonia. These have been linked to the worship and rites surrounding the goddess Ishtar and may have provided release for repressed sexual urges.[161]

We have only an oblique reference to homosexuality in Hittite Laws §189c: "If a man sins (sexually) with (his) son, it is an unpermitted sexual pairing." This law is unique in our ancient collections; its focus is on the taboo of incest, since it follows §189b, which forbids sexual relations between a father and his daughter. The law thus does not directly address the views of the Hittites on homosexuality; we cannot demonstrate, on the basis of this law, that it was considered a forbidden activity for unrelated parties.

1.8 BESTIALITY

In the Bible there are repeated laws against bestiality; in Exod 22:18 we read: "Whoever lies with a beast shall be put to death" (NJPS). The prohibition is repeated again in Lev 18:23:

> Do not put your semen into any beast and defile yourself thereby; and let no woman stand before a beast for it to have connection with her; it is perversion.

In Lev 20:15–16, we find this law repeated together with a statement of penalty:

And a man who put his semen into a beast—he shall be put to death; and you shall (also) kill the beast. And a woman who approaches any beast for it to have connection with her—you shall kill the woman and the beast; they shall be put to death; their bloodguilt is upon them.

The prohibition is again repeated in Deut 27:21: "Cursed be he who lies with any beast.—And all the people shall say, Amen" (NJPS). The fourfold repeated condemnation suggests that the practice of bestiality, although a perversion, was more than a remote possibility in the life of the times; indeed it is discussed in the Talmud and known to occur even in modern times.[162] In the Ugaritic myth about Baal, the god mates with a heifer prior to entering the netherworld; his act may reflect an annual fertility ritual.[163]

Putting the animal as well as the perpetrator to death seems to be a most harsh penalty. The Mishnah, *m. Sanh.* 7:4 thought likewise and asks:

> If a man sinned (and was thereby punished), in what way did the beast sin? Rather, because the offense came about for the man through her (the beast); therefore Scripture demands: let her be stoned (i.e., the death punishment customary for this offense). Another idea: so that this beast should not be passing through the market and they (i.e., onlookers) will say: "this is the one through which So-and-so was stoned."

161. See Bottéro and Petschow, "Homosexualität," 463–67.

162. Cf. Tigay, *Deuteronomy*, 256, 395 n.59. For talmudic passages discussing current practices of the time, cf. *m. Avod. Zar.* 1:6; 2:1; *b. Avod. Zar.* 14b–15b.

163. *ANET*, 139, 142.

This latter idea is echoed in *Sifra Qe-doshim* 10.10.5 (on Lev 20:16), which explains that the animal is killed to eradicate all memory of the act.

There was, however, some lingering discomfort even with these explanations. The medieval commentators Bekhor Shor and Hazzequni in their commentaries on Lev 20:15–16, note that the statement "their bloodguilt is upon them" is pertinent only when a male beast copulated with a woman. The female beast that was engaged by a man was a passive participant and, although put to death, incurred no guilt at all.

Bestiality is condemned in the Hittite Laws; punishments, however, can vary. Hittite Laws §§187–188 deal with sexual connection with a cow or sheep:

> If a man sins (sexually) with a cow, it is an unpermitted sexual pairing; he will be put to death. They shall conduct him to the king's court (lit. gate) [for trial]. Whether the king orders him killed or spares his life, he shall not appear (personally) before the king (lest he defile the royal person.) If a man sins (sexually) with a sheep, it is an unpermitted sexual pairing; he will be put to death. They shall conduct him [to the] king's [gate.] The king can have him executed or spare his life. But he shall not appear before the king.

Although in these cases only the human participant was punished, this was not always the case. Both human and animal were punished in Hittite Laws §§199–200a:

> If anyone sins (sexually) with a pig (or) a dog, he shall die. One shall bring him to the palace gate (i.e., the royal court) [for trial]. The king

may have them (i.e., the human and the animal) killed or he may spare them, but he (the human) shall not approach the king. If an ox leaps on a man (in sexual excitement), the ox shall die; the man shall not die. They shall substitute one sheep in the place of the man and put it to death. If a pig leaps on a man (in sexual excitement), it is not an offense. If a man sins (sexually) with either a horse or mule, it is not an offense, he shall not approach the king, nor shall he become a priest . . .[164]

These cases reveal the defilement that was believed to come from bestial acts. The punishment for the human actor varies according to the animal involved; generally, the death penalty is merited for a person who initiated connection with a cow, sheep, dog, or pig; but not with a horse or mule. The reason for this distinction is not known. The king may spare the life of the person, who, nonetheless, remains permanently defiled; that person must be kept away from the king's presence and is barred from serving the gods in a priestly capacity. These penalties may have been tantamount to banishment. From a slightly later period, an elaborate purification ritual is known, dealing with defilement coming from a man who has sinned with a sheep or goat; it is possible that this ritual might have been designed to eliminate the need for banishment.[165] The Hittite laws attach culpability to an ox that initiated sexual connection with a man; the man, being a passive participant, is also guilty but may escape the death

164. The second part of Hittite Laws §200a is treated in sec. 1.1.4.

165. Hoffner, "Incest, Sodomy, and Bestiality in the Ancient Near East," 85–90.

penalty by allowing a sheep to be killed in his stead. Rabbinic law, however, would consider a passive human party to be equally guilty.[166]

The Hittite laws supply important perspectives on the biblical laws in two respects. First, we see the ancient possibility for imposing the death penalty in cases of bestiality, which the Bible, however, applies without exception to all cases and includes the participating animal as well as the human offender. However, to some extent, a rationale for the severity of the biblical laws can be found in the state of defilement that the act of bestiality was presumed to create. In the Hittite laws, we see that the king's purity, like that of the gods and their temples, is always to be maintained, and the king must be safeguarded from contact with anyone who practices bestiality. The Bible, especially in Leviticus, aspired to extend this same quality and state of holiness to all persons in the community; this social expansion of purity may explain the severity of penalty and its uniform application.[167]

166. *Sifra Qedoshim* 10.2 (on Lev 20:15); *b. Sanh.* 54b.

167. See the comments of Milgrom, *Leviticus,* 1397–400.

2

Laws on Debtors and Debt Slaves

IN ANCIENT TIMES WHEN a person borrowed money, the debt obligation fell not only upon the borrower and his worldly goods but also upon the members of his family. In the absence of sufficient assets, the debtor or members of his family could be taken into debt slavery in order to repay the obligation through their labor. The Bible contains laws or injunctions whose aim was to help alleviate the situation of debtors and their families.

2.1 RELIEF GIVEN TO DEBT SLAVES ON AN INDIVIDUAL BASIS

In our previous discussion on families, we noted out that family households included non-free, i.e., slaves, as well as free individuals; therefore in the laws previously discussed, we have found provisions relating to slaves as well as to free persons. All of the slaves in some the laws that we have so far discussed are what one may term "chattel" or permanent slaves. These slaves could be a "house born" slave who was the child of a slave mother in his owner's household; one who was "purchased for money"; or a captive taken as booty in warfare.[1] Chattel slaves were different

from debt slaves, whose servitude was not, at least initially, intended to be permanent. However, the same Hebrew terms are used to describe both kinds of slaves; and this fact has lead to some confusion. But the difference between them was recognized in biblical times. Chattel slaves are typically described as non-Israelites, whose servitude was without termination. This is clearly stated in Lev 25:44–46:

> As for the male and female slaves whom you may have, it is from the nations around you that you may acquire male and female slaves. You may also acquire them from among the aliens residing with you, and from their families that are with you, who have been born in your land; and they may be your property. You may keep them as a possession for your children after you, for them to inherit as property. These you may treat as slaves, but as for your fellow Israelites, no one shall rule over the other with harshness. (NRSV)

The law appears to frown upon holding one's fellow Israelite as a slave; but the possibility is not ruled out because a fellow Israelite could fall into slavery through impoverishment and debt. In biblical as in other ancient societies, in the absence of other salable assets, unpaid

---

1. For the first two categories, cf. Gen 17:12–13, 23, 27; for captives, cf. Deut 21:10; Isa 14:2; 61:1. The three categories are enumerated in Philo, *Every Good Man is Free* 19.

debts would ultimately be satisfied by taking physical possession of the debtor himself or members of his family, who would be taken into bondage by the creditor in place of the debtor. The situation is poignantly depicted in 2 Kgs 4:1:

> A certain woman, the wife of one of the disciples of the prophets, cried out to Elisha: "Your servant my husband is dead, and you know how your servant revered the LORD. And now a creditor is coming to seize my two children as slaves." (NJPS)[2]

In this story, Elisha, through a miracle, enables to woman to fill up many jars of oil; she did so and in 2 Kgs 4:7 he told her: "Go sell the oil and pay your debt, and you and your children can live on the rest" (NJPS). This woman, happily, was able to repay her debt and have her children go free; but if she or her kinfolk were unable to repay the debt, debt slavery would have been the inevitable result. While, in theory, bondage for debt may not have been viewed as permanent, there were troubling questions. How many years of bondage were required in order to satisfy the claims of the creditor? Was the original debt reduced by the bondage or did it only reduce interest on the debt? Debt slavery was a serious social problem in ancient Israel and among her neighbors, because families of free persons, who fell into slavery, typically lacked the resources to redeem themselves from bondage and to regain their free status.

One solution was to set a limit upon the time of servitude for debt slaves, as described in Deut 15:12: "If a fellow Hebrew, man or woman, is sold to you, he shall serve you six years, and in the seventh year you shall set him free "(NJPS). A similar law appears in Exod 21:2–4:

> When you acquire a Hebrew slave, he shall serve six years; in the seventh year he shall go free, without payment. If he came single, he shall leave single; if he had a wife, his wife shall leave with him. If his master gave him a wife, and she has borne him children, the wife and her children shall belong to the master, and he shall leave alone. (NJPS)

As noted above, there is only one set of Hebrew terms for slaves and it is used without distinction both for chattel and debt slaves. Thus, adding the term "Hebrew" helps clarify that in these cases we are dealing with fellow Israelites, i.e., originally free individuals, who were sold into slavery to pay off their obligations. These laws support the notion that debt slaves should not serve in perpetuity. All obligations, whatever the amount, were extinguished through six years of servitude. At the same time, there was recognition that the Hebrew slave might not ever feel able to stand on his own feet economically and socially. Exodus 21:5–6 describes this possibility:

> But if the slave declares, "I love my master, and my wife and children: I do not wish to go free," his master shall take him before God. He shall be brought to the door or the doorpost, and his master shall pierce his ear with an awl; and he shall then remain his slave for life. (NJPS)

---

2. Another, figurative reference to selling one's children appears in Isa 50:1 where God chastises the Children of Israel: "Thus said the LORD: Where is the bill of divorce of your mother whom I dismissed? And which of My creditors was it to whom I sold you off?" (NJPS).

Deuteronomy 15:13–18 gives a similar provision but, at the same time, encourages creditors to provide their emancipated slaves with financial assistance:

> When you set him free, do not let him go empty-handed: Furnish him out of the flock, threshing floor, and vat, with which the LORD your God has blessed you. Bear in mind that you were slaves in the land of Egypt and the LORD your God redeemed you; therefore I enjoin this commandment upon you today. But should he say to you, "I do not want to leave you"— for he loves you and your household and is happy with you—you shall take an awl and put it through his ear into the door, and he shall become your slave in perpetuity. Do the same with your female slave. When you do set him free, do not feel aggrieved; for in the six years he has given you double the service of a hired man.[3] Moreover, the LORD your God will bless you in all you do. (NJPS)

The importunate tone of the last lines in Deut 15:13–18, while encouraging generosity, also reflects awareness of possible reluctance, on the part of creditors, to let their debt slaves go free. The act of boring of a hole in the slave's ear has been variously interpreted—as a slave mark, a sign of ownership, or as a symbolic joining of the slave to his master's home. The location "before God" is added in Exod 21:5–6 but omitted in the Deut 15:13–18 passage. It has been interpreted, in more

traditional fashion, as a legal act perhaps needing to taking place in the sanctuary or—taking it more literally since the plural form can be translated either as "God" or "gods—as the formal "presentation" of the slave, who is now become a permanent member of the family, to symbolic representations of the household gods or ancestors in a family shrine.[4]

In our Deuteronomy passages, Deut 15:12–18, male and female slaves were considered together and equally treated. But Exod 21:7–11 introduces a distinctive measure for females, apparently designed to protect vulnerable female slaves from sexual exploitation by adding marriage to their condition of bondage:

> If a man sells his daughter to become a female slave, she shall not go out (from slavery) as male slaves do. If she (afterwards) becomes unsuitable in the eyes of her master, who designated her for himself, he shall let her be redeemed; he shall not have the right to sell her to a foreign people, since he has deceived her. And if he designated her for his son, he shall deal with her as is customary with (free) daughters. If he marries another (woman), he must not diminish her food, her clothing, or her conjugal rights.[5] If he does not do these three things for her, she shall go free, without payment (of the debt for which she was sold).

This Exodus law does not seek to limit the woman's term of servitude to six years; in effect, there is a trade-off, giving her some

---

3. The translation "double" may be misleading; a more likely interpretation is that it describes a quantity of service equivalent to or comparable to that of a hired man; cf. the entry on this word in *HALOT*; this is also the sense given by the Septuagint, which translates "in lieu of an annual wage for the hired laborer."

4. Cf. Houtman, *Exodus*, 3:116–21; Horowitz, "'His Master Shall Pierce His Ear with an Awl.'"

5. For a discussion of the Hebrew term "conjugal rights" and their place in rabbinic Judaism, see Levine, *Marital Relations in Ancient Judaism*, 209–31.

trappings of marital status in exchange for a lifetime of connection to her new master's home. The creditor is made to act as a kind of guardian to the unmarried female slave; he can take her as a concubine for himself or else give her to another member of his family.[6] If the creditor fails to arrange a marriage for the daughter, then her family is able to "redeem her" although we are not told how they would now pay the underlying debt that led to the daughter being sold in the first place. This provision tells us only that in the absence of a marriage, her status will revert to that of a debt slave who, unlike a woman given in marriage, may be recovered by her family through redemption. (Redemption of debt slaves is discussed in Lev 25: 47–49 mentioned in sec. 2.2 and more fully discussed in sec. 2.5.2.)

There is some uncertainty about what is meant in Exod 21:11 by "these three things." Some have taken it to refer back to the three items of conjugal support. According to this reading, if a marriage takes place, the daughter must be treated according to conventional standards of wifehood or else is "divorced" i.e., allowed to leave her husband's house. But it is equally possible to follow the interpretation of some medieval rabbis— among them Rashi, Rashbam, Saadia, Ibn Ezra, Maimonides, and Nahmanides— who understood it simply to be one of the three options, namely, wedding her

himself, wedding her to his son, or allowing her father to redeem her. The notice about conjugal support would then be seen as a desideratum or addendum, making allowance for the likelihood that this young woman—essentially a slave concubine—might not be taken in as her husband's primary wife.

One cannot say when the Exod 21:7–11 law was put forward or the extent to which it was followed, because, as we shall see, debt slavery was a difficult, recurring social problem and a variety of remedies were put forward. In rabbinic interpretation of Exod 21:7–11 only a minor female, still under her father's authority could be sold; but then the case of the female in Deut 15:12 was a problem that needed to be explained; was she then also a minor or was she, more probably, an adult?[7] A rabbinic ban on the sale of adult women is affirmed in the Tosefta *t. Sotah* 2:9, Lieberman, and in the Mishnah *m. Sotah* 3:8, which adds that a father indeed may sell his daughter and that the court could sell a thief who could not pay for his crime; but also argues that an adult woman should not be sold. However, the Mishnah also knows of cases where women of various ages were taken as pledges to secure debts; *m. Ed.* 8:2 deals with a young girl who was taken as a pledge in Ashkelon; and *m. Ket.* 2:9 deals with a married woman who was taken to secure a financial obligation.[8]

In the ancient Near Eastern laws, we likewise find laws that sought to limit the term of servitude for originally free

6. The actual written consonantal text of the Hebrew Bible (the *Ketiv*) and Samaritan version both read Exod 21:8 to say: "who (because she was unsuitable in his eyes) did not (therefore) designate her (as a wife)," i.e., the master did not deem her fit for any male in his household. In my translation above I have maintained the traditional MT "corrected" reading (the *Qere*) "who designated her for himself."

7. See discussions of Tigay, *Deuteronomy,* 148–49; and Rashi's commentary on Deut 15:12.

8. For more discussion cf. Falk, *Introduction to Jewish Law,* 268–69; Jackson, *Theft in Jewish Law,* 139–44, discusses the insolvent thief.

individuals who fell into debt slavery. A measure limiting the term of bondage to three years appears in Laws of Hammurapi §117:

> If a (free) man—a debt has overtaken him (and) he has sold his wife, son, or daughter for money or else given them over into debt service, they shall work three years in the house of their buyer or the holder of their debt service; their release shall be set in the fourth year.

This law does not consider the possibility of a debt slave marrying during the time while he or she was fulfilling their term of debt slavery as in Exod 21:2–6, where a male debt slave married a woman who was a chattel slave belonging to the master. According to the law in Exodus, the wife—and any children born to them—will not be freed when male debt slave goes free. We do, however, find a description of similar restrictions affecting the marriage of two chattel slaves in Urnamma Laws §4:

> If a male slave took a female slave— his desired one (in marriage) (and) that male slave gained his freedom, she shall not leave the house (of her owner).

The result here mirrors the outcome in Exod 21:2–4: "If his master gave him a wife, and she has borne him children, the wife and her children shall belong to the master, and he shall leave alone" (NJPS).

The sale and marital arrangement for females seen in Exod 21:7–11 can likewise be partially compared with a form of adoption found in Near Eastern legal practice. In this arrangement, a young female becomes a legal dependent of her adopter who promises to marry her off at a future time. This form of "matrimonial" adoption, while not included in any of the surviving Near Eastern law collections, occurs in contracts of adoption, mostly from Babylonia and Nuzi. The adopted woman was often subsequently married to her adopter's son; this adoption was thus described by the term *kallūtu* or "status of daughter-in-law." But sometimes, as at Nuzi, the adopter might instead give the young woman in marriage to one of his slaves. In some transactions, the young woman was taken as either a daughter or daughter-in-law; in such cases, the adopter makes no initial commitment as to who will later marry the adopted woman. One has the definite impression that such contracts were entered into by poor families who were unable to arrange marriages of higher status for their young women.[9] It is possible that Exod 21:7–11 was modeled after such arrangements; but there are important differences. First is the fact that, in the ancient Near Eastern contracts, the young women were all free persons at the time of their adoption and remained so, whereas in the Bible, the young woman in Exod 21:7–11 is being sold as a slave and there is no mention of her being adopted. Second is that, in the Near Eastern contracts, the adopter, in his role as the young woman's guardian, does not intend to become the husband of the young woman, whereas in Exod 21:8 this is a possibility for a master "who designated her for himself."[10] The law in Exod 21:7–11

9. For examples of "matrimonial" adoption contracts see *CAD* K 85–86. For further discussion see Cardascia, "L'Adoption matrimoniale," and van Praag, *Droit matrimonial Assyro-Babylonien*, 79–84.

10. I know of only one exception to the usual pattern that may find resonance with the *Qere* or "corrected" reading of Exod 21:8 "designated for

can perhaps be viewed as an innovation, combining debt slavery with transfer of guardianship for matrimonial purposes.

We find another situation dealing with young female slaves in Middle Assyrian Laws §A 48. This law helps us see the situation of Exod 21:7–11 from yet another angle, namely, the value of the daughter as a marriageable woman:

> If a man (would give in marriage) the daughter of his debtor who was residing in his house as a pledge, he (!) must ask her father (and then) give her to a husband. If her father does not agree, he should not give (her in marriage). If her father is dead, he shall ask one of her brothers and that (brother) shall speak to the (other) brothers. If one brother says: "I will redeem my sister within one month," (and) within one month did not redeem (his sister), then the creditor, if he wishes, may clear her (title) and give her to a husband . . . [remainder broken].[11]

The creditor in §48 has been waiting for his payment but evidently did not need or else was unsatisfied with the amount of labor that the daughter of his debtor might provide to maintain herself, or to offset the mounting cost to the creditor of maintaining the hostage and leaving

the debt unpaid. (See further, below, in sec. 4.1, which discusses the treatment of hostages who were being held as security for unpaid debts.) The creditor wished to marry her off and receive her brideprice rather than the benefit of her labor. Her brideprice value might actually have exceeded the debt; and this is why her brother might wish to redeem her by paying the debt so that he himself could receive her brideprice when he gave her in marriage. But the brother had first to pay the outstanding debt owed by his father to the creditor; and he may have lacked the funds to do so. At this point, the creditor was entitled to marry off the daughter and receive her brideprice in satisfaction of the debt he was owed. Legally speaking, the creditor who has "cleared her (title)" becomes her guardian (by court action) in lieu of the unpaid debt; this action removes any residual claim upon her by her natal family; and the creditor uses her marriage as a way to recover his money. Her situation would be the same if her father were living and had given his consent to the marriage. In either case, the brideprice, which normally went to the woman's family, was now received by the creditor. With the perspective of Middle Assyrian Law §A 48, one may see the biblical case of Exod 21:7–11 in yet another light, namely, that of a father, as debtor, allowing his creditor to marry off his daughter, and the father forfeiting the value of his daughter's potential brideprice as a way to pay off his debt.

Another facet of debt slavery is revealed by the comment in Exod 21:8 "he shall not have the right to sell her to a foreign people." The term "foreign people" has been literally understood, e.g., in the Septuagint and by the medieval scholar

---

himself." In the Nuzi contract JEN 432, the adopter stipulates that he could give the young woman as a wife either to one of his slaves, or to a slave that he would manumit and adopt as a son, or perhaps even take this young woman for himself. For JEN 432, see Breneman, "Nuzi Marriage Tablets," 152–54. In this as in all of the "matrimonial adopton" contracts, the woman's offspring are to be raised as slaves belonging to the adopter.

11. Driver and Miles, *Assyrian Laws*, 418–19 suggest reading further into the break and based on the signs remaining to restore: "[or if he (the creditor) wishes, he may give] her [for money] according [to (his) tablet] . . ."

Hazzequni, as referring to gentiles. But the phrase was also subject to a less literal interpretation in order to bring the biblical text into conformity with a later rabbinic dictum found in the Tosefta, *t. Sotah* 2:9, Lieberman: " A (Hebrew) man may be sold once and then a second time; but a (Hebrew) woman cannot be sold a second time." Thus, some readers, both ancient and modern, have wanted to reinterpret this statement more narrowly, e.g., in *Targum Onqelos* as "another man" i.e., to any other master or, as restated by at least one modern scholar, to "anyone who is not a member of the nuclear family."[12] The medieval scholar Bekhor Shor attempted to reconcile these two views by interpreting the phrase to mean that the master may not give her to "his own non-Jewish (Canaanite) slave in order to breed children from her in the fashion that one might give a non-Jewish (Canaanite) slave woman to a Hebrew male slave (as in Exod 21:4)." Nahmanides, however, insists the plain meaning of the biblical phrase can only be that she (i.e., the female slave) is not to be sold to gentiles; the rabbinic use of this verse to support a ban on a further sale is only a secondary, overlaid interpretation and is not an aspect of the original context. Moreover, in Lev 25:47–48 we do find reference to outright sale of debt slaves, perhaps female as well as male, with concern about their being sold to gentiles, residing locally or possibly abroad:

> If a resident alien among you prospers, and if any of your kin fall into financial difficulty with him and sells himself to the alien,

or to a branch of the alien's family . . . they shall have the right of redemption . . . (NRSV)

Rashi, Rashbam, and Hazzequni all understood this passage as referring to a buyer who was a gentile and even one living far away. These rabbis, however, do not comment on how to reconcile Lev 25:47–48 with Exod 21:4, perhaps because it does not necessarily deal with a second sale. The reason for the prohibition on foreign sale is not given; but there may be a clue in the phrase "he shall let her be redeemed" which is stated in Exod 21:8. Removing a debt slave to a foreign land would render unlikely any possibility of future redemption taking place by the slave's family repaying the debt on his or her behalf.[13]

We get additional perspective on the issue of subsequent sale, touched upon in Exod 21:4, from Middle Assyrian Laws §§C 2–3, which deal with a creditor who wishes to sell a person that he is holding as security for a debt that is due but as yet unpaid:

> §2 [If a man sells] to another man for money [someone's son] or daughter who is dwelling in his house for (a debt of) silver and as [(its) security pledge, like he would se[ll someone (permanently)] residing in his house], [(and) they prove the charge against him,] he shall forfeit his silver and give [an amount eq]uivalent to him[14] to the property owner (who paid him for a slave). [They shall smi]te him [. . .

13. Daube, *Studies in Biblical Law*, 39–62 discusses the importance of the biblical concepts of "redeemer" and "redemption" and their relationship to family solidarity.

14. Alternatively, "a person of equivalent value" as *CAD* M/2, 58.

12. Cf. Paul, *Studies in the Book of the Covenant*, 54; there he also cites other scholars who agree with this view.

blows with canes; (and) he shall do the king's labor for 20 days.

§3[If a man] sells for money to (a buyer) in a foreign country [another man's son] or daughter who is dw[elling in his house] for (a debt of) silver and as (its) security pledge, [they shall prove the charges and con]vict him; he shall forfeit his silver, and give [an equivalent amount to the (sale) pro]perty owner (who paid him for a slave and [blows with canes] they shall sm[ite him]; (and) he shall do the king's labor for forty days. Moreover, [if the person he so]ld dies in the foreign country, he shall pay in full [for the (lost) life]. (But) he is allowed to sell into a foreign country an Assyrian man or Assyrian woman who was purchased [for f]ull [value].

According to the first law in §2, the creditor could not sell to anyone else a person, whom the creditor held as security for a debt; the second law in §3 prohibits selling that person into a foreign country. However, if the ownership of that originally free person being held as a security pledged was transferred to the creditor as a way to settle the debt in full, then a foreign (in addition to any domestic) sale was allowed. In the biblical laws dealing with the female debt slave in Exod 21:7–11, I believe we are dealing with full transfer of ownership to satisfy unpaid debts; otherwise the new master could not have exercised his authority in arranging her marriage. But, in the biblical law, unlike what one sees in the Assyrian laws, the female debt slave was not ever to be sold abroad.

Hammurapi Laws §§280–281 deal with Babylonian slaves who are sold abroad. The law in §280 states a prohibition against selling into foreign lands a native Babylonian who became a debt slave and who then by some chain of events ended up in a foreign country and was there purchased by a trader:

§280 If a man has purchased another man's male slave or female slave in a foreign country (and) when he has come back into the country (i.e. the slave's native country), the (Babylonian) owner of the male slave or female slave identifies his male slave or female slave; if that male slave or female slave were indeed natives of the land, then their release should be made without (any additional payment of) silver.

Some scholars have argued that the native Babylonian slave should not be totally freed from bondage and that his Babylonian master should still be entitled to take back his slave into servitude. Questions have been raised about the original owner's economic loss as well as the loss sustained by the trader in §280; but most interpretations assume that trader must bear this loss, even if he purchased the slave in good faith. Moreover, there are other (unanswered) questions about the chain of events leading to the slaves being sent abroad; could they have been kidnapped? [15] In my view, however, because of the term "release" and other evidence given below, one may feel satisfied in taking the outcome as plainly stated: the native Babylonian slave, when repatriated, went free, with neither trader nor previous owner being compensated for their losses.

15. For discussion see Driver and Miles, *The Babylonian Laws*, 1:225, 485–86; and Charpin, Les Décrets royaux."

In Hammurapi Laws §281, we have the case about a slave, who belonged to a Babylonian master, but was not a native:

> §281 If they (the slaves) are rather (originally) natives [lit. children] of another country, the purchaser shall swear before a god (as to) the (amount of) silver he paid and the (original) owner of the male or female slave shall give the (amount of) silver that he paid to the merchant (who bought the slave back), and he may (thereby) redeem his male slave or female slave.

In this case, the trader must receive compensation from the owner before he relinquishes the slave he purchased abroad.

It is clear from §280—however one interprets the outcome—that there was strong sentiment against native Babylonians being sold abroad. The laws in §§280–81 do not state that these Babylonian slaves were originally free, although this seems to be the likeliest explanation for their being protected in this fashion. This was clearly the situation in a late Old Babylonian lawsuit involving a native Babylonian, originally free, who was sold by his master to a nearby country; after five years there, he fled and came home and was subsequently freed.[16] The rule appears to be an ancient one, because we find it also operative in Sumerian court cases from several centuries earlier, where penalties are imposed upon owners who sold their slaves—apparently native citizens—abroad.[17] There is a hint of a

similar policy in the Mishnah and Tosefta, although these laws are concerned about a Jew selling his gentile slave to another country and thereby depriving the slave of living a life under monotheism and, secondarily, thereby reducing the possibility of that slave being emancipated by his Jewish master and becoming a member of the Jewish community. The straightforward formulation of the rabbinic law may nevertheless reflect a general ban, similar to what is found in Exod 21:8 "he shall not have the right to sell her to a foreign people" and in our ancient Near Eastern laws. It is simply stated in *m. Git.* 4:6: "(In the case of) one who sells his slave abroad: he (the slave) has (in effect) gone forth to freedom." Other versions of this law in *t. Avod. Zar.* 3:16, 18, Zuckermandel, add a further requirement that a document of manumission (i.e., a formal document of emancipation) be written for that slave who must be freed.

2.2 VOLUNTARY RELIEF GIVEN DEBT SLAVES AS A GROUP

We have now seen that there were laws "on the books," found both in biblical and Near Eastern sources, stating that debt slaves should be freed after a number of years of service. In other words, a set number of years of servitude would be considered as sufficient to satisfy the total claim, whatever the underlying obligation and amount of the original debt. However, these laws were apparently widely ignored; I believe this to have been the case because additional measures had to be introduced in order to protect debt slaves. Evidently, when debt slaves were dealt with on a case-by-case basis, they escaped notice and the laws protecting them were not enforceable.

---

16. The case is *CT* 6 29, treated in Schorr, *Urkunden*, no. 37, and more recently in Yoffee, *Economic Role of the Crown*, 57–60. The originally free status of this slave is implicit in view of his stated desire to return to work the land of his father's house.

17. For cases and discussion see Falkenstein, *NSG*, 1:86, 138, 145.

A more effective strategy, therefore, was to deal with debt slaves as a class or group. We see this described in an episode, recorded in the Book of Jeremiah that took place during the siege of Jerusalem during the last days of Zedekiah c. 588 BCE. Apparently in order to secure the full participation of all citizens in the defense of the city, there was a solemn agreement made—a covenant—to release all debt slaves. This was also seen as a meritorious act insofar as it fulfilled heretofore-neglected laws about limiting the time of servitude for individual fellow Israelites who became debt slaves. The slaveholders publicly performed the release but then, cynically, in private, recaptured their debt slaves and held them again as if their release had never happened. This episode is described in Jer 34:8–11:

> The word which came to Jeremiah from the LORD after King Zedekiah had made a covenant with all the people in Jerusalem to proclaim a release among them—that everyone should set free his Hebrew slaves, both male and female, and that no one should keep his fellow Judean enslaved. Everyone, officials and people, who had entered into the covenant, agreed to set their male and female slaves free and not keep them enslaved any longer; they complied and let them go. But afterward they turned about and brought back the men and women they had set free, and forced them into slavery again. (NJPS)

For violating their oath and promise, Jeremiah in a vision received a message for the people expressing divine wrath. Jeremiah 34:12–20 proclaims the punishment that was to come:

> Then it was that the word of the LORD came to Jeremiah from the LORD: Thus said the LORD, the God of Israel: I made a covenant with your fathers when I brought them out of the land of Egypt, the house of bondage, saying: "In the seventh year each of you must let go any fellow Hebrew who may be sold to you; when he has served you six years, you must set him free." But your fathers would not obey Me or give ear. Lately you turned about and did what is proper in My sight, and each of you proclaimed a release to his countrymen; and you made a covenant accordingly before Me in the House which bears My name. But now you have turned back and have profaned My name; each of you has brought back the men and women whom you had given their freedom, and forced them to be your slaves again. Assuredly, thus said the LORD: You would not obey Me and proclaim a release, each to his kinsman and countryman. Lo! I proclaim your release—declares the LORD—to the sword, to pestilence, and to famine; and I will make you a horror to all the kingdoms of the earth. I will make the men who violated My covenant, who did not fulfill the terms of the covenant which they made before Me, [like] the calf which they cut in two so as to pass between the halves: The officers of Judah and Jerusalem, the officials, the priests, and all the people of the land who passed between the halves of the calf shall be handed over to their enemies, to those who seek to kill them. Their carcasses shall become food for the birds of the sky and the beasts of the earth. (NJPS)

The prophet in this passage describes a ritual of covenant making whereby a sacrificial animal was cut in half; and the covenanting parties, in undertaking the obligation, walked between the two halves. By this solemn act they placed a conditional curse upon themselves—to be cut up and die like the sacrificial animals—if they failed to live up to their promise. Now, inasmuch as they did fail to do so, they were cursed by God.[18] Jeremiah's speech contains a paraphrase of the law in Deut 15:12, cited above (sec. 2.1). It appears that the law or custom of release was known at the time of Jeremiah but, at the same time, it is also clear that this law had been ignored by those Israelites holding debt slaves.

The Bible describes another crisis involving accumulated debt that took place in the time of Nehemiah, around 440 BCE, Nehemiah gathered the people and made them swear to forgive the debts of their fellow Jews. He appealed to their consciences but made no reference to the biblical laws of release as a basis for this action. He essentially used the same technique we saw in Jeremiah 34, namely, a general agreement, enforced by oath and self-curse, taken by the creditors to offer relief to their fellow Jews. This passage mentions sale of children as well as sales of Jews to gentiles because of debt. This event is related in Neh 5:1–13:

> There was a great outcry by the common folk and their wives against their brother Jews. Some said, "Our sons and daughters are numerous; we must get grain to eat in order that we may live!" Others said, "We must pawn our fields, our vineyards, and our homes to get grain to stave off hunger." Yet others said, "We have borrowed money against our fields and vineyards to pay the king's tax. Now we are as good as our brothers, and our children as good as theirs; yet here we are subjecting our sons and daughters to slavery—some of our daughters are already subjected—and we are powerless, while our fields and vineyards belong to others." It angered me [i.e., Nehemiah] very much to hear their outcry and these complaints. After pondering the matter carefully, I censured the nobles and the prefects, saying, "Are you pressing claims on loans made to your brothers?" Then I raised a large crowd against them and said to them, "We have done our best to buy back our Jewish brothers who were sold to the gentiles; will you now sell your brothers so that they must be sold back to us?" They kept silent, for they found nothing to answer. So I continued, "What you are doing is not right. You ought to act in a God-fearing way so as not to give our enemies, the gentiles, room to reproach us. I, my brothers, and my servants also have claims of money and grain against them; let us now abandon those claims! Give back at once their fields, their vineyards, their olive trees, and their homes, and abandon the claims for the hundred pieces of silver, the grain, the wine, and the oil that you have been pressing against them!" They replied, "We shall give them back, and not demand anything of them; we shall do just as you say." Summoning the priests, I put them under oath to keep this promise.

---

18. This act of covenant formation is also described in Gen 15. Cf. Rashi on Gen 15:10 and Bekhor Shor on Gen 15:9. For more recent discussion, with ancient Near Eastern parallels, see Sarna, *Genesis*, 114–15.

I also shook out the bosom of my garment and said, "So may God shake free of his household and property any man who fails to keep this promise; may he be thus shaken out and stripped." All the assembled answered, "Amen," and praised the LORD. The people kept this promise. (NJPS)

We are not well informed about practices during the centuries between the time of Nehemiah and the rabbinical traditions describing late Hasmonean, Herodian, and Roman times. The practice of Nehemiah and the generosity it asked for apparently continued as a moral desideratum, capable of being practiced by individuals or groups even if it was not mandated by state laws under Persian, Ptolemaic, and Seleucid rule. The idea of continuing voluntary adherence to the spirit of the biblical laws is reflected in the Gospels, which contain repeated references to debt and praise for creditors who voluntarily forgave their debtors. Jesus in Matt 6:12 declares: "And forgive us our debts, as we also have forgiven our debtors" (NRSV). And, again in Matt 18:23–26 in a parable:

> For this reason the kingdom of heaven may be compared to a king who wished to settle accounts with his slaves. When he began the reckoning, one who owed him ten thousand talents was brought to him; and, as he could not pay, his lord ordered him to be sold, together with his wife and children and all his possessions, and payment to be made. So the slave fell on his knees before him, saying, 'Have patience with me, and I will pay you everything.' And out of pity for him, the lord of that slave released him and forgave him the debt. (NRSV)

Matthew 18:29–30 describes how the governmental authorities were, however, normally expected to help collect creditors outstanding debts:

> Then his fellow slave fell down and pleaded with him, 'Have patience with me, and I will pay you.' But he refused; then he went and threw him into prison until he would pay the debt. (NRSV)

Jesus in Matt 5:25–26 also describes how in his day a debtor might be thrown into prison: "you will be thrown into prison. Truly I tell you, you will never get out until you have paid the last penny" (NRSV). The use of imprisonment appears to reflect the practice of Roman law, which allowed a creditor to seize his debtor and have him put into fetters and prison in order to coerce repayment. If payment was not forthcoming, the debtor could be sold into slavery.[19] There is evidence for a still earlier development of some kinds of debtor's prison in Mesopotamia; but we are unclear about the role of this detention in the settlement of debts or whether these prisons were private, communal, or state-owned.[20]

Nehemiah 5:1–13 also indicates that with respect to debts owed to gentile creditors, there was no expectation of forgiveness. We see from Lev 25:47–49, that there was indeed no expectation

19. See Thomas, *Textbook of Roman Law*, 78–79, where he discusses the legal action of *manus iniectio* (found in *XII Tab.* 3.1–6) and later changes introduced by *lex Poetilia*.

20. See *CAD* H, 218 sub. *bīt hubulli*; *CAD* Ṣ, 157 sub *ṣibitti*; cf. also Veenhof, *Letters from the Louvre*, *AbB* 14 128; this is a letter, which speaks of a creditor placing a man's wife, sons, and slave-women into detention. See also *CAD* K, 360–61 sub *bīt kīli*. For Sumerian terms, cf. Civil, "On Mesopotamian Jails," 75.

that a gentile creditor would voluntarily release his Israelite slave; the freedom of that slave could only be accomplished by repurchase:

> If a sojourner or stranger among you grows wealthy, and your brother fall into poverty with one of them and is sold to that stranger, or to a branch of the stranger's family—after he has been sold, he shall have (the right of) redemption; one of his brothers may redeem him, or his uncle or his uncle's son may redeem them, or anyone of his kin from his family may redeem them; or if he (himself) should (somehow) become able, he can be redeemed (in this fashion).[21]

The Mishnah in *m. Git.* 4:9 later ruled that there was an obligation to redeem the children of a man who sold himself to gentiles but this did not apply to the man himself, i.e., their father.

We know of no ancient Near Eastern evidence for this kind of communal agreement on behalf of debt slaves. This form of relief appears to be an Israelite innovation, used by Zedekiah and Nehemiah as a voluntary, defensive act undertaken in order to rebuild and maintain social solidarity within a small community. This modality of voluntary action appears to have taken root within the post-exilic Jewish community, to judge from the injunction spoken by Jesus in Matt 6:12 (cited earlier).

2.3 RELIEF GIVEN TO DEBT SLAVES AS A GROUP BY ROYAL DECREES

We have already seen that the biblical laws relating to individual servitude were not followed. More effective were general actions of release, like the ones that were enacted by Zedekiah and Nehemiah, which targeted the entire population of free persons who had fallen into debt slavery. These may have been patterned after ancient Near Eastern royal releases, which were typically enacted at the beginning of a new king's reign and at irregular intervals thereafter, in order to celebrate milestones in a king's reign and to provide needed economic relief. There is a long tradition of such royal easements, which usually included forgiving debts, releasing debt slaves, and canceling certain taxes. These measures are known from the end of the third millennium into the first millennia BCE and involve rulers in Sumer, Babylonia, Mari, Hana, Alalakh, Hatti (i.e., territory of the Hittites), Nuzi, and Assyria. A variety of terms are used to describe these enactments; the most well known is *andurāru*—also *durāru* in first millennium Assyria—which is cognate to Hebrew *deror*, which is translated as "release" in Lev 25:10 (sec. 2.4 below) and Jeremiah 34 (sec. 2.2 above). Another term is *mīsharu*, which is cognate to Hebrew *mesharim*—often translated as "equity"—which in Psalms is used to describe the "messianic" conditions under the beneficent and just rule of God.[22]

---

21. The order in the obligation to redeem given here is: self, brother, uncle, nephew, cousin, or other relative. The debtor's son or his father are not mentioned. Milgrom, *Leviticus*, 2238, offers some possible reasons. This Leviticus passage is further discussed in sec. 2.5.2.

22. For references and bibliography see Weinfeld, *Social Justice*, 75–96. A large number of the ancient Near Eastern references are more briefly but completely listed in *CAD* A/2, 115–17 and M/2, 116–18 and, for Sumerian, *PSD* A/3, 208–10 art. *ama-ar-gi4*. Kraus, *Königliche Verfügungen*, presents the evidence from the Old Babylonian period in detail. For releases proclaimed by the

These conditions include the release of debts and debt slaves in order to achieve "equity." These psalms proclaim a lofty vision of a more perfect future time when God Himself will rule the earth and full justice will truly prevail, e.g., Ps 98:8–9:

> Let the rivers clap their hands, the mountains sing joyously together at the presence of the LORD, for He is coming to rule the earth; He will rule the world justly, and its peoples with equity. (NJPS)

Similarly, Ps 96:10:

> Declare among the nations, "The LORD is king!" the world stands firm; it cannot be shaken; He judges the peoples with equity. (NJPS)

These psalms portrays God as a king who is beginning his reign; among a new king's first acts would be the issuing of a decree to release debts and debt slaves. This custom is well known in the ancient Near Eastern releases mentioned above. From such passages and from the use of familiar cognate terms, some scholars have argued that a practice of royal enactments, alleviating debts, was in fact also practiced in ancient Israel during the time of the monarchy. A royal enactment of this type may indeed underlie the story preserved in Jeremiah 34 (sec. 2.2), which may have been further reshaped in order to highlight the ideas of covenant and to embrace the ideology of Deut 15:12 (sec. 2.1). Unfortunately, there are no other surviving records of royal releases enacted by the Judean or Israelite monarchs. The psalms preserve the concept of royal enactment at a time when the

Judean monarchy was gone. Therefore, the institution was apparently sufficiently well known—either from past history or from general ancient Near Eastern practice—to be used repeatedly as a motif in the psalmic image of divine rule. It is interesting to note, in connection with the language of the psalms and its notion of divine rule, that the Akkadian cognate terms for "equity" (*mīsharum*) along with "truth" (*kittu*) came to be "personified" as sons of the sun-god, who, as we repeatedly see (e.g., secs. 6.1, 8.2) was visualized as the god of justice.[23]

2.4 RELIEF GIVEN TO DEBT SLAVES AS A GROUP BY CALENDAR

Another strategy for the relief for debt slaves as a group appears in the biblical laws of remission (*shemitah*) and jubilee (*yovel*). These releases were not dependent upon the decision of any monarch but, rather, were built into the calendar. Remissions were to take place every seventh year; this is the law of Deut 15:1–3:

> Every seventh year you shall grant a remission of debts. And this is the manner of the remission: every creditor shall remit the claim that is held against a neighbor, not exacting it of a neighbor who is a member of the community, because the LORD'S remission has been proclaimed. Of a foreigner you may exact it, but you must remit your claim on whatever any member of your community owes you. (NRSV)

Neo-Assyrian kings in the seventh century BCE, see Radner, "The Neo-Assyrian Period," 284–86. There is also an early reference to release of debts in celebration of the building of a major temple in Gudea, Cylinder B xvii, 17.

23. For word meanings cf. *CAD* E, 352–63; K 468–70; M/2, 116–19. In Mesopotamia the gods *Kittum* and *Mishārum* have another sibling *Dajānum* i.e., the deified or prototypical (just) "Judge"; cf. *CAD* D, 33.

A different strategy and computation appears in Lev 25:8–10; there was to be a regularly instituted release—but only at intervals of fifty years:

> You shall count off seven weeks of years—seven times seven years—so that the period of seven weeks of years gives you a total of forty-nine years. Then you shall sound the horn loud; in the seventh month, on the tenth day of the month—the Day of Atonement—you shall have the horn sounded throughout your land and you shall hallow the fiftieth year. You shall proclaim release throughout the land for all its inhabitants. It shall be a jubilee for you: each of you shall return to his holding and each of you shall return to his family. (NJPS)

All transfers of property, presumably forced by financial pressure, as well as the term of debt slavery for those totally impoverished were cancelled at the end of the forty-nine year cycle. Debt is addressed in Lev 25:39–41:

> If your kinsman (lit. brother) living nearby becomes impoverished and is sold to you, do not subject him to the treatment of a (chattel) slave. He shall remain with you like a hired laborer or sojourner; he shall serve with you only until the jubilee year. Then he and his children with him shall leave you; he shall go back to his family and return to his ancestral holding.[24]

24. It is not clear why the children of the emancipated slave are included in Lev 25:39–41. Rabbinic commentators assume that his family entered slavery with him; but then why is there no mention of his wife in Lev 25:41? If the master supplied him with a wife as in Exod 21:4 (sec. 2.1), and these children were hers, then it is striking that they were enabled to exit slavery along with their father. For discussion see Milgrom, *Leviticus*, 2224.

These laws—addressed simply to "you"—do not reveal the identity of the governing body that was to promulgate the remission or release. We have already seen in Jeremiah 34 that individual releases were not being practiced in the time of the monarchy, although the people evidently knew the concept. The same was evidently true for royal releases for the benefit debtor populations, as we have seen in the psalms. The kings of Judea (and Samaria) had apparently not instituted such releases; either they had omitted the practice altogether or did so too infrequently for mention in the historical books or prophets. These failures may be the impetus behind the schemes of Deut 15:1–3 and Leviticus 25, which do not depend upon the cooperation of creditors or upon the generosity of kings. Instead, they appeal to the community of citizens to take the discipline upon themselves; and by tying remission and release to the calendar, one should not find it necessary to persuade the populace anew each time a release was needed. There is recognition regarding extended periods of service for debtors in the Talmud, in *b. Qidd.* 14b, which explains the jubilee as a needed remedy instituted for debtors who might have been forced to sell themselves for periods longer than the six year terms described in Exod 21:2–4 and Deut 15:12–18 (sec. 2.1). The rabbis—evidently seeking to harmonize the presentation of so many alternative methods of release in the Pentateuch—sought to limit the six-year term to court-imposed sale, as for a thief who lacked the wherewithal to pay the monetary penalties added as punishment for theft. (See secs. 5.5 and 5.6.) The longer, forty-nine year term, they argue, was a feature of self-sale. This distinction is presented in a *baraita* cited in that same discussion:

> He who sells himself may be sold for six years or more than six years; if sold by the court, he may be sold for six years only. He who sells himself—(his ear) may not be bored; if he is sold by the court, (his ear) may be bored (as in Exod 21:5–6 and Deut15:16–17). He, who sells himself, has no gift made to him; if sold by the court, a gift is made to him (as described in Deut 15:13–18). To him who sells himself, his master cannot give a Canaanite bondmaid; if sold by the court, his master can give him a Canaanite bondmaid (as in Exod 21:4). Rabbi Eleazar said: "Neither may be sold for more than six years; both may be bored; to both a gift is made; and to both the master may give a Canaanite bondmaid."

We know from ancient Near Eastern documents that thieves might indeed sold into slavery, either as a punishment or because they were unable to make restitution. This kind of forced sale is also mentioned in Exod 22:2 (sec. 5.5) in connection with a thief who is unable to make restitution. But reading this distinction into Exod 21:2–4 and Deut 15:12–18 appears to be a scholastic effort at harmonizing otherwise contradictory scriptural sources; and this fact may ultimately explain why Rabbi Eleazar rejected the anonymous "majority view" of the *baraita*.

Some scholars have argued that the jubilee was an institution of pre-monarchal times, later forgotten or neglected. But others see it as a never actualized, utopian program.[25] The latter position is

more likely, for indeed a rabbinic tradition asserts that, already during the eighth century BCE, during the Assyrian period, jubilees were only counted for calendrical reasons but their regulations on debt release were not in force.[26] Jubilee also appears tentative in Num 36:4 (see sec. 1.5.2) where the relatives of the daughters of Zelophehad say: "And if there will (ever) be a jubilee for the Children of Israelites . . ." Rashi in his commentary to this verse notes that their statement is the basis of the comment of Rabbi Judah who, reading this same verse, said: "The jubilee is destined to cease and (then) to be restored (in messianic times)."[27] One gets a similar impression of laws as yet unrealized, in Ezek 46:16–18 (partly cited in sec. 1.5.1), which describes future releases during the restoration of Israel under the rule of its own princely ruler. At that time, says Ezekiel:

> Thus said the Lord GOD: If the prince makes a gift to any of his sons, it shall become the latter's inheritance; it shall pass on to his sons; it is their holding by inheritance. But if he makes a gift from his inheritance to any of his subjects, it shall only belong to the latter until the year of release. Then it shall revert to the prince; his inheritance must by all means pass on to his sons. But the prince shall not take property away from any of the

---

25. Wright, "Jubilee"; Milgrom, *Leviticus,* 2214–15; on both biblical and rabbinic times see Hezser, "Slaves and Slavery," 168–71, 176.

26. This tradition is discussed *in b. Arakh.* 32b–33a and is accepted as historically true in Maimonides, *Mishnah Torah, Hilkhot Shemitah v'Yovel* 10: 8. For fuller discussion cf. Wacholder, "The Calendar of Sabbatical Cycles."

27. *Sifra, Vayiqra Dibura d'Nedava Parshata* 13.1 (on Lev 2:14). Similarly, Rashi on Num 36:4. Some modern translations seek to interpret the Hebrew word "if" as "when" but this is not, strictly speaking, indicated on linguistic grounds.

people and rob them of their holdings. Only out of his own holdings shall he endow his sons, in order that My people may not be dispossessed of their holdings. (NJPS)

Ezekiel's release resembles the jubilee of Leviticus 25, but does not use that term. The release pertains only to property; but as we have seen in Lev 25:39–41 above, loss of ancestral land was often a typical first step to poverty and debt slavery. According to Ezekiel, in the new age that will come, all ancestral holdings will revert to their original families at the time of release.

As for the seventh year or *shemitah* of Deut 15:1–3, it was apparently also later counted for calendrical reasons; otherwise it remained without legal effect. Rabbinic tradition attributed its nullification to an official act by Hillel the Elder (c. 5 BCE), who instituted a court procedure called *prosbul*. The court certified outstanding debts and allowed them to continue in force after the seventh year; Hillel is said to have done this in order that Jewish creditors would not refrain from lending money. This is stated in the Talmud *b. Git.* 36b:

> The Rabbis ordained that it (i.e., the seventh year) should be operative, in order to keep alive the memory of the Sabbatical year; but when Hillel saw that people refrained from lending money to one another, he decided to institute the *prosbul*.[28]

We know of similar practices in ancient Near Eastern records, where lenders could insert clauses into loan documents obligating the borrower to forgo the benefit of any royal release that might occur before the loan was repaid; this practice goes back to the second millennium BCE.[29] However, ancient Near Eastern sources do not attest to any analogue for calendar-based releases like the jubilee or the seventh year remission, which are found only in the Bible. One is therefore left to wonder whether during biblical times the remission of the seventh year, as well as the jubilee, were constructions based upon social ideals of justice, but not necessarily realized or realizable in actuality—unless, perhaps, these measures might have been instituted through self-imposed community discipline during the periods of Ezekiel and Nehemiah, and prior to Hillel. Instituting limitations on the duration of debt servitude would fit in with other changes of attitude towards debt service discussed below (sec. 4.1), in connection with the mistreatment of debt slaves.

2.5 REDUCING THE BURDEN OF DEBT UPON THE NEEDY

2.5.1 Usury and Security

The biblical laws sought to help debtors through a ban on usury; this measure could keep debt owed from increasing in amount during the time while it remained unpaid. The omission of interest could ease a debtor's condition even though it could not totally prevent him from falling

---

28. Cf. also *Sifre D Re'eh* 113.3 (on Deut 15:3) which adds that loans secured by pledged goods may be collected even without a *prosbul;* see also *m. Shev.* 10:2–4; *m. Git.* 4:3; *t. Shev.* 8:6, Lieberman, states that *prosbul* was only be used for loans secured by real property.

29. For the Old Babylonian period cf. *CAD* N/2, 141 (*nazbu*). For a Middle Assyrian example see Chavalas, "Nazbum in the Khana Contracts from Terqa," 182–83.

into debt slavery. The Bible refers to a number of ways through which interest was charged on loans. One term *neshekh* (literally "a bite") seems to describe how a creditor would deduct the interest in advance from the amount received the borrower. Another term *tarbit* (or *marbit)* literally, "increase," appears to describe interest added to the amount that was borrowed; both principal and interest would be collected at the time of repayment.[30] The Bible, recognizing that the taking of interest on loans was customary, permitted Israelites to take interest from non-Israelites. The prohibition on taking interest was therefore only requested when lending to fellow citizens, i.e., for fellow Israelites. This distinction is clearly stated in Deut 23:20–21:

> You shall not deduct interest from loans to your countrymen [lit. brother, kinsman], whether in money or food or anything else that can be deducted as interest; but you may deduct interest from loans to foreigners. Do not deduct interest from loans to your countrymen, so that the LORD your God may bless you in all your undertakings in the land that you are about to enter and possess. (NJPS)

Leviticus 25:36–37 states a similar prohibition:

> Do not exact from him (your kinsman) deducted or added interest, but fear your God. Let your kinsman live alongside of you. Do not lend him your money at deducted

interest, or give him your food at added interest.[31]

To judge from the tone of these statements, the prohibition on interest appears to have been a moral or religious injunction rather than an enforceable law in ancient Israel. As we saw earlier in connection with freeing debt slaves, it was difficult to monitor transactions between private individuals. Omission of interest was envisioned as an act of humanity; and its reward or punishment came from Heaven, not from the courts; we see this, e.g., in Ezek 18:17:

> He has refrained from oppressing the poor; he has not exacted advance or added interest; he has obeyed My rules and followed My laws—he shall not die for the iniquity of his father, but shall live. (NJPS)

Heavenly retribution, delayed but inevitable, is also reflected in Prov 28:8:

> One, who increases his wealth by loans at deducted or added interest, accumulates it for (another), who (one day) will be (more) generous to the poor.

Writing in the first century CE, Philo, in his writings on virtue, makes similar moral arguments for lending to the poor without taking interest; about persons acting in this fashion he says:

> For . . . in place of the interest which they determine not to accept they receive a further bonus of the fairest and most precious things that human life has to give, mercy, neighbourliness, charity,

---

30. The meanings of these terms have been subject to other interpretations on how the interest payments were arranged. See discussion in Tigay, *Deuteronomy,* 217 and 387n; and also Milgrom, *Leviticus,* 2209–10.

31. Other passages mentioning the taking of interest are Exod 22:24; Ezek 18:13; 22:12; Hab 2:7; Ps 15:5.

magnanimity, a good report and good fame. And what acquisition can rival these?[32]

The ban on taking interest was widely circumvented or ignored; documents in Aramaic, Greek from the fifth centuries BCE to the first century CE show manifold ways in which interest was being charged in loans given by Jews to other Jews.[33] Creditors, however, could be more disposed to lend without taking interest if pledged assets belonging to the borrower secured their loan. The giving over of a pledge or security to the creditor provided a guarantee of payment in case of default and might in fact be worth more than the loan itself. The taking of security was seen as necessary when dealing with strangers as well as with the poor, who might otherwise not be given credit because of the risk that their loans would not be repaid, either because of deceit or destitution. In the Bible, pledged assets were frequently taken by the creditor into his own possession, as well as hypothecated, i.e., bound by contract to the creditor but not physically transferred to his control.[34] There are various Hebrew terms used to denote "pledge" or "pawn" ('erabon, 'abot, habol) and it is indeed possible that there were some details of legal difference between them; but these differences, if they existed, are not presently recoverable on the

basis of the biblical contexts. Security in a transaction involving strangers appears in the story of Judah and Tamar mentioned earlier; in Gen 38:17–18 we are told that Tamar, in her disguise, asked Judah for a security that he would later pay her for her favors:

> He [Judah] answered, "I will send you a kid from the flock." And she [Tamar] said, "Only if you give me a pledge, until you send it." He said, "What pledge shall I give you?" She replied, "Your signet and your cord, and the staff that is in your hand." (NRSV)

The Bible sought to assist more needy borrowers by limiting the type of assets that their creditors could take as security for loans; vital possessions needed for daily life and food preparation should not be taken:

> Deut 24:6—A handmill or an upper millstone shall not be taken in pawn, for that would be taking someone's life in pawn.

> Deut 24:17—You shall not subvert the rights of the stranger or the fatherless; you shall not take a widow's garment in pawn. (NJPS)

The conduct of a creditor in taking a pledge–including the borrower's clothing– is also regulated in Deut 24:10–13:

> When you make any kind of loan to your fellow, you must not enter his house to seize his pledge (from him). You must remain outside, and the man to whom you made the loan will bring forth the pledge to you. If he is a poor man, you shall not go to sleep in [i.e., holding] his pledge; you should indeed return the pledge to him by (the time) the sun sets; he can (then)

---

32. Philo, *On the Virtues* 84, Colson.

33. Falk, *Introduction to Jewish Law,* 204–6. Earlier examples from the fifth century BCE are Cowley 10 and 11 (=B 3.1, B 4.2) in Porten and Yardeni, *Textbook of Aramaic Documents*, 54–57, 104–5.

34. Security given by a third party for another borrower was promissory in nature; cf. Prov 22:26; if the borrower defaulted, the consequence fell upon the person giving security; cf. Prov 20:16; 27:13.

sleep in his garment and bless you; and for you this will be (considered as an act of) righteousness before the LORD your God.

This conduct and its rationale is again found in Exod 22:25–26:

If you take your neighbor's garment in pledge, you must return it to him before the sun sets; it is his only clothing, the sole covering for his skin. In what else shall he sleep? Therefore, if he cries out to Me, I will pay heed, for I am compassionate. (NJPS)

We know the reality of this plight from an excavated Hebrew letter, written in the seventh century BCE, in which a victim pleads to an official for help in recovering his garment, apparently seized by a creditor:

When I had finished my reaping, at that time, a few days ago, he took your servant's garment. All of my companions will testify for me, all who were reaping with me in the heat of the sun—they will testify for me that this is true. I am guiltless of an in[fraction].[35]

The situation of poor debtors who were forced to give their garments in pledge as well as condemnation for those who, oblivious to their plight, hypocritically oppressed them, is found in Amos 2:8:

They lay themselves down beside every altar on garments taken in pledge, and in the house of their God they drink wine bought with fines they imposed. (NRSV)

The use of the pledge by the creditor who held it was itself a form of interest; this was even more pronounced when the security was real property, like a field, which yielded crops or a house, which could be occupied.[36]

In the larger ancient Near East, one finds evidence for a wide variety of financial instruments and arrangements; these include interest bearing loans, loans without interest, interest charged on delinquent loans only, pledges both possessory and hypothecary, third party security arrangements, commercial loans, as well as private loans, etc. There is also a rich terminology describing these transactions, which go back to the third millennium BCE.[37] While interest-free loans existed, we are not informed about the circumstances surrounding them; and there is no statement prohibiting the taking interest as a matter of social policy like one finds in the Bible. However, there were laws, which attempted to regulate interest and to keep it within reasonable bounds. In the Old Babylonian law collections one finds regulations setting standard rates of interest: 20% on silver and 33-1/3% on commodities (grain).[38] Loans to individuals were normally collected at harvest time; and lenders were not allowed to change the terms once the loan was given; thus Eshnunna Laws §§19–21:

36. In later, rabbinic law, some sages frowned on this type of use but many rabbis permitted it. See Falk, *Introduction to Jewish Law*, 206–7.

37. The literature on loans is scattered. A good place to start is Westbrook, "Conclusions," and the bibliographies included in the various essays in the volume in which his article appears, as well as in the index of terms at the end of that volume.

38. Cf. Eshnunna Laws §18a, Hammurapi Laws §L (Roth, *Law Collections*, §t).

35. Metsad Hashavyahu 1:8–12. See Gogel, *Grammar of Epigraphic Hebrew*, 423; for more discussion and literature see Weippert, "Die Petition eines Entarbeiters," 449–66.

A man who lends (one commodity) in exchange for its counterpart, he shall collect (that same commodity) at the threshing floor. If a man lent grain [. . .] and (then) changed the grain for silver, at harvest time he shall (nevertheless) receive grain and its interest (at the rate of) 1 (*pān*) (plus) *4* seahs per *kor* (i.e., 33 1/3%). If the man lent silver initially, he shall collect silver and its (appropriate) interest (at the rate of) 1/6 shekel and six grains per shekel (i.e., 20%).[39]

These interest rates for silver and grain were considered fair and just; in loan documents, they are often referred to as "the interest of Shamash (the sun-god)." However one can find many loan documents, in which other rates of interest, both higher and lower, were charged. One must assume, therefore, that the setting of interest rates responded to other social and economic factors, which were operative at the time and place of the loans.[40]

We find an echo of the biblical concerns about creditors, debtors, and the taking of pledges in an inscription published by Gudea of Lagash (c. 2100 BCE). He sought to banish all conduct creating stress, pain, and strife during the rebuilding of the major temple dedicated to his city god; one of his acts was to see to it that "the creditor did not enter into the house of another man"—apparently either to collect his debt or to take a pledge from

him.[41] This passage helps us understand why the Bible felt the need to regulate this procedure.

2.5.2 Rights of Redemption

There existed a traditional right of redemption pertaining to the person of the debtor, who was sold into debt slavery because of his unpaid debts. A debtor might exit from bondage and redeem himself by repaying what was owed. It was probably not likely the case that a debtor himself possessed any additional assets; for if he had some, he would have used them to satisfy his debts and escape being sold. But relief might come to him from a relative who stepped forward to ease his kinsman's burden. This is the situation described in Lev 25:47–53, which links it to the jubilee institution (discussed in sec. 2.4):

> If a sojourner or stranger among you grows wealthy, and your brother fall into poverty with one of them and is sold to that stranger, or to a branch of the stranger's family—after he has been sold, he shall have (the right of) redemption; one of his brothers may redeem him, or his uncle or his uncle's son may redeem them, or anyone of his kin from his family may redeem them; or if he (himself) should (somehow) become able, he can be redeemed (in this fashion). He (the redeemer) together with the one who purchased him shall count (the years) from the year in which he was sold to him up to the year of the (coming) jubilee; and the money given for his sale shall be (set) against that number of years; (this period of time) shall be (reckoned) like years that a hired laborer

39. The grain interest comes to 100 *qû* per a *kor* consisting of 300 *qû*; a kor was approximately 300 liters in volume. As for the silver, there were 180 grains per shekel; the interest equals 36/180 grains or 20%. A shekel at that time was 1/60 of a mina of approximately 500 grams in weight. See further Powell, "Masse und Gewicht."

40. Greengus, *Studies in Ishchali Documents*, 194–96.

41. Gudea, Statue B v, 10–11.

(might serve). If many years still lie ahead, he (the redeemer) shall pay for his redemption accordingly, (calculating) from the money of his purchase. And if (but) few years remain until the year of the jubilee, he shall calculate it according to his years (of service and likewise) pay for his redemption. He (the debt slave) is to be considered as a year-by-year hired laborer; he (the debt-slave owner) shall not (be allowed to) govern him with undue harshness before your eyes.

Leviticus considers the debt slave to be a kind of indentured servant. His "wages" would correspond to the amount of debt for which he was sold, divided by the years remaining until the coming jubilee; his years of service are valued according that rate. It is not clear why Lev 25:47–53 had chosen to mention a sale to alien; presumably because this would be a situation where relatives might be highly motivated as well as expected to help their hapless kinsman, in the fashion of what we have seen recounted in Neh 5:1–13 (in sec. 2.2 above).

Documents from the ancient Near East attest to the practice of benefactors— typically family members—redeeming their kin who were seized or sold for debts of various kinds. As for laws, we have already seen references (in section 2.1 above) to the practice of redemption: in Hammurapi Laws §117, where a man is forced to sell a member of his family into debt slavery, and in §§280–281, which deal with slaves. One can also point to Hammurapi Laws §§118–119, which deal with chattel slaves who are sold by their owners because of debt; in §118, the former owner has no right of redemption once his slave is sold. But in §119 the situation

is one where the slave is a woman who has borne children to her master. Because of this relationship, this slave woman is not treated like other slaves; she is given the status of a quasi-family member; and her former master, as her "husband," has a right to redeem her. The laws in §§118–119 are as follows:

> If he (the debtor) has given over a male or female slave into debt service, the creditor (literally, banker/merchant) may transport him (elsewhere and) sell (him) for silver; he may not be reclaimed. (However,) if a (free) man—a debt has overtaken him and he has sold his slave woman who has borne him children, the owner of that slave woman may weigh out the (amount of) silver that the creditor weighed out (to him in the original loan) and may he redeem his slave woman.

In the Bible, we also find the term for "redemption" figuratively transferred to the theological realm, in depicting God's deliverance of Israel from pain and foreign captivity; thus, e.g., Isa 52:3 preserves the link between redemption and the image of the debtor:

> For thus said the LORD: "You were sold for naught; and (therefore) shall be redeemed without (the need to pay) silver."

A similar, figurative transfer is found in Mesopotamian religion. In a religious ritual, we find the following:

> He will hold the balance in his hand and pay the silver of his redemption (and recite) "O Shamash, the silver of the redemption payment for myself, my chief wife, my (other) wives, my sons and daughters has been given to you . . ."

The petitioner in this ritual is offering a symbolic payment to the sun-god in return for "release" from ailments or the threat of such afflictions.[42]

The Bible also attempts to ease the burden or threat of poverty by attaching a right of redemption to family property. For there was the expectation that under normal circumstances, houses and fields would pass down to one's heirs; nevertheless if family property was used to secure debts, it could be seized by a creditor if the debt could not be paid. Loss of land was a major step towards impoverishment of a family; and in ancient Israel, as in other part of the ancient Near East, loss of family property was considered to be an unfortunate outcome that had a deleterious effect on the social fabric. Rights of redemption were not extinguished by the death of the debtor who gave up the property; this right was inherited and could be exercised by his sons or by surviving male relatives. We have already encountered this right of redemption in the story of Ruth and Boaz in Ruth 3:9—4:12. Boaz, in addition to taking Ruth in levirate marriage, also—in his role as "the redeeming kinsman"—repurchased the mortgaged family land of Naomi and her family (sec. 1.1.2). We find another exercise of this custom again described in Jer 32:8–15:

> And my cousin Hanamel came to me in the prison courtyard— as the Lord had said—and said to me, "Buy my field, which is in Anathoth in the territory of Benjamin; for a right of possession and redemption belongs to you, buy it." Then I knew that it was the word of the Lord. So I bought the field in Anathoth from my cousin Hanamel amd I weighed out the (price in) silver for him, seventeen shekels of silver. I wrote a deed, sealed it, and had witnesses witness it; and I weighed out the silver on the scales. I took the deed of purchase, the (rolled-up) sealed text— (containing) the "commandment" and the stipulations—and the open (i.e., the visible, outside) copy[43] and gave the deed to Baruch son of Neriah son of Mahseiah in the presence of my kinsman Hanamel and the witnesses who signed on the deed, before all the Judeans who were sitting in the prison courtyard. Before them (all) I commanded Baruch as follows: Thus said the Lord of Hosts, the God of Israel: "Take these documents, i.e., this deed of purchase—the sealed text and the open one—and put them into an clay jar, so that they may endure a long time." For thus said the Lord of Hosts, the God of Israel: "Houses, fields, and vineyards shall yet again be purchased in this land."

Jeremiah, urged on by his kinsman, here exercised the right of redemption; he paid the price of the property to his kinsman, who then must have handed the silver over to the creditor who had foreclosed

---

42. This passage is cited in *CAD* I, 172; it comes from *AMT* 72 1 rev. 28–30.

43. The obverse of the document contained the full text; and following the text, witnesses could write their names or have their names noted by the scribe. The document was then rolled up and sealed. But in Jer 32:8–15, their names were apparently (also) signed on the outside, i.e., after the document was sealed. Their names were thus visible on the outside of the rolled-up and sealed document. In this mode, witnesses could be questioned without having to break open the sealed document. Both of these practices are known from the contemporary Jewish Aramaic and Egyptian papyri. Cf. Porten, *Archives from Elephantine*, 198–99.

upon the property or was ready to do so. This "extra step" of paying the price to Hanamel, demonstrated Hanamel's agreement and his ceding to Jeremiah the family property, which, he, from his own resources, had been unable to release from debt.

In Lev 25:23–25, the origin of the customary right of redemption is attributed to the claim that the entire "promised land" originally belongs to God, who gave it to Israel:

> But land must not be sold irrevocably, for the land is mine; you are but strangers and sojourners (living) with me. Throughout all the land that you hold in possession, you must provide a redemption for that land. If your kinsman [lit. brother] is in straits and has to sell (a piece) from his land holding, his nearest "redeemer" (i.e., relative) shall come (forward) and redeem what his kinsman has sold.

However, Lev 25:26–28 also sought to restructure the right of redemption by making it part of the law of jubilee. Under the scheme of jubilee, a land sale transaction was redefined as lease; the sale price was to be divided into 49 parts and its redemption price adjusted according to the number of years that had elapsed between the time of "sale" and the next jubilee. The family who was redeeming would not pay for those years during which the "buyer" held the property and had the benefit of its use; in this way, redemption was became in effect the "cancellation" of a 49-year lease arrangement similar in character to what we have already seen in connection with redemption from debt slavery. Lev 25:26–28 state the following:

> And a man—if he has no one to redeem for him, but he (himself later) has means and acquires enough to redeem it, he shall count up the (number of) years it was sold and pay for whatever balance (of years remain until the jubilee) to the man to whom he sold it, and he may then return to his land holding. But if he lacks the means to pay him out, then (the land) that he sold shall remain in the possession of the person who bought it until the jubilee; but in the jubilee year it shall go out (from his possession) and he [i.e., the original owner] shall return to his land holding.

Leviticus 25:29–31 however adds one restriction: jubilee will not release houses located within walled cities; for them, the customary right of redemption will be available for only one year after a sale:

> If a man sells a dwelling house in a walled city, it may be redeemed until a year has elapsed since its sale; the redemption period shall be a year. If it is not redeemed before a full year has elapsed, the house in the walled city shall pass to the purchaser beyond reclaim throughout the ages; it shall not be released in the jubilee. But houses in villages that have no encircling walls shall be classed as open country: they may be redeemed, and they shall be released through the jubilee. (NJPS)

The reason for this restriction is not stated; one can only speculate. The medieval commentators Hazzequni and Bekhor Shor suggest that a distinction was drawn between property that might be cultivated and thus required for subsistence, as opposed to urban residences that do not sit on potentially cultivatable land. This same argument has been also been put forth by modern scholars.[44] Hazzequ-ni further suggests that a person would hesitate to maintain or improve a house that was subject to redemption on a long-term basis. But this restriction did not apply to priestly holdings; the homes of Levites could always be reclaimed, while their nearby fields could not be sold in the first place; as Lev 25:32–34 states:

> As for the cities of the Levites, the houses in the cities they hold—the Levites shall forever have the right of redemption. Such property as may be redeemed from the Lev-ites—houses sold in a city they hold—shall be released through the jubilee; for the houses in the cities of the Levites are their hold-ing among the Israelites.[45] But the unenclosed land about their cit-ies cannot be sold, for that is their holding for all time. (NJPS)

This law on Levitical property appears to reflect the superior—and protected—so-cial position of priests, whose leadership, in the absence of native kings, became more pronounced after the Babylonian exile.

The Mishnah elaborates upon the biblical laws of redemption and establish-es a two-year period following a sale, dur-ing which the seller of property, whether house or field, cannot exercise his right of redemption. Mishnah *m. Arakh.* 9:1 states:

> One who sells his field during the time when jubilee is (practiced) is

not permitted to redeem it for no less than two years as it is written (Lev 25:15) "according to the num-ber of harvest years he shall sell it to you." If there was a year of blight or mildew or Sabbatical, it is not included in the counting for him (the buyer). But if he (the buyer) cultivated it (without planting) or left it fallow, it is included in the counting.[46]

According to the Mishnah, the buyer must be assured of having the benefit of no less than two years of harvest.

The right of redemption through monetary payment is an ancient custom, found as well in the Near Eastern laws. Eshnunna Laws §39 states:

> If a man becomes (financially) weakened and sells his house, on the day the buyer offers it for sale, the (previous) owner of the house may redeem (it).

This law recognizes the claim of the original owner, not necessarily because his house is in the category of ancestral property—although this may have in fact have been the case—but because the sale was "forced" by economic hardship. The language is reminiscent of Lev 25:25 " If your kinsman is in straits" but, unlike Le-viticus, the occupancy of the buyer here cannot be disturbed until and unless he decides to sell the property. We should note, however, that there are Old Babylo-nian documents recording redemption of land even in situations where the contract states that "a full price" had originally been paid. But these transactions perhaps could not have taken place without the

---

44. See discussion in Milgrom, *Leviticus,* 2198.

45. The verses, Lev 25:33–34, present textual difficulties; for a fuller discussion see Milgrom, *Le-viticus,* 2202–3.

46. This law also appears in *Sifra Behar* 3:10, commenting on Lev 25:15; see further Rashi to that verse.

consent of the current owner who bought the land from that family.[47]

There are numerous sale contracts containing clauses relating to redemption; this right is allowed in sale documents ranging in time from the early second to the middle of the first millennium BCE.[48] Usually no time limits for redemption are stated; however, I know of one sale contract where, like in Lev 25:29–31 above, the time given for a seller of a house to exercise his right to redeem is limited to one year after the sale. This clause is found in a contract from the late second millennium BCE found at Emar, in northern Syria. The seller owed a total of 30 shekels silver to two different creditors but could not pay them. Two other persons came forward and bought the debtor's house for 30 shekels and thereby enabled him to discharge his debt.[49] The seller's right of future recovery or redemption is stated as follows:

> If in the future, Zu-ba'la (the debtor and seller)—up to one year of days—will pay these 30 shekels silver to the (new) owners (of the house) he may take it back.

There was apparently some cloud hanging over the seller's ownership title. Zu-ba'la had delivered up the antecedent deed, which was in his possession; but he could not verify the history of any earlier title to

the property. The contract therefore goes on to state that if a claimant one day comes forward, who will successfully contest the present owners' title to the property they purchased, then the claimant will be entitled to recover his property but only on the condition that he reimburse the present buyers for the 30 shekels they paid to Zu-ba'la, the current seller:

> Otherwise—after two years have gone by—whoever one day will contest (the validity of the sale of) that house let him pay the equivalent amount of silver and let him take possession of his house.[50]

The claimant must pay because the present transaction was carried out in good faith to the extent possible. After all, the potential future claimant and his family had already let many years go by without challenging possession of the house by Zu-ba'la or the party who had earlier sold it to him. But it is interesting that the contract mentions a two-year threshold for reclamation. This term is of course similar to what we have seen in the Mishnah cited above. Why the two years? It may have been customary to allow an honest purchaser to benefit from his acquisition for this minimum period. But circumstances could vary and affect the conditions of sale. Thus, for example, in other contracts from Emar, no time limit is set on redemption or repurchase. The identity of the "would-be redeemer" or contestant is not given. Perhaps it might be a kinsman of the seller. In another document, he is specifically identified as the seller's brother. Two brothers, currently in debt, sold a field for 20 shekels; but a

47. See Greengus, "New Evidence on the Old Babylonian Calendar," 264–65, which discusses MHET 2/1, 41 and *CT* 45 3.

48. Cf. *CAD* P, 293 sub *patāru*. See also Abraham, "The Middle Assyrian Period," 179–84, 221 app. G; and Radner, "The Neo-Assyrian Period," 280–84.

49. The document is Arnaud, *Emar* 123; its import was pointed out in Westbrook, "Social Justice in the Ancient Near East," 153; but my interpretation of the contestation clause differs from his.

50. This same clause appears also in Arnaud, *Emar* 80.

third brother was not around to confirm the sale. Therefore the contract stipulates:

> If one day Baal-qarrad, their brother, will show up (and) contest it (the sale), let him give an equivalent amount of silver to Ahi-Dagan son of Dagan-kabar (the buyer) (and) he may take possession of his house.[51]

All the cases discussed are sales arising from unpaid debts; and in such cases, there appears to be underlying recognition that the sellers were forced by necessity to give up their property so perhaps the price received did not represent full value. This might explain why in our cases, the redeemer has only to pay an amount equivalent to the price of sale. But there are other sales, at Emar and elsewhere, where a connection to debt is not mentioned. There are also cases where a higher amount had to be paid in order to redeem or where any redemption is expressly denied.[52] In the Bible, the right of redemption is supported by a concept of family property; a similar concept was certainly also operative at Emar (and at Nuzi); but one may not assume that the concept of family holdings was the prime motivation everywhere. In Babylonia, easing the situation of free persons who fell into debt seems in itself to have been a sufficient, motivating principle.

51. The document is Arnaud, *Emar* 115. The property included more than just a house; there was apparently a well. (The term describing the overall property is obscure.)

52. See Ries, "Lösegeld"; and for Emar, van der Toorn, "Domestic Cult at Emar," 41–47; see also references in *CAD* I, 171 and *CAD* P, 294–95.

3

Laws on Chattel Slaves

3.1 SALE OF CHATTEL SLAVES

W HILE THE BIBLE CONTAINS no laws on the sale of chattel slaves, such laws are preserved in rabbinic law collections, which display a remarkable degree of continuity with Near Eastern laws going back to the second millennium. Jews, like their ancient neighbors, continued to own chattel slaves. This Jewish practice of slave ownership continued throughout Roman times until the Byzantine emperors, under pressure from the Christian church, limited the rights of Jews to acquire and hold non-Jewish slaves. After that time, Jewish slave holding in the West was considerably decreased, but it continued in Babylonia, which was under non-Christian, Sassanian rule, for many more centuries.[1]

Among the things we find, in connection with the sale of slaves, are concerns about epilepsy and other defects; laws addressing such concerns are found in Tosefta *t. B. Bat.* 4:5, Lieberman:

1. Linder, *Jews in Imperial Roman Legislation*, 82–85, presents imperial legislation, from the fourth through sixth centuries CE, against Jewish ownership of pagan and especially Christian slaves. A more tolerant situation obtained in Babylonia, as can be seen in formulary for slave sale documents authorized by R. Hai Gaon in the tenth–eleventh centuries CE (presented below).

If one sold a female slave to his neighbor with the understanding that she possessed defects and (also) told him, "This female slave—she is sickly, an idiot, an epileptic, and a dullard;" and she possessed (none of the enumerated defects but did possess) another (even lesser) defect, which he (did not identify but by implication) included among the (unspecified) defects; it is a sale in error. (But if the seller said, "She has this defect," which she actually possessed), "and another too," (but without specifying any other defect,) it is not a sale in error.

The Tosefta in *t. B. Bat.* 4:7, Lieberman, then adds some additional matters that could affect the sale because of the slave's character, namely, his criminal behavior, as well as potential loss of ownership rights by the buyer due to his slave being wanted by the authorities for punishment or penalty:

> If one sells a slave to his fellow and he (the slave) is found out to be a thief or a gambler, he becomes his (the buyer's) property. (i.e., it does not void the sale; however, if the slave is found to be) a robber or he

is under sentence for a crime, it is a sale in error.[2]

The Babylonian Talmud in *b. Git.* 86a offers specific, comprehensive language, which became mandatory in sales of slaves:

> R. Judah ruled (the following provisions be included) in slave sales: That his slave is rightfully his property and he is free and clear of disputes or legal challenges and from claims of king and government;[3] and that no slave mark of another owner is upon his body; and that he is free of all physical defect; and from skin disease that may have erupted, whether recently or formerly.[4]

We know that the formulation of Rabbi Judah in fact continued to be used in Babylonia as late as the eleventh century CE, where it still appears in a slave sale document template in the formulary manual prepared by R. Hai Gaon.[5]

Laws and provisions in documents of sale from the ancient Near East reveal the long history of similar concerns, outlining the responsibility of sellers to warrant the condition and behavior of their chattel slaves. Hammurapi Laws §§278–279 state:

If a man buys a male (or) female slave and his (the slave's first) month has not elapsed and "falling sickness" befalls him, he may return (the slave) to his seller and the buyer shall take back the silver that he paid. If a man buys a male (or) female slave and he (or she) has (prior) claims (against them), the seller must pay those claims.

Here we see that the seller of a slave must assume some responsibility for the health and condition of his slave. "Falling sickness," almost certainly epilepsy was seen as a hidden defect capable of invalidating the sale. The seller was also responsible for clearing the title of the slave he sold, i.e., defending the rights of the buyer to enjoy untroubled ownership of his newly acquired slave. Sale documents from the period of Hammurapi's successors in fact contain clauses providing a guarantee of one month for "falling sickness" as in the law above. The sale documents frequently mention another sickness or condition—as yet unidentified, which is guaranteed however only for 1–3 days. Babylonian slave sale documents likewise make the seller responsible for defending the title of the slave he sold. In keeping with the law, contracts typically include the statement: (the seller) will be responsible (to respond) to claimants as required by the king's ordinance.[6]

A remarkable continuity of formulary tradition is evidenced by a Neo-Assyrian slave sale written at the town of

---

2. Gulak, *Legal Documents in the Talmud*, 130 cites paragraphs from later Roman law (*D.* 21.1.19.1 and *D.* 21.1.1.1) in the name of Ulpian, where similar concerns and terms are found. Parallels to the Tosefta passage appear in *b. B. Bat.* 92b; *b. Ket.* 58a; *b. Qidd.* 11a; *j. B. Bat.* 15d.

3. The reading "government" accepts the emendation from "queen," discussed in Gulak, ibid. 131–32.

4. This Talmudic passage and its terminology, is discussed in detail in Gulak, ibid. 128–41.

5. The full text is given in Gulak, *Otzar Hashtarot*, 356–57.

6. For the Babylonian sale documents and discussion of the *tebītum* ailment, see *CAD* B, 206, 360; *CAD T,* 305–6; and Greengus, "The Selling of Slaves," 3. Another suggestion is that this term refers to a "window" of time, allowing the buyer to inspect the slave in closer fashion. Cf. Stol, *Epilepsy in Babylonia*, 134–35.

Gezer, in Judea, in 651 BCE, which states that the slave is guaranteed against "seizure (and) 'falling sickness' for 100 days; for crime, in perpetuity. Note that the guaranty period for epilepsy is here extended to 100 days rather than being just one month as earlier.[7] This same clause is likewise found in Neo-Assyrian slave sales written in the land of Assyria.[8] The Assyrian term for "crime" (*sartu*) refers to criminal or fraudulent acts in general; it sometimes also denotes stolen property and penalties imposed for theft. This concern for a slave's criminal behavior is similar to what we see later in *t. B. Bat.* 4:7 cited above. The Tosefta appears to be more tolerant of slaves who are petty thieves and gamblers than for slaves who are robbers or convicted felons. I do not know whether the Assyrians would have embraced this distinction.[9] Criminal behavior is enumerated along with still other issues affecting title in Neo-Assyrian slave sales from Nineveh. In one sale, we find the seller's guaranty "against crime, against the slave having been assigned for security (i.e., to secure a financial obligation), or subject to (a prior) debt." In this sale, a slave woman, daughter of the seller, is being sold with the understanding that she will be given in marriage to the son of the buyer. Three persons are listed who will stand behind the guaranty and who are ready to recompense the buyer, should the guaranty fail.[10] The Tosefta also mentions guarantees relating to mental defects along with physical ones. These are also mentioned in Neo-Assyrian transactions as well, but only infrequently.[11]

One should consider the possibility that a full range of guarantees, even if unmentioned, may have been implicit in Hammurapi Laws §§278–279 and in other ancient Near Eastern transactions, as well as in R. Judah's formulary in *b. Gittin* 86a. They may perhaps have become part of a generally assumed, customary obligation that sellers were required to defend their title of ownership for the item or slave being sold to another party. Thus, for example, in an Aramaic slave sale from Samaria, dated to the last half of the fifth century BCE we find:

> If another party will contest with Jehopedeni (the buyer) [or with his son after him], he (the seller) will clear (the claim and) restore (the slave) to Jehopedeni.[12]

"Defension" clauses or stipulations similar to this one have been found in Aramaic real estate documents from Egypt

---

7. Becking, "Two Neo-Assyrian Documents from Gezer."

8. Examples are cited in Greengus, "The Selling of Slaves," 4 nn. 9–10. A comprehensive list of Neo-Assyrian documents (112 examples!) containing such clauses and their archaeological find-spots appears in Radner, *Die Neuassyrischen Privaturkunden*, 174–88. She also notes contracts, which add exclusions for madness (?)—cf. *CAD* Š/2, 266 sub *šēhu*—blindness, and another defect, *šibirru*, as yet not satisfactorily interpreted.

9. Gulak, *Legal Documents in the Talmud*, 130 maintains that Roman law would likewise not have considered theft (and gambling) as rendering the sale invalid, unless the sale document specifically asserted that a slave was free from such defects.

10. This document, Postgate, *Fifty Neo-Assyrian Documents*, no. 13, is discussed by Postgate, ibid., 26; and Greengus," The Selling of Slaves," 5 n. 12. Radner, *Die neuassyrische Privaturkunden*, 168, discusses their joint liability and on 175 notes that this guarantee was intended only to cover the slave's past conduct up to the time of sale.

11. Radner, ibid., 179–80, notes the presence of guarantees for "madness" in twelve documents. These guarantees were valid for one month.

12. Gropp, "The Samaria Papyri," 63 no. 3:5–6. Cf. also Cross, "Samaria Papyrus 1."

during the Persian period and in a Syriac slave sale from Dura–Europus from Roman times. The same verb "clear" (*mrq*) used in the example above also appears frequently in defension clauses in Late Babylonian slave sale documents of the Persian period; and it is likewise found, alongside of synonymous verbs, in a defension formula preserved in the Babylonian Talmud (*b. B. Metz.* 15a), where in a discussion about improved property, Raba states: "You know, (it is for this reason) the seller writes for the buyer: 'I will arise and will smoothe, cleanse, and clear these purchases . . ."[13]

Rabbi Judah's formulary also mentions markings upon the slave's body that are associated with another owner. Slave marking in the form of a style of hairdo are mentioned in the Old Babylonian laws together with prohibitions against helping slaves remove them without their owner's permission.[14] Slave marks in the form of brandings or tattoos are attested in Neo-Assyrian and Neo-Babylonian sources.[15] In the fourth century BCE, we have a Jewish slave sale document from Samaria that mentions a slave being free of blemishes and having no slave mark upon her.[16]

Despite there being a biblical law that forbids tattooing in Lev 19:28, the ear of the permanent slave is required to be marked in Exod 21:5–6 and Deut 15:12–18 (discussed in sec. 2.1). A more general acceptance of the custom of branding or tattooing slaves during the biblical period is also implicit in the figurative description of Isa 44:5, which states:

> One shall say, "I belong to the Lord," Another shall call (himself) by the name of Jacob. And still another shall write (upon) his hand "belonging to the Lord." And (yet another) identify (himself) by the name of "Israel."[17]

In a somewhat related fashion, the Tosefta (*t. Makk.* 4:15, Zuckermandel) exempts a slave owner from the prohibition against marking or tattooing in Lev 19:28 if he marks his slave in order to keep him from running away: "(An owner) who marks his slave so that he will not run away, is exempt (from the biblical prohibition)."

3.2 RETURN OF LOST OR RUNAWAY SLAVES

The Bible in Deut 23:16–17 states:

> You shall not (imprison and) deliver to his master a slave who seeks escape from his master with you. He shall live with you in your midst, in any place he may choose,

13. For these later documents see Greengus, "Selling of Slaves," 5–6 nn. 13–15.

14. For references see *abbuttu CAD* A/1, 48–50, where we find that the custom of *abbuttu* continued down to Late Babylonian times.

15. Dandamaev, *Slavery in Babylonia*, 229–38; and Reiner, "Runaway—Seize Him." Cf. also *CAD* A/3, 9–11. The Aramaic term *shnitah* is cognate to Akkadian *shindu* (*shimtu*) and is found in the Elephantine papyri, Cowley 28 and Kraeling 5; also a verbal form in Kraeling 8; see Porten and Yardeni, *Textbook of Aramaic Documents,* 48–51, 72–73, 84–85.

16. Samaria Papyrus 2:2 states: "[a female slave of his], without blem[ish, upon whom is no] tattoo/mark." This document is published in Cross, "Report on the Samaria Papyri."

17. Cf. the discussion in Dandamaev, *Slavery in Babylonia,* 229 n. 205; he finds a context for Isa 44:5 in the markings appearing on the hands of slaves described in the Elephantine papyri, Cowley 28 and Kraeling 5 cited above. The sense of the passage in Isa 44:5 is recognized also in Bekhor Shor's comment on Lev 19:28, where he says: "it (tattooing) is a custom of idolatry, as they (idolaters) often inscribe the name of (their) idolatrous (god) on their skin." See further Milgrom, *Leviticus,* 1694–95.

among any community [lit. of your gates], wherever he pleases; you must not mistreat him.

While the Bible requires a finder to return stray animals and lost articles belonging to others (sec. 5.9), here, exceptionally, the law advocates allowing the slave to remain a runaway, despite the resulting property loss to his owner. At the same time, the person observing this law is not enriched, because the fugitive slave is left to live on his own as a free person. There is also no mention of penalty. The reason behind this law is not stated; nor does the Bible anywhere state its intention to abolish the institution of chattel slavery, which, as we know, continued to be practiced among the Israelites. We may also wonder about the identity of the parties, both master and slave: were they fellow Israelites or foreigners?

Most interpreters—ancient and modern—have taken this law as referring to a non-Israelite chattel slave who flees from a foreign land into Israelite territory. This reading, as we shall presently see, is supported by the fact that provisions on extradition and return of fugitives, whether free persons or slaves, are well-attested obligations in ancient Near Eastern treaties. In ancient diplomatic relations, there was the expectation that runaways should be taken captive and held for return to their owners. But the biblical law removes from the individual citizen the moral duty to actively assist the king or ruler in implementing his treaty obligations dealing with fugitives. According to Deut 23:16–17, no effort should be made either to conceal the fugitive or to hold him; and there is, likewise, no duty to facilitate the owner's recovery of the runaway by bringing his whereabouts to the attention of the

authorities. This law therefore tells Israelites to do nothing: neither to the slave nor to assist his master in recovering his fugitive slave. This reading, assuming a fugitive from a foreign land, is probably the most likely interpretation. However, the biblical text is brief; so other interpretations cannot be ruled out. The law could be a response to other, unstated assumptions, e.g., a slave running away from an overly cruel local master. The biblical law might even reflect a populist attitude of sympathy to the condition of chattel slaves; this would be especially likely if the fugitive was in fact a native Israelite who was sold into foreign bondage. We have already seen in previous discussions (in secs. 2.1 and 2.5.2) a sympathetic concern for native debt slaves, who were sold into foreign lands; we could view the law in Deut 23:16–17 very differently if, indeed, it related to Israelite slaves who were sold into foreign bondage.

A second biblical argument against handing over a runaway is preserved in a variant Greek version of Prov 30:10 found in the Septuagint, which declares: "Do not deliver a domestic [i.e., a slave] into the hands of a master lest he curse you and you vanish."[18] The Hebrew text of Prov 30:10 states: "Do not slander a slave to his master, lest he curse you and you be (found) guilty." The idea here seems to be that the apprehended runaway slave will pronounce an angry curse, against his captor or "betrayer." Moreover, this curse

18. The Syriac version follows the Greek and reads: "Do not hand over a slave to his master, lest he curse you and you be condemned." The Greek in this verse (and elsewhere in Proverbs as well as in other places) translates "slave" with Greek term for "household slave, domestic"; but this nuance is not necessarily present in the Hebrew text, which uses the more general Hebrew term *'ebed*.

in some sense would be both justified and dangerous, presumably, because God, in whose name the curse would be invoked, will have greater sympathy for the slave than for his captor or "betrayer." The slave's curse, supported by a sympathetic God, would come true.

We get a glimpse of a very different policy of dealing with runaways who crossed the border in the story dealing with Shimei son of Gerah; Solomon had received a warning about Shimei from his father David. While on his deathbed, David told Solomon (1 Kgs 2:9):

> And now do not leave him unpunished; for you are a wise man and you will know what to do with him and you will and send his gray hair down to Sheol with blood.

Solomon had no legal reason to kill Shimei so he restricted his freedom, saying (1 Kgs 2:36–40):

> "Build yourself a house in Jerusalem and stay there—do not ever go out from there anywhere else. On the very day that you go out and cross the Wadi Kidron, you can be sure that you will die; your blood shall be on your own head" . . . Three years later, two slaves of Shimei ran away to King Achish son of Maacah of Gath. Shimei was told, "Your slaves are in Gath." Shimei thereupon saddled his ass and went to Achish in Gath to claim his slaves; and Shimei returned from Gath with his slaves. (NJPS)

The circumstances surrounding the recovery of Shimei's runaway slaves fits in well with the diplomatic relationship between Solomon and his neighbor Achish. Their cooperative diplomatic relationship was a continuation of the political alliance previously existing between Achish and Solomon's father David.[19] Cooperation on returning runaway slaves would be an expected feature of such political alliances; and one can thereby explain why Achish held Shimei's runaways in custody and then sent notification to some unnamed official in Solomon's palace who then in turn must have informed Shimei.[20] Shimei's absence from the city, in violation of his confinement agreement, provided grounds for Solomon to have Shimei executed (2 Kgs 2:41–46). Yet Shimei probably assumed that he had both customary right and permission to recover his property.

The rabbis interpreted Deut 23:16–17 in a narrow fashion; and did not take it as the basis of a general condemnation of chattel slavery. This is illustrated by a story told in the Talmud (b. Git. 45a):

> A slave of Rabbi Hisda's escaped to the Cutheans. He sent word to them that they should return him. They quoted to him in return the verse, "Thou shalt not deliver a slave unto his master . . ." He sent to them to say: "That refers to a slave who escapes from abroad to Eretz Israel, as explained by Rabbi Ahi son of Rabbi Josiah." Why did he quote to them the interpretation of Rabbi Ahi son of Rabbi Josiah? Because it accords more with the literal meaning of the verse.

19. See 1 Sam 27:1–6; 28:1–2; 29:8–9.

20. Cf. Tigay, *Deuteronomy*, 387 n. 57. Since the palace was the likely conduit of notification, Shimei may have erroneously assumed that King Solomon had given his implicit approval for Shimei to leave the city in order to recover his property. This was a fatal mistake.

This episode took place in Babylonia; and Rabbi Hisda felt that he was justified in seeking recovery of his runaway slave. The point of the story is that even the Samaritans—called by the Rabbis in a pejorative manner "Cutheans"—who adhered to the literal text of Scripture, were persuaded that Rabbi Hisda's narrow interpretation of the Deut 23:16–17 was the correct one. This law therefore held no currency for slaves and their owners living outside of the land of Israel.

When we look at the ancient Near Eastern laws, we consistently find an obligation to return slaves to their owners, whether near or far. This expectation appears in many of our law collections. In Urnamma Laws §17 we read:

> [If a male or] female slave . . .] has gone beyond the boundary of his city (and) a man returned him, the owner of the slave shall pay [. . .] shekel(s) silver to the man who returned him.

Harboring a runaway is the focus of Lipit-Ishtar Laws §§12–13:

> If a female (or) male slave of a man flees inside of a city (and) he has proven that he or she has dwelt in another man's house for one month, he (that man) must give (as penalty) one (additional) slave for the slave (he kept). If he has no slave (to give) then he shall pay 15 shekels of silver.

Hammurapi Laws §16 deals with runaway slaves belonging to the palace or to royal clients. Their ownership are vigorously protected; there is a duty to restore them without expectation of reward:[21]

If a man has confined in his house a missing male or female slave of the palace or of a commoner (i.e., a royal client)[22] and has not brought (him or her) out at the herald's call, that house owner shall be killed.

Hammurapi Laws contain further cases dealing with lost or fugitive slaves; §§17–20 also deal severely with those who clandestinely held slaves belonging to other citizens:

> If a man captured a missing male or female slave in the open country and has conducted him back to his owner, the owner of the slave will pay him two shekels silver. If that slave will not name his owner, he shall conduct him to the palace; his background shall be determined and they shall return him to his owner. If (on the other hand) he has held that slave in his own house, after the slave has been seized in his hands, that man will be killed. If the slave has escaped from the hand of the person seizing him, that man shall swear an oath by a god to the owner of the slave and he will be free of responsibility.

The final section of Hammurapi §§17–20, dealing with a slave who escaped after being seized, is instructive on the policy found in Deut 23:16–17. In Hammurapi's

21. A fragmentary passage in §15 of the Middle Assyrian Palace Decrees likewise requires finders of slaves to report them to the king; nothing more is preserved. Cf. Roth, *Law Collections,* 203.

22. The appropriate translation of these individuals, who are called *mushkēnu* in Old Babylonian times, has been much discussed and debated. They were freemen but lower in social class to the *awīlu*—usually simply translated as "man," who is the typical subject of most laws. They could own slaves. Some have suggested translations like "serf, fiefholder, commoner, *Bürger*." The commoners are linked with the king and with the needs of the palace in the Hammurapi Laws, in the Eshnunna Laws, and in documents of the period. For discussion, see Stol, "Muškēnu"; and Greengus, "Legal and Social Institutions," 476.

laws, the person who tried to hold him is held responsible if he captures and does not return the runaway. However he is not blamed or punished if the slave subsequently escaped. Deuteronomy goes a step further and avoids any interaction between the person and fugitive. There can be no legal responsibility since there was no apprehension. There is no blame or punishment for inaction and therefore no oath was necessary.

The Hittite laws likewise seem not to impose a duty upon a third party to apprehend a runaway slave; but there is provision for reward to one who seized the runaway held him for his owner. Thus in Hittite Laws §22 we read:

> If a male slave runs away and someone brings him back, if he captures him nearby, he shall give him (i.e., the finder) [a pair of] shoes. If (he captures him) on the near side of the river, he shall pay 2 shekels silver; if on the far side, he shall pay him 3 shekels silver.

In this law, the runaway was apprehended close to home. Hittite Laws §23 considers a situation where the slave was taken in a neighboring country; it then depends upon the nature of the diplomatic relations maintained it and the Hittite kingdom:

> If a male slave runs away and goes to the land of Luwiya, (his owner) shall pay 6 shekels of silver to whomever brings him back. If a male slave runs away and goes into an enemy country, whoever brings him back shall keep him for himself.

Luwiya, a friendly neighbor, was situated outside of the Hittite lands. The bounty paid to the finder is thus increased over that paid within the homeland. By contrast, the runaway slave who reached enemy territory was, in effect, lost to his owner. One may assume that the original owner would have been able to keep his runaway slave had he himself been able to enter the enemy territory and apprehend him. We are also not given details about how the finder established his formal legal title to the runaway or how his right would be defended against that of the first owner.

Hittite Laws §24 deals with a finder who apprehended a runaway but kept him in his own possession; the finder was obligated to pay for his use of another person's slave:

> If a male or female slave runs away, he/she at whose hearth his/her owner finds him/her shall pay one month's wages: 12 shekels silver for a man, 6 shekels silver for a woman. (Later text: shall pay one year's wages: 2 1/2 minas (=100 shekels) of silver for a man, 50 shekels of silver for a woman.)

It is possible that there is no conflict between the earlier and later disposition; the later text may simply be offering a more extended formulation, indicating that compensation was owed for every month during which the slave was held and used by his captor.[23]

Earlier, in connection with Shimei and his slaves, I referred to the fact that provisions requiring extradition of fugitives frequently occur in ancient Near Eastern treaties—and there are many that have been found. A few examples will suffice for illustration. An Old Babylonian peace treaty c. 1800 BCE, from the area of Eshnunna contains a provision on the

23. Hoffner, "On Homicide in Hittite Law," 306 n. 17.

return of fugitive slaves who had fled into the neighboring territory before the war, i.e., before the current treaty of peace had been signed:

> The slave of a man who before the war (had fled) and whom after "the ass was slaughtered" (i.e., the ritual sacrifice marking the formal inauguration of the current peace treaty) they are (still) holding (in their possession)—(that slave) shall return (home to his owner).[24]

Another example of a cooperative extradition provision is found in a treaty from c. 1500 BCE from northern Syria, between the kings of Alalakh and Tunip:

> If a runaway, male (or) female slaves of my country, flees to your country, if you cannot seize and return him (but) someone (else) can seize him and bring him to you, [you should hold him] in your prison. When his owner comes you shall give (him) back to [that owner.] If he (the slave) is not staying (with you), you should provide an escort and in whatever city he stays, let him (the owner) seize him (there).[25]

The ancient treaties deal with many types of fugitives in addition to chattel slaves; these include rebels, criminals, captives taken as booty in war and now fled, deserters, and free subjects who left to avoid taxes or obligations. Extradition was a

fundamental feature of foreign relations in antiquity just as it still is in many modern diplomatic treaties.[26]

The laws of Deut 23:16–17 thus represent a radical departure from ancient Near Eastern conventions. If it does involve foreign fugitives, then it counsels taking no action; but, at the same time, Deuteronomy does not enjoin performing any obstructive act, like hiding a fugitive or helping him to escape. Such action of course might be considered as a criminal act and could be punished by the authorities or at the very least might require a "finder" who apprehended but did not return a runaway to pay compensation, as in Hittite Laws §24. From Hittite Laws §23, we see that in the absence of treaties, there was no real expectation on the part of an owner that he would recover his slave who fled to a foreign land. The biblical law may perhaps be viewed as a form of "quiet protest," expressing sympathy to fugitive slaves by taking no overt steps to assist in their recapture. This was about as much as a person could legally do in those ancient times. Deuteronomy 23:16–17 is therefore stated purely as a moral injunction, without adding any earthly punishment to be imposed upon those who did not heed but chose to continue with customary norms of apprehension and return of runaways with the expectation of reward from the owner.

24. Greengus, *Studies in Ishchali Documents,* 74–77, no. 326:34–36, with an improved reading as given here.

25. Wiseman, *Alalakh Tablets,* 26–29, no. 2:22–27; also translated in *ANET,* 531.

26. For Hittite and Akkadian language examples cf. the many references in Beckman, *Hittite Diplomatic Texts,* 206 Index sub "fugitives." Cf. also a provision in the Aramaic Sefire treaty (iii, 20) from the eighth century BCE translated in *ANET,* 661. For discussion of originally free fugitives and refugees, see Altman, "Basic Concepts in the Law of People Seeking Refuge."

4

Laws Relating to Personal Injury and Homicide

THE BIBLICAL LAWS ON injury and homicide are not laid out in one place; they are, rather, to be found scattered in connection with cases involving debt slaves, fatal attack by domestic beasts, theft, fights and brawls, and killing of parents by children. Rabbinic sources add additional cases not found in the Bible: injury to chattel slaves belonging to others, acts causing another person public embarrassment. I will take up the cases belonging to this broad category of "Personal Injury and Homicide" in their individual sub-groups.

4.1 MISTREATMENT OF DEBT SLAVES AND HOSTAGES

The Bible recognized that debtors being held as slaves could at times be subject to mistreatment. Thus Lev 25:39, in connection with the debt slave (cited earlier in sec. 2.4), enjoins creditors who held debt slaves: "do not subject him to the treatment of a (chattel) slave. He shall remain with you like a hired laborer or sojourner." This caution is repeated several times more in this chapter: e.g., in Lev 25:43: "Do not govern him with undue harshness him ruthlessly and you shall fear your God."[1]

The Bible offers two laws where a slave owner struck his slave. In Exod 21:20–21 the master beat his slave to the point of death or near death. If the slave died immediately afterwards, it is considered to have been an act of homicide and the owner must answer to the charge. If the slave lingered for a day or two and then died, the death is not considered to be homicide; because an owner has a right to beat his slave who, in the ancient view, is property. In Exod 21:26–27, a slave owner struck his slave and caused him to lose an eye or tooth; in compensation, the slave is to be set free by the master who caused this injury. The laws are as follows:

> Exod 21:20–21—If a man strikes his male slave—or female slave—with a rod, and he (the slave) dies under (the blows) of his hand, then he must be avenged. But if he survives [lit. stands] a day or two, he is not to be avenged, since he is his (i.e., the master's) money.[2]

> Exod 21:26–27—If a man strikes the eye of his male slave—or female slave—and destroys it, he shall let him go free in compensation for (destroying) his eye. If he

---

1. Also in Lev 25:43 and 25:53 (sec. 2.5.2).

2. My translation "his (i.e., master's) money" follows the literal Hebrew, which is adopted by the LXX and KJV. Some modern translations rephrase as "his property."

knocks out the tooth of his male slave—or female slave—he shall let him go free in compensation for (loss of) his tooth.

There has been discussion, going back to rabbinic times, concerning the character of the slaves in these passages: are they chattel slaves—about whom (as shown in sec. 3) hardly any laws relating to them are stated in Scripture—or are they Hebrew debt slaves, who are the subject of debt-slave laws as in Exod 21:2–11 (sec. 2.1) and elsewhere? In Exod 21:20–21, the phrase "he must be avenged" suggests that the beaten slave has Israelite relatives who could demand justice on his behalf. On the other hand, the phrase "he is his (i.e., the master's) money" speaks of ownership and well as control, which would be especially true for chattel slaves. This very question of the slave's identity is repeatedly posed in the Mekhilta on these verses; and the rabbis there clearly prefer to interpret these verses as referring to chattel slaves.[3] This interpretation is invariably upheld in rabbinic tradition; but Ibn Ezra, in his (shorter) commentary to Exod 21:20 and 21:26 notes that the "deniers," i.e., the Karaites, maintain that these laws actually refer to Hebrew debt slaves. However, says Ibn Ezra, if one must decide between these two opinions, one must clearly yield to the "authority" of rabbinic tradition. Ibn Ezra's statements suggest that, in his mind, the truth of this question was not really certain at all; but he felt obliged to respect and affirm rab-

binic tradition, even if that interpretation were not persuasive to an unbiased reading of the text. A similar sentiment and constraint is stated by Joseph Ibn Kaspi (c. 1300 CE), who in connection with Exod 21:20, writes:

> Let it (i.e., the status of the slave) be (as) deliberated in the Talmud (i.e., a chattel slave); because for this (passage) and the one later, our intention must suffice for us (alone). If I were permitted, I would explain it. Therefore I leave (this matter) entirely (without comment).[4]

Modern scholars are, of course, less intimidated; and some of them support the Karaite understanding that our laws are in fact dealing with Israelite debt slaves; but we are far from any consensus on this question.[5]

In Exod 21:26–27, I find it easiest to imagine that an injured debt slave rather than a chattel slave is being set free. The debt slave is, after all, a freeman; and his release would be the equivalent having his debt cancelled, as in Hammurapi Laws §116 (see presently below). But, if as the rabbis interpret, the biblical slave in question is a chattel slave, then he (or she) is being most exceptionally compensated, being suddenly catapulted from a permanent servile status into the legal position of a free person. For as we shall see below (sec. 4.2), in connection with injuries inflicted upon chattel slaves belonging to another owner, the laws, both Near Eastern and rabbinic, are content with the remedy that only compensation be given to the owner of that slave.

3. *Mekhilta Mishpatim* 7, 9 on these verses. Cf. also *t. Qidd.* 1:6, Lieberman, where it states that a "a (Canaanite) slave goes free when (losing) vital parts (of his body through his master's actions.) This understanding is more fully stated in *b. Qidd.* 24a.

4. Ibn Kaspi 2:212 This passage is partly cited by Lockshin, *Rashbam on Exodus*, 239 n. 59.

5. See Chirichigno, *Debt Slavery in Israel,* 148–85; Jackson, *Wisdom Laws,* 240–54.

An unexpected curiosity of rabbinic exegesis is that because of their position that Exod 21:20–21, 26–27 refer to chattel slaves, the remedies they provide for chattel slaves will not be made available for the Hebrew debt slaves, who are clearly identified as the subject of Exod 21:1–11. For the rabbis, non-fatal injuries to one's own Hebrew (debt) slave must be compensated for in the same way as an injury to a free Hebrew; moreover, if one's Hebrew (debt) slave were injured by another person, the owner of that Hebrew slave would be entitled to compensation for the lost labor of his Hebrew slave. However, in either instance, a Hebrew (debt) slave would not be set free, even for loss of his eye or tooth; he would be required to complete his full term of service even in the house of the very creditor who abused him![6] This seems quite unjust; and some modern scholars, therefore, want to argue that the intent of the biblical passages is to embrace injuries to any and all slaves—whether debt slave or chattel. But such "global" intent, while laudable social policy, is not clearly evident in the ancient biblical text. One would have expected more explicit language if this were indeed intended.

In the ancient Near Eastern law collections, one finds many laws expressing concern about injuries sustained by debt hostages. The taking of debt hostages was a recognized legal right in the ancient world, as well as in ancient Israel (sec. 2.1)

that allowed a creditor to seize slaves or family members of the debtor in order to coerce repayment of their debt. If the debtor did not pay, then the debt hostage would remain in the possession of the creditor and must labor to pay off the debt and, possibly, its interest, too, if interest was being charged and added to the unpaid principal. Eshnunna Laws §§22–24 are cases where a person, who was not certified as a *bona fide* creditor, nevertheless seized another person's slave or family member as a debt hostage and also caused their death through mistreatment. The seizer is subject to the death penalty if he harmed free individuals; but for harming slaves belonging to another he owed only compensation: two slaves for each one that he killed:

> §22 If a man has no claim upon another man and has seized the female slave of that man as a debt hostage, the owner of the female slave shall swear an oath by a god (asserting) "You have no claim upon me" and (the person seizing) shall weigh out silver as much as is the [value] of the female slave.
>
> §23 If a man has no claim upon another man but has seized as a debt hostage the female slave of that man (and) has confined the seized debt hostage in his house and caused (her) death, unto the owner of the female slave he will replace (with) two female slaves.
>
> §24 If a man has no claim upon him but has seized as a debt hostage the wife of a commoner (i.e., royal client) or son of a commoner (and) has confined the seized debt hostage in his house and caused (his/her) death, it is a capital case; the hostage seizer shall die.

6. Cf. Rashi to *b, Qidd.* 16a. These principles are summarized by Maimonides, *Mishnah Torah, Hilkhot Hovel u Maziq* 4:10, 13. Maimonides here summarizes in a more orderly fashion, statements of rabbinic discussion preserved in *m. B. Qam.* 8:3, 5; *b. Gitt.* 12b; *b. B.Qam.* 86a; *b. Qidd.* 24a. He adds further, limiting factors in *Mishnah Torah, Hilkhot Avadim* 5:5.

Hammurapi Laws §§114–116 begins with the same issue of unjustified seizure but adds the important case where a claim existed and seizure was justified, but the debt hostages died while in custody of the seizer:

> §114 If a man has no claim for grain or silver upon another man but has seized a debt hostage from him, he shall weigh out one third mina silver for each seized debt hostage.

> §115 If a man has a claim for grain or silver upon another man and has seized a debt hostage from him and the debt hostage has died a natural death [lit. because of her fate] in the house of the (lit. her) hostage seizer, that case has no (basis for) complaint.

> §116 If a debt hostage in the house of the one who seized her has died from beating or from (other) mistreatment, the owner of the debt hostage shall convict his creditor [lit. trader/merchant] and if (the debt hostage was) a (free) man's son, they shall kill his son; if the slave of the man, he shall weigh out one third mina silver; and (in all cases) he will forfeit whatever he lent (to the debtor).

Hammurapi Laws §114 is a case similar to Eshnunna Laws §22; in both cases, a debt hostage was taken without legal grounds but not injured; compensation must nevertheless be paid. Hammurapi Laws §§115–116 deal with legally taken debt hostages who died; if, as stated in §115, the hostage dies from natural causes, there is no blame. However, in §116—just as in Eshnunna Laws §§23–24 and in Exod 20:20–21—if the hostage died from his beating; this would be considered a capital crime if the victim was a free individual. One can also infer, from what is stated in Exod 21:21, that it was considered reasonable for a master to beat his debt slave, "since he is his money." Holding the master liable for capital crime, however, would serve as a caution against his egregious mistreatment of a free person taken as a debt hostage or slave. On the other hand, as in Eshnunna Laws §23, the master's liability for causing the death of a chattel slave whom he held as a debt hostage was settled by compensation. One finds no parallel to the biblical concept of the injured person surviving for one or two days after his severe beating. But such calculations may have anciently figured into how judges determined the legal cause of death and its possible relationship to prior corporal punishment.

In Middle Assyrian Laws §A 44, we read about the right to apply physical chastisement to a free person who was held as a debt slave; this law focuses on the transition in status from pledge or hostage to debt slave:

> If an Assyrian man or if an Assyrian woman—who was dwelling in the house of another man (i.e., a creditor) as a pledge for (an debt equal to) his full purchase price (i.e., were he to be sold as a slave)— was (now) taken over for that full amount, he (i.e., the creditor) may whip, pluck hair, mutilate or pierce his (i.e., the debt slave's) ears.

It thus appears that more gentle treatment was initially warranted for persons in the status of debt hostage, during the time while the creditor was waiting for his payment and there was still expectation that the debt could be paid. However, if the debt could not be paid, then the creditor as here assumed full control of the hostage, who would now remain with him as a debt slave to work off the debt. The point of mentioning "full purchase price" is to simplify the case and the progress of the creditor's execution. In §A 44 the value of the debt and that of the pledge were balanced. However, from contracts of the period we learn that if the value of the pledge exceeded the value of the debt, then the pledged item, whether person or field, would first have to be valued and then sold to a third party. Any amount in excess of the debt would go to the debtor, not the creditor.[7] In Middle Assyrian Laws §A 48 (sec. 2.1) we also saw that a period of time would be given to the debtor before execution. The chastisements permitted in A 44 are, to be sure, harsh to modern sensibilities; but they were no more severe in character than the treatment that Middle Assyrian Laws §A 59 allowed a husband to use against his wife:

> In addition to (any of) the punishments for [a man's wife] that are [written] in the tablet (of laws), a man may [whip] his wife, pluck her hair, mutilate or st[rike] her e[ars]; there is no penalty (for these actions).

It seems therefore that the purpose of both laws, §§44 and 59, was to establish some—at least in their view, justifiable—limits on mistreatment of originally free individuals who fell under the legal authority of a husband or a creditor.

Because of the extensive similarities, I think it is more than likely that the biblical laws, like those of the ancient Near Eastern collections, deal with the treatment of free citizens who, because family debts were not paid, became debt slaves. The biblical laws of Exod 21:20–21, 26–27 look to a point in time after debt hostages became full debt slaves. Full debt slaves are in fact also the subjects of Exod 21:1–11 (as in Deut 15:12–18); these have been discussed in sec. 2.1. If debt slaves were not also the subject of Exod 21:20–21, 26–27, then one would have expected some additional qualification in the biblical text since the texts are placed so close together. Otherwise, apart from the doubtful cases of Exod 21:20–21, 26–27, either in the Bible or in the ancient Near East, one finds no laws governing the treatment of one's own chattel slaves! It was apparently assumed that the master owned these outright; and that he could treat them as he wished, moderated by his economic interest in not losing their value.[8] But the labor of debt slaves, on the other hand, did not permanently belong to the creditor. Debt slaves needed protection because, as originally free persons, they were eligible to be redeemed from slavery by their families. This is also why, as we have already seen, there were attempts to set some time limit on the servitude of debt slaves. Redemption was a remedy that was available to debt slaves; it is widely attested in ancient Near Eastern practice; and, in the Bible, this very point is made in Lev 25:47–49, which was presented above in sec. 2.5.2.[9]

8. The *Theodosian Code* 9.12.2 (decree dated to 329 CE) makes this same point concerning a master's self-interest with respect to his own chattel slaves.

9. For ancient Near Eastern examples of redemption over the centuries, see *CAD* I/J, 171–73; for some Neo-Assyrian examples, see Radner, "The Neo-Assyrian Period," 280–84.

7. Abraham, "The Middle Assyrian Period," 185; the documents giving evidence to this practice are *KAJ* 150 and 168; the relevant passages are cited in *CAD* A/2, 158–59.

All of these measures became less important over time. Historical changes in the condition of debt slaves may explain why the rabbis, in their interpretation of Exod 21:20–21, 26–27, came to view these biblical laws as applying to chattel slaves. Beginning in the seventh century BCE we find widespread movement to curtail the practice of debt slavery, which, because it involved potential enslavement of free citizens, was increasingly recognized as injurious to the health of a society and its people. The measures taken by Nehemiah (c. 450 BCE) (cited in sec. 2.2) are paralleled by the reforms of Solon in Athens. Solon (c. 600 BCE), as reported by Aristotle, not only cancelled public and private debts—an act of release—but also enacted a law that prohibited using persons as security for any future loans.[10] Scholars have also noted the near-disappearance of loans secured by persons in Neo-Babylonian and Persian times.[11] This process of change is also visible in Rome, when after the enactment of the Poetilian law (c.326 BCE), a defaulting debtor could no longer be shackled in imprisonment nor sold into slavery, but was merely obliged to work off the amount of his debt.[12] What we see, therefore, is a widespread, general movement in the Near East and Mediterranean lands to transform the older institution of debt slavery into a form of indenture, requiring labor to pay off the obligation; the debtor now remained a free person and would not be sold as a slave. This is perhaps the status that Lev 25:39–40 had in mind when it stated:

> If your fellow citizen [lit. brother] living with you (i.e., in your community) becomes impoverished (through debt) and sells himself to you, do not use like a (chattel) slave. He shall stay with you as (i.e., in the condition of) a hired or bound laborer; he shall serve with you only until the jubilee year.

The date of composition for Leviticus is unknown; but a majority of scholars see it as having emerged in its present form during the Persian Period.[13] This statement in Leviticus may signal the new attitude of the times.[14]

There were also new measures to ameliorate the condition of chattel slaves. In Athenian law, it was declared an act of homicide for an owner to kill his slave, even one who had confessed to murder.[15] The emperor Hadrian (d. 138 CE) forbade masters to kill their slaves who were guilty of a crime without court permission; and his son, the Roman emperor Antoninus Pius (d. 161 CE) allowed cruelly treated slaves to seek sanctuary and directed magistrates to investigate. The courts could force the master to sell his slave with a ban to prevent him from ever being returned to his cruel owner.[16] The rabbis, therefore, writing during imperial Roman times, confronted a world economy which had generally abandoned

10. Aristotle, *Athenian Constitution* 6.1.

11. Dandamaev, *Slavery in Babylonia,*179–80.

12. Thomas, *Textbook of Roman Law,* 79, citing among others, *Livy* 8.28. See also Gaius, *Inst.* 3.189; Aulus Gellius, *Attic Nights* 20.1.46–52.

13. Westbrook, "Conclusions," 336, comments on Lev 25:39–40 and its conceptual link with the *lex Poetelia.*

14. According to Milgrom, *Leviticus,* 1694, 2214–15, Leviticus 25 implies that a real change in the treatment of debt slaves by fellow Israelites had actually taken place.

15. Todd, *The Shape of Athenian Law,*190; he cites *Antiphon* 5.47–48 and 6.4. Antiphon wrote c. 425 BCE.

16. Thomas, *Textbook of Roman Law,* 394–95, citing Gaius, *Inst.* 1.53 and other sources.

the practices of debt slavery that we find in the ancient Near Eastern laws and that had existed earlier in Greece and Rome. There was thus no basis for them to assign Exod 21:20–21, 26–27 to debt slavery; they had no knowledge of these more ancient traditions. Therefore they could only relate these passages to chattel slavery and saw them as a parallel—and a more generous one at that—to Roman reforms against mistreatment of chattel slaves. Moreover, based upon Lev 25:39–40 and, in view of what was Roman law during their time, they easily envisioned the condition of the Hebrew slave as indenture; and thus, predictably, re-interpreted the debt slave passages in Exod 21:20–21 and Deut 15:12–18 as mandating nothing more than indenture. By their time, the former conditions and abuses of debt slavery had fortunately vanished from memory.

4.2 INJURIES TO CHATTEL SLAVES

Rabbinic sources include laws dealing with injuries to chattel slaves belonging to others; this situation is not covered in the Bible but it would have been a logical addition to laws dealing with injuries inflicted upon one's own slaves. The penalty is always compensation, which is paid to the owner of the slave. The Mishnah, *m. B. Qam.* 8:3 states:

> If one injures a Canaanite (i.e., chattel) slave belonging to others, he (the party causing the injury) is liable for all (categories of compensation, i.e., damage, physical pain, medical care, loss of work time, and humiliation.) Rabbi Judah says: there is no payment for humiliation made to slaves.

A more harsh response is described the Talmud in *b. Git.* 12b:

> Come and hear: R. Johanan says that if a man cuts off the hand of another man's slave, he must make good to his master his loss of work time and the cost of his medical attention, and the slave will (henceforth) live on charity.

In the view of Rabbi Johanan, compensation, as always, goes to the master; but a master also has the legal right to abandon his incapacitated slave to public charity.

The remedy of giving compensation for injury is an ancient one and is seen in Hammurapi Laws §199:

> If he (a free citizen) blinds the eye of another man's slave or has broken a bone of another man's slave, he shall pay one-half of his value.

The Babylonian law helps us understand the position taken by Rabbi Johanan; a serious, incapacitating injury will significantly reduce the market value of a slave, by impairing his ability to work.

A fixed rate of compensation appears in the Hittite Laws §8, which deals with injuring to a slave belonging to another person:

> If anyone blinds a male or female slave or knocks out his tooth, he shall pay 10 shekels of silver; he shall look to his house for it.[17] (Later version) If anyone blinds a male slave in a quarrel, he shall pay 20 shekels silver. If it is an accident,[18] he shall pay 10 shekels of silver.

17. This phrase is understood as requiring the striker to pledge his property as security for this obligation. See Hoffner, *Laws of the Hittites*, 168–69.

18. The meaning of this phrase is discussed in ibid., 170; a variant form "his hand sins" occurs in

The juxtaposition of eye and tooth in the earlier version of Hittite Laws §8 is reminiscent of Exod 21:26–27. One can readily understand the impact of partial blindness on a person's ability to work; but the loss of a tooth seems less serious. The Talmud in *b. Qidd.* 24a brings a Tannaitic ruling on this question citing a *baraita*, which may supply an answer, explaining these as representing injuries to any part of the body, which cannot regenerate: "A Tanna taught: (The slave) goes out [free] through [the loss of] his eye, tooth, and projecting limbs, which do not return." Although, according to the interpretation of the rabbis, this particular ruling, concerns chattel slaves who are injured by their own master rather than by outsiders, the concern over permanent loss seems to be the operative principle. The Hittite Laws, apparently sharing this view about permanent loss, go on to include injuries to a slave's arm, leg, ear or nose. The Hittite Laws, however, do not reckon every such loss as equal in gravity; compensation will therefore accordingly vary, depending upon the injury; we see this in Hittite Laws §§12, 14, and 16:

> §12 If anyone breaks a male or female slave's arm or leg, he shall pay 10 shekels (variant text: 6 [shekels]) of silver; he shall look to his house for it. (Later Version) If anyone breaks a slave's arm or leg, if he is disabled (?), he shall pay 10 shekels silver. But if he is not disabled (?), he shall pay him 5 shekels of silver.

> §14 If anyone bites off the nose of a male or female slave, he shall pay 3

shekels of silver, and he shall look to his house for it.[19]

> §16 If anyone tears off the ear of a male or female slave, he shall pay him 3 shekels of silver. (Later version) If anyone tears off the ear of a male or female slave, he shall pay him 6 shekels of silver.

Later versions of other Hittite Laws juxtapose injuries to slaves with injuries to free persons within a single law. We will thus look at these paragraphs (§§7–8 and 10) when I discuss injuries to free persons (sec. 4.3). We will also see that injuries to chattel slaves are compensated in lesser amounts than similar injuries to free persons and that doctor's fees were covered.

As mentioned earlier, one finds no law dealing with injury to one's own chattel slave in the extant ancient Near Eastern sources. The rabbis deal with this situation only in part, as stated above (sec. 4.1), in their interpretation of Exod 21:26–27, which they apply to chattel slaves. The rabbinic interpretation, as I have mentioned, is awkward in that a chattel slave was to be freed only in the event of an injury to an eye or tooth or to any part of the body, which cannot regenerate. But in situations of "lesser" non-fatal injuries, the rabbis agree that the master would bear no legal responsibility! This is summarized in *m. B. Qam.* 8:5:

> One who injures a Canaanite (i.e., chattel) slave of his own is not liable for any of these (five categories of compensation that were paid for injuries to free persons).

Hittite Laws §§3–5 discussed below (sec. 4.8) in connection with homicide.

19. A later version of §14 sets payment at 15 minas, which Hoffner, ibid. 27, 178, following others, suggests must almost certainly be a scribal error—perhaps intending 15 shekels.

The five categories—damage done, pain, medical attention, loss of work, humiliation—are more fully discussed below, in my presentation of *m. B. Qam.* 8:1 (sec. 4.3), which deals with injuries to free persons. A similar law removing these benefits from chattel slaves appears in the Tosefta, *t. B. Qam.* 9:21, Lieberman:

> One who injures his own male or female Canaanite (i.e., chattel) slave is free (with respect to compensation) between him and them because any such payment is a fine (and is not applicable to chattel slaves).[20]

4.3 INJURIES TO FREE PERSONS

I have already discussed injuries to originally free debt slaves, which are described in Exod 21:20–21 (sec. 4.2); these verses are preceded by Exod 21:18–19, which opens the topic of injuries with a case involving fully free persons:

> If men quarrel and one strikes his fellow with stone or fist, and he does not die but must lie [lit. fall] in bed, if he then gets up and walks about outdoors upon his staff, the one who struck him shall be free of blame, but he must pay for his inactivity (i.e., loss of work) and have him completely healed (i.e., pay for his medical care).

More permanent injuries are the subject of Lev 24:19–20:

> And a man—if he inflicts a permanent injury upon his neighbor, as he has done so shall it be done to him: broken bone for broken bone, eye for eye, tooth for tooth. Just

> as he inflicted a permanent injury upon the (other) man, so it should be inflicted upon him.

The plain language of this law appears to describe imply a physical retaliation against the perpetrator of a permanent injury. According to this principle, the injured party has the right to subject his assailant to the same injury that he himself has suffered. This right is referred to as "talionic reprisal." According to Josephus, the injured victim in fact had a choice of accepting money in place of exacting talionic retribution:

> He that maimeth a man shall undergo the like, being deprived of the limb whereof he deprived the other, unless indeed the maimed man may be willing to accept money; for the law empowers the victim himself to assess the damage that has befallen him and makes this concession unless he would show himself too severe.[21]

Philo, who likewise understood the law in literal fashion, goes so far as to condemn those who would replace physical retaliation with money or alternative punishments:

> The legislators deserve censure who prescribe for malefactors punishments which do not resemble the crime, such as monetary fines for assaults, disfranchisement for wounding or maiming another, expulsion from the country and perpetual banishment for willful murder or imprisonment for theft . . . Our law exhorts us to equality when it ordains that the penalties inflicted on offenders should correspond to their actions, that their property should suffer

20. This ruling follows a principle declared in *m. Ket.* 3:8 "In situations (where a power) of sale (is present), no fine (can be levied)."

21. Josephus, *Ant.* 4.280, Thackeray.

if the wrongdoing affected their neighbor's property, and their bodies if the offense was a bodily injury, the penalty being determined according to the limb, part or sense affected, while if his malice extended to taking another's life his own life should be forfeit.[22]

However, later rabbinic Jewish interpreters (e.g., *b. B. Qam.* 83b–84b) rejected talion for non-fatal cases and argued against the plain reading of the biblical text, saying that the option of physical retaliation should never be taken literally, nor could such remedies be made available to an injured victim. For these rabbis, only monetary compensation could be allowed in the cases of non-fatal wounding and injury; they thus applied the response that was appropriate to a non-fatal injury in Exod 21:18–19 to the cases of permanent injury and loss of limbs that are presented in Lev 24:19–20. This is the position of the Mishnah, *m. B. Qam.* 8:1:

> If one injures his fellow man, he is liable to him for five categories (of compensation): for the damage (done), for pain, for medical attention, for loss of work, and for humiliation. How (does one calculate) damage? (If for example) he blinded his eye, cut off his hand, broke his leg, they (the judges) evaluate him as if he were a slave being sold in the market and estimate how much he would have been worth (before the injury) and how much he is worth (now). As for pain? (If for example) he wounded him with a (burning) spit or nail and even on just his fingernail, a place that doesn't leave a wound, they (the judges) estimate how much a person like him would require to suffer in this fashion. As

> for healing? (If) he smote him, he must be responsible for his healing; if ulcers developed, if they were the result the blow, he is liable; if not from the blow, he is free from responsibility. As for loss of work? They (the court) evaluate him as if he were the guard of a cucumber field (only) because he (the assailant) has already paid for loss of his hand or foot. As for humiliation? It is all according to the (social status of the) persons causing and suffering humiliation.

The five categories of compensation are the same that I have previously mentioned above (in sec. 4.2) in connection with injuries to a chattel slave belonging to another. The Talmud (*b. B. Qam.* 85a) in reference to payment for pain asks how is the Mishnah's estimate is to be reckoned? They propose that the criterion is a case where a criminal is being punished by the king and ordered to suffer the same injury as in our case but then has the choice of easing the wounding or amputation by being given anesthetic drugs. How much would the criminal pay to avoid such pain?[23]

Post-Talmudic rabbinical authorities, albeit in guarded language, gave voice to their recognition that the plain wording of the biblical texts went against the received teaching of the rabbis, who advocated only compensation for non-fatal injuries. Ibn Ezra, Maimonides, and Abraham, the son of Maimonides acknowledge this in their commentaries.[24]

---

22. Philo, *Spec. Laws* 3.181–82, Colson.

23. Cf. also Maimonides, *Mishnah Torah, Hilkhot Hovel u Maziq* 4:10.

24. Cf. Ibn Ezra on Exod 21:24; Maimonides, *Guide* iii, 41; Abraham son of Maimonides, *Perush Hatorah Lerabenu Avraham,* on Exod 21:21. See further the discussion in Weiss Halivni, *Peshat and Derash,* 85–87, 200 n. 75.

Maimonides in his law code concedes that the rabbinic interpretation rejecting talion is not supported by the biblical text and must therefore be attributed to an ancient oral tradition going back to Moses.[25]

The rabbis may have felt morally justified to reject talionic reprisal, which is a cruel form of justice; and surely a victim was better off with compensation than with revenge. Talionic reprisal, which had once also been practiced in Roman law, had long been replaced by compensation. So the practice was obsolete in the Roman Empire by the time of the rabbis.[26] This obsolescence may have promoted a desire to reinterpret the ancient biblical laws. However, we also know that the practice of talionic justice had a previous history in the ancient Near East and continued to be practiced in tribal Arabia down to the time of Muhammad.[27] The custom of allowing physical reprisal in fact still survives in modern Saudi Arabia, where the ancient customs known from the Quran are still followed.[28] It therefore seems

likely that the practice of talionic reprisal was both known and practiced centuries earlier in biblical times. Moreover, as we shall see below, the formula "eye for eye, tooth for tooth" is repeated twice more in the Pentateuch, in contexts dealing with homicide, where the context and intent to apply corporal punishment are clear.[29] We will, presently, also see how talionic reprisal and compensation were not necessarily mutually exclusive; and that both could coexist within the same legal system as alternative solutions for cases of injury and homicide.

When one looks at the ancient Near Eastern sources, we see the practice of compensation as a well-established remedy for injury. We also see a "catalog" of injuries to specific body parts similar to those of Lev 24:19–20. A sequence of injuries and their "values" is given in the Laws of Urnamma:

§18 [If a man with respect to another man . . .] his [. . .] cuts off his [fo]ot (?) he shall pay 10 shekels silver.

§19 If a man with respect to another man using a club, utterly

25. Maimonides, *Mishnah Torah, Hilkhot Hovel u Maziq* 1:6.

26. Thomas, *Textbook of Roman Law,* 349–50. He notes that earlier, as seen in *XII Tab.* 8.2–4, (cited later in this sec.), a victim suffering maiming injuries was still given a choice between talionic reprisal and accepting compensation.

27. See Schacht,"Kiṣāṣ." He states that the institution was based on the customs of pagan times and confirms that it included talionic retaliation for non-fatal injuries as well as for homicide. (I thank Prof. Daniel C. Snell for pointing out this reference.). For earlier studies, see also Th. W. Juynboll, "Crimes and Punishments (Muhammadan),," who points out that talionic retaliation was limited to those parts of body that could be severed without killing the victim.

28. Talion, the taking of "an eye for an eye," survives even today and was reported in an article on Saudi Arabia appearing in an article "Saudi Arabian Justice" appearing in *The Economist* vol.

259 no. 8226 (June 16–22, 2001) 46: "Nowhere else are the *qisas,* or retaliatory punishments allowed under Islam, applied with such punctilio: last August, an Egyptian worker's eye was surgically removed at the insistence of a man who lost the use of his own eye after the Egyptian had thrown acid in his face." Cf. also, in the New York Times, "Hospitals Are Asked to Maim Man in Punishment, " August 20, 2010, national edition, A9. This article reports on a search being made in Saudi Arabia to identify ways to damage an assailant's spinal cord in order to cause paralysis in him similar to that of his victim. The victim's family is quoted as saying "There is no better word than God's word, an eye for an eye."

29. Similar formulas are found in Exod 21:24 (sec. 4.7) and Deut 19:21 (sec. 8.1).

destroys the limb that he was striking, he shall pay 1 mina silver.

§20 If a man with respect to another man using a knife(?) cuts off his nose . . . he shall pay 2/3 mina silver.

§21 If a man with [respect to another man, using . . .] cuts off [. . .] he shall [pay . . . shekels silver.]

§22 [I]f [a man with respect to another man, using . . .] his tooth, he sh[all pay] 2 she[kels silver].[30]

A similar—and better-preserved—sequence is found the Laws of Eshnunna, some two centuries later; here, too, compensation will vary according to the injury:

§42 If a man bit the nose of another man and severed it, he shall pay 1 mina silver; an eye—1 mina; a tooth—1/2 mina; an ear—1/2 mina; a slap on the cheek—he shall pay 10 shekels silver.

§43 If a man has cut off the finger of another man, he shall pay [1]/3 mina silver.

§44 If a man knocked down another man in the street(?) and has broken his hand, he shall pay one-half mina silver.

§45 If he has broken his foot, he shall pay one-half mina silver.

§46 If a man struck another man and has broken his collarbone, he shall pay 1/3 mina silver.

§47 If a man in a violent fight, has caused an injury(?), he shall pay 10 shekels silver.

30. I here follow the numbering of paragraphs in Roth, *Law Collections*, 19, but have added readings based on those of Kramer and Finkelstein as given in Finkelstein, "Laws of Urnammu."

The injuries mentioned in §§42–43, with the exception of the slap on the cheek, create permanent loss; the slap, as we shall see below in a separate discussion (sec. 4.4), represents more of an assault on a person's dignity than on his body. The injuries in §§44–46 deal with broken bones that may or may not heal properly. The injury in §47 is not clear but was evidently not as serious, to judge from the lesser penalty.

The Laws of Hammurapi include both compensation and talionic reprisal; in this system, however, the right of talionic reprisal is only available for members of the highest social class of freemen:

§196 If a freeman has blinded the eye of the son of another freeman, they shall blind his eye.

§197 If he has broken the bone on a freeman, they shall break his bone.

§198 If he has blinded the eye of a commoner or the bone of a commoner, he shall pay one mina silver.

§200 If a freeman has knocked out a tooth of another freeman, his social equal, they shall knock out his tooth.

§201 If he has knocked out a tooth of a commoner, he shall pay 1/3 mina silver.

§206 If a freeman in a brawl has struck another freemen and set a wound upon him, that man shall swear "I did not strike him, knowing (that I would so injure him)" and he shall pay the doctor (for his victim's medical care).

The sequence of laws in §§196–206 also includes a number of paragraphs that I discuss in other sections. §199, which deals with a freeman who has injured a slave belonging to another, has already been discussed above (sec. 4.2). The laws in the intervening §§202–205, deal with slaps on the cheek; these are discussed more fully below in sec. 4.4. In this present list of laws discussed here, we see that talionic reprisal only applies between social equals of the highest class; a commoner who is injured by a freeman of higher status, i.e., a "gentleman," must be content with compensation. The resolution in §206 brings to mind Exod 21:18–19, where the assailant does not pay compensation but must pay for loss of work time and medical care. There is, however, no mention of loss of work time in §206, which, however, also adds the need for of the assailant to swear an oath. The oath introduces the factor of intention, which the other laws do not consider as a mitigating factor. Perhaps this is because both parties were fighting; and this changes the calculation. In the Hittite Laws discussed below, intention reduces but does not eliminate the penalty. The sequence of injuries in Hammurapi Laws: eye, bone, and tooth is similar to "broken bone for broken bone, eye for eye, tooth for tooth" found in Lev 24:19–20.

The Hittite Laws know only compensation, which, as in Babylonia vary in amount according to the nature of the injury. In the following citation, we will be looking at §§7–15. One should note that in a later version of §§7–8, the law dealing with free persons, which is the content of §7, is combined together with §8, which deals with injuries to slaves. (The slave provisions were mentioned earlier in sec. 4.2 together with those in §§12, 14, and 16, in the discussion of injuries to chattel slaves.) The later version of §§7–8 also considers the number of teeth lost. We should also note that §7 by itself has

been preserved in two versions: the earliest version, like Exod 21:18–19, combines injuries to eye and tooth within the same law. The Hittite Laws are as follows:

§7 If anyone blinds a free person or knocks out his tooth, they used to pay 40 shekels of silver. But now he shall pay 20 (variant: 10) shekels of silver, and he shall look to his house for it.

§7 (Later Version) If anyone blinds a free man in a quarrel, he shall pay 40 shekels of silver. If it is an accident [lit. "the hand sins"], he shall pay 20 shekels of silver.[31]

§§7–8 (Later Version) If anyone knocks out a free man's tooth—if he knock out two or three teeth—he shall pay 12 shekels of silver. If it is a slave, he shall pay 6 shekels of silver.

§9 If anyone injures a person's head, they used to pay 6 shekels of silver: the injured party took 3 shekels of silver, and they used to take 3 shekels of silver for the palace. But now the king has waived the palace share, so that only the injured party takes 3 shekels of silver.

§9 (Later Version) If anyone injures a (free) man's head, the injured man shall take 3 shekels of silver.

§10 If anyone injures a (free) person and temporarily incapacitates him, he shall provide medical care for him. In his place he shall provide a person to work on his estate until he recovers. When he recovers, (his assailant) shall pay him 6

31. The meaning of this phrase is discussed in Hoffner, *Laws of the Hittites,* 170; a variant form "his hand sins" occurs in Hittite Laws §§3–5 discussed below (sec. 4.8) in connection with homicide.

shekels of silver and shall pay the physician's fee as well.

§10 (Later Version) If anyone injures a free man's head, he shall provide medical care for him. And in his place he shall provide a person to work on his estate until he recovers. When he recovers, (his assailant) shall pay him 10 shekels of silver and shall pay the 3 shekel physician's fee as well. If it is a slave, he shall pay 2 shekels of silver.

§11 If anyone breaks a free person's hand or foot,[32] he shall pay him 20 shekels of silver, and he shall look to his house for it.

§11 (Later Version) If anyone breaks a free man's hand or foot, if (the injured man) becomes disabled (?), he shall pay him 20 shekels of silver. If he does not become disabled (?), he shall pay him 10 shekels of silver.

§13 If anyone bites off the nose of a free person, and he shall pay 40 shekels of silver, and he shall look to his house for it.

§13 (Later Version) If anyone bites off the nose of a free man, he shall pay 30 shekels(!)[33] of silver, and he shall look to his house for it.

§15 If anyone tears off the ear of a free person, he shall pay 12 shekels of silver, and he shall look to his house for it.

§15 (Later Version) If anyone tears off the ear of a free man, he shall pay 12 shekels of silver.

32. For the reading "hand" rather than "arm" and "foot" rather then "leg," see Hoffner, ibid. 25 n. 33.

33. The text has 30 minas, i.e., 1200 shekels, which—as Hoffner, ibid. 27 n. 32 notes—is almost certainly an error, since one sees a consistent pattern of reductions rather than increase of compensation in the later versions of the laws.

When we encounter compensation, it is evident that the ancient legal systems preferred to establish rates of compensation, rather than to leave every situation to be argued out in an individual fashion. The omission of compensation rates in the Bible is therefore surprising if compensation were indeed the usual, ancient biblical practice. Their omission supports the supposition that talionic reprisal was in fact the primary or "statutory" response in cases of personal injury involving free persons. There are traces of rates for compensation in other situations, as we shall see below, e.g., in Exod 21:32 in connection homicide caused by an animal (sec. 4.10); and there, too, we see a difference between free persons (talionic reprisal) and slaves (compensation only). Status was an unavoidable fact of life in ancient societies; the rates of compensation for slaves were less than for free persons; this is well illustrated in the Hittite and Babylonian Laws that have been cited.

Hittite Laws §10 offers a good parallel to Exod 21:18–19, containing provisions both for medical care and for loss of work. The Hittite laws, however, also add compensation for the victim, which is omitted in the Bible. But, the rabbis, as we saw in *m. B. Qam.* 8:1 (cited earlier in this section), do add a provision for additional payments for damage, pain, and humiliation. Expectation of such additional compensation is reasonable in any system based upon the practice of compensation. One might then ask why the rabbis, having added these payments, did not also specify a schedule of rates such as we find in Babylonian and Hittite laws? One reason may be because there was no mention of these payments and rates in the biblical case of Exod 21:18–19; there was thus no biblical foundation upon which the rabbinic law could be constructed. But perhaps a more likely reason is the fact that in Roman law of their times, the set penalties likewise found in earlier Roman law had long been replaced by the practice having damages assessed by judges.[34] The rabbis conformed to contemporary Roman legal practice in their reformulation of the archaic biblical laws on injury. The earlier Roman law, preserved in the Twelve Tables (c. 450 BCE), considered compensation as an alternative to talionic reprisal and also set rates of payment. Thus, for injuries, *XII Tables* 8.2–4:

> If one has maimed another person's limb, let there be retaliation in kind unless he makes agreement for composition with him. If he has broken or bruised a bone of (a) freeman with hand or club, he shall undergo a penalty of 300 pieces. If (he has broken a) slave's (bone), 150 [pieces]. If one has done simple harm [to another], penalties shall be 25 pieces.[35]

We here have categories identical to what we see in our ancient Near Eastern systems: talionic retaliation, compensation with set amounts, distinction by status, and recognition of insult as an actionable offense (which is discussed in sec. 4.4). Compensation and talionic retaliation were alternatives; and the possibility of imposing the latter may have served to

help motivate offenders to come to agreement with their victims. It is therefore reasonable to imagine that in biblical times, compensation also existed as an option alongside of talionic reprisal. This was certainly true in connection with homicide, as we shall see below in sec. 4.8.

4.4 ASSAULT ON DIGNITY

Some attacks were considered hurtful, not because of the physical pain they inflicted but, rather, because they symbolized insult and profound disrespect. In the archaic period, we are dealing with physical actions rather than defamatory remarks. This is the type of offense described in the Mishnah, *m. B. Qam.* 8:6:

> A man who struck his fellow man on the ear, must pay him a *sela*. Rabbi Judah in the name of R. Jose the Galilean says (he must pay him) one mina. If he slapped him, he must give him two hundred *zuz*; (if he slapped him) with the back of his hand, he must give him four hundred *zuz*. If he pulled his ear, plucked his hair, spat and his spittle reached him, removed his garment from upon him, uncovered a woman's head in the marketplace (i.e., publicly), he must give 400 *zuz*. This (however) is the general rule: all is in accordance with the person's honor.

It is interesting that, in the case of assaults on dignity, the rabbis who edited this Mishnah, even while they preserved the ancient schedule of compensations, also confirm their preference of allowing judges discretion to set penalties. Their general rule was clearly stated in Mishnah *m. B. Qam.* 8:1 (cited above in sec. 4.3): "As for humiliation? It is all according to

34. Thomas, *Textbook of Roman Law*, 349–50.

35. Warmington, *Remains of Old Latin* III, 476–77. Words in parentheses are added for clarity; words within square brackets represent Warmington's restorations. The category "simple harm" or *iniuria*, by the time of Gaius (c. second century CE), had been expanded to include verbal insult or defamation. Cf. Gaius, *Inst.* 3.220–21 and De Zulueta, *The Institutes of Gaius: Part II Commentary*, 216–20.

(the social status of) the persons causing and suffering humiliation."

Medieval rabbinic commentators try to harmonize the two approaches. Rashi takes the scheduled amounts to be supplementary fines in addition to what the judges might determine. Maimonides, however maintains that they are in fact the schedule to be followed in cases where no actual physical harm was involved; and the appended comment "all is in accordance with the person's honor" will allow judges to diminish the sum for victims of lesser social status.[36] In the Mishnah's schedule, striking the ear was set at one *sela*—a coin worth about 2 shekels—but other opinions would raise the compensation amount to a mina—approximately 50 shekels. The compensation for slapping the face was doubled if one slapped with the back of his hand. A *zuz* was worth approximately one-half shekel; thus 200 and 400 *zuz* added up to about 50 and 100 shekels.[37] It can be seen therefore that the suffering of indignity was considered every bit as "painful" as the pain of a broken limb.

The Tosefta, in another passage, *t. B. Qam.* 9:31, Lieberman, makes this point very clear in a scene of dispute between two scribes:

> If he struck him with the back of his hand or with a sheet of paper or with an account book (or) with undressed leather skins (or) with a sheaf of documents which (he held) in his hand, (in all of these cases) he must pay him 400 *zuz*; and this (penalty) is (so high) not

because (we are dealing with) an injury causing physical pain but because (each one is) an injury causing public shame.

While there is no biblical law dealing with insult, there are frequent references in the Bible to suffering the indignity of being slapped. Thus, e.g., in Job 16:10:

> They open wide their mouths at me; Reviling me, they strike my cheeks; they inflame themselves against me. (NJPS)

This act is associated with the lowest stage of despair in Lam 3:30–32:

> Let him offer his cheek to the smiter; let him be surfeited with mockery. For the Lord does not reject forever, but first afflicts, then pardons in His abundant kindness (NJPS)[38]

A similar counsel in given in Luke 6:27–29:

> But I say to you that listen, Love your enemies, do good to those who hate you, bless those who curse you, pray for those who abuse you. If anyone strikes you on the cheek, offer the other also; and from anyone who takes away your coat do not withhold even your shirt. (NRSV)[39]

The New Testament passage is interesting in that it mirrors the same sequence of actions listed in *m. B. Qam.* 8:6 quoted above, i.e., moving from a slap on the face to pulling off someone's garment. I suggest that this ordering of cases in Jesus' sermon

---

36. Rashi on *b. B. Qam.* 91a; Maimonides, *Mishnah Torah, Hilkhot Hovel Umaziq* 3:8; also his Mishnah commentary on our passage.

37. These monetary equivalences are taken from Steinsalttz, *Talmud Reference Guide,* 291.

38. Other biblical references to slapping the face as a gesture of indignity appear in Isa 50:6; Mic 4:14; Ps 3:8.

39. Another version of this statement appears in Matt 5:38–40.

emerges from the oral tradition of laws that was current at that time among the people of Judea. These two cases, together with the images in Lam 3:30–32, supplied important grounding for the message of this sermon, encouraging the people to bear with equanimity the indignities of their political and economic oppression.[40] In a change of pace, the Talmud preserves a humorous story about one Hanan, who was known to be a rascal:

> The scoundrel Hanan, having boxed another man's ear, was brought before R. Huna, who ordered him to go and pay the plaintiff half a *zuz*. As [Hanan] had a battered *zuz* coin, he desired to pay the plaintiff the half *zuz* [which was due] out of it. But as it could not be exchanged, he slapped him again and gave him [the whole *zuz* coin].[41]

Assaults on dignity are found in the ancient Near Eastern sources. We have already noted above (sec. 4.3) Eshnunna Laws §42: " a slap on the cheek—he shall pay 10 shekels silver." Measures both of compensation and corporal punishment also appear in the Hammurapi Laws:

> §202 If a freeman has smitten the cheek of a freeman who is greater than him (in status), he shall be struck sixty (lashes) with an ox whip in the public assembly.

§203 If the son of a freeman has smitten the cheek of the son of a freeman who is the same (status) as he is, he shall pay one mina silver.

§204 If a commoner has smitten the cheek of another commoner, he will pay 10 shekels silver.

§205 If the slave of an free man has smitten the cheek of a son of a freeman, they shall cut off his ear.

§202 is interesting in that it points to greater nuances of social stratification—at least among the higher class group—that go beyond what we have seen thus far between the three broad classes of slave, commoner, and gentleman (or freeman). The laws omit the case where a commoner strikes a freeman, who is higher than him in status; presumably the result would be the same as in §202. The pattern of corporal punishment for violating class barriers appears again in §205; the presumptuous slave is marked permanently by mutilation. Both the flogging in §202 and the mutilation in §205 are harsh penalties indeed; but the perceived gravity given to insults to dignity are evident in §203 where a mina must be given in compensation; this was a very large sum in those days.

We have a document relating to a trial for insult dating from the Old Babylonian period; the tablet was found in the region of Eshnunna; but unfortunately, as was sometimes the case, the document was not dated:

> Pir-ilishu, an Amorite soldier struck the cheek of Apil-ilishu son of Ahum-nasir and has acted in a hostile manner. (But at the trial) he said as follows: "I did not strike him." The governor and the judges sent Pir-ilishu the Amorite soldier

---

40. A discussion of these interconnections appears in Greengus, "Filling Gaps," 154–55.

41. This story appears in *b. B. Qam.* 37a and *b. Bekh.* 50b–51a; in the latter discussion, there is an attempt to explain the meagerness of Hanan's penalty *vis-à-vis* the *sela* penalty that *m. B. Qam.* 8:6 imposes for inflicting a blow on the ear. An argument is made that the *sela* in the Mishnah was in fact a provincial coin, worth only 1/2 *zuz*.

to the gate of (the temple of) Ishtar; (there) he would stand (and) swear (an oath in support of his statement); he could then walk away (free). (However) he did not stand and did not swear and (so) he will pay 3 1/2 shekels silver. [Names of three witnesses follow] [42]

The soldier lost the case because he was unwilling to swear an oath in support of his testimony, which would have satisfied the court and enabled him to rebut the accusation. Evidently there were no witnesses who could conclusively testify that he had actually slapped Ahum-nasir; but witnesses may have been able to corroborate the hostility that was manifested in the encounter. This circumstance could explain why the court placed the burden of proof upon the soldier, since he, rather than the alleged victim Ahum-nasir, was required to take the oath. The payment of 3 1/2 shekels is less than the 10 shekels seen in Eshnunna Laws §42 mentioned above. Perhaps the amount was less because there were no witnesses that someone's face had in fact been slapped. It is also possible that, in this community, a different rate of compensation was applied; or perhaps the rates in our law collections were intended only as general guides, leaving final determination to the judges.

4.5 STRIKING A PARENT

In Exod 21:15 we read: "He who strikes his father or his mother shall surely be put to death." The biblical text does not clarify the extent of the harm caused by this blow; did it cause a wound and was

it fatal? The rabbis interpret the situation as involving a non-fatal blow; but, at the same time, it was their view that the blow was severe enough to cause a wound. They reasoned by analogy from other cases: its non-fatal character from the fact that the text doesn't indicate a fatality,[43] and from other uses of this verb to describe striking, leading to wounding or maiming.[44]

Support for understanding the biblical case as non-fatal striking comes from Hammurapi Laws §195; at the same time, we find no support there for the idea that such striking necessarily involved wounding. That law states: "If a son has struck his father, they shall cut off his hand." One might here infer that this blow was not one of wounding. The verb used "to strike" is the same as used in connection with slapping the face; and from Hammurapi Laws §206 cited above (sec. 4.3): "If a free man in a brawl has struck another freeman and set a wound upon him . . . ." we see that wounding is not implicit in striking. Therefore, in Hammurapi Laws §195, one may likewise assume that wounding was not a necessary consequence of the son who struck his father. This law thus is more about insult rather than physical harm. As we have seen above, in Hammurapi Laws §202 and §205, corporal punishments—albeit less severe than cutting off a hand—were given for assaults on dignity. The penalty in §195 is harsh but it is still less severe than the death penalty given in Exod 21:15! Was the harshness of the biblical law due to a wound being

---

42. This text is published in Lutz, *Verdict of a Trial Judge.* For restorations and the current reading, see Greengus, "Filling Gaps," 153 n. 9.

43. This argument is made in *b. Sanh.* 84b; and *Sifre N Mas'ey* 159 on Num 35:11.

44. This argument appears in *Mekhilta Mishpatim* 5 on Exod 21:15 and in *Sifra Emor* 14.20 on Lev 24:21. See further *m. B. Qam.* 8:3, 5; and *m. Sanh.* 11:1.

inflicted, as the rabbis wanted to assume; or was it intended to serve as a strong response to insult regardless of any degree of physical harm? I am unable to answer this question. Moreover, the Babylonian case does not mention mother alongside of father; was this formulation merely an omission, or were mothers intentionally excluded from the protection given by this law? We do not know more on the basis of the present data. Nor can we determine whether such laws, either in the Bible or in Babylonia, were ever enforced.

4.6 INJURY TO MALE GENITALS

The subject matter of Deut 25:11–12 is about injury to a man's private parts, which took place in consequence of a fight between two men. The wife of one of the men, initially a bystander but apparently fearing for her husband, sought to help him by grabbing the testicles of his assailant. The law describes the injury in a somewhat veiled manner:

> If two men get into a fight with each other, and the wife of one comes up to save her husband from his antagonist and puts out her hand and seizes him by his genitals [literally, "shame parts"], you shall cut off her hand; show no pity. (NJPS)

The penalty for this injury is resolved in talionic fashion; the woman who caused the injury loses her hand. This is as close as one can come to physiological parity since she is a female; and her hand was the agent of the injury. Rabbinic commentators note that the injunction "show no pity" also appears in Deut 19:21 followed by the talionic formula: "Nor must you show pity: life for life, eye for eye, tooth for tooth, hand for hand, foot for foot"

(NJPS). Since the Rabbis had already reinterpreted non-fatal talion as being punished by monetary compensation (sec. 4.3), they likewise take the penalty in Deut 25:11–12 to be interpreted as monetary compensation.[45] But Ibn Ezra, in his commentary to this verse, is unwilling to abandon the plain meaning of this verse. He agrees that compensation should be offered; but if it were not, then her hand would indeed be cut off.

One is left to wonder why the biblical text was not more explicit about the injury. Was there actual physical damage or was the offense simply the woman's boldness in grabbing a strange man's testicles? This second theme of indecency is suggested by rabbinic commentators in the Mishnah; in *m. B. Qam.* 8:1 they use Deut 25:11–12 to justify adding a payment for humiliation in addition to other payments for damage, pain, etc. (cited above in sec. 4.3). They look to the descriptive language used in the phrase "she seized him by his genitals," or literally "by his shame parts." They thus are able to "locate" the added payment for humiliation within the biblical text.

Middle Assyrian Laws §§A 7–8 may give us further insight–both to the theme of injury and to the theme of indecency:

> If a woman has laid a hand upon a man (and) they have proven her guilty, she must pay 30 minas of lead (and) they will flog her 20 (blows) with canes. If a woman in a fight has crushed a man's testicle,

---

45. Cf. Rashi on Deut 25:12; but he also found it necessary to cite the hermeneutical argument used by R. Judah in *Sifre D Ki Tetze* 293 in order to defend this rabbinic reinterpretation. Saadia, on the other hand, takes the cutting as literal but sees it as a defensive act taken to protect the man during the fight.

they shall cut off one of her fingers. Moreover, if a physician has bandaged it, and the second testicle has been affected from the first and it becomes infected (?), or, if she (also) crushed the second testicle in the fight, then they shall tear out her [nipples].[46]

In the first case, the woman is punished because she physically attacked a man, even if, apparently, she did him no lasting physical harm. She not only has to pay a significant penalty but also suffers corporal punishment. It is possible to understand her offense as deriving from the bold or forward nature of her action; perhaps also the humiliation suffered by the man who was attacked by a woman in this manner. In the second case, both parties—the woman and the man—are involved in a fight with one another; but the woman acts "out of bounds" and inappropriately, by attacking the man "below the belt" and causing an injury. Her action here may likewise have been considered indecent. The penalties are now talionic. The tearing out of her nipples may mirror the likely impairment of the injured man's procreative abilities. The "lighter penalty" of cutting off of her finger is reminiscent of the biblical cutting of the hand, although it is not as harsh. The Assyrian laws likewise support the rabbinic understanding of the biblical case as involving injury rather than a simple "grasping," for otherwise the punishment of cutting off a hand seems vastly out of proportion for indecency

alone. It is troubling, however, not to have a more explicit mention of an injury in Deut 25:11–12. Moreover, in Middle Assyrian Laws §A 8, the woman was herself a protagonist in the fight, while in biblical case the woman only entered the fray to help her husband who was evidently losing the fight. For all of these reasons, it seems that women—both in Assyria and in biblical Israel—were being punished on two counts: first, because of "crossing the line" of appropriate gender behavior; and second, for the injury they caused to an assailant. The evidence overall shows that there was a shared prejudice concerning women who "stepped out of line" and attacked men; they were to be severely punished for doing so.

4.7 STRIKING A PREGNANT WOMAN

A special case of injury dealing with a pregnant woman and her foetus appears in Exod 21:22–25:

> If men fight, and they strike a pregnant woman and her (unborn) children come forth, but there was no (other) harm, he (i.e., the one responsible) shall be penalized according (to the amount) that the woman's husband may determine for him and give (payment) based on reckoning. But if there is (other) harm, you must set the penalty as life for life, eye for eye, tooth for tooth, hand for hand, foot for foot, burn for burn, wound for wound, bruise for bruise.

This law has been subject to a variety of interpretations. While it is clear that a miscarriage resulted after the woman received the blows, question has been raised as to whether the children lived or died when they came forth in this untimely

---

46. For this restoration—and for other ideas incorporated in this discussion— see Paul, "Biblical Analogies to Middle Assyrian Law," 337. Other scholars, however, have restored "eyes." Both penalties occur in the laws. Valuable discussion of these cases can also be found in Tigay, *Deuteronomy*, 484–86 (Excursus 24).

fashion. A second question relates to what is meant by "(other) harm." Does it relate to the woman or to her children who came forth and then died? These questions arise because of the translation of these verses in the Septuagint, in which all injuries mentioned relate only to the children and not to their mother. In the first instance, where one reads "but there was no (other) harm," the Greek version read: "and her child[47] comes forth not fully formed," i.e., the foetus or foetuses were very premature and could not have survived outside of the womb. In this case, the woman's loss can be satisfied by compensation. But in the second instance, where one reads "But if there is (other) harm," the Septuagint reads: "but if it is fully formed, he shall pay life for life." In this case, the striker is to be punished by death, i.e., life for life. Philo, who follows the Septuagint explains:

> But, if the offspring is already shaped and all the limbs have their proper qualities and places in the system, he must die, for that which answers to this description is a human being, which he has destroyed in the laboratory of Nature who judges that the hour has not yet come for bringing it out in to the light, like a statue lying in a studio requiring nothing more than to be conveyed outside and released from confinement.[48]

On the other hand, Josephus and subsequent rabbinic interpreters—on the basis of reading the Hebrew text—understood the first case as involving foetuses, which were born prematurely and died. They then understand "(other) harm" to relate to the woman herself, who may have suffered one of the various injuries enumerated or even death from this mishap.[49] The interpretation of Josephus and the rabbis is supported by a number of factors. The first factor is the variety of injuries: " life for life, eye for eye, tooth for tooth, hand for hand, foot for foot." It makes greater sense if this list refers to the woman rather than to foetus, which in the Greek version is dead in both instances. Second is that the word "harm" while obscure, seems elsewhere to refer to loss of life due to a fatal accident. So, for example in Gen 42:4: "And Jacob did not send Joseph's brother Benjamin with his brothers, since he feared that he might meet with harm." Third, as we shall presently see, this suggested sequence of events—first, death of foetus; second, death of mother—is repeatedly paralleled in the ancient Near Eastern law collections, in their versions of what was apparently an ancient "paradigm" law case.

The earliest example comes from a Sumerian scribal exercise tablet:

> If (a man) pushed the daughter of a (free) man and caused her to abort the contents of her womb [lit. the thing inside her], he shall pay 10 shekels silver. If (however) he struck the daughter of a (free) man and caused her to abort the content

47. The Greek version reads "child," singular, in place of "children," plural, in the Hebrew text.

48. Philo, *Spec. Laws* 3.108, Colson. This distinction between fully formed and not fully formed seems to be a Greek concept. Stol, *Birth in Babylonia and the Bible*, 43 cites a Hellenistic inscription that evaluates the degree of "defilement" of a woman who had a miscarriage according to whether her expelled foetus was clearly formed or not.

49. Josephus, *Ant.* 4.278, *Mekhilta Mishpatim 8 ad loc.* Cf. also Rashi, Ibn Ezra, Hazzequni, Rashbam, Bekhor Shor, etc. on Exod 21:22–25.

of her womb, he will pay one-third mina of silver.[50]

These laws are interesting in that they distinguish levels of responsibility on the part of the person causing the abortion according to the severity of the physical contact. In the first instance there was pushing; in the second an actual blow. Such distinction is not preserved or revisited in the later ancient Near Eastern law formulations—nor, for that matter, in Exod 21:22–25. In all the other laws, as we shall see, the injury is described as being caused by someone striking the woman.

Another early version of this case as well as a sequence of harm to foetus and mother is found in an unplaced fragment of Lipit-Ishtar Laws:

> If a [man . . . str]uck the daughter of a freeman (and) caused her [to expel] (the contents of) [her] womb, he shall [pay] one-half mina silver. If she dies, that man [lit. male] shall be killed. If a [. . .] struck a female slave belonging to (another) man (and) caused her to expel (the contents) of her womb, he shall pay 5 shekels silver. If . . . [text broken off].[51]

A more complete version of the case appears in Hammurapi Laws §§209–214:

> §209 If a freeman struck the daughter of another freeman and caused her to abort the content of her womb, he shall pay 10 shekels silver for the content of her womb.

§210 If that woman has died, they will kill his daughter

§211 If he has caused the daughter of a commoner to abort the content of her womb by (his) striking, he shall pay 5 shekels silver.

§212 If that woman has died, he will pay one-half mina silver.

§213 If he struck the female slave of a freeman and caused her to abort the content of her womb, he will pay 2 shekels silver.

§214 If that female slave has died, he will pay one-third mina silver.

This group of laws reveals the same social stratification that we have seen in connection with non-fatal physical injuries, separating the cases according to whether the victim was gentry, commoner, or slave. The death of the foetus here, as in the previous cases, is not considered as full homicide. But causing the death of the mother is more serious and; in the case of the higher class, is punished not just by death but also by talionic reprisal, i.e., the death of the striker's daughter. But what if the striker in §209 had no daughter? One may imagine that the striker himself would then be subject to the death penalty as in Lipit-Ishtar. One may surmise that this would also happen to a striker if he were commoner or slave who caused the death of a higher social class mother in §210.

A grouping of similar and related cases appears in the Middle Assyrian Laws §§A 50–53:

> §50 [If a man] struck [a woman] and [caused] her [to abort the content of her womb, the wif]e of the man w[ho struck her]—they shall do to [her as he di]d to her (i.e., the

50. The text is YOS 1 28 iv 1–10, which are SLEx §§1–2 in Roth, *Law Collections*, 43. Stol, *Birth in Babylonia and the Bible*, 39 interprets the contrast between "pushing" and "striking" to imply "accidental" and "deliberate."

51. This fragment is UM 55-21-71 published in Civil, "New Sumerian Law Fragments"; our cases are iii, 2'–15.' See also Roth, ibid. 26–27 §§d–g.

woman whom he struck) [In place of the] contents of her womb he must pay (the payment for) a life. And if that woman dies, they will kill that man; (and) he must (also) pay for the content of her womb. And if there is no son of that woman's husband whose wife he struck and she aborted the content of her womb, they shall kill the striker in place of the content of her womb. (But) if the content of her womb was female, he will (only) pay (the payment for) a life.

§51 If a man struck another man's wife who does not raise (children) and causes her to abort the content of her womb, it is (nevertheless) an offense; he must pay two talents of lead.

§52 If a man struck a prostitute and caused her to abort the content of her womb, they shall (nevertheless) reckon it as (requiring) blow for blow; he must pay (the payment for) a life.

§53 If a woman by her own (action) aborts the content of her womb, they shall probe (the charge against) her and convict her. They shall impale her on a wooden (pole); they shall not bury her. If she dies in aborting the content of her womb, they shall (likewise) impale her on a pole; they shall not bury her. If persons have [conceal]ed that woman when she aborted the content of her womb. [. . .] they said [. . .] (remainder broken).

§50 contains the principle of talionic reprisal, striking the pregnant wife of the striker because her husband had struck another man's pregnant wife. The text does not tell us what would be done if the striker had no pregnant wife; presumably if lacking a wife, the penalty would fall upon him directly. §50 adds an additional case not found elsewhere, allowing the court to kill the striker if he caused a childless man to lose the chance of male progeny by causing his wife to abort her foetus. In other words, causing the loss of a potential male heir was a capital offense. This is unexpectedly harsh but also shows us how important it was for an Assyrian man to have male progeny.

Like Hammurapi Laws §§211–214, §§51–52 deal with female victims, who were not treated as other women. The woman "who does not raise children" may be a priestess who normally would have no children or perhaps a slave. Another suggestion is that she was physically handicapped in some way so as to prevent her from carrying a child to full term in previous pregnancies.[52] The circumstances of this case cannot at present be further elucidated. This law also introduces a set figure of compensation, which is not done in any of the related cases of this group. §52 extends the full protection of the law to a prostitute, presumably even though the loss of a foetus carried by a prostitute could not be assigned with certainty to a particular husband; compensation, however, must be paid for the life of her foetus as for any other. The talionic principle, articulated in §52, with the words "blow for blow" evokes for us the biblical statement of talion "wound for wound, bruise for bruise" found in Exod 21:22–25 cited earlier. It reminds us also that although talion, in ancient times, normally represented physical retribution; it might also be satisfied by compensation as here. We therefore have another indication of how talion and compensation coexisted

52. Cardascia, *Les Lois assyriennes,* 243.

together in the ancient scheme of penalties. In these Middle Assyrian Laws, monetary compensation was the usual penalty made for the life of the foetus that was aborted. Like the biblical case, we do not see a set amount as in the Laws of Lipit-Ishtar and Hammurapi Laws §§209–214, but rather a negotiated reckoning. Moreover, just as in the Bible and in our other ancient Near Eastern law cases, if the woman dies, it is considered as homicide and the striker must pay with his own life.

§53 is unique in being the only case we know dealing with self-induced abortion. There is no biblical parallel.[53] The law is brutal, giving this woman the death penalty by torture and denying her burial. Her punishment is more severe than would befall anyone who may have induced an abortion by striking her; a striker would have paid only compensation. This law reminds us again about how Middle Assyrian society—or at least its laws—was repressive of women.

Surprisingly, there is yet one additional case dealing with a striker causing abortion in the Middle Assyrian Laws; it appears somehow out of order, placed among sexual offenses. The case is Middle Assyrian Laws §A 21:

> If a man struck the daughter of (another) man and caused her to abort the content of her womb, they shall probe (the charges against him, (and) convict him. He shall pay 2 talents 30 minas of lead (and) they shall (also) beat him 50 (blows)

with canes; he must (also) do the king's labor for a month of days.

Scholars have justifiably wondered about how to connect this case with §§50–53. It has been suggested that the woman here was unmarried since she is described as a "daughter" and not a "wife" and thus there was no loss of progeny to any husband as in those cases. She is also of a higher status than the prostitute in §52; there is thus greater compensation to be paid; but with no mention of the talionic reprisal allowed to a husband in §50.[54]

The basic case of causing abortion through striking a pregnant woman is also found in the Hittite Laws §§17–18:

> §17 If anyone causes a free woman to miscarry, [if] it is her tenth month,[55] he shall pay 10 shekels of silver, if it is her fifth month, he shall pay 5 shekels of silver. He shall look to his house for it.

> §17 (Late Version) If anyone causes a free woman to miscarry, he shall pay 20 shekels silver.

> §18 If anyone causes a female slave to miscarry, if it is her tenth month, he shall pay 5 shekels of silver (Variant: 10 shekels of silver.)

> §18 (Late Version) if anyone causes a female slave to abort, he shall pay 10 shekels of silver.

The fact that the Hittite Laws calculate compensation according to the age of the foetus suggests a possible meaning for the obscure Hebrew word *pelilim* in Exod 21:22, which, with NJPS, I have translated

53. Josephus, *Against Apion* 2.202, Thackeray, appears, however, to assume its existence when he states: "The Law orders all the offspring to be brought up, and forbids women either to cause abortion or to make away with the foetus; a woman convicted of this is regarded as an infanticide, because she destroys a soul and diminishes the race."

54. The interpretation here follows Cardascia, *Les lois assyriennes*, 136–38.

55. Hoffner, *Laws of the Hittites*, 179, explains this calculation as being based upon approximately 10 lunar months or 40 weeks.

as "reckoning" in the phrase "and give (payment) based on reckoning." An idea, perhaps somewhat related, is found in the Septuagint's translation: "he shall pay with judicial assessment." This interpretation is followed in the Targums and favored by many commentators.[56] It is curious that in the later versions of the Hittite Laws §§17–18, graded compensation is replaced by set sums, depending upon the social status of the mother.

In the Mishnah, the rabbis discuss how to arrive at an appropriate method of compensation for the woman who lost her foetus due to being struck. They also restate their understanding of the unintentional nature of the injuries inflicted in the biblical case. We read in *m. B. Qam.* 5:4 as follows:

> And a man who was intent upon (striking) his fellow but (instead) hit a woman; and her (unborn) children aborted—he must pay compensation for these (aborted) children. How does he pay compensation for the children? They estimate the value of the woman— how much she is worth (were she to be sold as a slave) before she gave birth and how much she is worth since she gave birth? Rabbi Simeon son of Gamaliel said: if (this is) so, since the woman gave birth (i.e.,

she is proven to be fertile) she is (now) worth more in value. Rather, they should evaluate the (unborn) children—how much they would have been worth (had they lived) and give (this amount of compensation) to (her) husband.

Note that the majority (i.e., the first opinion) shifts the calculation from the foetuses to the change in value in the woman herself; the minority view of Rabbi Simeon retains the focus on the foetuses, which I believe was the ancient focus both in the Bible and in the ancient Near East. The majority view of the rabbis resembles more sophisticated methods used in Roman law, which consider the values before and after the damage.[57] These rabbis were thus ready to abandon the ancient methods of compensation used in this case.

The rabbis further modified the punishment in the biblical case if the woman herself died. For the rabbis, the consequence stated in Exod 21:22–25 "you must set the penalty as life for life" would not be interpreted as capital punishment so long as the striker did not intend to hit the woman. In this situation, the biblical "life for life" can at best only indicate monetary compensation.[58] The rabbis thus reduced the consequences in order to remove the possibility of the striker suffering death for an unintentional homicide; this outcome, they felt, would be unjust. However, as we shall see below, while the Bible indeed does recognize the distinction between intentional and unintentional acts,

56. Cf. Houtman, *Exodus,* 3:162–63. The obscurity of the terms "harm" and "reckoning" has opened the door to other interpretations. Westbrook, "Lex Talionis and Exodus 21, 22–25," interprets the cases in Exod 21:22–25 as revolving around whether the person who actually struck the woman and caused her to abort could be identified or not. Jackson, *Wisdom Laws,* 218–26, accepts the notion of judicial supervision for "reckoning" but maintains that the cases revolve around the issue of whether the woman's foetus, prematurely born, survived or died. For additional discussion see Cohen, "Exodus 21:22–25 and the Current Debate on Abortion."

57. Cf. Thomas, *Textbook of Roman Law,* 363–65, discussing versions of the *lex Aquilia* preserved in *D.*9.2.2 and Gaius, *Inst.* 3.210, 218.

58. This discussion appears in the Talmud, *b. Sanh.* 79a–b. Yet another opinion given there argues that one who kills in error should be totally exempt, even from compensation.

we will also see later in connection with adult homicide (sec. 4.8), that even one who killed unintentionally could nevertheless lose his own life by a justifiable act of talionic retribution through vengeance taken by the victim's family. For in biblical times, the absence of motive could never erase a person's full responsibility for the consequences of his actions.

4.8 HOMICIDE

Biblical and ancient Near Eastern laws and related sources have a great deal to tell us about homicide. However, as we shall presently see, the ancients did not think of homicide in terms of our own modern categories. In order to appropriately embrace the full range of data and ideas, I have divided the presentation into three sections. The first two sections deals with biblical and later Jewish materials; the third section will introduce the ancient Near Eastern sources into the discourse.

4.8.1 Homicide: Intentional, Unintentional, Accidental

In modern Anglo-American law, homicide is typically divided into categories of (1) murder, which involves premeditation and malicious intent; (2) manslaughter, which may be the result of passion or combat; and (3) criminally negligent homicide, which came about indirectly, through one's failure to act in a responsible manner. Death that came about through an unavoidable accident would not be considered as an act of homicide.[59] In biblical times there was a different grouping of categories. To begin with, all of the categories mentioned were considered as homicide. The biblical laws

put murder and manslaughter together in a single group; any person, whether murderer or manslayer, merits capital punishment. Involuntary manslaughter that came about through an accident was also considered as an act of homicide but the slayer was allowed to seek sanctuary. Criminally negligent homicide was likewise considered a capital offense, but will be looked at in a separate section (4.9). The subjects for the present section are: murder, manslaughter, and death through unavoidable accident.

The Bible deals with homicide in a number of passages. We begin with Exod 21:12–14:

> He who strikes a man and he dies, he shall certainly be put to death. But (for) one who did not lie in wait (to kill) and God made it happen through his hand, I will assign you a place to which he can flee. If (however) a man plotted against another to kill him with cunning, you shall take him from my altar to die.

The first sentence is a general statement that one who commits homicide deserves to die.[60] The next two verses introduce distinctions based on motive. For one who killed inadvertently, i.e., only God knows why it happened, that person will need to seek protection and refuge, most likely, from the outrage of the victim's family or friends who might nevertheless seek vengeance. The vengeance of the victim's family is not described in this passage but we know of this practice from other biblical laws on homicide that we

---

59. Black, *Black's Law Dictionary*, 751–52, 983.

60. The general principle is also stated in Gen 9:6 "Whoever sheds the blood of man, By man shall his blood be shed; For in His image Did God make man" (NJPS).

shall look at presently. However, if it can be established by the judgment of a court that the slayer acted with premeditation, then he can be removed from his refuge to face justice and punishment. The role of the courts is likewise not described in this passage, but is found in other, more detailed laws, which are treated below.

As for altars and shrines serving as places of refuge, this practice is vividly described in the power struggle between Adonijah and Joab and their brother Solomon for the throne of David. About Adonijah we read in 1 Kgs 1:50–52:

> Adonijah was in fear of Solomon and (so) he arose and went (to the Tent of the Lord) and seized upon the horns of the altar. It was reported to Solomon: "Adonijah is in fear of King Solomon and has seized upon the horns of the altar, saying, 'Let King Solomon now swear to me that he will not slay his servant by the sword.'" And Solomon said, "If he is a worthy man, not a hair (of his head) shall fall to the ground; but if evil be found in him, he shall die."

After initially sparing him, Solomon in fact later decided to have Adonijah killed. At that time, Joab upon hearing this news—and realizing that, having previously supported Adonijah's claim to the throne, he, too, was likely to be killed—also fled to the altar in attempt to forestall his fate. This is told in 1 Kgs 2:28–31:

> When the news reached Joab, he fled to the Tent of the LORD and grasped the horns of the altar—for Joab had sided with Adonijah, though he had not sided with Absalom. King Solomon was told that Joab had fled to the Tent of the LORD and that he was there by the

altar; so Solomon sent Benaiah son of Jehoiada, saying, "Go and strike him down." Benaiah went to the Tent of the LORD and said to him, "Thus said the king: Come out!" "No!" he replied; "I will die here." Benaiah reported back to the king that Joab had answered thus and thus, and the king said, "Do just as he said; strike him down and bury him, and remove guilt from me and my father's house for the blood of the innocent that Joab has shed. (NJPS)

Solomon here overlooked the sanctity of the shrine as a place of refuge. He justified his action by referring to the premeditative nature of earlier murders committed by Joab during the reign of King David—heretofore not punished; and Solomon imposed sentence without trial.

A more detailed law dealing with homicide is found in the book of Deuteronomy. Here again we find the custom of asylum but the places of refuge are limited, initially to three cities.[61] We are not told how these cities were selected or whether they contained religious shrines with altars. But Deuteronomy does give us details about the wrath and vengeance of the victim's family, as well as attempting better to define the contrast between premeditated and accidental killings. Deut 19:1–7 first presents the case of accidental homicide:

61. There appears to have been some ancient editorial efforts to bring the three cities in Deut 19:1–7 in line with the total of six cities in Num 35 (discussed below). First is the additional comment of Deut 19:8–10 on the possible future need for three more cities; second is in Deut 4:41–43, where we are told that Moses already at this time designated three cities of refuge in Transjordan. See *j. Makk.* 31c–32a; and for modern scholarship see Tigay, *Deuteronomy*, 377 n. 27, and 354 n. 116.

When the LORD your God has cut down the nations whose land the LORD your God is assigning to you, and you have dispossessed them and settled in their towns and homes, you shall set aside three cities in the land that the LORD your God is giving you to possess. You shall survey the distances, and divide into three parts the territory of the country that the LORD your God has allotted to you, so that any manslayer may have a place to flee to.—Now this is the case of the manslayer [lit. homicide],[62] who may flee there and live: one who has killed another unwittingly, without having been his enemy in the past. For instance, a man goes with his neighbor into a grove [lit. forest] to cut wood; as his hand swings the ax to cut down a tree, the ax-head [lit. the iron] flies off the handle and strikes the other so that he dies. That man shall flee to one of these cities and live.—Otherwise, when the distance is great, the blood-avenger, pursuing the manslayer in hot anger, may overtake him and kill him; yet he did not incur the death penalty, since he had never been the other's enemy. That is why I command you: set aside three cities. (NJPS)

The case of premeditated homicide is given in Deut 19:11–13:

If (however) a man is an enemy [lit. hater] of his neighbor and lies in ambush for him and rises against him and murderously strikes him

so that he dies and then flees to one of these towns, the elders of his town shall send (agents) and they shall remove him from there and they shall give him into the hand(s) of the blood-avenger and he shall die. Let your eye not pity him. Thus you will this innocent blood from Israel, and it is appropriate for you (to do so).

Yet another law on homicide appears in Numbers 35. It begins with a preface dealing with establishing six cities of refuge for persons who unintentionally committed homicide. These cities were selected out of a larger body of forty-eight cities belonging the Levites; but again we are not told why these six Levitical cities were specially qualified for the purpose of asylum. The appointment of cities appears in Num 35:6:

The towns that you assign to the Levites shall comprise the six cities of refuge that you are to designate for a manslayer [lit. homicide] to flee to, to which you shall add forty-two towns. (NJPS)

More elaboration follows in Num 35:9–15:

The Lord spoke to Moses saying: Speak to the children of Israel and say to them: When you cross the Jordan into the land of Canaan, you shall designate cities for yourselves cities—they shall be for you cities of refuge so that a manslayer who has killed a person by mistake may flee there. The cities shall be for you as a refuge from the avenger, so that the manslayer [lit. homicide] may not die until he has stood before the assembly for judgment. The cities that you designate shall be the six cities of refuge for you. You shall designate three cities beyond the Jordan, and three

62. The same Hebrew term, *rotzeach,* is alternatively translated either as "manslayer, slayer, or murderer" in order to accommodate our modern definitions of the ancient situation. It would be easier if one could simply translate "homicide" i.e., perpetrator of a homicide. But this term is not a familiar usage and so I have retained the situationally conditioned translations.

cities you shall designate in the land of Canaan: they shall serve as the cities of refuge. These six cities shall serve as refuge for the Israelites and well as for the stranger and sojourner among them so that anyone who kills a person by mistake may flee there.

Num 35:11 introduces a new term, "by mistake," which evokes for us a case of "unwitting" homicide similar to that in Deut 19:1–7, where the ax-handle flew off, striking and killing someone.

The next section, Num 35:16–21, further defines the category of non-accidental homicide to exclude circumstances that are equivalent to premeditation:

> If (however) he struck him with an iron implement and he (the person struck) died, he (the striker) is a murderer [lit. a homicide]; the murderer must be put to death. And if he struck him with a stone (in his) hand that one could die thereby, and he (the victim) died, he is a murderer; the murderer must be put to death. Or if he struck him with a wooden implement (in his) hand that one could die thereby, and he (the victim) died, he is a murderer; the murderer must be put to death. The blood-avenger— he shall put the murderer to death; when he meets up with him, he may kill him. (So, too) if he pushed him in hate or hurled (something) upon him (while lying) in wait and he died; or if he struck him with his hand in enmity and killed him, the striker shall surely be put to death; he is a murderer. The blood-avenger may slay the murderer when he meets up with him.

Numbers 35:16–21 in effect expands the category of premeditation by adding circumstantial factors, involving use of a "weapon," as well as there being a prior history of enmity between the parties, that we have already seen in Deut 19:11–13. Thus, if someone struck another person using an implement of iron—of unspecified size—or a stone or wooden (club) of sufficient size or weight to cause a lethal outcome, such use in itself "crosses the line" and raises the fatal injury to the level of premeditation. The use of a "weapon" removes this blow from the category of accidental homicide, apparently even if the striker, in his own mind, did not necessarily actually intend to kill the victim he struck. The intent of the striker is not otherwise evaluated. The passage then moves to a more overt situation of premeditation, evidenced by the assailant "lying in wait" to attack his victim; we have already seen language similar to this in Deut 19:11–13 and Exod 21:12–14. Finally, premeditation is assumed by assessing the prior relationship of the assailant towards his victim. Just like in Deut 19:11–13, a history of "hate" or "enmity" between the parties will supply a motive, again regardless of the assailant's actual intent at the time when the fatal blow was struck.

The rabbis noted that the Bible in Num 35:16 did not specify the size of the iron implement or how it was used; the Talmud in *b. Sanh.* 76b used this omission to explain it as follows:

> Samuel said: why is "(in his) hand" not mentioned in connection with iron? Because iron can kill no matter what its size. It has been taught likewise: Rabbi said; It was well known to Him who spoke and the world came into being that iron, no matter how small, can kill;

therefore the Torah prescribed no size for it. This however, is (true) only if one stabbed him; (otherwise size must be considered).

In other words, a pointed iron instrument—a knife or needle of any size—is considered to be a lethal weapon; but used as a blunt instrument it falls under the rule for needing to be of sufficient size, like wood or stone objects or implements. The rabbis also seek to add additional judicial determinations based upon what part of the body was struck and the force of the inflicted blow; these distinctions are of course absent in the biblical laws but added by the rabbis through their process of exegesis.[63] The lethal nature of a small pointed instrument is also recognized in the Sumero-Babylonian tradition. In a catalogue of malevolent ghosts, among those who, having died in an untimely fashion and come to trouble the living, there is the one who "died from the prick of a pin."[64]

Numbers 35:22–28 presents its understanding of accidental homicide, which is defined by the absence of the factors mentioned previously in connection with premeditated homicide:

(However) if he pushed him momentarily without enmity or threw upon him some object without (having lain) in wait, or some stone that one could die thereby without looking he let fall upon him and he (the victim) died, and he (the

63. See *b. Sanh.* 78a, based on *m. Sanh.* 9:2 and incorporating *Sifre N Maseʿy* 160 on Num 35:17, 20. The rabbinic principles are summarized in Maimonides, *Mishnah Torah, Hilkhot Rotzeah Ushmirat Nefesh,* 3:1–6.

64. The ghost is mentioned in line 89' within the text of an incantation in Geller, *Evil Demons,* 113, 205.

slayer) was not his enemy nor did he wish him harm. Then an assembly shall judge between the smiter and the blood-avenger according to such determinations [lit. judgments]. The assembly shall rescue the (accidental) manslayer [lit. homicide] from the blood-avenger, and the assembly shall return him to the city of refuge to which he fled, and there he must dwell until the death of the high priest who was anointed with holy oil. But if the (accidental) manslayer ever goes outside the limit(s) of the city of refuge to which he has fled, and the blood avenger should find him outside the limit(s) of his city of refuge, and the blood avenger kills this (accidental) manslayer, then there is no bloodguilt (for this killing). For he (i.e., the manslayer) must dwell within his city of refuge until the death of the high priest; but after the death of the high priest, the (accidental) manslayer may return to his home [lit. land of his holding].

This section does not employ the term "by mistake" that was mentioned above in Num 35:11 but seems to have in mind a case similar to the "flying ax-handle" of Deut 19:1–13, where the term "unwittingly" is used there. The absence of any history of enmity between the parties, as well as the manslayer not "(having lain) in wait" here again are determining factors.

It is important to note that both Numbers 35 and Deut 19:1–7 recognize the right of the blood avenger to kill the manslayer "in hot anger." In other words, he may kill the manslayer, who is not within a place of refuge, summarily without requiring judicial permission. Homicide was primarily viewed as a private grief, suffered by the family and kinfolk of the victim. Moreover, even if a trial took place, capital punishment was still visualized as being administered by the blood avenger rather than by a magistrate or officer of the court. We have already seen other situations where the kinship network was paramount, e.g., in connection with levirate marriage rights (sec. 1.1.2), inheritance (sec. 1.5), and redemption of property (sec. 2.5.2). Closest kinsmen had both the right and the duty to avenge a homicide; they acted in their capacity as "blood avenger" (literally, "redeemer of the blood (of the slain victim)." The blood of the victim needed to be "soothed" by the death of his slayer. Vengeance to be taken by the family of the victim was used by the larger community as the means to punish the slayer. But if the family failed to act, it did not mean that the slayer escaped justice. Other persons could then step in and punish a manslayer, who deserved to die.

The concept that the blood of the victim requires vengeance, the use of refuge in the form of escape to safety in exile, and the vulnerability of the manslayer, are ideas that are visible elsewhere in the Bible. One place is the story of Cain and Abel. When Cain slew Abel, God confronted him and declared: "What have you done? Listen, your brother's blood is crying out to me from the ground! (Gen 4:10 NRSV).[65] In this story, God punished Cain by banishing him into exile; God also protected Cain from being slain by any other person by giving him a sign. Thus, in Gen 4:13–15, we are told:

> Cain said to the LORD, "My punishment is greater than I can bear!

> Today you have driven me away from the soil, and I shall be hidden from your face; I shall be a fugitive and a wanderer on the earth, and anyone who meets me may kill me." Then the LORD put a mark on Cain, so that no one who came upon him would kill him. (NRSV)

The "mark of Cain" is a feature that is not found in our refuge laws and has been the subject of much speculation. Some understand it to be an actual mark upon his face or body; others take it to be some external device or talisman. One midrash even suggests that God gave him a protective dog to accompany him on his wanderings.[66] We will have more to say about the "mark of Cain" presently; but first we need to look at another biblical tale involving the operation of family justice; it relates to the murder committed by Absalom and the judgment given by David in the case brought before him by a woman of Tekoa.

Background to the woman's tale is found in 2 Samuel 13, which tells the story of how Amnon, David's son, lured his half-sister Tamar into his house and then raped her (See sec. 1.4.2). Absalom, Tamar's full brother, was furious but could do nothing against his half- brother Amnon. But at a later time, as told in 2 Sam 13:23—14:24, Absalom hatched a plot; he invited all of the royal princes—all the sons of David—to a feast; and there he ordered his servants to murder Amnon. Absalom then fled the kingdom to a foreign country, the city of Geshur, where his maternal grandfather was king. David

---

65. Cf. on this expression also Job 16:18 "Earth, do not cover my blood; Let there be no resting place for my outcry!" (NJPS).

66. *Bereshit Rabbah* 22:12 (on Gen 4:15), *Bamidbar Rabbah* 7:5 (on Num 5:2). Hazzequni (on Gen 4:15) however states: " He (God) gave him a sign; and he (Cain) believed in it; but the text does not disclose it (further).

loved Absalom and missed him sorely but did nothing. After three years had passed, Joab invited a woman from Tekoa to come and pretend to be a supplicant before David. Joab instructed her to present herself as a widow with only two sons, one of whom had killed his brother; in 2 Sam 14:5–11, she is standing before the king:

> The king asked her, "What is your trouble?" She answered, "Alas, I am a widow, my husband is dead. Your servant had two sons, and they fought with one another in the field; thee was no one to part them, and one struck the other and killed him. Now the whole family has risen against your servant. They say, 'Give up the man who struck his brother, so that we may kill him for the life of his brother whom he murdered, even if we destroy the heir as well.' Thus they would quench one remaining ember, and leave to my husband neither name nor remnant on the face of the earth." Then the king said to the woman, "Go to your house, and I will give orders concerning you." The woman of Tekoa said to the king, "On me be the guilt, my lord the king, and on my father's house; let the king, and his throne be guiltless," The king said, "If anyone says anything to you, bring him to me, and he shall never touch you again." Then she said, "Please, may the king keep the LORD your God in mind, so that the avenger of blood may kill no more, and my son not be destroyed." He said, "As the LORD lives, not one hair of your son shall fall to the ground." (NRSV)

The woman then, in a further speech, made the king mindful of the strife in his own house; the king, now understanding the import of what he himself had said to her earlier, agrees to bring Absalom back from exile. David at first shuns him but later they are reconciled.

David, during the time when he still believed the woman of Tekoa's tale to be true, gave her assurance that no harm will befall her surviving son. But we are not told how the king intended to restrain the kinsmen, bent on vengeance, from executing her son. Was it sufficiently safe to rely on the king issuing an order of protection? In Numbers 35 and Deut 19:1–7, the blood avenger was able to kill a manslayer, who ventured forth from his place of refuge. If this could happen, then how was King David able to fully curb the basic right of the woman of Tekoa's family's to take vengeance? What's more, there is nothing said here about having the woman's son escape into exile or refuge. We may here now think back to the "sign for Cain," which, perhaps, may have been something like a royal talisman, emblem, or some other article to be worn by the son that would proclaim the king's protection over him; or perhaps even a tattoo or distinctive scar upon the face or body of the manslayer.[67] Such marking could proclaim that the slayer was under royal (or in the case of Cain, divine) protection.

As for Absalom, his remedy had been to seek exile. He was unwilling or unable to avail himself of royal protection; perhaps that measure was added later, after he returned and regained his father's favor. The location of Absalom's exile was external, the same as that of Cain, who

---

67. Gaster, *Myth Legend and Custom,* 1:55–56, 62, put forward the idea of bodily marking for Cain, adding many examples from ancient and pre-modern cultures. Cf. also *Pirqe Rabbi Eliezer* 21, where it is suggested that God placed a letter of the alphabet (as a tattoo) on Cain's arm.

had to flee his country. There are customs similar to this attested among other early societies, where manslayers might be punished with enforced exile or being declared outlaws; if they did not flee, their lives could be taken with impunity; and those who slew them—like the kinsmen of the victim—would not be subject to retribution. Cain's exile was permanent; but in other societies, like in the treatment of Absalom, we see that exile could be temporary.[68]

In Numbers 35, the cities of refuge function as a form of internal exile or banishment, used for a manslayer, who, in the view of society, did not deserve to suffer capital punishment by blood vengeance. Asylum would be granted even though, in the eyes of the victim's family, the blood of the victim still "cried out" for vengeance and the kinsmen might never be convinced that this act of homicide was truly inadvertent. The law in Numbers 35:22–28 was unable to extinguish a family's right of vengeance; the law could only give refuge to the slayer for a period of time, until hot emotions, hopefully, would settle. The law is there to interpose a barrier of protection or restraint between the blood avengers and the manslayer. Num 35:22–28 does include a limit on the manslayer's exile, limiting it to the lifetime of the current high priest. In Deut 19:1–13, on the other hand, there is nothing said about how long the asylum seeker could remain in the city; nor is there any reference there to the high priest. Numbers 35 does not tell us what would happen if the

blood avenger killed the slayer years later, after the term of exile was ended, when he would be legally permitted to leave his refuge. The Mishnah, however, does imagine a situation where there was no high priest; in such a case, the exile, like that of Cain, would become life-long.[69]

We thus find in the biblical laws—in addition to external exile as in the narratives—three sites for asylum or internal exile: religious shrines containing altars, designated cities of undefined character, and "Levitical" cities, i.e., cities historically inhabited by Levites. These differences may reflect an historical process, with changes in the concept of asylum over time. Scholars have posited an historical relationship between altar shrines and the cities—especially the Levitical ones. Were these perhaps former sites of shrines, where altars stood prior to the religious reforms of Josiah, who abolished—and certainly discredited—altars located outside of the Jerusalem temple (2 Kgs 23:15–20)? Their formal designation as cities of refuge could be viewed as a way of utilizing some of the former sacred places, which previously had functioned as places of asylum.[70] Some rabbis indeed maintain that all forty-eight of the Levitical cities had functioned as places of temporary, i.e., pre-trial, asylum; and that the smaller number of three or six were

---

68. For examples in archaic Europe, cf. Diamond, *Primitive Law Past and Present,* 76. For other, pre-modern peoples, cf. e.g., Llewellyn and Hoebel, *The Cheyenne Way,* 137, 158. Cf. also the Hittite instructions for border guards cited below in sec. 4.8.3.

69. Cf. *m. Makk.* 2:7. Maimondes also adds a ruling on an avenger of blood, who killed the slayer after his release from refuge; he considers this to be a fresh homicide for which the avenger himself must now be punished; see *Mishnah Torah, Hilkhot Rotseah Ushmirat Nefesh* 7, 13. But this case is not formally dealt with in the Talmud and, of course, does not appear in the Bible.

70. See the discussions in Weinfeld, *Deuteronomy,* 236–37; Rofé, "History of the Cities of Refuge," 207, 214–21.

designated to serve as places of long-term residence for manslayers whose actions were judged to be accidental.[71]

In the account about Absalom's flight, and in the flights of Adonijah and Joab, there is no mention of the existence of secular or Levitical cities of refuge, as described in the laws of Deuteronomy 19 and Numbers 35. Some scholars therefore suggest that they may have been instituted during the reigns of kings who came after David and Solomon; and perhaps in the era of Josiah, when he abolished the regional shrines. There are yet other factors that may have had an impact on how one views the time frame of their use. A *baraita* cited in the Talmud, *b. Sotah* 48b, declares:

> When the first Temple was destroyed—the cities with pasture land were abolished, the Urim and Thummim ceased, and there was no more a king from the House of David.

The "cities with pasture land" refers to the forty-eight Levitical cities, including the six cities of refuge commanded in Num 35:6, as discussed above. The Urim and Thummim were divinatory devices carried in the breastplate of the high priest. This rabbinic tradition would considerably narrow the available time period for the actualization of the cities of refuge. They could have then existed only during the late monarchy. There are, to be sure, other biblical traditions, which link the institution of asylum cities to Moses and

Joshua.[72] Some scholars consider these to be valid historical references and thus place their use to a period before the monarchy was established. However, other scholars believe that these traditions are pseudo-historical, supplying moral argument in support of a later program, which may or may not have come into actualization.[73] The truth is, that at this stage of our knowledge, one does not know for certain when—leaving aside the question if ever—a system of cities of refuge was in operation.

At the same time, it seems that the practice of temples serving as places of at least temporary refuge did not ever disappear or become obsolete. The Bible tells us that religious shrines functioned in this capacity in the time of David and Solomon. And during the Persian period, this practice was still recognized, as we can see from the story told in Neh 6:10–13; Nehemiah is recounting what happened to him:

> One day when I went into the house of Shemaiah son of Delaiah son of Mehetabel, who was confined to this house, he said, "Let us meet together in the house of God, within the temple, and let us close the doors of the temple, for they are coming to kill you; indeed, tonight they are coming to kill you." But I said, "Should a man like me run away? Would a man like me go into the temple to save his life? I will not go in!" Then I perceived and saw that God had not sent him at all, but he had pronounced the prophecy against me because Tobiah and

---

71. See *b. Makk.* 10a, whose statement is followed by Hazzequni and Bekhor Shor in their commentaries on Num 35:6. Cf. also Nahmanides, who is not fully persuaded, in his comments on Num 35:14.

72. Deut 4:41–43; Josh 20:1—21:40; 1 Chr 6:42–66.

73. For literature, cf. Barmash, *Homicide in the Biblical World*, 84 n. 49; Rofé, "History of the Cities of Refuge," 207–10.

Sanballat had hired him. He was hired for this purpose, to intimidate me and make me sin by acting in this way, and so they could give me a bad name, in order to taunt me (NRSV).

Nehemiah, not being a priest, was reluctant to enter the sanctuary; not only might this be an admission of guilt but he might also be criticized for his unwarranted entry.[74] From a much later time, Josephus records that the Seleucid king Demetrius (c. 145 BCE) wrote a generous letter to Jonathan the Jewish High Priest promising him release from many taxes along with many privileges for the Judeans; he also proposed that the Jerusalem temple be recognized as a place of asylum:

> And all those who take refuge in the temple at Jerusalem or in any place to which its name is attached, whether because they owe money to the king or for any other reason, shall be set free, and their possessions shall be left untouched.[75]

This proposal may not have included asylum for homicide; and we have no certainty that it was acted upon by Jonathan or his successors. But we do see that the custom of using religious shrines as places for asylum was still very common.[76]

There are also passages in the Psalms that describe the Temple as a place of refuge; for example, Ps 27:4–5:

> One thing I asked of the LORD, that will I seek after: to live in the house of the LORD all the days of my life, to behold the beauty of the LORD, and to inquire in his temple. For he will hide me in his shelter in the day of trouble; he will conceal me under the cover of his tent; he will set me high on a rock (NRSV).

Similarly, Ps 59:17:

> But I will sing of Your strength, extol each morning Your faithfulness; for You have been my haven, a refuge in time of trouble. (NJPS)

We also know of at least one instance where a synagogue functioned as a place of refuge. There is stated in a Greek inscription from Egypt which records that Ptolemy Euergetes II (145–115 BCE) proclaimed a certain synagogue as a place of asylum.[77]

---

74. Barmash, *Homicide*, 73 n. 10, suggests that perhaps at the time of Nehemiah, the altar was off-limits to laity, but not the temple itself, because in Neh 13:8, it appears that Nehemiah did enter the temple in order to empty the room previously used by Tobiah.

75. Josephus, *Ant.* 13.56, Thackeray. A similar passage appears in the account given in 1 Macc 10:43: "And all who take refuge at the temple in Jerusalem, or in any of its precincts, because they owe money to the king or are in debt, let them be released and receive back all their property in my kingdom" (NRSV).

76. The history of asylum in ancient Israel has been subject to different reconstructions; see, e.g., for their own views and for previous scholars, the discussions in Barmash, *Homicide in the Biblical World*, 71–93; Milgrom, *Numbers*, 504–9; Rofé, "History of the Cities of Refuge." For pagan temples and later churches and mosques used as places of asylum cf. Westermarck, "Asylum."

77. Horbury and Noy, *Jewish Inscriptions of Graeco-Roman Egypt*, 214, no. 125. This reference is also discussed in Ben Zeev, *Jewish Rights in the Roman World*, 263–64. The custom of designating Philistine, Phoenician, and other temple cities in the region as places of asylum is well attested for Seleucid and Ptolemaic times; there is also some earlier evidence for this practice during Persian and even late Assyrian times. See Greenfield, "Asylum at Aleppo."

We lack postbiblical statements concerning the practice of private blood vengeance for homicide; we may therefore wonder whether this practice became obsolete. The omission of any mention of cities of refuge in Ezekiel's proposed plan of government—in Ezekiel 40–48—has been taken to indicate that blood vengeance was suppressed during the Persian period.[78] A number of later rabbinic traditions testify that following independence from the Seleucids, civil and criminal jurisdictions were taken over, initially by the Hasmonean and later by the Roman rulers of Judea. The Palestinian Talmud, in *j. Sanh.* 18a states:

> Forty years before the destruction of the (second) Temple (i.e., c. 30 CE), the power over capital cases was removed (from the local Jewish courts); and in the days of Simeon ben Shetah (c. 75 BCE) the power over monetary disputes.[79]

It is virtually certain that the practice of private, kinship-based blood vengeance would not have survived under Roman rule, if the Hasmoneans and Herodians did not already suppress it before them. Capital punishment would, of course, continue; but we would expect that it would then have been administered by the sovereign or his appointed magistrates. We know, however, that the custom of offering asylum, probably temporary, in religious shrines did continue

into Roman times, as well as the punishment of exile.[80] But the custom of asylum, according to the historian Suetonius, was ended during the reign of the emperor Tiberius, who ruled 14–37 CE, because "he abolished the customary right of asylum in all parts of the empire." [81] The Romans nevertheless retained an ancient custom of punishing homicide with exile in cases when capital punishment was not given. Both earlier and later laws are described by the jurist Marcianus, who lived c. 200 CE:

> The penalty of the *lex Cornelia* (67 BCE) on murderers and poisoners is deportation to an island and the forfeiture of all property. However, nowadays capital punishment is customary, except for persons of a status too high to be subject to the (modern) statutory punishment; those of lower rank are usually either crucified or thrown to the beasts while their betters are deported to an island.[82]

4.8.2 Compensation for Homicide

There is another important dimension in the handling of homicide in biblical times about which we are told, with an attitude of condemnation, in Numbers 35. This is the custom of offering monetary compensation to the family of a victim—"buying off," so to speak, the bloodguilt connected with the homicide and its call for vengeance. We have seen earlier, in connection with personal injury, about

---

78. Cf. Milgrom, *Numbers,* 509.

79. A variant of this text, which appears in *j. Sanh.* 24b, replaces Simeon ben Shetah with Simeon bar Yohai, who lived over a century later. Another similar tradition appears in *b. Shabb.* 15a. John 18:31 also testifies to Judean powerlessness over capital punishment under Roman rule. Similarly, Acts 18:14 on criminal prosecution, and of course, the trial of Jesus by Pontius Pilate.

80. *D.*21.1.12 records the practice in the time of the jurist Labeo (c. 4 BCE).

81. Suetonius, *Tib.* 37. The actions of Tiberius are also reported in Tacitus, *Annals* 3, 60–62, which is discussed in Greenfield, "Asylum," 278.

82. *D.*48.8.5.

how talionic reprisal and monetary compensation were part of a single justice system. Thus in Deut 32:35, Moses, in God's name, is able to declare:

> (Blood) vengeance and compensation are mine (waiting only for) the time that their foot falters because their day of disaster is near, and things destined hasten towards them.

Blood vengeance is an expression of talionic reprisal—the life of the manslayer for the life of the victim; and the kinsmen of the deceased act as the agents of justice. Compensation was an alternative resolution. Despite the unity of compensation and talionic reprisal that we saw in connection with non-fatal injuries, we find a strongly worded position against monetary compensation for homicide expressed in Num 35:31–34:

> And you must not accept a ransom for the life of a murderer [lit. homicide] who is (judged) guilty (and sentenced) to die for he must surely be put to death. Nor may you accept ransom (for one) to flee to a city of refuge, (or for one) to return to live in the land before the death of the (high) priest. You shall not pollute the land in which you (dwell); for blood—it will pollute the land, and for the land no expiation can be made for blood that is shed on it, except by the blood of the one who shed it. You shall not defile the land in which you dwell, in which I (likewise) dwell, for I the LORD (will) dwell among the Israelite people.

For the author of Numbers 35, the blood of the murderer needed to be spilled in order to atone for the blood of the victim. The vehemence of this law suggests that the practice of offering monetary compensation for homicide was known in ancient Israel but was now being opposed. Indeed we have already noted the existence of possible compensation in the discussion of adultery (sec. 1.3.1). The juxtaposition of compensation and capital punishment in connection with homicide was still a possibility in the narrative about David's dealing with the Gibeonites in 2 Samuel 21 (which I mentioned earlier in the discussion about Rizpah, the concubine of Saul in sec. 1.1.2) In this narrative we see not only the juxtaposition of compensation with capital punishment, but also a deeper level of talionic reprisal taking place against family members of the offender. In 2 Sam 21:3–4, David negotiated with the Gibeonites in an effort to remove bloodguilt from the land. David earlier had learned from an oracle that the famine came because of Saul having slain some of the Gibeonites. So David offers them a choice:[83]

> And David said to the Gibeonites, "What shall I do for you and in what way can I make expiation, so that you may bless the LORD's inheritance (i.e., the land and its people)?" And the Gibeonites replied to him, "We have not (any wish to receive) silver or gold from Saul and his household; and we have not (any wish) to put to death any person in Israel." And David responded, "What do you say I must do for you?"

The Gibeonites refused compensation but instead, as was evidently their right, then asked for talionic retribution, taking the lives of Saul's surviving close

---

83. This act of Saul is not otherwise recorded in the Bible; *b. B. Qam.* 119a offers a suggestion.

relatives since Saul was now dead. David felt he had no choice but to agree with their demand for blood vengeance over compensation. What is surprising here is that we find talionic retribution being taken against members of Saul's family— even against those who may not have participated in the slaying of the Gibeonites! This transfer of responsibility was seen as just in ancient Israel, for it was in keeping with the ancient idea of "visiting the sins of the father upon the children." In this form of "collective responsibility," blame for one person's misdeeds could be passed down upon other members of his kinship group, especially upon his children who were after all, in all other respects, his heirs. This policy of transferred or collective retribution was believed to be present in divine justice, as stated in Exod 20:5 and Deut 5:9: "visiting the sins of the father on the sons until the third and fourth generation for my enemies." In a similar fashion, when Achan was stoned for stealing sacred property (Josh 7:20–26; see sec. 5.7), the members of his family were punished together with him. We again see this concept again expressed in relation to the sins of Ahab. In 1 Kgs 21:28–29 God spares Ahab and defers punishment for him, transferring it to his son:

> And the word of the LORD came to Elijah the Tishbite, saying, "Have you seen how Ahab humbles himself before me? Because he humbles himself before me, I will not bring the evil in his days: but in his son's days will I bring the evil upon his house."

However, thinking on this subject changed during biblical times; the concept of transferred liability was rejected in Deut 24:16:

> Fathers shall not be put to death for children, neither shall children be put to death for the fathers: every man shall be put to death for his own sin (only).[84]

But the practice was deeply rooted and not easily relinquished. A discourse filling an entire chapter in Ezekiel was devoted to presenting the newer ideal in great detail. We cite here a short excerpt from Ezek 18:19–20:

> And now you say, "Why should a son not carry (responsibility) for his father's sin?" But the son has done what is just and righteous and has observed and performed all my statutes; he shall surely live! (Only) the person who sins shall die. A son shall not bear (responsibility) for a father's sin, nor shall a father bear (responsibility) for the sin of the son; the righteousness of the righteous shall belong to him (alone) and the wickedness of the wicked will belong to him (alone).

One may assume that the concept of collective or transferred responsibility was abandoned after the time of Ezekiel. The laws on cities of refuge in Deuteronomy 19 and Numbers 35 do not mention the possibility of liability being transferred to members of the slayer's family; the slayer alone is responsible; and—unlike what we saw for the family of Achan or Saul—not

---

84. Conformity with the new principle of individual responsibility is attributed to King Amaziah in 2 Kgs 14:5–6: "And it came to pass, when kingship was firmly in his hand, he killed those of his servants who had slain his father the king. But he did not put to death the children of the murderers, as was written in the book of the teaching of Moses, where the Lord commanded, saying, "The fathers shall not be put to death for children, nor children be put to death for fathers; each person shall be put to death for his own sin."

his family nor his kin. This aspect of extended liability evidently disappeared or was suppressed at the time when the texts of our laws on cities of refuge were written. However, there still remained a shared role for the kinship group with respect to the duty of blood avenger. According to what we have seen in the account given by the woman of Tekoa in 2 Sam 14:7 (sec. 4.8.1), the role of avenger could apparently be assumed by any person belonging to the victim's family. The changes in liability for homicide may very well be connected with the disappearance of tribal identity that began during the monarchy; for by postexilic times, kinship groups were smaller; tribal designations retained historical interest but they no longer had any legal function and relevance in society.

4.8.3 Homicide in Ancient Near Eastern Sources

In ancient Near Eastern sources, we find overall many of the same concepts that we have seen in biblical and rabbinic sources. But there were differences among the Near Eastern societies, affecting the manner in which these concepts were applied.

In the Sumerian laws dealing with homicide, the death penalty is meted out by the state, not by the kinship group of the victim. The death penalty for homicide is stated in Urnamma Laws §1: "If a man slays (another man), that man will be killed." Additional details on how the death penalty for homicide was administered comes from a "classic" Sumerian homicide trial, which was preserved as part of a scribal school curriculum. In the trial, three men are sentenced to death for killing a priest; the wife of the slain priest is also implicated as an accessory to the murder. The sentence is described as follows:

> Being men who have killed, they may not remain living; the males– all three of them– and that woman shall be executed before the chair of (the deceased) A son of B.[85]

The murdered man's chair can be seen as creating a symbolic contact with the deceased victim; in this sense the place of punishment is similar to what we see in a Neo-Assyrian trial (cited below), where the slayer is executed on the grave of the victim. The delivery of capital punishment is here controlled by state authority; there is no legal role for an "avenger of the blood."

Under certain circumstances, compensation could also be given; this is not stated in the laws but we find this resolution in a judicial decision from a few decades after Urnamma:

> Final Verdict: Whereas Kuli son of Ur-Eanna slew Babamu, the musician, it was decided in the presence of the vizier that since Kuli killed (a man), his wife, his daughter, and his estate were given over to the sons of Babamu. Lu-Girsu was baliff.[86]

It appears that Kuli himself could not be brought to justice; apparently he had fled. Compensation was the alternative;

---

85. Jacobsen, "An Ancient Mesopotamian Trial for Homicide"; the excerpt presents lines 30–35. I have replaced the Sumerian personal names with letters of the alphabet for clarity.

86. The case is Falkenstein, *Die neusumerischen Gerichtsurkunden* 2 no. 41. Falkenstein, ibid., 1:132–33, notes that Kuli himself was not punished for his murder and compares another case, Falkenstein, ibid., 2 no. 42, where a robber fled and his family members were given over to the victims in compensation.

and Kuli's financial debt was borne by his wife, daughter, and estate. They were given over as debt slaves to supplement the forfeiture of Kuli's property. The case continues; five years later, Kuli's wife and daughter themselves fled from the sons of Babamu; but they were apprehended; and their status as slaves was confirmed again by the court. We are not informed as to how long they were required to serve. Their servitude might have been permanent as in Hittite Laws §§1–4 (discussed below). Because the slayer's punishment was borne by his wife and daughter, we can view this case as an example of transferred responsibility.

Capital punishment was applied for homicide in Babylonia. We know of a case where talionic reprisal for an intentional homicide was imposed by Rimsin, a Babylonian king who was an older contemporary of Hammurapi, in a letter issued to his officials in Larsa:

> Thus (says) Rimsin your lord: "Since he cast a boy into a furnace, you (too) cast (that) slave into the furnace."[87]

At the same time, the possibility of imposing compensation as an alternative to the death penalty appears in an Old Babylonian treaty document from the area of Eshnunna. One of the treaty provisions states:

> If one brings a capital charge, if it (the homicide) involves one (manslayer), he will die. If it involves from two to three—up to five or more (manslayers), they shall (all) be seized for this capital crime; anyone whom they (the court) *convict* will die [and . . .] all of them

will (together?) pay one and two-thirds mina silver.[88]

The death penalty falls upon the person who struck the fatal blow whether he acted alone or in a group; however, other members of the group (and perhaps the slayer as well) must pay compensation. The punishment for homicide varied with the circumstances of the case.

In Babylonia, in Eshnunna Laws §§47A–48, the stated punishment for homicide is monetary when the assailant and the victim were in a fight together; in modern terms, such homicide caused by altercation or passion would be considered manslaughter. All capital cases needed to come before the king:

> §47A If a man in a brawl caused the death of another man's son, he shall pay two-thirds mina silver.

> §48 And in a case involving money from one-third mina to one mina, the (local) judges shall handle his case; but a matter (involving the taking) of a life, is for the king.

Monetary payment for fatal injury in a brawl appears in Hammurapi Laws §§207–208, (which follow just after the case of non-fatal injury in §206 discussed above in sec. 4.3):

> §207 If he (the party injured in a brawl) has died from his blow(s), he (the striker) shall likewise swear ("I did not strike him knowing [that I would kill him]"); if he (the victim) is the son of a freeman, he (the striker) shall pay one-half mina silver.

---

87. *BIN* 7 10; the document is treated most recently in *AbB* 9 no. 197.

88. Greengus, *Old Babylonian Tablets from Ishchali and Vicinity,* 74–77 (no. 326:22–27).

§208 If he (the victim) is the son of a commoner, he (the striker) shall pay one-third mina silver.

§207 shows the concept of unwitting or accidental homicide. This injury did not rise to the level of talionic reprisal but was, rather, to be settled by compensation. In an Old Babylonian document from Mari, we find the expression "silver pertaining to a capital case" together with the payment of three and one-half minas silver. This sum is substantially higher than the less than one mina amounts found in Eshnunna Laws §48 and the one half or one-third mina in Hammurapi Laws §§207–208.[89] But in a diplomatic dispatch found at Mari, one does find a report of negotiations offering a ransom of one-third mina, five shekels silver, later raised to one-half mina silver. The brother of the victim, however, was unwilling to accept ransom in any amount; and he was allowed to execute a most brutal vengeance upon the murderer.[90]

It is interesting that while the biblical laws cited above (secs. 4.8.1–4.8.2) in Deuteronomy 19 and Numbers 35 contrast premeditated homicide with accidental homicide, they do not consider the category of non-intentional fatal injury resulting from a brawl. That case may however be partially implied in Exod 21:18–19 (sec. 4.3), where the non-fatal striking of another person in a fight, even intentionally and using a stone as a weapon, is satisfied by compensation. But if that striking were fatal to the victim, it would have merited capital punishment, even if the striker did not intend to kill his victim. This would certainly be so according to Numbers 35:16–21, where any striking, using a stone or other object, is equivalent to premeditated homicide as long as it led to a fatality.[91] Numbers 35 gives no consideration to the state of mind of the striker. The Bible there gives no opportunity to the slayer to swear to his lack of intent as in Hammurapi Laws §§207–208. The Bible, rather, relies upon circumstances like use of a weapon or prior history of enmity between the parties. On the other hand, the Babylonian laws do not tell us whether any of the combatants used a stone or weapon in the brawl. So we do not know if that would have made a difference. Some scholars theorize that in earlier biblical times, accidental or unintentional homicides might have been more readily settled by compensation, as in Babylonia. They find indirect evidence

89. On this amount see further ARM 8 1, which is mentioned in Barmash, *Homicide in the Biblical World*, 171–72; also *CAD* N/1, 300–301 sub *dīn napištim* "capital case." The context there is not a case of homicide; the reference appears in a no-contest clause sworn by the parties in an adoption contract; it appears as an aside, describing the high forfeiture penalty demanded in this agreement.

90. The text is A. 3680, published in Joannès, "L'absence d'Atamrum," 336–38, and restudied in Durand, "La vengeance à l'époque amorrite. The murderer was made to suffer gruesome mutilations and then was dragged thirty times around the city. For the slaying of a murderer by a kinsman of the victim see also the Mari reference in *CAD* N/2 251, sub *niqmum*.

91. This is also the understanding of Josephus, *Ant.* 4.277, Thackeray: "In a fight without the use of the blade, if one be stricken and die on the spot, he shall be avenged . . ." Josephus here distinguishes between "stone or fist," which are mentioned in Exod 21:18, and the use of a weapon, which is not mentioned there. Josephus may here reflect Roman law, where, according to the *lex Cornelia* (67 BCE), the use of a weapon was in itself grounds for a charge of homicide. Cf. also *D*.48.8.1–3 and the rescript of Hadrian: "if someone draws his sword or strikes with a weapon, he undoubtedly did so with the intention of causing death."

for a scheme of compensation in Deut 19:1–13, because the law there makes no provision for long-term residence in the place of asylum. The same might have been true for slayers who took refuge in sacred shrines. Refuge then would have served as a temporary measure, whose purpose was to allow time for the parties to arrange for compensation.[92]

The adjudication of homicide cases by the king and settlement of homicide through compensation is again seen in a document of the Middle Babylonian period, written shortly after 1000 BCE. The document records a series of settlements reached between two quarreling families whose enmity went back to a time when a member of one family had slain the female slave of his neighbor; the slain woman was wife to a member of his household:

> . . . A son of B, struck the *slave* of C *the bowmaker*—whom D married—with an arrow and killed her. C and A son of B went to law and Ninurta-kudurri-uṣur the king declared unto A as follows: "Go, give seven slaves unto C. . . ."141[93]

No further information is given about the details of the killing; it is not certain whether compensation was given because the victim was a slave or because the circumstances indicated an unintentional or accidental homicide.

A juxtaposition of talionic reprisal with monetary compensation, closer in character to what we have seen in the Bible in connection with the choice given by David to the Gibeonites, is clearly visible in laws and documents from Assyria. We also find evidence for the role of kinfolk in determining the punishment. Middle Assyrian Laws §B 2 deals with a manslayer whose assets are jointly held with other persons in his family who were innocent of wrongdoing. As with the Gibeonites, the family of the victim has a choice:

> If a man—(one) of brothers (who had) not divided (their property)—has ended (someone's) life, they shall hand him over to the "life owner" (i.e., the next of kin to the victim). If the "life owner" chooses, he may kill him; or, if he chooses, he may come to an agreement [and] take his (i.e., the slayer's) share (in the family property).

Middle Assyrian Laws §A 10 deals with another case where the family of the victim is given a choice between taking reprisal or accepting compensation:

> [If] either a man or woman entered [into the house of another person] and killed [either a man o]r woman (there), [they shall hand over] the killers [to the master of the household]. If he chooses, he shall k[ill] them; [if he chooses, he may come to an agreement and] take [their property. And if] there is noth[ing of giving in the hous]e of the kill[ers, he shall take] either a son [or daughter] . . . (remainder of the text is lost).

We have a number of Neo-Assyrian documents, relating to actual trials for homicide, in which compensation was offered and accepted. One document is

---

92. Cf. Rofé, "The History of the Cities of Refuge in Biblical Law," 254–56; Jackson, "Reflections on Biblical Law," 41–50; idem, *Wisdom Laws*, 133 and n. 77. These scholars, however, also consider the possibility that compensation might have been paid as well in cases of intentional homicide.

93. *BBSt* no. 9, col. i, 2–10. Except for the king, I have replaced the other personal names with alphabet letters in order to present the circumstances of the case more clearly.

especially revealing. It involves a proposed settlement, handing over the slayer's daughter, just as in Middle Assyrian Laws §A 10:

> (Beginning lost) Now it is mutually agreed: the man (i.e., the slayer) will hand over A, the daughter of B (who is the slayer) to C son of D (the victim) in lieu of the blood and will wash away the blood (thereby). If he does not hand over the woman, they will kill him (the slayer) upon D's grave. Whoever stirs up strife (over this agreement) will pay ten minas silver (and) Ashur, Shamash, and the oath of the king will call him to account . . . (the tablet breaks off; traces of date and names of witnesses follow).[94]

This document reveals the custom of having talionic reprisal take place at the grave of the victim; furthermore, if compensation were offered and accepted by the victim's family, then the blood of the victim would be considered as "washed off." Blood would no longer "cry out" for vengeance. The handing over of a daughter by the slayer looks like transferred liability; but it may perhaps be more a reflection of the absolute patriarchal power of a father over his children. The father was able to give members of his family as compensation for his own actions.

Clear instances of transferred liability are known in Mesopotamia. We have already noted transferred liability in Hammurapi Laws §210, where a daughter suffers death for her father's causing

the death of a pregnant woman (sec. 4.7). Transferred liability is also seen in Hammurapi Laws § 116 (cited above sec. 4.1)) where a son will be put to death if his father caused the death of another man's son taken by the father as a debt hostage. The same fate befalls the son of the builder of a faulty house in Hammurapi Laws §230 (discussed below in sec. 4.9). We also saw transferred liability in Middle Assyrian Laws §§A 55–56, where a free man's wife suffers sexual reprisal for a rape committed by her husband (sec. 1.4.1). We also find transferred liability in Hittite Laws §44a where the offender's son pays for his father's crime (discussed below). However, we do not know of any cases of collective responsibility exactly like that seen with the Gibeonites and the descendents of Saul—that is, where after the culprit died, talionic reprisal could be taken against his children. This form of transferred responsibility was, however, preserved among the Bedouin tribes of pre-Islamic Arabia. Their customs were accepted by Islam and thus even survive into modern times. We will have more to say about these Arabian customs below, after we have discussed the rest of what we know from earlier ancient Near Eastern evidence.

The Hittites generally punished homicide with compensation. There is also evidence of a historical shift in societal attitudes, since we find, in their laws, other situations where the older practices of capital punishment were replaced by measures of compensation.[95] Hittite Laws

---

94. This document, *ADD* 321, and other documents dealing with homicide and compensation are treated in Roth, "Homicide in the Neo-Assyrian Period"; Jas, *Neo-Assyrian Judicial Procedures*, 62–67; and Barmash, *Homicide in the Biblical World*, 56–70. In the translation I have given above, I have replaced the personal names with alphabet letters.

95. Cf. Hittite Laws §§92, 121, and 166–167 (see below in secs. 5.6.2, 6.6); removal of corporal punishment is also present in Hittite Laws §101 (not quoted here).

§§1–4 on homicide clearly present this practice:

§1 [If] anyone kills a man or a woman in a [quarr]el, he [i.e., the slayer] shall [bring him (for burial)] and shall give 4 persons (lit. heads), male or female respectively, and he shall look [to his house for it.]

§2 [If] anyone kills [a male] or female slave in a quarrel, he shall bring him (for burial) [and] shall give [2] persons (lit. heads), male or female respectively, and he shall look to his house for it.

§3 [If] anyone strikes a free [man] or woman so that he dies, but it is an accident [lit. his hand sins], he shall bring him (for burial) and shall give two persons (lit. heads), and he shall look to his house for it.

§4 [If] anyone strikes a male or female slave and he dies, but it is an accident [lit. his hand sins], he shall bring him (for burial) and shall give one person (lit. head), and he shall look to his house for it.

§3–4 (Later version) [If anyone . . .]s(?) [a woman] so that she dies, but it is an accident [lit. his hand sins] [he shall pay 4? minas of silver.] But if the woman was a slave, he shall pay two minas of silver.

§§3–4 deal with unintentional killing; and the compensation is thus less than in §§1–2 where the killing, if not fully intentional, nevertheless occurs during a quarrel. The circumstance of a quarrel raises the level of the striker's responsibility.

The difference between the Hittite and the Babylonian treatment of murderers was the subject of a letter written by the Hittite king Hattusili III to Kadashman-Enlil II of Babylon (c. 1270 BCE). In his letter, the Hittite king attempts to explain why the murderers of traveling Babylonian merchants were not being put to death. Hattusili tells the Babylonian king:

. . . they do not kill (as punishment) in Hatti . . . They apprehend the murderer [and deliver him] to the relatives of the dead man; [but they allow] the murderer [to live. The place] in which the murder occurred—they purify. If his relatives will not accept [the compensation], they may make the murderer [their slave]. If a man who has committed an offense against the king [escapes] to another land, killing him is not the practice. Ask, my brother, and they shall tell you . . . thus. Would those who do not kill a political criminal (enemy of the king now) kill a merchant (who killed another merchant)?[96]

Hattusili adds the illustration of treason to make his point; the punishment for one who commits an offense against the king is not death, thus one can more readily understand the Hittite custom regarding other acts of homicide. Killing of a merchant is in fact the subject of Hittite Laws §5:

If anyone kills a merchant (var. Hittite merchant), he shall pay 100 minas of silver and he shall look to his house for it. If it is in the lands of Luwiya or Pala, he shall pay 100

96. For this passage, *KBo* I 10: r. 14–23, see Beckman, *Hittite Diplomatic Texts*, 136; see also Greengus, "Some Issues," 65–70 for discussion on Hittite societal changes relating to homicide and on the protection given to merchants in the ancient Near East. Barmash, *Homicide in the Biblical World*, 178–201, adds additional references and discussion.

minas of silver and also replace his goods. If it is in the land of Hatti, he himself shall (also) bring the afore-mentioned merchant (for burial).

(Later version) If anyone kills a Hittite [merchant] in the midst of his goods, he shall pay [. . . minas of silver] and he shall replace the goods threefold. But [if] the mer-chant is not in possession of goods, and someone kills him in a quarrel, he shall pay six minas of silver. If it is only an accident [lit. the hand sins], he shall pay two minas of silver.

Here we see that compensation was given to settle the slaying of a Hittite merchant, just like in the case of a foreign merchant. The later version of this law adds provi-sions for restitution of goods. If goods were not involved, then the case is han-dled like other homicides, but again with compensation.

From neighboring Syria we have a number of treaties, which likewise call for compensation being paid to fami-lies of merchants who were killed. These settlements also appear in treaties be-tween kings of Ugarit who were vassal to Carchemish, which was, itself, a satellite kingdom of the Hittite empire. The sums to be given range from three and one-half to approximately twelve minas. The trea-ties also provide that one who has mur-dered a merchant from the other ruler's country, if apprehended, must in addition restore the value of lost goods.[97]

From Hittite Laws §§3–4 (and 5) dis-cussed above, we see that, within a gen-eral policy of compensation for homicide, the Hittites recognized circumstances of

accidental homicide and felt that it was appropriate to reduce the penalty in cases of unintentional homicide. There are also laws where the act of homicide was seen as intentional—or nearly so. This is found in Hittite Laws §43:

> If a man is crossing a river with his ox (var. oxen) and another man pushes him off (the ox's tail), grasps the tail of the ox, and crosses the river, but the river carries off the owner of the ox [i.e., he drowns], they (the dead man's heirs) will take that very man who pushes him off [i.e., as a slave].

The man who pushed the owner off of his ox may not have intended to drown him but at the same time he is not free of responsibility for creating a situation of peril for the other person. He should have known this. The penalty here is thus more severe in that the offender must himself be enslaved, rather than being permit-ted to offer other persons in his stead as is done in Hittite Laws §§1–4 (above).[98] Another case of intentional homicide—or an action practically considered so—is described Hittite Laws §44a. Here, again, the penalty hits the offender personally:

> If anyone makes a man fall into a fire, so that he dies, he (the guilty party) shall give a son in return.

It may be argued that the penalty here is perhaps less severe than in §43.[99] It will of course depend upon whether the enslave-ment of a son was viewed as more hurtful to a father than his own enslavement. The seriousness of the perpetrator's action, which is described as directly causing

97. For references cf. Greengus, "Some Issues," 66–68; Barmash, *Homicide*, 184–99.

98. See Hoffner, "On Homicide in Hittite Law," 306–8.

99. Ibid., 309.

the victim's death, with no mitigating circumstance, leads me to believe that it was the more painful penalty.

The Hittites were aware that their avoidance of capital punishment was not customary elsewhere; thus, they did not attempt to impose their own view upon neighboring peoples in global fashion. A Hittite document containing instructions for the governing officials counseled:

> Furthermore, the commander of the border guards, the town commandant, and the elders shall judge and decide legal cases in accordance with the law. As it has been from olden days—in a town in which they have been accustomed to imposing the death penalty, they shall continue to do so. But in a town where they have been accustomed to imposing exile, they shall continue that (custom).[100]

There is also some evidence that the Hittites, at an earlier time in their history, imposed capital punishment for homicide—at least for one who slew a person of royal blood. The royal edict of Telepinu, who reigned some two centuries before Hattusili III (of the royal letter mentioned above) in an effort to reduce bloodshed and feud between members of the royal family, decreed that the family members of the person committing homicide would no longer be subject to capital punishment, only the perpetrator himself. Telepinu also introduced the option of compensation as an alternative to capital punishment:

> Whoever commits murder, whatever the heir [literally: owner of the blood] himself of the murdered

man says (will be done). If he says: "Let him die," he shall die; but if he says: "Let him make compensation," he shall make compensation. The king shall have no role in the decision.[101]

From the range of practices involved in the social response to homicide, we can see that this is an area in which there was, anciently, no uniformity. The customs of Assyria come closest to those of ancient Israel—more so than those of the Babylonians or the Hittites. It may therefore be possible to imagine that the institution of the biblical cities of refuge could have developed and flourished during the period from 722 to 612 BCE., after Assyria conquered the northern kingdom of Israel; and Judea, much reduced in geographical size, was embedded within the larger, surrounding Assyrian empire. I have already mentioned a possible link between the establishment of cities of refuge and king Josiah, whose religious reform eliminated the use of shrines outside of Jerusalem; Josiah ruled towards the end of the Assyrian period, from c. 640–609 BCE. The new ideas on collective responsibility, found in Ezekiel and Deuteronomy, which removed liability from the relatives of the manslayer, may likewise have emerged during the Assyrian period. For, as we have seen, in Assyria, responsibility rested only upon the slayer and was not transferred to his relatives.

It is difficult to determine when the section on the rejection of compensation

---

100. For this document, preserved in several ancient copies, see *ANET*, 210–11.

101. Cf. Hoffner, On Homicide in Hittite Law," 311, who discusses and rejects an alternative translation favored by others: "But to the king, he shall not pay compensation." See also in Roth, *Law Collections,* 237, Barmash, *Homicide in the Biblical World,* 31–32, 219, and Greengus, "Some Issues," 69–70.

found in Num 35:31–34 was written; it, too, may have been during or just after this period of strong Assyrian dominance. For the Assyrians, as we have seen, did allow compensation to be paid for homicide. One can see that the juxtaposition of compensation and talionic reprisal was still possible a century or so earlier; and appears in a parable in 1 Kgs 20:38–43, used by an unnamed prophet, disguised as a wounded soldier, in his confrontation with king Ahab:

> Then the prophet departed, and waited for the king along the road, disguising himself with a bandage over his eyes. As the king passed by, he cried to the king and said, "Your servant went out into the thick of the battle; then a soldier turned and brought a man to me, and said, 'Guard this man; if he is missing, your life shall be given for his life, or else you shall pay a talent of silver.' While your servant was busy here and there, he was gone." The king of Israel said to him, "So shall your judgment be; you yourself have decided it." Then he quickly took the bandage away from his eyes. The king of Israel recognized him as one of the prophets. Then he said to him, "Thus says the LORD, 'Because you have let the man go whom I had devoted to destruction, therefore your life shall be for his life, and your people for his people.'" The king of Israel set out toward home, resentful and sullen, and came to Samaria. (NRSV)

The prophet pretended that he was a soldier who had been given the responsibility of guarding an important prisoner but let him get away. He conveyed his fictional assignment as a command whose violation would expose him to punishment—either

"life for life" or a heavy compensation of one talent, which was far beyond the reach of all but the wealthiest of people. The point of his charade was to point out to king Ahab that by letting his adversary Ben-Hadad, king of Damascus, go free, Ahab, too, must suffer divine punishment for this indiscretion. The prophet—and the biblical account—could employ this scenario, juxtaposing compensation and talionic reprisal, because this alternation of penalties was clearly well understood and seen as plausible.

It is difficult to know why Numbers 35 advocated against compensation. Some scholars have argued that the biblical rejection of compensation represented a moral advance, informed by an increased respect for the sanctity of human life. This is an attractive idea. At the same time, however, others have made similar claims of moral advance for the Hittites, who abandoned talionic reprisal and capital punishment in favor of compensation! I am unable to judge; and the debate over the appropriateness of capital punishment for homicide continues even today.[102]

We can gain further insight into the biblical treatment of homicide by considering pre-Islamic practices which were accepted by Islamic law, i.e., the Qur'an, as well as continuing in Ottoman law and even twentieth century Syrian law. Most notable is the juxtaposition of corporal punishment and compensation, which is similar to what we have already noted in connection with personal injuries. The family of the victim had the choice: exacting blood vengeance or accepting compensation. Vengeance could be taken

102. Cf. Barmash. *Homicide in the Biblical World*, 142–45; and Greengus, "Law: Biblical and ANE Law," 249.

against other relatives of the slayer. Compensation had to be accepted in cases of accidental homicide but was optional in other situations, e.g., if a weapon was used or if there was evidence of intent. The amounts of this payment, called *diya* was set by custom; women would merit half of the compensation given to men; and the compensation paid for the death of a slave belonged to his owner. The setting of customary rates of evaluation based on status and gender follows what we have already noted in the Bible and in our ancient Near Eastern sources.

Although our evidence for these customs comes from a time after the Bible, they do appear to reflect the approach and thinking found in tribal societies, not just in the Near East, but also familiar to us from tribal groups in Europe, Asia, Africa, and North America.[103] As such, they offer useful descriptions, which help illuminate for us the practices depicted in the Bible for the early Israelite monarchy and earlier, tribal periods. Also present in pre-Islamic and Islamic law are features of collective responsibility, both in contributing to the payment on behalf of relatives and in sharing of payments made, although the rights of the victim's heirs were paramount.[104] This feature, too, reminds us of what we have seen about transferred liability in the stories about David and the Gibeonites (sec. 4.8.2)) and about Achan (sec. 5.7). Asylum is also known in the early Islamic societies; refuge could be sought at mosques and tombs of saints. The use of shrines as places of asylum is in

fact widely known in many places outside of ancient Israel; we therefore assume that the use of tent or altar in the Bible is indeed the most ancient Israelite practice.[105] It can also be seen that such practices are more typical in tribal societies, where a central authority is not present or fully established.

The Near Eastern sources, as we have seen, frequently mention homicide victims who were slaves instead of free persons. The Bible in Exod 21:20–21, according to my interpretation above (sec. 4.1), deals with the death of free persons who became debt slaves through mistreatment by a creditor holding power over them. It thus would not, as has been maintained, deal with killing a chattel slave. We therefore have no biblical law dealing with an act of homicide perpetrated by or against chattel slaves. But a law on this subject is found in rabbinic collections. The Mishnah, *m. Makk.* 2:3 (and a parallel passage in *t. Makk.* 2:7, Zuckermandel) states:

> All must go into exile[106] or suffer flogging for (injury or death to) an Israelite; and an Israelite is likewise (so punished) on their account.

This laconic text is explicated in the Gemara in *b. Makk.* 8b which asks:

> What is this (statement) "All must go into exile . . . for an Israelite" intended to include?—Is it to include (chattel) slaves or Cutheans (i.e., Samaritans)?

Their answer is affirmative and they cite a *baraita* whose language is more explicit:

103. Cf. the series of discussions, covering various societies, in Gray, Schrader et al., "Blood Feud."

104. See Tyan, "Diya"; Juynboll, "Crimes and Punishments (Muhammadan)."

105. See Westermarck, "Asylum" and literature cited there.

106. The Mishnah (*m. Makk.* 2:4) understands "exile" as being sent to one of the cities of refuge.

We learn (thus) from what our Rabbis taught (elsewhere in a *baraita*): A slave or Cuthean goes into exile or receives a flogging on account of an Israelite, and an Israelite goes into exile or receives a flogging on account of a Cuthean or slave.

The link between exile and homicide is clear; but the rabbis were at a loss to imagine a case where flogging would take place. Clearly it would be a situation where the injury was non-fatal, but then why was compensation not being given? They finally determine that flogging could be imposed upon a freeman in cases where monetary compensation would be insignificant. However, no specific illustration is offered on the flogging of a slave. The case of a slave who insulted the dignity of a freeman comes to mind as one possibility. The flogging provisions of this law remain obscure.[107]

4.9 INJURY AND HOMICIDE THROUGH NEGLIGENCE ON PROPERTY

The Bible holds property owners responsible for consequences that follow upon failure to protect others from harm; a serious case is described in Deut 22:8:

If you build a new house then you should construct a parapet on your roof so that you do not put blood (guilt) upon your house if a person should fall from it.

The law is laconic but it clearly reveals the fact that an accidental fall from an unprotected roof rood terrace will leave the house owner subject to a charge of homicide as the result of his negligence. This law can be seen as an early form of a community building code, setting a safety standard to which every structure should conform. According to later rabbinic law, responsibility for the parapet passed with the house to a renter who was living in the house and left the roof undefended. The Talmud, in *B. Metz.* 101b, cites a *baraita* which states:

Our Rabbis taught: If a man rents a house to his neighbor, the landlord must install doors, make windows open, repair the ceiling, and support (any) beam. The tenant must provide the ladder (for ascending to the roof, build up its) parapet, fix its gutter spout, and plaster his roof (with mud plaster).

The biblical law does not include details on lesser injuries; but we may well assume that the owner is liable for all injuries. More detail on general liability, which would extend to lesser, non-fatal, injuries appears in two rabbinic laws dealing with property. In the Tosefta, *t. B. Metz.* 11:7, Lieberman, we read:

If a wall fell due to tremors or due to wind or rainfall (damage) and if he (the owner) had constructed it properly, he is free from liability; (but) if (he did) not, he is liable. If (the authorities) gave him time (to repair his wall and) it fell during that time, he is free from liability; (but) if after the time (given) he is liable. And how long is the time (period)? It should not be less than 30 days.

This law seems to focus upon the builder of the structure, like in Deut 22:8.

---

107. The flogging of the freeman is mentioned in Maimonides, *Mishnah Torah, Hilkhot Sanh.* 16:12. According to *m. B. Qam.* 8:3 (cited above in sec. 4.2), there was no compensation to be paid for insulting or humiliating a slave.

A second case in the Mishnah, *m B. Metz.* 10:4, is less specific and includes a tree as well as the wall of a house.

> A wall or a tree that fell into public domain and caused damage—(the owner) is free of liability to compensate. If (the authorities) gave him (notice and) time to trim the tree or to repair the wall and they fell during that time (period), he is not liable. If after the time (period allotted) he is liable.

These rabbinic laws, which deal with builder and owner, reveal the participation of community authorities in supervising and warning property owners. The biblical law on the parapet in Deut 22:8 seems to be addressed to an owner who is also the builder; it does not make reference to the community (who may indeed have played some role) but focuses instead on the most serious consequences of negligence.

The ancient Near Eastern laws likewise focus upon the most serious consequences; but at the same time, like the rabbinic sources, also include the role of community authorities. In Eshnunna Laws §58 we read:

> If a wall (of a house) was buckling and the district (officials) have made this known to the owner of the wall and he did not strengthen his wall; and then the wall collapsed and killed the son of a (free) man, it is a capital case; (this is) the decree of the king.[108]

The severity of this law parallels the punishment given in Deut 22:8 and is addressed to the owner.

However, Hammurapi Laws §§229–231, like the biblical law, refers to the responsibility borne by the builder of a house:

> If a builder constructs a house for a man and has not made his work sound and the house he built collapsed and has caused the death of the owner of the house, that builder shall be killed. If it (i.e., the collapse) has caused the death of the son of the house owner, the son of that builder shall be killed. If it (i.e., the collapse) has caused the death of a slave belonging to the house owner, he (the builder) must give (another) slave in place of the (dead) slave to the owner of the house.

We see that the builder of an unsafe dwelling is criminally negligent for his act; and he, as well as his family, can be punished—in talionic reprisal—in the same fashion as if he directly struck a fatal blow upon his victim. Talionic reprisal extending to the builder's son is harsh; and we may ask whether this more severe level of capital punishment was added because the person responsible was the builder, not the owner, whose responsibility was only maintenance of an already built, existing structure? In light of this Babylonian law, the language in Deut 22:8 is interesting because it does not specifically tie the capital punishment to the builder alone but states responsibility in a more general fashion. Did the "blood guilt" upon his house extend to persons in the family other than the builder himself, and did responsibility also pass to the renter of the house, as the rabbis maintained? Alternatively,

---

108. The link between the rabbinic cases and Eshnunna Laws §58 was discussed by Levinson, "A Lost Chapter in Rabbinic Legal History: The Wall Topos of the Edubba."

might this general statement have served as an opening for payment of compensation or "ransom" since the fatality came about by indirect means? Compensation, as we shall presently see (sec. 4.10), was possible when death came about through an owner's negligence with respect to the actions of his domestic animals.

4.10 INJURY AND HOMICIDE CAUSED BY DOMESTIC ANIMALS

The slaying of a human by a domestic animal is the subject of Exod 21:28–32:

> Exod 21:28 If an ox gores a man or a woman and he (or she) dies, the ox shall indeed be stoned, and its flesh shall not be eaten; but the owner of the ox is (considered) blameless.

> Exod 21:29 But if the ox has been a habitual gorer in the past, and its owner has been warned but has not guarded it, and it kills a man or a woman, the ox shall be stoned, and its owner also shall be put to death.

> Exod 21:30 If a ransom demanded of him (the owner), then he shall pay (for) the redemption of his life as much as is demanded of him.

> Exod 21:31 Or (if) it gores a (person's) son or daughter, he (the owner) shall be dealt with according to this same ruling.

> Exod 21:32 If the ox gores a male or female slave, he (the owner) shall pay to the slave's owner thirty shekels of silver, and the ox shall be stoned.

In Exod 21:28, where the ox has gored a human for the first time, the owner of the ox is not blamed for the mishap; but the ox will be destroyed. In the second case, beginning in Exod 21:29, the ox was

known to be a gorer and its owner had been warned; the owner should then either have destroyed the ox or had henceforth to watch over it with special care. Its reputation as a gorer must have been based upon the behavior of this ox with other animals; because had this ox previously gored a human, it should have been already destroyed, at least according to Exod 21:28. The Bible (nor for that matter, the Babylonian laws below—as we shall presently see) does not supply any parameters for determining how many acts of repeated goring would qualify as "habitual."[109] The key element here is that the ox was so identified by the community and a warning to that effect had been given to the owner by the authorities. We will see that the judgment of the authorities was a precondition, in Babylonia as well as in the Bible. Alternatively, the rabbis imagined a much more restricted and "narrow" case, e.g., an ox gored for the first time but escaped stoning by running away or where there were insufficient witnesses to the goring.[110] They also exempted some oxen from stoning due to cognitive impairment of their owners or animals made unruly from being used in the gladiatorial arena.[111]

109. For the rabbis, the ox that gored another ox (not a human) would have become "habitual" when it had done so on at least three separate times. See *m. B. Qam.* 1:4, 2:4, and *t. B. Qam.* 2:2, Lieberman. This "three time rule" is inserted into *Targum Pseudo-Jonathan* on Exod 21:29. The talmudic discussion in the Palestinian Talumd, *j. B. Qam.* 2b elaborates and argues about the time intervals between acts of goring. One rabbi was of the opinion that even a first time gorer must be slaughtered in order to prevent a second such mishap; cf. *m. B. Qam.* 4:9 (and *Mekhilta Mishpatim* 10 to Exod 21:29). For a possible "echo" of this view in the Septuagint, see Houtman, *Exodus*, 3:179.

110. *See b. B. Qam.* 41a.

111. Cf. *m. B. Qam.* 4:4.

The owner of the goring ox is liable for capital punishment because of his negligence and his inadequate control of this dangerous animal. But the text then takes an interesting turn, allowing the owner to escape the death penalty by paying compensation. Exod 21:30 employs a passive verbal construction "If a ransom is demanded of him." Philo interpreted this to mean that it is left up to a court to decide "what punishment he must suffer or what compensation he must pay."[112] Following this line of reasoning, it has been argued that the amount of ransom is left unstated, on the assumption that an assessment determined by a court would be seen as fair.[113] Some scholars have further argued that, in leaving the ransom unspecified, the biblical writer is consciously rejecting the practice of setting a schedule of specific sums for the lives of humans— at least for the lives of all free persons, since in Exod 21:32 a specific amount is set for slaves.[114] But this may be reading too much into our text, for one might also argue that the court, while having discretionary powers, would remain mindful of customary levels of compensation. Thus any court assessment might well have been set and guided by existing scales of monetary compensation that were known in biblical society, as well as in neighboring societies of the ancient Near East.

Awareness of levels of compensation based upon age may be the reason why Exod 21:31 adds a separate provision on death of children. When the text states "according to this same ruling," it seems on the surface to invoke the same handling mentioned earlier for adults, namely capital punishment or an amount of compensation was to be determined. But some scholars have read into this language a provision requiring judges to impose *exactly* the same level of penalty for the death of children as for the death of adults.[115] We know that the lives of children—and sometimes women, too—were not always valued at the same level as the lives of male adults. There is actually evidence within the Bible itself, for the existence of scaled valuations adjusted for age and gender. One finds this in Lev 27: 1–8:

> Speak to the Israelite people and say to them: When a person [lit. man] makes a special vow to the LORD for your value equivalence as a human being, (the following shall be your calculation): (For) a male, from twenty to sixty years of age, your equivalence will be fifty shekels of silver by the sacred shekel (weight of the sanctuary); if she (the focus of the vow) is a female, your equivalence is thirty shekels. If (the focus person's) age is from five years to twenty years, your equivalence is twenty shekels for a male and ten shekels for a female. If the age (of the focus person) is from one month to five years, your

112. Philo, *Spec. Laws* 3:145, Colson. *Targum Pseudo-Jonathan* also inserts mention of the court into its translation of Exod 21:30.

113. Finkelstein, *The Ox That Gored*, 30–31.

114. So, for example, Finkelstein, ibid., who follows Müller, *Die Gesetze Hammurabis,* 166, and states that the omission of a table of sums represents " a deliberate repudiation of the *wergild*, or assessment of loss principle, as it is exemplified in the Laws of Hammurabi." (See presently in this section below). Other scholars following this view are noted in Jackson, *Wisdom Laws,* 283.

115. Cf. Finkelstein, *The Ox That Gored,* 33: "He [the biblical writer] feels constrained to reject explicitly the practice by which the indemnity was fixed on the basis of the victim's status or age, and prescribes a uniform penalty instead."

equivalence for a male is five shekels of silver, and your equivalence
for a female is three shekels of silver. If the age (of the focus person)
is sixty years or over: if a male, the
equivalence is fifteen shekels and
for a female ten shekels. But if he
is too poor for your (customary)
equivalence, one shall present him
before the priest, and the priest
shall assess him; the priest shall
assess him according to what the
vower can afford to pay.[116]

It is clear that the calculation of monetary scale or equivalence (Hebrew 'erekh)
is here being set according to age and
gender, in a fashion that is reminiscent
of the Old Babylonian treaty provisions
on compensation—apparently for accidental homicide—mentioned below. We
know, moreover, that this kind of scaled
monetary equivalence was actually employed in ancient Israel. From the time of
the late monarchy, in 2 Kgs 23:33–35, we
are told that king Jehoiakim was required
to tax Judeans in order to raise the tribute
tax imposed upon him by Pharaoh Neco.
He imposed the tax in a proportionate
manner—"each person according to his
monetary equivalence ('erekh)." Note that
in Lev 27:8, the Bible allowed the priest
to adjust the customary monetary equivalences according to the economic situation of the person involved. Perhaps this is
exactly what Exod 21:30–31 was actually

trying to accomplish by leaving the ransom to be paid by the owner of the goring
ox unspecified. In other words, the judges
were given leave to deviate from the customary scale of monetary equivalence—
except possibly in Exod 21:32, where the
ransom for a slave who was killed seems
to have been fixed at thirty shekels. That
sum, incidentally—and perhaps not surprisingly, is also the equivalence in Lev
27:1–8 for a woman and it is half of the
sixty shekels equivalence for an able-bod-
ied free male adult.

The monetary "ransom," or compensation paid by the owner presumably was
paid to the family of the victim in the same
fashion as in the case of the slave, where it
would go to the owner of the slave. Yet the
ancient rabbis were uncomfortable with
the idea of compensation; there was, after all, the biblical prohibition against accepting compensation for a homicide that
is expressed in Num 35:31–34 "And you
must not accept a ransom for the life of
a murderer who is (judged) guilty (and
sentenced) to die for he must surely be
put to death." (See sec. 4.8.2). If this law
had truly been followed, then how could
any payment have been made in Exod
21:30–31? Some rabbis therefore argued
that the payment in Exod 21:30–31 could
not be a payment representing the monetary "value" of the victim's lost life but,
rather, an exculpatory payment based
upon the monetary "value" of the owner
of the ox, who was redeeming his own life
through monetary payment. But other
rabbis maintained the interpretation that
it was indeed a payment of compensation
for the life of the victim, with the sum to
be determined according to the "value" of
the life of the victim.

116. From the use of second person "your
equivalence," it appears that this law was addressed
to the supervising priests or to the head of a family
making the financial pledge. The latter is certainly
the situation in Lev 27:6 which deal with infants
and children and in Lev 27:9 (not quoted here),
which deals with animals, which end up being sac-
rificed. Milgrom, *Leviticus*, 2369, 2410–11, considers that this law may have evolved as a replacement
for earlier, now abandoned practices of donating
humans directly to the Temple.

A majority of rabbis, however, preferred to follow *Targum Pseudo-Jonathan* in describing the death penalty there as "death that will be sent upon him from Heaven." In other words, this death penalty for the owner of the ox was not really actionable in any earthly court. These rabbis did not think it appropriate for an earthly court to mete out a death penalty to the owner of the ox for an action committed by his beast.[117] If there was not to be any court-imposed death penalty, then compensation—now the only recourse—was therefore "permissible" here; and its value was indeed to be calculated solely according to the loss sustained by the family of the victim and not on the life of the ox owner.[118] This majority understanding, namely, that the ransom is calculated according to the life value of the victim, is in line with ancient Near Eastern practices; and, as noted by Finkelstein, "it is indeed the same principle that governs remedies for wrongful death in almost every jurisdiction today."[119]

The medieval commentator Bekhor Shor, while maintaining the view that the ransom was based upon valuing the life of the owner of the ox, also points out that, according to the plain meaning of the text, one could argue that the death penalty could actually have been imposed in this case. Moreover, he says that compensation could then have been paid only with the consent of the family who agreed to receive it![120] We have already seen that in ancient Assyria, such choice was actually given to the victim's family; they could either accept compensation or they had the right to have the murderer executed upon the grave of the victim. Yet, at the same time, the homicide in our case was committed by a beast, not by the owner himself; and in the ancient Near Eastern laws—as we shall see—the negligent owner of the ox was not subject to the death penalty, but only paid compensation. So we may raise the question—like the rabbis did—as to whether, in the biblical ox case, the death penalty was a necessity. Is it possible that in the Bible the penalty of death was "announced" as a moral statement but that it was never intended to be acted upon, since ancient custom and practice had long dictated compensation as the fair settlement in such cases where homicide was committed by one's beast? Alternatively, is it also possible that the biblical law, by leaving the matter up to judges, was—as Philo anciently maintained—still leaving room for capital punishment if the circumstances were exceptional and more severe punishment was merited?

In these goring ox cases, the Bible introduces a new idea not present in the ancient near Eastern laws (cited below), namely, a provision that the ox that killed a human being, must be stoned to death. This takes place even if the ox was a first time gorer of a human and despite the fact that compensation might also be paid; the ox was always to be put to death. This was a rule. The mandatory death of the ox may

117. Cf. *b. Sanh.* 15b "One executes for homicide that he himself committed, not for a homicide committed by his ox."

118. Talmudic discussion is found *in b. Makk.* 2b and *b. B. Qam.* 27a, 40a. This discussion mirrors the argument in *Mekhilta Mishpatim* 10 on Exod 21:30.

119. Finkelstein, *The Ox That Gored,* 31–32. Finkelstein, however, personally believed (ibid., 30 n.11) that in Exod 21:28, the "ransom" was originally meant to be calculated by valuation of the life of the owner rather than upon the lost life of the victim.

120. Bekhor Shor's comments appear within his comments on Exod 21:30.

have weighted the argument in favor of not imposing the death penalty upon the owner; after all, if the actual "perpetrator" of the killing was put to death, then was it really necessary to kill the owner?

The reason for punishing the animal is not stated; and its omission has opened the door to many explanations. Nahmanides links the stoning of the ox with Gen 9:4–6, where Noah is told by God that every homicide must be requited; it also states: " from every animal I will require it [i.e., blood] and from human beings, each one for the blood of another, I will require a reckoning for human life" (NRSV).[121] In this view, the animal would be subject to the same punishment as a human offender. And there are, indeed, examples from other cultures, from as far away as India and as close as ancient Greece, where animals that killed humans were put to death. There is also a significant body of evidence of such animal trials that took place in ancient Greece, medieval Europe and, more recently, even in the United States.[122]

But there may be more in the death of the ox than simple guilt and responsibility. First, the execution of the ox is carried out via the ritual of stoning which carries with it features of communal participation and religious solemnity.

Second, the Bible forbids eating the flesh of the executed animal. Both features require comment. In connection with stoning, the Mekhilta described the action of the ox as "rendering the earth unclean and causing the Divine Presence to depart."[123] Modern scholars, similarly, have suggested that the ox became "taboo, unclean"; or, as having negated "the hierarchically differentiated order of creation by which man was granted sovereignty in the physical world."[124] Stoning is a reaction to the disturbing, "unnatural" behavior of this animal.

Death by stoning, in the biblical tradition and elsewhere in the ancient Near East, is reserved for crimes of a special character. In those cases there is no special "executioner," for the community assembled is the mass executioner of the sentence. Offenses that entail this mode of execution must therefore in theory or in fact, "offend" the corporate community or are believed to compromise its most cherished values to the degree that the commission of the offense places the community itself in jeopardy.[125]

Biblical parallels for the punishment of animals may be found in Lev 20:15–16, where the person committing an act of bestiality and the animal are both condemned to death; similar provisions are found in the Hittite Laws §§187–188, 199 where both the person and the animal merit the death penalty for participating in these sexual acts. The offense of bestiality is, of course, not the same as the homicide committed by the ox. However, there

121. Nahmanides, commentary on Gen 9:5. This same comment was offered by Abraham, son of Maimonides, *Perush Hatorah,* 342–43 in his commentary on Exod 21:28. One may compare a much later episode recorded in *m. Ed.* 6:1, where a sage reported that "a cock was stoned in Jerusalem because it killed a man."

122. Gaster, *Myth, Legend, and Custom in the Old Testament,* 243–50; Finkelstein, *The Ox That Gored,* 47–73. Finkelstein attributes the later, more recent survivals of this practice, to biblical influence! However, note the killing of oxen in Hittite Laws §166, discussed below in sec. 6.6.

123. Statement of R. Isaac in *Mekhilta Mishpatim* 10 on Exod 21:28.

124. Finkelstein, *The Ox That Gored,* 28–29.

125. Ibid., 26–27. For discussion and other perspectives see Jackson, *Wisdom Law,* 258–66.

is similarity in that animals as well as humans are punished for their behavior. (The laws on bestiality have been treated more fully above in sec. 1.8).

As to not eating the flesh of the stoned ox, it has been argued that there is indeed "religious evaluation inherent in this law . . . evidenced by the prohibition of eating the flesh of the stoned ox. The beast is laden with guilt and is therefore an object of horror."[126] Most commentators follow the opinion of Philo, who anciently stated: "It is required by the law of holiness that the flesh of an animal that has killed a man should not be used as a foodstuff for men or to make their food more palatable."[127] All of these explanations, while attractive, must however be viewed as suggestions only; for the biblical text, as is so often the case, seldom states the explanation for its rules.

Turning to the ancient Near East, we find the goring ox case in Eshnunna Laws §§54–55, which goes directly to the case of "repeated offense":

> If an ox is a habitual gorer and the district has made this known to its owner and he did not guide his ox with care[128] and it gored a man and caused his death, the owner of the ox shall pay 2/3 mina (i.e., 40 shekels) silver. If it gored a slave and caused his death, he shall pay 15 shekels silver.

The case of accidental, i.e., first time goring of a human victim found in Exod 21:28, should have preceded this paragraph, based upon what we have seen in Exodus 21. Why is it missing? It is important to recall that our copies of the Eshnunna laws are school texts, which exhibit other scribal errors and omissions; so omission or "skipping" seems to be the simplest explanation.[129]

The case of a beast accidentally goring a human victim is, however, preserved in the presentation of the cases in Laws of Hammurapi §§250–252:

> §250 If an ox, walking along the street, gores a man and causes him to die, that case has no claim.
>
> §251 If the man's ox was a habitual gorer and his district had notified him that it was a gorer and he had not polled its horns (or) closed it in, and the ox then gored the son of a free man and caused his death, he (the owner) shall pay one half mina (i.e., thirty shekels) silver.
>
> §252 If (the ox gored) a man's slave, he (the owner) shall pay one third mina (i.e., twenty shekels) silver.

We can see a gradation of penalties: two thirds of a mina or forty shekels for killing an adult freeman in Eshnunna Laws §§54–55; one half mina or thirty shekels for the death of a minor in Hammurapi Laws §251; and lesser sums for the death of a slave: one-third mina or twenty shekels in Hammurapi Laws §252 and fifteen shekels in Eshnunna Laws §55. Hammurapi Laws omits the case of the adult victim; we may assume that the compensation for an adult would have be more

---

126. Greenberg, "Some Postulates of Biblical Criminal Law, " 11.

127. Philo, *Spec. Laws* 3.144, Colson.

128. The verb here is corrected to *ušеširma*; cf. Yaron, *The Laws of Eshnunna,* 77 and Roth, *Law Collections,* 67.

129. Yaron, *The Laws of Eshnunna,* 21–30 gives examples of such errors and omissions. For other, more complex explanations of the omission of the expected case, see Yaron, ibid. 296–97; and Finkelstein, *The Ox That Gored,* 24.

than thirty shekels—perhaps 40 shekels as at Eshnunna.[130]

An Old Babylonian treaty from the region of Eshnunna contains a schedule of payments in a similar range, based upon age, gender, and social status:

> The son of a free man—(his value is) two-thirds of a mina silver (i.e., forty shekels). The slave of a free man—(his value is) fifteen shekels silver; and (for) a female, ten shekels silver. An old man or an old woman [. . .] like a child in value.[131]

The reason for making these payments is not included in our document, which may have been a draft of the final treaty text. However, one can see from the amounts to be paid, that they could have been intended as the agreed schedule of compensation for victims of accidental homicide. The amounts are very similar to the schedule of compensation for victims slain by a goring ox seen in the laws. The breakdown in age and gender reminds us of what we have seen in the biblical ʿerekh or valuation discussed above in Lev 27:1–8. The amount of compensation for elderly (victims) was known but is not spelled out; the statement "like a child in value" may have referred back to a

provision for children that was omitted by the ancient scribe.

The Eshnunna Laws add two further cases not found in the Hammurapi Laws or in the Bible; but they are, as we shall presently see, partly addressed in rabbinic sources. The cases deal with a vicious dog which, like the ox, is known to be dangerous and which commits homicide.[132] Such cases are perhaps a more common occurrence than death from a goring ox; but the point made is the same. In Eshnunna Laws §§56–57, we read:

> If a dog is vicious and the district has made this known to its owner and he did not guard his dog and it bit a man and caused his death, the owner of the dog shall pay 2/3 mina (40 shekels) silver. If it (the mad dog) bit a slave and has caused his death, he shall pay 15 shekels silver.

The amounts of compensation to be paid are identical with the amounts paid by the owner of the goring ox in Eshnunna Laws §§54–55.

The Talmud, b. B. Qam. 15b, addresses the danger of a vicious dog in a baraita which states:

> Rabbi Nathan says: From where (do we learn) that a man should not bring up a vicious dog in his house, or keep an unsound ladder in his house? Because the (biblical) text (Deut 22:8) states: "so that you do not put blood (guilt) upon your house."[133]

This dictum draws upon Deut 22:8, which deals with death of a person falling from

---

130. Many scholars prefer to understand "son of a free man" in Hammurapi Laws §252 to be a social designation of class, i.e., unless one is required by context to see a minor present, as clearly is the case in some paragraphs of the Hammurapi Laws. For more discussion see Yaron, *The Laws of Eshnunna*, 146–48, who shows that the usage of this term is by no means uniform. Westbrook, "Reflections on the Law of Homicide in the Ancient World," 147–51 maintains that one should always translate "son of a man," with the understanding that this individual was legally subordinate to a father who was the head of a free and independent household.

131. Greengus, *Old Babylonian Tablets from Ishchali and Vicinity*, 74–77 (no. 326:4–8).

132. See Yuhong, "Rabies and Rabid Dogs in Sumerian and Akkadian Literature," 33.

133. This dictum is again cited in b. B. Qam. 46a and b. Ket. 41b.

the roof because of a missing parapet. According to the *baraita* cited in my discussion of this law above, in sec. 4.9 above (*b. B. Metz.* 101b), responsibility for the parapet and for the ladder ascending to the roof was passed on to the tenant or occupant of the house. Thus Rabbi Nathan finds the tenant or occupant also responsible if the ladder was faulty and a person fell to his death in using it.

As for a vicious dog, however, the rabbis still maintain the distinction between a first and repeated attack that we have seen both in the biblical and Babylonian laws. In rabbinic law, the dog, like the ox, would of course be stoned if the victim died, as in the Bible. But if there was no prior history of the dog attacking and the owner had not been warned about his dog by the authorities, then a first time fatal dog attack, like that of an ox, did not create liability for the animal owner. The rabbis extend this understanding even to certain situations where the first attack occurred on the premises of the animal owner. This point is made in Tosefta, *t. B. Qam.* 6:27, Lieberman:

> A worker who entered the courtyard of a house owner (who was his employer) without his permission—even if (in general) he had permission to enter and collect his pay—(and) the ox of the house owner gored him or the dog of the house owner bit him, he (the house owner) is not liable. (However) if he (the house owner was (actually) present and) said "Enter," then the house owner is liable.

The Talmud, in *b. B. Qam.* 33a, discusses this case of the worker further and attempts to refine how rabbinic law should regard the circumstances relating to the worker's right or expectation to

enter the house of his employer. The rabbis there conclude that regular employees in effect may have had permission to come to their employer's house to collect their wages. But the employer, i.e., the house owner, would not incur liability even if he were at home, in a situation where he had had told his employee to wait at the door of the house and the employee then entered on his own. [134] Hammurapi Laws §250, interestingly, describes the goring ox as walking in the street; but one does not otherwise see any distinction between public and private domains in any of the other Babylonian laws. In any case, one can see from the rabbinical law statements, that laws on fatal dog bite were widely known and that the dog bite law was naturally—and perhaps even historically—linked to discussion of the goring ox case, as we have it in Eshnunna Laws §§56–57.

4.11 UNSOLVED HOMICIDE

Deuteronomy 21:1–9 deals with the situation of unsolved homicide. The Bible is concerned about bloodguilt and where to fix responsibility. Since it is not known who committed this hateful act, a degree of responsibility attaches itself to the community closest to the area where this crime occurred:

> Deut 21:1–2 If, a (slain) victim is found in the land that the Lord your God is giving you to possess, fallen in an open field, and it is not

---

134. The Talmud there (*b. B. Qam.* 33a) cites additional *baraitot* which present similar cases of accidental death involving with workers who come to collect their wages. The conclusions reached by the rabbis are summarized in Maimonides, *Mishnah Torah, Hilkhot Nizqey Mammon* 10:11–12. The required stoning of the ox is addressed there in 10:1, which follows *t. B. Qam.* 5:13, Lieberman.

known who struck him down, then your elders and your judges shall go out to measure the (distances) to the towns that are near the body.

Deut 21:3–4 The elders of the town nearest the victim shall take a heifer that has never been worked and that has never pulled in a yoke. The elders of that town shall bring the heifer down to a stream with running water, (at a spot) which is neither tilled nor sown, and shall there break the heifer's neck in the stream.

Deut 21:5 And the priests, the sons of Levi, shall come forward, for the Lord your God has chosen them to minister to him and to pronounce blessings in the name of the Lord, and by their pronouncements all (such) cases of dispute and "blows" (shall be handled). Deut 21:6–8 All the elders of that town nearest the victim shall wash their hands over the heifer whose neck was broken in the stream, and they shall speak up and declare: "Our hands did not shed this blood, and our eyes did not see (this happen). Absolve, O Lord, your people Israel, whom you redeemed; and do not let (the guilt of) innocent blood remain in the midst of your people Israel." Then they will be absolved of the blood (guilt).

Deut 21:9 And (so) you shall purge the innocent blood from your midst, because you will do what is right in the sight of the Lord.

Because of proximity, the elders of the city closest to the corpse had the responsibility to carry out a ritual of expiation for the murder; the death of the heifer, in effect, "atones" for the spilt blood of the victim. The entry of the priests into these proceedings is not fully described,

since only elders are described as acting in Deut 21:6–8. The medieval commentator Bekhor Shor thus concludes that the priests were involved in ritual aspects only; and that the references to "dispute" and "blows" refers to the range of situations for which rites were needed. Thus, e.g., in Numbers 5, in cases like the waters drunk by the suspected wife with whom her husband is quarreling (sec. 1.3.2), and in the present ritual of the heifer. Following a similar line of reasoning, *Targum Onqelos* on Deut 21:5 translates "dispute and plague of leprosy."[135] Rashi and Nahmanides, following a mishnaic tradition, further suggest that the elders recited "Our hands did not shed this blood" while the priests recited "Absolve, O Lord, your people Israel, whom you redeemed."[136] But it is equally possible to read the text in Deut 21:6–8 and understand it to say that the elders recited all of both declarations. In other words, these are actually the operative words of an oath statement, to be sworn by the elders; and the participation of the priests was simply to administer the sacred oath to the elders.[137] As for the reference to redemption in Deut 21:8, Ibn Ezra suggests: "As you redeemed them from Egypt by you gracious kindness, so redeem them (also now) from this blood and the punishment due for it." This, of course, mirrors the language found in some versions of the Septuagint, which expands the Hebrew text to state: "whom you redeemed, O Lord, from the Land of Egypt."

The rabbis, in their study of the passage of the heifer raise questions that go

135. Bekhor Shor makes this point in his commentary to Deut 17:8.

136. *m. Sotah* 9.6.

137. See Tigay, *Deuteronomy*, 475.

beyond the text of the biblical passage. For example: what should happen if the murderer was found after the ritual of the heifer? Was the murderer then free from punishment since the blood of the heifer had been spilled? The rabbis say no; if he is found, he must be punished by death.[138] Another question arises because the biblical text does not tell us what is the disposition of the heifer after it is killed. In the opinion of the rabbis, its manner of death rendered it unfit for consumption; they therefore reason that it must be buried at the location of the ritual.[139] They also ask how this ritual of the heifer was able to atone for a murder committed by an unidentified third party. A perceptive and, in my opinion, correct answer is offered by Nahmanides, in his commentary to Deut 21:8:

> In my view, the reason for the heifer is similar to that of other sacrifices performed away from the altar, namely those of the "scapegoat" (Lev 16) and the "red heifer" (Num 19); for this reason the rabbis classify these among those statutes (whose reasons are known only to God).

In other words, Nahmanides describes our ritual as a kind of sacrifice—which it definitely appears to be—and relates it to two others, which likewise take place away from any temple or shrine; their common function is expiation.[140] Because of this apparent link with sacrifice, the rabbis did not prescribe a replacement ritual for the ceremony of the heifer for their own time, after the Temple was destroyed. But apparently also reluctant to identify it unambiguously as a sacrifice—since it took place away from the Jerusalem altar—they maintain that the ritual of the heifer was anciently abandoned even before the Temple was destroyed, because murder became so prevalent.[141] The origins of the ritual of the heifer were no doubt better understood in biblical times; and perhaps it was then considered as an acceptable form of sacrificial slaughter.

There is a another reference to breaking the neck of a donkey in Exod 13:12–13, again in a cultic-sacrificial context:

> You will pass on to the Lord every first issue of the womb: every first issue, increase of the cattle you own—the males (specifically)—shall be for the Lord. But every first issue of a donkey you shall redeem (i.e., replace) with a sheep; and if you do not redeem it, you must break its neck; but every first-born human male among your children you must redeem.

There was an underlying belief that all firstborn animals belonged to God and must therefore be offered as sacrifices. However, the firstborn donkey, whose flesh according to Lev 11 was considered unclean, could be replaced with a surrogate offering from a clean animal; otherwise its neck was to be broken. This act

138. *Sifre N Mas'ey* 161 on Deut 21:4, which appears in their comment to Num 35:33.

139. The rabbis found this omission troubling and so it repeatedly comes up; see e.g., *m. Ker.* 6.2; *b. Ker.* 6a, b; *b. Bek.* 9b; *b. Hullin* 82a; *b. Sanh.* 47b; *b. Sotah* 46b.

140. A similar analysis, more briefly stated, appears in Hazzequni on Deut 21:4 who compares Lev 16:22, where the scapegoat is sent forth to a "an uninhabited place." For, as Hazzequni says: "because both (rituals) have the same meaning."

141. This is implicit in *m. Sotah* 9:9 and *t. Sotah* 14:1, Lieberman. See also Tigay, *Deuteronomy*, 475–76 who sees similarities with the later Jewish expiatory ritual of *kapparot*.

took place away from the Temple altar.[142] The firstborn of human beings could only be redeemed.

There is also reference to the ritual breaking of the necks of other animals in Isa 66:3, albeit in a condemning fashion; it is there grouped with other sacrificial rituals, which were to be abandoned:

> Whoever slaughters an ox is like one who kills a human being; whoever sacrifices a lamb, like one who breaks a dog's neck; whoever presents a grain offering, like one who offers swine's blood; whoever makes a memorial offering of frankincense, like one who blesses an idol. These have chosen their own ways, and in their abominations they take delight (NRSV).

In the Bible we also find the practice that when priests slaughter small birds for sacrifice, they do so by pinching off their heads at the neck; this method of slaughter was not approved by the rabbis for non-cultic, domestic use.[143]

When we look to the ancient Near East, we find that the Hittite Laws contain provisions that supply perspective to Deut 21:1–9. In Hittite Laws §6 we read:

> If a person, man or woman, is killed in another (?) city, he (the victim's heir) shall deduct 100 gipeššar (= 3

acres) from the land of the person on whose property the person [i.e., the victim) was killed and shall take it for himself.

A later version of the laws states:

> If a man is found killed on another person's property, if he is a free man, he (the property owner) shall give his property, house, and 60 shekels of silver. But if (the dead person) is a woman, (the property owner) shall give (no property, but) 120 shekels of silver. But if it (the place where the dead body was found) is not (private) property, but uncultivated open country, they shall measure 3 danna [approx. 3 miles] in all directions, and whatever town/village is determined (to lie within that radius), he shall take those same (payments from the inhabitants of the village).[144] If there is no town/village [i.e., within the radius], (the heir of the deceased) will forfeit (his claim).

According to the Hittite view, an owner was responsible for what took place on his land, even if he, himself, did not commit the murder. We also see that, if the victim lay dead in the open country, i.e., "no-man's land," a comparable degree of responsibility extended out to any neighboring community that was within a statutory radius of 3 miles distance. But if the distance between the crime spot and the community was beyond the 3 mile radius, then the victim's family could make no claim upon anyone. The theme of the

---

142. Num 18:15 restates the law, giving redemption as the only option for all unclean animals: "you shall redeem the firstborn of every unclean animal." The two verses are in conflict. In the light of Num 18:15, the Samaritan version "corrects" Exod 13:13 to read "every first issue of an animal" rather than "every first issue of a donkey." On the other hand, the rabbis go on to re-interpret Num 18:15 to mean only a firstborn donkey! Cf. *Mekhilta Bo* 18 and Rashi on Exod 13:13.

143. This practice is described in Lev 1:15; 5:8. For its restriction for sacred use only cf. *b. Yebam.* 32b; *b. Menah.* 5b.

144. Hoffner, "On Homicide in Hittite Law," 303–4, discusses other interpretations of the phrase, literally, "he shall take those same ones." Some suggest that the heirs of the dead person were entitled to take the inhabitants of the community as slaves. This would greatly exceed the 120 shekels paid by an inhabited locale.

Hittite laws is larger community responsibility for crimes committed within its precincts. According to the letter of Hattusili III (cited above in sec. 4.8.3) the Hittites also had a practice of purifying the crime spot even when compensation was paid: "[The place] in which the murder occurred—they purify."

We can now more clearly understand the purpose behind measuring of the distance to the neighboring communities in Deut 21:1–9; the victim lay in no one's territory and his slayer was unknown. The biblical law, unlike the Hittite, says nothing about a limit on the distance between the slain body and the surrounding communities. Moreover, there is, in the Bible, no provision for compensation, perhaps because this custom came to be rejected as we have seen in our discussion of homicide (sec. 4.8.2). However, it is also possible that the biblical case involved a situation where the identity of the victim and his heirs were unknown, since nothing is said about relatives of the victim. The biblical law deals only with the necessary ritual of purification, the details of which are not described in the Hittite sources. In Deut 21:7 the elders of the nearest community wash their hands, apparently a symbolic gesture indicating that they are free from the blood. They then must also—probably under oath—declare their innocence with respect to the murder. We in fact know of similar declarations taken under oath as part of the treaty obligations between the city of Ugarit and Carchemish referred to above in our discussion of homicide (sec. 4.8.3). In these treaties, if the killer is not known and the goods of the merchant are missing, then the city representatives—apparently the elders or magistrates—must travel to the other city,

pay his family compensation for the homicide, and then publicly swear: "We do not know the men who killed them (the slain merchants) and the property and goods of those merchants are missing."[145]

We also find the principle of community responsibility in Hammurapi Laws §§23–24, which deal with robbery:

> If a robber has not been caught, the robbed man shall render account (of) his lost property before a god, and the city and the chief magistrate in whose territory and district the robbery was committed shall restore to him (the value of) his lost property. If the life (of the robbed man was taken), then the city and magistrate shall pay one mina silver to his kinfolk.

We see, therefore that the principle of community responsibility was deeply established in ancient societies, including that of ancient Israel. The biblical law, as we have noted, contains no provision for giving financial compensation to the family for the homicide that took place. There is only a ritual of purification and a solemn declaration by the elders and magistrates in order to remove all blame from their community.

4.12 KIDNAPPING

The Bible has two laws on kidnapping. In Exod 21:16 we read:

> And he who kidnaps (lit. steals) a man and has sold him or is found

145. RS 17.146 and RS 18.115 and a shorter oath in RS 20.22 (no mention of property) cited by Barmash, *Homicide in the Biblical World*, 184–99. A reference to oath also appears in RS 17.145. Hoffner, "On Homicide in Hittite Law," 305, wonders if an oath was not also a feature of the purification ritual mentioned in the letter of Hattusili III.

(holding him) in his possession (lit. hand) shall surely be put to death.

A second law is found in Deut 24:7:

> If a man is found kidnapping (lit. stealing) a person who is one of his Israelite brethren, and he has bound him to (his) service or sold him, that kidnapper shall die; so you will remove this evil from your midst.

The biblical cases focus more on adult victims than on children; the motive for the crime is for the kidnapper to use the victim as his own slave or to make a profit from the victim by selling him into slavery, as did the brothers of Joseph in Gen 37:28: "And (when) Midianite traders passed by, they pulled Joseph up out of the pit and they sold Joseph for twenty (pieces of) silver to the Ishmaelites; and they brought Joseph to Egypt."[146] In both of the biblical laws, the kidnapper's punishment is death. The first situation, where the victim was discovered while still in the possession of the kidnapper is not well stated in Exod 21:6. The phrase "or is found in his possession" could grammatically also refer to the purchaser, except that we assume that the purchaser would not be held responsible for the kidnapping. Likewise obscure, in Deut 24:7, is the phrase "bound him to (his) service," which employs a little attested verb, which the ancient Greek translated as "overpowered" and the Targums as "do commerce with (him)." We have followed the Targums and most commentators who understand this verb to indicate that that kidnapper put the victim to use in his own service.

We are aided in this understanding by comparing the laws dealing with kidnapping with those of livestock theft (sec. 5.5), where we see that a legal difference was made there in punishment, depending upon whether the animal was sold or still in the possession of the thief. The punishment after sale was more severe. We may assume acknowledgment of this same distinction in the kidnapping laws, except that this distinction is here to be overlooked. Capital punishment was to be imposed in both situations, i.e., whether the victim remained in the power of the kidnapper or was sold to another person.

The rabbis, nevertheless, chose to modify the plain meaning of the biblical texts; they narrowed the circumstances under which a kidnapper might be subject to the death penalty. In scholastic fashion, they reshaped the law in conformity to a cumulative reading of both passages. First they limited liability for kidnapping and sale to situations where witnesses can testify to the sale. Second, following Deut 24:7, the victim must be "one of his Israelite brethren," thus a free person, not already a slave. Third, on the basis of the verb "steal," which is also used for "kidnapping," they argued if the victim could be recovered before a sale took place, then the kidnapping would fall under the general law of theft, but the kidnapper would not yet merit the severe punishment of death applicable to the offense of kidnapping; he would then only be required to amend his crime through payment of compensation. The rabbis thus re-institute the distinction between holding and selling that the biblical laws appear to have expressly rejected! We see their amended understanding in the Tosefta *t. B. Qam.* 8:1, Lieberman:

---

146. On the juxtaposition of Midianites and Ishmaelites in this same verse, see Levenson, "Genesis, Introduction and Annotations," 76.

If one kidnapped him (i.e., the victim) but did not sell him or if he sold him but he is (still) standing in the market (i.e., a sale is not completed), he is free from liability (for the death penalty of the crime of kidnapping). (Similarly) one who kidnaps slaves (i.e., persons who were already enslaved) is (likewise) free of liability (for the death penalty punishment).

Another modification of this law was added in a *baraita* cited in *b. Sanh.* 85b, based upon the reading of Exod 21:16 "is found (holding him) in his possession (lit. hand)." The rabbis there argued that the victim must be fully in the power of the kidnapper (and not still in the possession of his original owner) in order for the death penalty to apply:

If one kidnapped him but did not sell him or if he sold him but he (the victim) was still in his own domain, he is not liable . . . One who kidnaps slaves is free of liability (for the crime of kidnapping).

And finally, according to the Mishnah, *m. Sanh.* 11:1, the kidnapper who retained his victim would be not be culpable until he himself had used the victim as his own slave:

One who kidnaps a person from (the people of) Israel is not liable until he brings him into his possession. Rabbi Judah says: "Until he brings him into his possession and has used him (as a slave), as it is written (Deut 24:7) "he has bound him to (his) service and sold him.'"

Maimonides went even one step further and required that all these pre-conditions must be present for the death penalty to be applied; thus the victim needed to be in the power of the kidnapper, he must himself have used the victim as his slave, and he sold him and the sale was completed.[147]

When we look to the ancient Near East, we find a plainly stated law on kidnapping in Hammurapi Laws §14:

If a man has kidnapped (lit. has stolen) the young son of (another) man, he shall be killed.

This case seems to deal with the kidnapping of a child who, presumably, could not protest or otherwise come to his own defense. The kidnapping of an adult would no doubt also be a crime, but perhaps might not be punished by death, as we shall see in other contexts. The law in §14 does not address the situation of a subsequent sale; like in Exod 21:16, it would appear to be blameworthy enough that that the kidnapper himself holds his victim. Eshnunna Laws §49 deals with the kidnapping of slaves; here however, the penalty is not death but, rather, two-fold compensation:

If a man has been seized with a stolen male slave (or) female slave, a male slave must follow the (recovered) male slave (as a penalty); (similarly) a female slave (must follow) the (recovered) female slave.

The different treatment of stolen slaves conforms to what we have seen in the later rabbinic laws, namely, that the threat of capital punishment for kidnapping was only applied in the case of free persons.

Provisions concerning the dislocation, removal, and abduction of free citizens and slaves are found in an Old Babylonian peace treaty c. 1800 BCE, from the area of Eshnunna:

147. Maimonides, *Mishnah Torah, Hilkhot Geneva,* 9:2–3.

A (free) resident of the territory of Shadlash and its environs (or) of the territory of Neribtum and its environs who fled (their country) because of war and who was cut off (from home); his lord (i.e., his king) shall not seize him. If it (his removal) was a result of a kidnapping (lit. removal by force) or *banditry*, he shall be investigated. (If) the person was not (originally) a hostile party, he may go back; if he is a hostile party he will be seized (by the king to whom he was hostile) . . . If (the removed person is) the son of a free man, he (the abductor) shall return the son of the free man and he will pay one mina silver. If a slave of a free men, he shall go back (to his owner) and the (the abductor) will pay one-half mina silver.[148]

In these situations, the death penalty was not imposed for kidnapping, evidently because these acts had occurred during a time of hostility between the two kingdoms. Harassment of enemy powers might then have been seen as laudable; and in this kind of climate, some people might have assumed that laws normally in force were to be suspended. Therefore, upon the restoration of peace and civility, restitution along with an appropriate penalty was judged as a fair way to settle such cases. We do see, however, that kidnapping of minors—who were less capable of acting defensively—was considered to be a more grievous offense than the kidnapping of adults.

Here again, we see that the kidnapping of slaves was not viewed with the same degree of condemnation as in the taking of free persons. The reason for this distinction is not given in our ancient sources; it could reflect the different levels of protection given to persons of higher and lower degrees of social status. But, it might also be due to the assumption of different responses on the part of free and slave victims. The latter reasoning is what we find in Roman law, in a rescript from the emperor Hadrian (c. 135 CE) states that "It should, however, be clearly understood that a person can be liable to a charge of theft for stealing others' slaves without immediately being reckoned a kidnapper on that account." The reasoning there seems to have been that it was not always clear whether a slave was actually kidnapped or whether he was just a runaway; in the latter case, the offense was less serious than kidnapping. Thus a charge of ordinary theft would always remain as a reasonable basis for judgment.[149]

The Hittite Laws that deal with kidnapping focus upon persons who were kidnapped and taken across political boundaries, from the Hittite heartland into the neighboring, territory of Luwiya—and in one instance also into the neighboring kingdom of Arzawa. These were close neighbors with whom the Hittite kings enjoyed friendly relations, although one can see from the laws that the Hittites were in a superior position and that their own economic interests were paramount. Thus Hittite Laws §19a–b:

> §19a If a Luwian man abducts a free person, man or woman, from the land of Hatti, and leads him away to the land of Luwiya (var. Arzawa), and subsequently his

---

148. Greengus, *Old Babylonian Tablets from Ishchali*, 74–77 (no. 326:9–15, 18–21; lines 16–17 are fragmentary and have not been restored.)

149. Hadrian's rescript is cited in *D.*48.15.6. The Talmud in *b. Sanh.* 85a does not undertake to explain the exemption for slaves.

owner [i.e., the head of his household] recognizes him, he shall confiscate (?) [lit. bring] his (i.e., the abductor's) own estate [lit. house].

§19b If a Hittite abducts a Luwiyan man in the land of Hatti itself, and leads him away to the land of Luwiya, formerly they gave 12 persons (lit. heads) but now he shall give 6 persons, and he shall look to his house for it.

The Hittite laws, characteristically, do not impose the death penalty for abduction; but the penalties given in compensation are significant in amount. A second set of laws deals with abducted slaves; in this situation, as we have seen in rabbinic and Babylonian laws, penalties were less severe. Thus Hittite Laws §§20–21:

§21 If a Hittite man abducts a male slave belonging to a(nother) Hittite man from the land of Luwiya, and leads him to the land of Hatti, and subsequently his (i.e. the abducted person's) owner recognizes him, the abductor shall pay him 12 shekels of silver, and he shall look to his house for it.

§22 If anyone abducts the male slave of a Luwian man from the land of Luwiya and brings him to the land of Hatti, and his owner (later) recognizes him, he (the owner) shall take only his own slave; there shall be no compensation.

The Hittite Laws on kidnapping, like the biblical laws, focus solely upon adults; we have no way of knowing if different penalties would have been imposed upon those who kidnapped minors. We can also see that the abduction of Hittite citizens and their slaves was punished more severely than when the cases involved other nationalities. Such distinction brings to mind the interpretation of the rabbis who would limit liability to Israelite victims only. We would therefore not exclude the possibility that the biblical laws—at least Deut 24:7—were likewise intended to limit capital punishment to cases where the victim was one of their own people.

5

Laws Relating to Movable Property

5.1 DEPOSIT OF GOODS FOR SAFEKEEPING

IN SOCIETIES LACKING BANKS and other such secured storage locations, one could encounter the need to find a safe place for one's valuables, especially during periods of absence from home or while traveling. This need is the background for Exod 22:6–7. The deposited objects are evidently small, capable of being held within the house.[1]

> If a man delivers to his neighbor money or goods for safekeeping, and the (deposited) item is stolen from the man's house, then the thief, if he is caught (lit. found), shall pay double. If the thief is not caught, the owner of the house shall be brought before God, (to swear) that he (himself) had not laid hands on his neighbor's (deposited) property.

Exodus 22:6 opens with a ruling on the penalty to be imposed upon the thief who stole the deposited item; we will look at this ruling again in our discussion below (sec. 5.6.2), where I deal with additional laws on theft. The focus here is on deposit, where if the deposited items are missing, the owner of the house is required to takes an oath in order to clear himself from any suspicion of being involved in their theft. Curiously, the text does not actually contain the verb "to swear"; but an oath is implicit in the situation and it was so anciently understood by the Septuagint which, in the Greek, adds the verbal phrase "and (he will) swear." Philo, who no doubt read and made use of the Septuagint, explained the situation in this way:

> ... the receiver of the trust [i.e., the deposit] must go of his own freewill to the court of God and with hands stretched out to heaven swear under the pain of his own perdition that he has not embezzled any part of the deposit nor abetted another in so doing nor joined at all in inventing a theft which never took place.

This is also the understanding of the situation by Josephus and the rabbis.[2]

In Exod 22:6–7, there are no details given about the theft; only that the

---

1. This is the understanding given by Rashbam and other commentators on this verse; for these see Paul, *Studies in the Book of the Covenant*, 93 n. 2.

2. Cf. Philo, *Spec. Laws* 4.34, Colson; Josephus, *Ant.* 4.287; and *Mekhilta Mishpatim* 15 on these verses.

deposited items are now missing and that they were in fact stolen. But how did one determine that a theft had occurred and that one needed to be looking for an "outside" thief? What would happen if there were no evidence that a theft had occurred? The Bible, in its brief account, does not present this alternative case and gives no details on the theft. However, details concerning how theft of deposited items could be assumed or established are found in the Mesopotamian laws. In these laws, in the absence of such confirming circumstances, the house owner would not be permitted to escape responsibility by swearing an oath. In the Eshnunna Laws §§36–37 we read:

> §36 If a man gave his goods for deposit to an innkeeper and the house was not broken into, the door jamb not pried open, (nor) the window frame torn out, (yet) he has allowed the deposited goods he gave him to become lost, he (the house owner) must replace the goods for him.

> §37 If (however) that man's house has been broken into (and) together with the goods of the depositor which he deposited with him there was (also) loss by the house owner, then the house owner shall swear (an oath) for him by the life of the god at the gate of (the temple of the god) Tishpak (saying) "my goods have indeed also been lost together with your goods; I have not committed fraud or (illegal) removal;" and there is no claim against him.

In the situation described in §36, there is no evidence upon which to accuse the house owner himself of being a thief. But the puzzling and suspicious circumstances will not allow him to escape

responsibility by swearing an oath. The lack of any signs of break-in suggests that the house owner may have been lax in the way he guarded his house. The thief seems too easily to have entered the premises; and so the house owner cannot escape responsibility. The house owner is required to compensate the depositor by replacing the items or their value; but, at the same time, he is not given a more severe penalty, which would have been the case if it could be proved that he himself was the thief.

The second case in §37 adds a further qualification. If there were signs of a break-in but only the deposited item was taken, then this circumstance would raise questions and will prevent the house owner from taking an oath, which would release him from responsibility. The determining circumstances are thus two-fold: telltale signs of break-in, along with loss by the house owner of items of his own property. The Eshnunna Laws require the house owner to swear to his own loss as well as to solemnly assert that he had no part in the loss of the deposited items.

These same considerations appear again in Hammurapi Laws §125, which however introduces an additional factor: how the house owner conducted himself as caretaker of the deposited goods:

> If a man has given over his good(s) for safekeeping, and from the place of deposit his good(s) along with goods of house owner are (now) missing, either because of break-in or burglary, the owner of the house who was negligent must make it good and replace for the depositor whatever he gave him for safekeeping and which he then allowed to become lost. The house owner may continue to search for his own lost

property and may recover it from the thief.

This law of Hammurapi tells us that one must also consider the quality of care given to securing the deposit on the part of the house owner who received it. Since the house owner was found to be negligent, he is required to compensate the depositor even if there was a break-in and some of his own property was taken along with the deposited items. There is no mention of an oath because the house owner's negligence seems to have precluded it. Hammurapi Laws, however, omit telling us what would happen when the householder was *not negligent*; in such a case, based upon what we have seen, one may presume that the law would have allowed the house owner to swear an oath, absolving him of blame just as in Eshnunna Laws §§36–37.

Hammurapi Laws §125 does not give us details on how one would evaluate the house owner's conduct in order to decide whether or not he had acted negligently. I think it unlikely that the house owner was held to be negligent solely because a break-in took place; for surely then no house owner would be willing to receive deposited goods if he would always and in all circumstances be held responsible when loss occurred. Negligence, as a recognized category of behavior, is frequently mentioned elsewhere; but to our knowledge, it is not defined in the extant ancient Mesopotamian sources. There is, for example, a letter written during the reign of Hammurapi's son, where the sender cautions the recipient against negligence:

Concerning the half mina silver of mine, which I sent it to you to buy sesame oil—I have heard the

(words of) your letter which you sent me. Since you looked around and did not find sesame oil (to buy), keep that silver in your hand; do not be negligent in guarding the silver!"[3]

One may find more details about how to define negligent conduct in connection with deposits in later rabbinic laws. There, we find laws, where deposited money was stolen and the house owner is held responsible—not just because a theft occurred, but because the receiver did not secure or protect the item according to the standard of care expected of custodians. For this failure to exercise the customary prudence and care, the house owner is required to compensate the depositor. The Mishnah, *m. B. Metz.* 3:10, states:

If a man deposited money with his neighbor, who bound it up and slung it over his shoulder or entrusted it to his minor son or daughter, and locked up before them but not properly, he is liable (if the money was stolen) because he did not guard it in the (appropriate) manner of custodians. But if he guarded it in the (appropriate) manner of custodians, he is free of liability.

The Talmud's discuses this Mishnah, in *b. B. Metz.* 42a; and there one finds still more descriptive comments describing what were appropriate ways to protect money or valuables kept in one's house:

Samuel said: Money can only be guarded (by placing it) in the earth.

3. YOS 2 11:4–11 most recently treated in *AbB* 9. This passage is partly cited in *CAD* E, 49. For other cases in Hammurapi Laws involving negligence see Driver and Miles, *Babylonian Laws,* 1:461–66. The verb "be negligent" or "careless" also appears in Eshnunna Laws §5.

Said Raba: But nowadays that there are those skilled in sounding (out hollow spaces in the earth), it can be properly guarded only (by placing it) under the roof beams. But (it was rejoined:) nowadays that there are house-breakers (who break into the roof); it can thus be guarded only between the bricks . . . it may be (hidden) within the wall. But nowadays that there are 'rappers' (skilled in finding such hollows), it can be guarded only in the handbreadth nearest to the earth or to the uppermost beams.

Samuel and Raba lived in Babylonia during the 3rd and 4th centuries CE in dwellings made of mud-brick; the structural characteristics of their houses were not so different from those of earlier centuries. Thus, in Hammurapi Laws §125, one may reasonably imagine that negligence was defined in a similar fashion. In other words, the owner of a mud-brick house in the time of Hammurapi was seen to be negligent for not having exercised sufficient care, either in placement of the deposited items—as described in the Babylonian Talmud, or in his handling of the deposit, as suggested in the Mishnah.

Further elaboration on negligent behavior is found in the Palestinian Talmud, in a discussion on *m. B. Metz.* 3:1, which states that the owner in whose house a deposit was stolen or lost is given the option of swearing an oath or paying compensation and not swearing an oath. But a house owner who was negligent must pay compensation and is not given the option to swear. This last situation is very similar to what is described in Hammurapi Laws §125. The Talmud in its discussion states:

When does one say, "an unpaid[4] custodian may swear an oath and be free (of liability, only) if he guarded them in the (appropriate) manner of custodians." (Thus, for example) he stored them away in an appropriate manner; he placed them (i.e., the money) in his purse, tied them up in his cloak and kept them before him; placed them in a strongbox or chest or coffer. If they were then stolen or lost, he owes only the oath and is free of financial obligation. And if there are witnesses (to testify) that he (appropriately) did so, he need not (even) take the oath. (However) if he stored them away in an inappropriate manner; tied them up inappropriately; left them (hanging) at his back; set them on top of his roof and they were stolen, he is required to pay for them. (In sum:) if he set them in a spot that was appropriate for keeping them safe, he is free of liability; but if not, he is liable.[5]

One can thus arrive at a more in-depth description of deposit in Exod 22:6–7 with the help of the insights provided by near Eastern and rabbinic laws. While not all of the legal points are found in every one of the preserved laws, I take this to be the result of the incomplete and somewhat random drafting of the ancient law collections, which are all selections out of a larger body of material. Nevertheless, the varied nature of the cases described above have led some modern scholars to

4. The Rabbis used the cases in Exod 22:6–14 as an exegetical basis for making formal distinctions between custodians or "bailees"; these are discussed below (sec. 5.3) in connection with Exod 22:13–14. The rabbis understand the receiver of the deposit in Exod 22:6–7 to have been unpaid since there is no mention in the Bible of a fee or charge for this service.

5. *j. B. Metz.* 9b.

argue for a less integrated and more "evolutionary" view of the laws of deposit.
For example, some would say that adding negligence in Hammurapi Laws §125
is a later redactor's contribution, adding a
new test to an earlier, simpler standard of
proof which was based only upon signs of
break-in and home owner's loss. This earlier standard is present in Eshnunna Laws
§37.[6]

This "evolutionary" view assumes
that the concept of negligence was not
universally recognized in these ancient
societies and only emerged in stages of
"development." I cannot agree. One cannot ignore the fact that there is, after all,
not a great distance either in geography
or in chronology between the Eshnunna
and Hammurapi Laws; less than one hundred miles of geographical distance and
fifty years or less of time separate them.
The verb "to act negligently," moreover,
is found in both law collections in other
cases; and it can therefore easily be argued
that the concept is in fact implied in Eshnunna Laws §36, in the phrase "(yet) he
has allowed the deposited goods he gave
him to become lost." As for the biblical
laws, they are terse and there are clearly
many missing details, e.g., the circumstances whereby theft was determined to
have taken place and any consideration
of possible concomitant loss of personal
goods by the house owner. While negligence is not specifically mentioned in
Exod 22:6–7, the concept was however
known and is evident in other biblical
laws, e.g., the owner of the goring ox (in
sec. 4.10) or the careless digger of a pit in
Exod 21:28–36.[7]

I am persuaded, as I earlier stated,
that Exod 22:7 involves the swearing of
an oath before God. However, others have
argued that being "brought before God"
does not indicate an oath at all but, rather,
a more "primitive" procedure, an ordeal
or oracle to test the house owner's veracity when challenged by the depositor. (A
similar claim has been made for Exod 22:8
which is discussed below in sec. 5.6.2.)[8]
As additional support for our seeing the
taking of an oath in Exod 22:7, I can point
to Exod 22:10 which deals with the deposit of animals and their loss. There, it
is clearly stated "an oath before the LORD
shall decide" (discussed below in sec. 5.2).
One can also point to Lev 5:20–24 where
oath was the expected mode of proof for
the receiver of deposits:

> The LORD spoke to Moses, saying:
> If a person sins and commits an of-
> fense against the LORD (in that) he
> had lied to a member of his com-
> munity in a matter of a deposit or
> a pledge, or by robbery, or has ex-
> ploited his neighbor, or has found
> something lost and lied about it—
> and swore falsely regarding any of
> these various things that one may
> do and commit a sin thereby. And
> if it comes to pass if he has sinned
> (in this manner) and has (now) felt
> guilty, then he must restore what
> he took by robbery or what he took
> by fraud, or the deposit that was
> entrusted to him, or the lost thing
> that he found, or anything else
> about which he has sworn falsely,
> then he shall repay the principal
> amount and shall add one-fifth to

---

6. For discussion see Koschaker, *Rechtsvergleichende Studien*, 26–33.

7. This law, Exod 21:33–34, deals with an animal injured by falling into a pit carelessly left open

and unguarded by its digger. I have not included
it in the present study because I have been unable
to find a matching case for it in our extant ancient
Near Eastern legal sources.

8. For a review of opinions—pro and con—see
Jackson, *Wisdom Laws*, 338–41, 343–44.

it. He shall pay it to its owner when he realizes his guilt.

Here we find a person expressing subsequent remorse over his false oaths; and deposit is one of several situations listed for which his guilt might be eased through giving restitution.[9] But in order fully to atone for having taken his false oath, Lev 5:25–26 requires an expiatory sacrifice:

> And he shall bring to the to the LORD (as) his guilt offering, a ram without blemish from the flock, or the [lit. your] equivalent (in money) for a guilt offering to the priest The priest shall make atonement on his behalf before the LORD, and he shall be forgiven for any one of these things that one may do to incur (such) guilt.

I find further support for the oath being present in Exod 22:7 in noting that Morgenstern, a modern scholar, who assumed that the Pentateuch is composed of documents written at different times, did not appeal to Leviticus 5 in order to exclude the possibility of ordeal in Exod 22:7. For he might have argued that these two passages belong to different times and literary strata. He in fact expressed reservations about reconstructing an ordeal in Exod 22:7 on the basis of customs among the Bedouin of the nineteenth century. He observed that:

> . . . trial by ordeal is as a rule, resorted to only when the case seems extreme and the oath alone does not suffice . . . The oath is regularly employed in cases of theft of animals or other property . . . where

there is no direct evidence but only suspicion of guilt; while the ordeal is resorted to, as a rule, only in cases of rape, adultery or murder, when all direct evidence is lacking and the circumstances are unusually shocking."[10]

To this observation I would further note that, even in situations of ordeal, the test is linked to requiring the party or parties involved to swear a solemn oath. In other words, the peril created by the ordeal is designed to punish the person who swore falsely. We have seen this in Num 5:19, where the wife suspected of adultery first swears an oath before undergoing her ordeal. The same procedure of linking oath with ordeal is found in Babylonia in cases of adultery and treason using the river ordeal. (These situations have already been discussed above in sec. 1.3.2.) For all of the above reasons, I remain confident about the presence of oath in Exod 22:6–7 (and also in 22:8 as we will see below in sec. 5.6.2)— just as it appears to have been the case in the ancient Near Eastern parallel cases dealing with deposit.

5.2 ANIMAL KEEPERS AND THEIR RESPONSIBILITIES

The Bible contains a law on the responsibilities of those who are entrusted with the care of animals belonging to another. There are also additional references, in

9. False oath is the common thread uniting all of the sins mentioned. Cf. also Sprinkle, "Theft and Deprivation of Property."

10. Morgenstern, "The Book of the Covenant," 112–16. His view is followed by Fishbane, *Biblical Interpretation in Early Israel*, 173. However, Jackson, "Modelling Biblical Law: The Covenant Code. Part I," 1807–14 still raises the possibility of an oracular process in Exod 22:7. He argues that deposit was a transaction culturally viewed as creating a sacred obligation touching upon God. This view is maintained in Jackson, *Wisdom Laws*, 337–44.

the narratives and in the prophets, to the legal responsibilities of shepherds with respect to the animals in their care. In Exod 22:9–12, the law is stated as follows:

> If a man gives over to his neighbor a donkey, ox, sheep, or any other animal for keeping, and it dies or is injured or is carried off, without (another) witness (to what happened), an oath before the LORD shall decide between the two of them, (with the keeper swearing) that he did lay his hand on his neighbor's property; and its (i.e., the animal's) owner shall accept (what he says), and he (the keeper) shall not be required to pay its (i.e., the animal's) owner (for this damage or loss). But if it was indeed stolen from him, he must pay its owner. If it was torn apart by wild beasts, he should bring it (dead or alive) as evidence; he need not pay for what was torn by wild beasts.

The keeper normally has full responsibility for the animals in his charge and thus is responsible to protect them from theft;[11] but he is not liable under certain circumstances: natural death, non-fatal injury, or the animal being carried off by force of arms, e.g., by bandits or taken as plunder in military action.[12] In the absence of witnesses, Exod 22:10 allows the keeper to confirm his story by swearing an oath. This is understandable, considering

the animals are usually kept outside of densely populated urban areas. The keeper, however, also has a responsibility to prevent theft; this, after all, is the animal owner's expectation; therefore Exod 22:11 requires him to pay the owner in cases of theft. The keeper is given relief when animals are taken from his care by wild beasts; but only if the keeper can bring back some physical evidence of this event, which also testifies that he was, at the time, protecting his animals. The Bible does not mention a necessity to bring physical evidence in case of natural death, but the carcass or hide would surely remain and be available for return even though the text makes no mention of this; perhaps it was self-evident.[13] No trace, however, would remain of animals carried off by bandits or soldiers. The Bible seems to allow the oath of the shepherd to stand in place of physical evidence in these cases.

There are a number of biblical parallels that bear out details of the biblical law stated above. They deal primarily with animals attacked by wild beasts. There is a description of loss through wild beasts in Amos 3:12, where the prophet describes the future plight of Israel at the hands of her enemies.

> Thus says the LORD: Just as the shepherd rescues from the mouth of the lion two legs, or a piece of an ear, so shall the people of Israel who live in Samaria be rescued,

11. This analysis of the keeper's responsibility appears in Rasbam to Exod 22:6.

12. The verb "carried off" refers to acts of plunder or robbery; cf. Hazzequni to Exod 22:9. As for "injured," Jackson, *Wisdom Laws,* 346–48 says this refers to accidental injury or non-fatal maiming caused by attack of wild beasts. Nahmanides on Exod 22:12 similarly considers the possibility of accidental injury. However Rashbam on Exod 22:9 relates it to wild animal attack, but where the animal was not carried off by its animal attacker.

13. Mesopotamian administrative records from all periods contain entries for dead animals, whose carcasses were apparently brought in from the steppe by herders. See, for example passages cited in *CAD* M/2, 101–2 and especially the Neo-Babylonian contracts cited below, where the owner promises pay a bonus consisting of one hide and 2 1/2 shekels worth of sinew per one hundred recovered dead animals.

with the leg of a bed or fabric from a couch.

The protective actions of a shepherd are described in a speech between David and Saul in 1 Sam 17:33–37:

> Saul said to David, "You cannot go against this Philistine to fight with him; for you are just a lad, and he has been a warrior from his youth." But David said to Saul, "Your servant has been a shepherd for his father for the flock; and when a lion or a bear came, and carried off a lamb from the flock, then I would go after it and strike it down, and rescuing (the lamb) from its mouth; and if it turned on me, I would take hold of its beard, strike it down, and kill it. Your servant has killed both lion and bear; and this uncircumcised Philistine shall be like one of them, since he has scorned the arrayed armies of the living God." And David said, "The Lord, who saved me from the paw of the lion and from the paw of the bear—he will save me from the hand of this Philistine." Then Saul said to David, "Go, and may the Lord be with you!"

The responsibility of the shepherd as animal keeper is also the background of Jacob's angry speech to Laban in Gen 31:38–41:

> These twenty years I have been [a shepherd] with you; your ewes and your female goats have not miscarried, and I have not eaten the rams of your flocks. That which was torn by wild beasts I did not bring to you; I bore the loss myself; from my hand you required it, whether stolen by day or stolen by night. It was like this with me: by day the heat consumed me, and the cold by night, and my sleep fled from my eyes. These twenty years I have been in your house; I served you fourteen years for your two daughters, and six years for your flock, and you have changed my wages ten times. (NRSV)

Jacob protests that he did more for Laban than was legally required of him. His first point deals with his care of pregnant female animals and responsibility for their offspring. His second point deals with his refraining from eating rams, i.e., (male) animals from the flock belonging to Laban. His third point is that he might have brought home as evidence the remains of animals torn by wild beasts but refrained from doing so and bore these losses himself. His fourth point is that there was no distinction between daytime and nighttime thefts. His final point deals with Laban willfully changing his wages.

We can further our understanding of these five points, as well as of our other biblical citations, by looking at Near Eastern evidence, starting with the Hammurapi Laws §§263–267 on herding:

> §263 If he (the herder) has allowed an ox or sheep that was given over to him become lost, he must restore ox for ox and sheep for sheep to its owner.

> §264 If a shepherd, to whom has been given either cattle or sheep for tending, has received his full wages (and) is satisfied, (then) reduces the number of cattle or sheep (or else) diminishes their offspring, he must give back (to the owner) offspring and product(s) according to his (original) contract.

> §265 If a shepherd to whom has been given either cattle or sheep for tending has acted falsely (and) changes a marking or sells (an

animal), they shall convict him and he shall restore the cattle or sheep he stole ten-fold to their owner.

§266 If there was an outbreak of sickness (literally: stroke of a god) in the fold or a lion made a kill, the shepherd shall clear (himself by oath) before a god and the owner of the fold shall accept the loss in the fold.

§267 If the shepherd was negligent and a crippling illness (?)[14] occurred in the fold, the shepherd who allowed a crippling illness to occur in the fold shall make good and pay to their owners (for the loss of these) cattle or sheep.

Let us begin with §§263 and 266, which contrast lost animals with those animals killed through attack by wild animals. In §263, the situation seems self-evident: the animals were lost through the shepherd's negligence or inattention. The shepherd was hired to tend his animals; so, if there is no mitigating circumstance, he must pay for this loss. But in §266, there were events beyond his control—unforeseen sickness or a lion's attack. In these situations, the shepherd who is ready to swear an oath will not be charged for the loss of these sick or slain animals. Jacob, however, in his third point of argument with Laban, testifies that he

refrained from any attempt to free himself of responsibility for animal attack. Following what appears to have been common custom and law, he could have done so without taking an oath by his bringing forward parts of the carcass as evidence for the animal attack, Jacob could then legitimately have deduct these losses from the flock; instead, Jacob bore these losses himself.

There is an interesting variation on the response to animal attack found in Hittite Laws §80, which presents a slightly different economic arrangement for animals torn by wild beasts:

> If any (shepherd) abandons (a sheep) to a wolf, its owner shall take the meat but (the shepherd) shall take the sheepskin.[15]

According to this law, a shepherd would be rewarded for this act of bravery in snatching the sheep from the jaws of the wolf, receiving the additional economic benefit of the hide. I imagine that this would be in addition to the shepherd receiving credit for the lost animal. But, unfortunately, the Hittite Laws do not elaborate on this point. There is some evidence for a practice involving hides in herding contracts from the Persian period in Mesopotamia, as we shall see presently. But we have no comments on the disposition of hides and meat in the Bible.

Hammurapi Laws §264 mentions the existence of a contract between the owner and the shepherd's wages.[16] There

---

14. The Akkadian term *pissatum* has been explained as "mange" in *CAD* B, 156; but perhaps more likely as a "crippling disease" in *AHw* 85. The outbreak is assumed to be the result of negligence by the shepherd, unlike the outbreak of sickness (literally: "the stroke of a god") in §266; cf. Finet, *Le Code de Hammurapi*, 128. Postgate, "Some Old Babylonian Shepherds and Their Flocks," 6 notes that in Old Babylonian herding contracts, liability for this problem is juxtaposed with responsibility for lost animals that the shepherd must replace for the owner. For specific citations see also Roth, "Scholastic Exercise Laws," 133 n. 19.

15. Hoffner, *Laws of the Hittites*, 195, in his commentary to this law notes that the wolf did not succeed in carrying off the carcass. The shepherd succeeded in wresting the dead animal away from the wolf.

16. Hammurapi Laws §261 (not cited here) sets a "standard" wage or food supplement for herders of sheep and cattle at 8 kors of grain per year.

is also reference to the expected propagation of offspring while the flock is under the shepherd's care; but no further details are given. We learn more about offspring and wages from shepherding contracts from Mesopotamia. We learn more about expectations from Old Babylonian period documents, which record the transfer of sheep and goats to the custody of shepherds. Some of the contracts add provisions on wages and on expected rates of increase for the flock and for diminution through natural causes. The rates of increase specified require the shepherd to deliver between 60 to 80 lambs out of 100 births; the shepherd would thus be allowed to take for himself any lambs that survived beyond those numbers. Some contracts contain provision for a natural mortality rate of 10 to 15 out of every 100 animals. There are also adjustments depending upon whether or not the shepherd received wages and sometimes also an amount for food and clothing. Norms similar to these appear in later herding contracts from the Persian period, where we find shepherds undertaking to supply 66 2/3 (sic) lambs per hundred female sheep in addition to fixed amounts of wool and butter. The shepherd is allowed a mortality rate of 10 percent but is allowed to salvage the hide plus an amount of sinews; the rest presumably belonged to the owner. These ancient contracts may be further compared with provisions known from shepherding arrangements in Iraq and Palestine in the first half of the twentieth century.[17]

Jacob, in his speech to Laban in Gen 31:38–41, did not use the term "contract" but his complaint about wages presupposes that one existed; I will say more about wages below. Jacob also mentions offspring in his statement to Laban. Jacob seems to be saying that he reckoned miscarriages together with live births and adjusted his deliveries of lambs to Laban accordingly, thus giving Laban a flawless fulfillment of his contract.

Jacob's statement on eating the rams is not mentioned in our Near Eastern sources. It may however be implied in the provisions in Hammurapi Laws §264 where the shepherd "reduces the number of cattle or sheep (or else) diminishes their offspring" or in §265 "has acted falsely (and) changes a marking or sells" (an animal or exposed them to avoidable illness as in §267). It is possible that Jacob added animals to Laban's share, that, by customary right, would have been reckoned either as belonging to Jacob's share of increase or within a quota for dead animals. The fourteenth-century commentator Isaac Abrabanel observed that it would be contrary to nature and experience for twenty years to pass without a miscarriage in the flock; without some animals lost to predatory beasts; and without a ram being taken out by Jacob for his family to eat. The point, says Abrabanel, is that Jacob paid for every animal, even those for which he would have been entitled to claim exemption.[18] In addition, Jacob's comment on suffering from the weather lead us to doubt that he received a clothing allowance, as noted in

---

17. For Mesopotamian and later herding contracts and their details see Finkelstein, "An Old Babylonian Herding Contract and Genesis 31:38f," and literature cited there. For Old Babylonian period contracts see further Postgate, "Some Old Babylonian Shepherds and Their Flocks"; Stol,

"Fragment of a Herding Contract"; and Greengus, *Studies in Ishchali Documents*, 132–33.

18. Abrabanel, *Commentary on the Torah*, 148–49.

some of the Old Babylonian shepherding contracts.

There are other references to Jacob's "wages"; in Gen 30:28–43; 31:7–9, 41; in Gen 30:31–34 we read about one "contract":

> He (Laban) said, "What shall I give you?" Jacob said, "You shall not give me anything; if you will do this for me, I will again feed your flock and keep it: let me pass through all your flock today, removing from it every speckled and spotted sheep and every black lamb, and the spotted and speckled among the goats; and such shall be my wages. So my honesty will answer for me later, when you come to look into my wages with you. Every one that is not speckled and spotted among the goats and black among the lambs, if found with me, shall be counted stolen." Laban said, "Good! Let it be as you have said." (NRSV)

These passages describe the bargain that Jacob finally made with Laban to take as his share those animals with rare markings; his share, therefore, was based upon the vagaries of nature rather than upon the overall numbers of offspring, which was customary for Near Eastern shepherds. Laban, in his greed, accepted the bargain eagerly because Jacob was agreeing to forgo more typical arrangements between owners and shepherds. Although Jacob and Laban had arranged the above contract, it—or previous ones— are described as being subject to changes and frequently renegotiated; so Jacob later complained to his wives. But Jacob got the best of Laban notwithstanding, through his manipulation of the breeding process, which is extensively described in Gen

30:37–42. Speaking later to his wives in Gen 31:6–9, Jacob remembered:

> You know that I have served your father with all my strength; yet your father has cheated me and changed my wages ten times, but God did not permit him to harm me. If he said, 'The speckled shall be your wages,' then all the flock bore speckled; and if he said, 'The striped shall be your wages,' then all the flock bore striped. Thus God has taken away the livestock of your father, and given them to me. (NRSV)

The Near Eastern materials have helped illuminate four of the five points in Jacob's argument with Laban mentioned earlier. But we have not been helped with respect to Jacob's remark about night theft. His statement seems to imply that the customary responsibility of a shepherd might be mitigated if a theft occurred during the night. This is a detail that is not mentioned either in the biblical or in the Near Eastern laws. The commentator Abrabanel here understood Jacob to be claiming that he was not required to recompense animals stolen during the darkness of night; and what's more, that Jacob's fatigue described in Gen 31:40 came about through his valiant attempts to stand guard and protect the flock at all times.[19] The medieval Jewish commentator Hazzequni attempted to explain it in a slightly different way as follows: "It was customary to herd during the day but at night to return the sheep to spend the night with their owner so that if one was stolen at night, the loss would be the owner's" but Jacob paid for such losses, too.[20] The legal implication

19. Ababanel, *Commentary on the Torah*, 148–49 begins his discussion with looking at Gen 31:31.

20. Hazzequni on Gen 31:39.

of Jacob's remark about night theft is not otherwise taken up and developed by the rabbis in their halakhic discussions, evidently because they understood the shepherd's responsibility for lost animals to be total and unconditional. Thus *m. Shevu.* 8:1 and *m. B. Metz.* 7:8 state: "a paid guardian or a hirer may take an oath if the beast was lamed or driven away or dead, but he must make restitution if it was lost or stolen." One would imagine that nighttime would be a time of special challenge as long as the flock remained in the care of a shepherd. But so far, evidence from outside of the Bible for the possibility of such mitigation is lacking.[21]

Hittite Laws §87 offers a case that may indirectly bear on (night?) theft of animals in the care of a shepherd:

> If anyone strikes the dog of a herdsman a lethal blow, he shall pay 20 shekels of silver and shall look to his house for it.

This law exacts a high penalty for anyone who kills a sheep dog, apparently because of its importance to the job of herding and the fact that such dogs might not easily be replaced. A lien will be placed against the killer's house and assets if he does not pay.[22] Subsequent paragraphs in the Hittite Laws (§§88–89) impose lesser penalties for killing the dog of a hunter (12 shekels) or watchdog (1 shekel) and do not add the clause extending liability to placing a lien on the killer's property. Biblical shepherds, however, are

pictured as acting alone; if they used dogs, these are not mentioned.

All in all, the biblical laws and practices relating to herding are fairly close to what we find in the ancient Near East; herding was an important economic component of the times and one should not be surprised that similar norms prevailed over the entire region of the fertile crescent and continued into recent times. The biblical and Near Eastern sources clearly resonate with each other and with what we know about herding from ancient documents of everyday life. The biblical laws in Exod 22:9–12 add a more explicitly stated exclusion for the shepherd whose flock has been plundered by force, allowing him to be free of blame when he swears an oath in such cases as he does for theft. The Near Eastern laws do not mention this possibility in connection with shepherds; perhaps it did not need mentioning, being self-evident. This provision might perhaps have been the subject of Hammurapi Laws §262, which starts with entrusting animals to a shepherd but then breaks off; and the lost text of this paragraph is not preserved in any of the extant ancient copies of the laws.

5.3 BORROWED OR HIRED ANIMALS AND TOOLS

Borrowing and hiring are not the same transactions; but the Bible treats them together in Exod 22:13–14:

> (13) If a man borrows (an animal) from another and it is injured [lit. broken] or dies, its owner not being with it, he must surely pay.

> (14) If its owner was with it, he shall not pay; if he was hired, he is (still) entitled to his wage.

21. In a Talmud discussion of Jacob's statement, *b. B. Metz.* 93b, Raba suggests that it would be normal for a shepherd to sleep a little during the night, so losses that occurred should therefore not be charged against him. Jacob, therefore, had assumed greater responsibility than expected.

22. See Hoffner, *Laws of the Hittites,* 168.

Verse 13 is most likely a case where one individual borrows an animal to assist him in carrying out agricultural or other labors. The possibility of dying supports the idea that animals are indeed included in these verses, even though the borrowed or hired items are not otherwise identified in the Hebrew text. In verse 13, the phrase "it is injured or dies" is the same that is used for animals left with the herder in Exod 22:9 (sec. 5.2). The ruling appears to be that in the absence of the owner of the borrowed item, total responsibility falls upon the borrower. This is the sense whether one translates "its owner not being with it," i.e., the borrowed animal, or "with him," i.e., alongside of the borrower.

Verse 14 introduces a second, alternative case, where the owner of the borrowed (animal) is present and apparently working along with his beast. The last part of v. 14 also introduces a third case, where the arrangement was one of hire. The last part of v. 14 is troublesome, because the subject of the verbs "was hired" and "entitled" is not clear; it is the masculine pronoun "he," which one could likewise translate "it." So we have a choice. Is the grammatical subject of the verbs the owner of the animal who was hired to come along with his beast to help manage it, and that he will be paid regardless of the accident to his animal? (This is how I have taken it in our translation.) Or is it the animal that was hired, rather than borrowed, as in the previous case given in v. 13? In this view, we might have translated: "If it (i.e., the animal) was hired, it has still earned its hire (despite having been injured or died while working)."

Deciding between translations has been made more difficult because the rabbis sought to use this part of the verse as a

textual anchor for the *sokher* or "hirer" of an animal, e.g., a worker who did not borrow but rather hired an animal belonging to another. The Hebrew term for "hirer" does not appear in our passage, which employs the passive term *sakhir*, i.e., (the) "hired (person or item)." The Bible knows both the "active" term "hirer" and the passive term "hired" elsewhere; but they are attested only for the hiring of persons, not animals. The rabbis nevertheless wish to translate the last part of v. 14 as if it said: "If it (i.e, the animal) was hired (by a hirer and it was injured or died), he (the hirer of that animal) has (still) earned his wage." The rabbis were seeking to establish scriptural foundations for the four types of custodians or "bailees" listed in the Mishnah: an unpaid guardian, a paid guardian, a borrower, and a hirer, i.e., one who rents an animal belonging to another to assist him in his labors.[23] The rabbis, in the Talmud,[24] want to argue that the receiver and guardian of deposits in Exod 22:6–7 (discussed above in sec. 5.1) was an unpaid custodian; this is of course very possible, although, to be sure, nothing is said about the presence or absence of a fee in the biblical text. They assume that the herder in Exod 22:9–12 (sec. 5.2) was a paid custodian; and this is certainly the case for the herder. The borrower is clearly mentioned in verse 13; but where in Scripture was the fourth custodian, the hirer or renter? The rabbis, following the Mekhilta on Exod 22:13–14,[25] want to use the last part of v. 14 as the scriptural base for the category of hirer or renter. Rash-

23. These four categories are given in *m. Shevu.* 8:1, and *B. Metz.* 7:8.

24. The rabbis base this on a *baraita* cited in *b. B. Metz.* 94b.

25. *Mekhilta, Mishpatim* 16.

bam sums up the rabbinical position as follows: "It is that he hired the beast of the other person in order to use it in his labor." If the animal then dies of natural causes, "he (the hirer) is exempt for accidental mishaps" because "he is paying its (the animal's) hire and (thus) he is no longer treated like a borrower."

However, medieval commentators Joseph Bekhor Shor and Hazzequni see this as a forced interpretation of the verses; and I have followed them in my own translation above. These commentators argue that the *peshat* or plain meaning of the verses requires that the phrase "he is entitled to his wage" must refer back to the owner of the animal mentioned in the first half of v. 14, who was hired to assist with the work to be performed; this is how he came to be present on the scene when the animal died or was injured. This would be a natural continuation of v. 13, where the owner was *not* present. The borrower in v. 13 is liable because the owner was not there to witness the circumstances of the loss or damage. But the owner was present in v. 14; and the final clause in that verse therefore states that if the owner was there and, moreover, had he himself been hired, apparently to assist with the work or to manage his beast, then the owner must be paid for his service, even if the animal in the process of work accidentally died or was lamed. And the Mishnah, *m. B. Metz.* 8:1 in fact puts forth this very understanding, and identifies the owner as the one hired:

> If a man borrowed a cow together with the service of its owner or hired its owner together with the cow, or if he borrowed the service of the owner or hired him and afterwards borrowed the cow, and

the cow died, he is not liable for it is written: "If the owner is with him, he shall not pay."

But the uncertainty of the pronouns still enables even many modern as well as earlier translators to understand "its (the animal's) hire rather than "his (the animal owner's) hire." And there is no way to settle the question decisively. Thus, for example, NJPS offers "if it [i.e., the beast] was hired, he [i.e., the owner] is entitled to the hire [i.e., of his dead animal)." Similarly, NRSV "if it [i.e., the beast] was hired, only the hiring fee is due." Driver and Miles translate similarly: "if it [i.e., the beast] be a hired thing, it came for its hire" which they explain that "the hirer is not responsible if he has paid the price; for the risk is then with the owner," who rented out his beast for profit.[26]

Daube offers yet another direction in the interpretation of the last part of Verse 14: "If he (the borrower of the cattle that has suffered damage or died) be a labourer (employed and paid by the owner of the cattle), it shall be set against his hire (he shall make amends up to the amount of his wages)." Daube takes the phrase "if he was hired" to refer not to the owner of the animal but to the person who was described as the borrower in v. 13![27]

Leaving aside the interpretation of the latter part of v. 14, it is clear that the presence of the owner made a difference. His presence would prevent or would seem to rule out charging the temporary user with the misuse or mishandling of the borrowed animal. Therefore the

26. Driver and Miles, *Babylonian Laws*, 1:440.

27. Daube, *Studies in Biblical Law*, 16–17. See further Houtman, *Exodus*, 3:205 for similar interpretations setting the loss against the hiring fee; these include the Septuagint.

borrower is not liable. But if the owner were not present, then the borrower in Exod 22:13–14 would be responsible to pay for a beast that died while working. We find confirmation of such unmitigated liability by a borrower for loss during use in the story of the borrowed axe retrieved by Elisha in 2 Kgs 6:1–7. When the axe fell into the river, the prophet using it cried out "Alas my lord and it was borrowed!" The borrower was evidently under an obligation to return the very object that he borrowed, intact. This conforms to the general principle that one finds in *m. B. Metz.* 7:8 and *m. Shevu.* 8:1: "a borrower must make restitution in every case."

The later rabbis who lived during the centuries after the Mishnah, however, wished to ease the borrower's liability so that, even if the owner were not present, the borrower of the animal could also be exempt from liability as long as he was using the animal or item in an appropriate fashion and for the agreed-upon purpose; for why else did he borrow it in the first place? [28] The rabbis narrow the focus of the biblical case to times when the animal was in his possession but not being employed at the task for which it was borrowed. But in *b. B. Metz.* 97a we are also told that the borrower must also bring witnesses who can testify that he was using the borrowed item in the appropriate manner: "A man borrowed a bucket from his neighbor, and it broke. When he came before R. Papa, he said to him, 'Go and bring witnesses that you did not put it to unfitting use, and you

will be free from liability." This exemption is thus to be narrowly applied; and the rabbis also did not exempt the borrower from responsibility even if the beast was carried off by bandits. This is their position, even though this mishap was not explicitly mentioned as a liability for the borrower in Exod 22:13.[29]

It is understandable that the Rabbis were motivated to find scriptural roots for cases dealing with animals that were hired to assist workers with laborious tasks; indeed, such cases are frequently presented in the Mishnah and were commonplace everyday transactions. Such laws occur in the Mesopotamian laws, as we shall presently see; and one would thus expect that similar laws must have operated in biblical times. But they are not preserved; in fact—as mentioned above—every time the terms "hire, hired, hireling" occurs in Scripture, it is a person who is being hired, never a beast—unless perhaps in the unclear and disputed last phrase in Exod 22:14.

Scriptural evidence for the hirer of animals is thus scant. The Mishnah therefore attempts to "fill this gap" and in the tractate *m. B. Metz.* devotes several paragraphs to cases where hired animals are injured or died. We should note that in the case of loss or theft, the hirer is responsible just like the borrower was in Exod 22:13–14; but unlike the borrower, the hirer is free from liability in case of unforeseen accidents; his liability is like

---

28. See *b. B. Metz.* 96b–97a. The rabbinic position is summarized by Maimonides, *Mishnah Torah, Hilkhot She'elah Upiqadon,* 1.1. The rabbinic position on responsibility conforms to *commodatum* , i.e., loan for use, in Roman law; cf. Thomas, *Textbook of Roman Law,* 274–75, citing D.13.6.4–5.

29. This mishap is mentioned in the laws of the shepherd in Exod 22:9 and there the law does remove liability from the shepherd (who was hired). See discussion in *b. B. Metz.* 94b–95a, and in Maimonides, *Mishnah Torah, Hilkhot She'elah Upiqadon,* 1:1.

that of the herdsman.[30] The Misnhah in *m. B. Metz.* 7:8–10 states:

> A paid guardian or a hirer may take an oath if (the beast was accidentally) lamed or carried off (by bandits or wild beasts) or died (from natural causes) but he must make restitution if it was lost or stolen . . . A brigand counts as unavoidable accident. A lion or a bear or a panther or a serpent counts as unavoidable accident . . . If a beast died a natural death, this counts as unavoidable accident but not if it died of cruel treatment.

Ordinary people were not expected to prevent attacks by wild animals as was exceptionally done by the king David in his youth, who recounted his heroic actions in 1 Sam 17:33–37 cited above.

The circumstances of injury, animal attack, and natural death also appear in the Mesopotamian laws dealing with hired work animals. In Hammurapi Laws we find them dealt with in some detail. The laws specify a tariff of damages for non-fatal but maiming injuries; the tariffs are not expressed in specific sums but rather as a percentage of the value of the animal when it was still healthy and intact. The Hammurapi Laws mention both ox and donkey, but focus upon oxen, since these were vitally important for plowing the hard soil of that arid region. The laws are as follows:

> §244 If a man hired an ox or donkey and a lion kills it in the open steppe, (the loss) is the owner's.

---

30. The rabbis, however, are divided on whether the hirer should be given the opportunity to swear an oath, freeing him from responsibility for loss or theft. Cf. *b. B. Metz.* 80b, and *b. B. Qam.* 45a–b, cited by Rashi and Rashbam on Exod 22:14.

> §245 If a man hired an ox and has caused it to die by neglect or by beating, he shall replace ox for ox to the owner of the ox.

> §246 If a man hired an ox and has broken its leg or cut the sinew of its neck (var. tears off its skin), he shall replace ox for ox to the owner of the ox.

> §247 If a man hired an ox and has destroyed its eye, he shall give half its value in silver to the owner of the ox.

> §248 If a man hired an ox and has broken its horn, cut its tail, or injured the tendon of its hoof, he shall pay one fifth of its value in silver.

> §249 If a man has hired an ox and a god smote it so that it died, the man who hired the ox shall swear an oath by a god and is free (of liability).

The oath of the hirer in §249 is similar to the oath sworn in the Mishnah cited above. Just as in the Mishnah, the Hammurapi Laws give exemption for natural death and for the attack of wild beast but offer no relief to the hirer in cases if the hirer on his own caused injury or damage to the animal. Hammurapi Laws also describe in more detail the kind of injuries that the hirer may have inflicted upon the ox. §249 mentions accidental death but does not say anything about accidental laming as cited in the Mishnah. Otherwise the laws correspond to what we see in the Mishnah.

We find some hint of exception for normal "wear and tear" in connection with rental of a tool in Eshnunna Laws §9A. If someone rents a sickle and it breaks, apparently during harvesting, the renter is required to return the broken pieces; the rental fee is still owed but there is no mention of the renter having to pay anything further for the broken tool.

> One seah (plus) 5 "quarts" barley is the rental of a sickle; and (if broken) he must return the pieces to its owner.[31]

But it is not clear whether the laming of a beast would have been considered as normal "wear and tear." Hiring contracts from the period of Hammurapi and his dynasty at times include provisions assigning to the hirer specific responsibility for injuries to animals; these contracts then list parts of the anatomy, as in the laws: eyes, horns, hooves, and tail.[32] The addition of these clauses may have served to assign responsibility to the hirer even in case of accidental injuries. Because we do not know for certain whether the Mesopotamian laws would have been as forgiving as is the Mishnah with respect to any non-fatal accidental injuries. In all other respects, however, the laws are similar.

In Hammurapi Laws §244 we are not told how the hirer would prove the occurrence of the lion's attack to the owner. The law somehow assumes that the facts of the case were clearly known. One might think of witnesses and maybe also physical evidence of attack, as required of the shepherd in Exod 22:12 (sec. 5.2). Perhaps the hirer was required to take an oath, as in §249 and in *m. B. Metz.* 7:8–10. This seems to be the most plausible understanding, as we can see also in the Hittite Laws §75 presented below. But the reason

for the absence of mentioning the oath in §244 is not clear.

Laws on injuries to oxen have a long history, going back to Sumerian times. The Laws of Lipit-Ishtar contains a tariff of set compensations for a series of injuries caused by the hirer:

> §34 If a man hired an ox (and) and cut its hoof tendon, he shall pay one third of its value.

> §35 If a man hired an ox and destroyed its eye, he shall pay one half of its value.

> §36 If a man hired an ox and severed its horn, he shall pay one fourth of its value.

> §37 If a man hired an ox and severed its tail, he shall pay one fourth its value.

Laws on animal injuries also appear in ancient school exercises, where student scribes wrote down and memorized Sumerian laws and legal phrases. Their formulation is at times less precise than in the formal laws; many, for example, do not include that part of the law, which tells that the ox was hired. They simply describe the injury and its consequence:

> §1 If he [destroyed] the eye of the ox, he shall pay one half of its value.

> §2 If he cu[t off] its horn, he shall pay one third of its value.

> §3 If he severed(?) the hoof tendon of the ox, he shall pay one fourth of its value.

> §4 If he cut off the tail of the ox [rest of the line is lost].[33]

---

31. *CAD* K, 616 discusses this law and textual problems relating to the term "(broken) pieces."

32. Examples are cited in Roth, "The Scholastic Exercise Laws About Rented Oxen," 133 and in *CAD* S, 253; see also YOS 13 370.

33. Roth, "Scholastic Exercise Laws About Rented Oxen," 129–36. See also Roth, *Law Collections*, 40–41.

In a later, bilingual text of school exercises from the Middle Assyrian period, we have a parallel version of §1 and one additional law on broken bones apparently caused by overloading the ox:

> If because of an (overly) massive pack, he shattered a bone of the ox, he shall pay its full value in silver.
>
> If he destroyed the eye of an ox, he shall pay one-half its value.[34]

These school exercises also preserve evidence for the contrast between the hired animal being attacked or wandering off and becoming lost, i.e., between accident and negligence. The case of loss offers an important parallel to *m. B. Metz.* 7:8–10 cited above. The cases are preserved in an ancient school text from Old Babylonian times:

> §9 If a lion devours an ox while walking about, the misfortune falls to its owner.
>
> §10 If an ox walking about becomes lost, he (the hirer) [will replace] the ox (with) a like ox.[35]

This is the very same principle that applies in rabbinic law; the hirer, like the shepherd, is liable for an animal that is lost or runs away; release from liability is possible only for major calamities or accidents.[36]

Another school exercise text brings three additional laws dealing with fatal injuries, including two involving lion attack:

If a drover (went) from the residential area (and) entered a reed thicket (outside of the town and) a lion killed (an ox), he (the drover) shall not replace the ox.

> If an ox dies (i.e., drowns) in crossing a river, he (the hirer) shall replace (it with) a healthy ox along with (paying) the hire (of the drowned ox).
>
> If a lion kills a yoked ox, he (the hirer) shall not replace the ox.[37]

One can assume that the drover was a paid keeper, who, like a herder, was not responsible for a sudden animal attack. The other two laws deal with hirers. Lion attack was considered an accident; but the hirer was responsible when taking an ox across a body of water, which was to be done with caution and care.

There are also provisions dealing with injuries to oxen found in the Hittite laws; the oxen were presumably hired although the text does not state this clearly.

> §74 If anyone breaks the horn or leg of an ox, he shall take that (ox) for himself and give an ox in good condition to the owner of the (injured) ox. If the owner of the ox says: "I will take my own ox," he shall take his ox, and he (the offender) shall pay 2 shekels silver.
>
> §75 If anyone hitches up an ox, a horse, a mule, or an ass, and it dies [or] a wolf devours [it], or it gets lost, he shall replace it at fair value. But if he says: "It died by the hand of a god," he shall take an oath (to that effect).

34. Landsberger, *MSL* 1, 168–69; this text is an appendix to the scribal series *ana-ittišu* iv.

35. YOS 1 28 v 26—vi 1. See Roth, *Law Collections,* 44.

36. Cf. Maimonides *Mishnha Torah, Hilkhot Skhirut,* 1:2 treats the "hirer" and the "hired custodian" in the same category.

37. Roth, "Scholastic Tradition and Mesopotamian Law," 44, 80–86; and Roth, *Law Collections,* 52. The translation given above for the first law above is an alternative, based upon her discussion.

Laming and mutilation are the subjects of §74; here there is adjusted liability if the owner agrees to take his injured animal back. This suggests that liability for injuries fell uniformly upon the hirer, unless the owner was persuaded or willing to forgive the hirer in part. In §75, most losses, including natural death, are the responsibility of the hirer; but if the animal died because of "an act of God," then the hirer can swear an oath and be free from liability. We know from Hammurapi Laws §266 in connection with shepherds, that sickness is described by the expression "the stroke of a god."[38] The shepherd there must take an oath affirming the outbreak just as does the hirer in Hittite Laws §75.

But in Hittite Laws §75, death of an animal due to an attack of a wolf is not viewed as an exemption; why is it not viewed in the same way as an attack of a lion? We have seen in many laws already cited—Hammurapi Laws §244 and Old Babylonian school exercises—that the hirer would not be held responsible for the attack of a lion. Moreover, the shepherd in Hammurapi Laws §266 is able to escape responsibility for loss due to the attack of a lion by swearing an oath. The situation is the same in *m. B. Metz.* 7:8–10, which removes responsibility due when an animal is killed by a lion, bear, or panther. These animals are presumably included in the expression "hand of a god" in Hittite Laws §75; but not the wolf. We find a similar exclusion and some underlying reasoning in *m. B. Metz.* 7:9,[39] which, in discussing

liability for animals in the keeping of a herdsman or rented by a hirer, states:

> If one wolf attacked, it is no accident but two wolves count as an unavoidable accident. R. Judah says: when wolves come in a pack, even one wolf is to be considered as an unavoidable accident. Two dogs do not count as an unavoidable accident.

There seems to have been an expectation that one could drive off a lone predatory wolf or even two dogs; but an attack by a pack of wolves would rise to the level of a lion, bear, or panther.

It is curious that we have no ancient Near Eastern laws dealing with the borrowing of animals, like in Exod 22:13, while in the ancient Near East, we have numerous laws on hiring of animals yet none in the Bible! Both borrowing and hire were practiced and there may have been a continuum between these transactions, based on expectations for the use and care of property belonging to another. We find a kind of merging of the two categories, for example, in a late second millennium Babylonian document where tools borrowed will be subject to a hiring fee if they are not returned by a set time. In another document from the first millennium, we find a time limit set on a borrowed draft animal.[40] We have no knowledge of such "conversions" in the Talmud. Yet, here too, in my view, the incomplete spectrum of evidence reflects the incomplete and often random nature of our surviving sources.

38. For other examples of this phrase, describing illness, pestilence, and plague, see *CAD* L, 201–2

39. A parallel passage is *t. B. Metz.* 8:16, Lieberman.

40. These are cited in *CAD* E, 387b. The free lending of animals also took place using the form of *hubuttatu* (interest free) loans; cf. *CAD* H, 221.

5.4 HIRING OF BOATS AND LOSS THROUGH NEGLIGENCE

Navigable rivers and open waters adjacent to coastal areas played a significant role in ancient commerce and transportation; this was especially true for Babylonia in rabbinic times as well as centuries earlier. But navigating these bodies of water could at times be treacherous. In the Tosefta, *t. B. Metz.* 11:26, Lieberman, the following provision is preserved:

> Boatmen may state (in a contract): "anyone whose boat is lost—we will arrange another boat for him." (But) if it was lost through negligence, there is no requirement to arrange (a replacement) for him. (However) if it was not lost through negligence, one is obligated to arrange (a replacement) for him, Moreover, if he veered off to a place where boats do not traffic, one is not obligated to arrange (a replacement boat) for him.

In this law, we have what appears to be a "self-help" contract made by a group of boatman, who agree to help one another by lending each other a replacement vessel in times of special need. But the agreement would not be binding upon the parties if a boatman damaged or lost his craft through negligence.[41]

The Talmud, in *b. B. Qam.* 116b, discusses this law and raises a question:

> But is this (i.e., the disqualification for negligence) not obvious?—No; (there may be a place where) during Nisan (i.e., high water) they generally travel one rope's length

(away from the shore,) whereas during Tishri (i.e., low water) they travel two ropes' length (away from the shore). And (if it happened that) during the days of Nisan, he sailed in the place (fit for sailing) during Tishri (and the boat was overwhelmed and sank). Would you then say that he maintained his customary way (and therefore it should not matter)? So (in this law) we are told, no, (such variant conduct would be considered negligence on his part).

The Talmud is here describing boats on the great rivers Tigris and Euphrates and their canal systems. These waterways were vital for life, cultivation, and commerce in Babylonia; most habitable communities were thus situated close to the waterways. During the spring, in the season of high water, it was advisable to keep a boat and its towropes closer to the shore to avoid turbulence and floating debris. On the other hand, during the low water season of late summer and early fall, it would be prudent to have the boat travel further out where the water was deeper, so as not to run aground. In addition to towropes, the river and canal boats of Babylonia were also propelled by punting poles and oars; wind and sail power could only be relied on sporadically.[42] Due to the scarcity of trees and lumber in Babylonia proper, the vessels that were used—including rafts, coracles, and gufas—were

41. The Tosefta, *t. B. Metz.* 11:25, Lieberman, describes a similar, self-help agreement made by donkey drivers to lend replacement animals to one another. Here, too, their agreement is not binding in a situation of negligence.

42. The requirement for timely shift in navigation is explained by Rashi *ad loc.* For identical conditions continuing in the early twentieth century cf. Salonen, *Die Wasserfahrzeuge in Babylonien*, 1. Salonen (ibid. 110) also comments on the prevailing winds, which only infrequently supported upstream travel. Salonen, *Nautica Babyloniaca*, 43–50, further discusses the use of towing, rowing, and sailing.

often constructed out of materials more readily available like reeds, hides, ropes, and pitch. The ancient texts contain many references to damage, grounding, sinking, and repairs to such vulnerable vessels.[43]

Liability for loss could also be the result of overloading a craft and making it sink. The Tosefta, *t. B. Metz.* 7:10, Lieberman, declares:

> And how much might one add to a burden to become culpable thereby? Samchum said—or it is attributed to Rabbi Meir: a *qab* for a porter (lit. a shoulder); 3 seahs for a wagon; but for a boat—any amount (of extra weight is too much).

A *baraita* cited in *b. B. Metz.* 80b is similar but adds some slight margin of latitude, according to the size and capacity of the vessels:

> Our rabbis taught: (Anyone is culpable who causes loss by overloading by as little as) 1 *qab* for a porter (lit. a shoulder); an *ardab* for a "tub boat"; a *kor* for a (small) boat; 3 *kors* for a larger Liburnian boat (with a sail).[44]

The Talmud, in its discussion, seeks further to clarify the implications of this law. Rabbi Papa presents his view, that for boats, the additional quantities represents one-thirtieth of their customary capacity, which, he says, is thirty kors for an average vessel. According to Maimonides, this proportional metric of one-thirtieth applies as well to the "over-loading" of a porter or a beast of burden.[45]

If negligence was not involved and a boat simply sank of its own accord, there was no obligation to pay for the boat; the situation was similar to having an ox fall dead while working that we have seen above (sec. 5.3); it was a hazard that must be endured. However, just as in the case of the stricken animal, there was the matter of the hiring fee. This question is addressed in a *baraita* cited in *b. B. Metz.* 79a–b:

> (In the case of) one who hired a boat and it sank half way into its journey, Rabbi Nathan said: "if he (already) gave (the money for its hire), he cannot take it back; if he has not given (the money), he need not give (it now)."

In a further discussion, the Talmud, in the name of Rabbi Papa, modifies this law to say that it will apply only if there was no specificity in the transport contract. In other words, the two spoke only of "a boat and its cargo." However, if either a specific boat or a specific cargo was mentioned in the transport agreement, then the boatman and owner must each give up one–half of the hiring fee.[46]

When we turn to the ancient Near Eastern sources, we also find a series of

---

43. See Salonen, *Die Wasserfahrzeuge in Babylonien*, 5, 66–74, 138–50, on construction; and ibid., 47–51, on damages and repairs.

44. The metrical units can only be approximated; but the relationship between them is better known. If we assume that one *qab* was equal to 1 liter in volume, then one seah would equal 6 liters, and a *kor* would be 180 liters. The *ardab*, originally a Persian unit, was apparently equal to 36 liters in volume. Cf. Powell, "Masse und Gewichte," 499, 505, and *CAD* S, 421–22 on the sizes of the *seah* (*sūtu*) and its units. See Steinsaltz, *The Talmud*, 289 for the nearly similar relationship between these units in rabbinic texts.

45. Maimonides, *Mishnah Torah, Hilkhot Schirut* 4:7–8, affirms this standard but also states that one must be ready to adjust these measures to customary, local practices.

46. The Talmud's modification is recapitulated in Maimonides, *Mishnah Torah, Hilkhot Schirut* 5:3; some reasons are given there.

laws dealing with boatmen and expectations on how they must live up to their contracts. In Lipit-Ishtar Laws §5 we read:

> If a man hires a boat (and) one set a route for him (and) he altered its route (and at that) time and place the boat was lost (?), (and) he has acted in a harmful manner; the man who hired the boat must [replace] the boat [and must (also) pay its hire].[47]

The reading and general understanding of this law is helped by a similar formulation found in a Sumerian collection of legal passages:

> If a man [hired a boa]t and one [set] for him his determined route (but) he changed its route (and) in that place the boat was sunk and he (thus) acted [in a har]mful manner. He must replace the boat and (also) pay its hire (AT).[48]

In another Sumerian scribal exercise tablet, there is a fragmentary passage giving another possible resolution to the boatman's negligence:

> If he alters the stated route (and) causes the boat to founder, until he renews the boat, he must pay for one half of its hire unto its owner.[49]

In this situation, there was the possibility of the boatman raising the sunken boat and repairing it. The view here is that the boatman will therefore receive some offset against the full penalty of replacing the boat together with its full hire that would otherwise be due from him. I imagine that this reduction comes about since the boatman is capable of restoring the rented boat to future use and perhaps the reduction to half of its hire is in recognition for his labors in doing so. But if he failed to restore the boat, he should then have to pay for it in full as in the previous laws.[50]

While the Sumerian laws focus upon the loss of the boat and the hiring fee, the Old Babylonian laws include consideration of the boat's contents when sunk. Eshnunna Laws §5 puts it simply:

> If a boatman was negligent and caused the boat to sink, he must pay (for) as much as caused to sink.

This same theme of a boatman's negligence are more elaborately taken up in Hammurapi Laws §§236–238:

> §236 If a man gave out his boat for hire to a boatman and the boatman was negligent and caused the boat to sink or be lost, the boatman must replace the boat for the owner of the boat.

> §237 If a man has hired a boatman and a boat and loaded it with grain, wool, oil, dates, or anything else, (and) that boatman was negligent and caused the boat to sink and what it carried to become lost, the boatman must replace the boat he sank and whatever in it that was lost.

47. My reading of the text supplements what is given in Roth, *Law Collections,* 27 and offers for fragment N. 3058 line 19 the reading: *ki-ud má zá[h-a]*. For the text and copy of this fragment see Steele, "An Additional Fragment."

48. This law is Roth, *Law Collections,* SLHF iv 42—v 11 on p. 51.

49. This law is YOS 1 28 iv 11–18; cf. Roth, *Law Collections,* 43–44.

50. A fragmentary Sumerian school exercise tablet from the Middle Assyrian period mentions returning a boat and paying its hire; the preserved lines state: "he shall return the boat to its dock and pay its hire to its owner." But there is no certainty that this boat had foundered. Cf. *MSL* 1 69.

§238 If a boatman caused another man's boat to sink and (subsequently) has raised it (from the water), he (the boatman?) shall give silver (equal) to one-half its value.

The Babylonian laws describe the obligation resting upon a negligent boatman to replace or pay for the boat he lost as well as to take responsibility for repaying the value of any cargo that was in the boat. In both §236 and §237 of the Hammurapi Laws, as in Eshnunna Laws §5, the compensation paid for boat and cargo would evidently erase any further obligation by the boatman for the lost craft. But Hammurapi Laws §238 is a different case. To begin with, there is no mention of negligence; the boat sank but it was recovered; and the boatman himself, as it appears, raised and refloated the craft. So why was the boatman required to pay half the value of the boat? One possibility is that even after raising the boat, there may have been further repairs needed to make sure the craft was sound; and that, after raising the boat, the boatman's liability for such repairs was limited to half the value of the recovered boat. There is in fact evidence of such obligations in certain Old Babylonian period boat rental contracts. For example, in one document from the reign of Hammurapi's son, Samsuiluna, a boat is rented for one month; the renters agree in advance to set amounts of liability: 10 shekels if the boat is lost and 5 shekels if the boat sinks.[51] The 5 shekel provision may therefore envision the recovery of the vessel, with the renters then paying one half of the agreed-upon 10

shekel value of the rented boat. Their arrangement appears to be the same as what is described in Hammurapi Laws §238.

As for the hiring fee, no mention is made of it either in Eshnunna Laws §5 or in Hammurapi Laws §§236–238. This omission is surprising since the earlier, Sumerian laws consistently do include this in the settlement. We may perhaps assume that the hiring fee had been paid in full at the time of rental; or if not, liability for any balance was specified and secured by the rental contract.[52] But it is also surprising that our Sumerian laws do not address the matter of cargoes. In my view, this is because the ancient law collections were not intended to be comprehensive in content or scope.

None of the ancient Near Eastern laws give us details describing the nature of the boatman's negligent behavior. Here, as in the laws on deposit (sec. 5.1), the rabbinic sources may be helpful. They tell us that it was the boatman's responsibility to monitor the depth and flow of the river as well as to be careful not to overload his vessel. These cautions might be self-evident; but we do welcome having such supplemental details expressed in our rabbinic sources. There are no laws on boats or boat rentals in the Bible; but from their recurrence and preservation both in earlier and later centuries, we should have little reason to question the existence of nautical regulations and performance expectations in the cultural milieu of the times.[53]

51. This document is YOS 12 111. Additional examples of this same 2:1 relationship between loss and sinking are given in Stol, "Miete," 169.

52. The practices of giving full payment at the outset as well as at the conclusion of business are attested in Neo-Babylonian boat rentals; cf. Ries, "Lösegeld," 179. The same was true in boat rentals in Old Babylonian times; see Stol, "Miete," 169.

53. There are numerous references to boats in the Mishnah and Tosefta; for laws involving boats,

5.5 THEFT OF LIVESTOCK

Theft of livestock is a well-known problem in farming societies, exacerbated by the fact that animals are movable and capable of being led away by someone other than their rightful owner. We read in the Bible:

> Exod 21:37 If a man steals an ox or a sheep, and slaughters it or sells it, he shall pay five cattle for the ox, and four sheep (or goats) for the sheep.

> Exod 22:1 If the thief is found tunneling in, and is beaten and dies, there is no bloodguilt for him; Exod 22:2a but if the sun shone upon him, there is bloodguilt for him.

> Exod 22:2b He (the thief) shall make restitution; (but) if he hasn't the means, he shall be sold for his theft.

> Exod 22:3 If the stolen item, whether an ox or donkey or sheep, is indeed found in his possession alive, the thief shall (just) pay double.[54]

The verses Exod 22:1–2a are a parenthetic insertion which interrupt the flow of discourse; the case could be more smoothly read if they were not in their present location. The subject of Exod 22:2b, "He (the thief) shall make restitution . . . ," refers back to the livestock thief in Exod 21:37; this connection has long been recognized.[55] Some modern Bible translations therefore rearrange these verses and place Exod 22:1–2a after Exod 22:3, although there is no ancient version that contains this improvement.[56] The inserted verses introduce the possibility of a thief dying for his theft; this represents an "escalation" of response, beyond the monetary or financial punishments that appear in the two verses that frame this insertion. I will postpone our discussion of the "inserted verses" (Exod 22:1–2a) until the next section (sec. 5.6), where I discuss theft of property other than livestock.

Exodus 21:37 offers no explanation for the higher penalties in situations where the thief slaughtered or sold the stolen animal. Bekhor Shor suggests it is because the owner personally feels the loss of familiar animals with which he worked, which he may also have raised and thus have been more familiar with in handling. The difference between four and five times, he argues, relates to the fact that one does not use a sheep as a work animal. However, if the stolen animals could be recovered intact, then the thief pays a twofold penalty, or, as *Targum Onqelos* and the Samaritan versions have it: "two for one" i.e., two animals (or their value) for each one stolen.[57]

---

cf., e.g., *m. B. Bat.* 5:1; *m. Maksh.* 5:7; *t. Demai* 1:11, Lieberman; *t. Qidd.* 1:7, Lieberman. For further discussion of vessels, with focus upon Palestine and the Mediterranean, see Sperber, *Nautica Talmudica*.

54. 4Q22 (paleo Exodus^m) reads here, with the Samaritan, "he shall pay two (for) one." Cf. Sanderson, *An Exodus Scroll from Qumran,* 90 who suggests that this phrasing seems to represent an editing of an earlier text, represented by MT and LXX. This language is also used in the Targum and the Mekhilta (see below).

55. The continuity between these verses was seen and noted, e.g., by Rashi, Ibn Ezra, and Hazzequni in their commentaries on these verses. Philo, *Alleg. Interp.* 3.32 also considered Exod 22:1–2a to be a separate law.

56. Cf. e.g., KJV and NRSV; these Bibles also renumber Exod 21:37 as the first verse of Exodus 22.

57. So Rashi ad loc., following *Mekhilta Mishpatim* 13 "two live animals or the value of (two) live animals."

We encounter a fourfold (Septuagint reads there: sevenfold!) penalty for theft and slaughter in 2 Sam 12:5–6, in a livestock case related to David by the prophet Nathan; the case turns out to be fictional and a parable condemning David for taking Bathsheba, the wife of Uriah. The story begins as follows:

> 2 Sam 12:1 And the LORD sent Nathan to David. He came to him, and said to him, "There were two men in a certain city, the one rich and the other poor.
>
> 2 Sam 12:2 The rich man had very many flocks and herds;
>
> 2 Sam 12:3 but the poor man had nothing but one little ewe lamb, which he had bought. He brought it up, and it grew up with him and with his children; it used to eat of his bread, and drink from his cup, and lie in his bosom, and it was like a daughter to him.
>
> 2 Sam 12:4 Now there came a traveler to the rich man, and he was loath to take one of his own flock or herd to prepare for the wayfarer who had come to him, but he took the poor man's lamb, and prepared that for the guest who had come to him."
>
> 2 Sam 12:5 Then David's anger was greatly kindled against the man. He said to Nathan, "As the LORD lives, the man who has done this deserves to die;
>
> 2 Sam 12:6 he shall restore the lamb fourfold, because he did this thing, and because he had no pity." (NRSV)

The fourfold penalty is similar to what is found in Exod 21:37; but then how should we understand David's additional comment that the thief deserved to die? Some commentators follow Qimhi who considers David's statement to be hyperbolic since, at least according to rabbinic understanding, there would be no death penalty for this theft. Many modern scholars have also discounted it, suggesting that the parable did not reflect legal reality.[58] But one must not assume that we actually know the full legal realities of the monarchy period. Furthermore, as we have already seen in Exod 22:1–2a cited above and shall again see from other biblical and ancient Near Eastern law cases (secs. 5.6 and 5.7), the death penalty for theft, while severe, was not unknown in ancient times—albeit it was not usual for stealing livestock! Moreover, as the biblical tale unfolds, we see that the death penalty is an integral feature of David's punishment; in 2 Sam 12:14–23, David himself is spared the death penalty that he pronounced upon the fictitious thief in 2 Sam 12:5; but his infant child born of Bathsheba is condemned by God to die in his place. The entire story loses its impact if David's reference to the death penalty is not taken seriously as a pivotal feature. Because, in this story, it is the death penalty and not the fourfold payment that is mirrored in Nathan's scathing admonishment and elaboration on his earlier parable.

A sevenfold penalty for theft is stated in Prov 6:30–31:

---

58. Whitelam, *The Just King,* 123–29 with earlier literature cited there. Jackson, *Theft in Early Jewish Law,* 146–47, argues that the death penalty was a later addition to the story, inserted by later readers who were unhappy with David not being assigned responsibility, in the parable, for the death of Uriah.

They do not despise one when he steals to satisfy his appetite because he is hungry. Yet (if) he is caught, he will pay sevenfold; he must give up all the wealth he possesses (lit. of his house) (to pay the penalty).

The sevenfold penalty here seems to be applied to thefts of an undetermined nature; it is unclear whether this would have pertained to livestock. In any case, it is interesting for us to note the multiple degree of the penalty.

In Mesopotamia we find that theft of livestock was ordinarily punished by twofold penalty as it was in Exod 22:3. In a Sumerian scribal school collection we read:

> If (a man) has stolen a pig, he shall double (its value) for compensation.[59]

This law is juxtaposed with another dealing with theft of a boat, where the punishment is also twofold compensation.

Livestock theft is the subject of many paragraphs within the Hittite Laws; the animals are classified according to the severity of penalty associated with stealing them. The most valuable group is one of animals kept apparently for breeding: bulls, stallions, or rams. These animals and their classifications are subject of Hittite Laws §§57–59:

> §57 If anyone steals a bull—if it is a weanling calf, it is not a "bull"; if it is a yearling, it is not a "bull"; if it is a 2-year old bovine, that is a "bull." Formerly they gave 30 cattle. But now he shall give 15 cattle: 5 two-year olds, 5 yearlings, and 5

weanlings, and he shall look to his house for it.

> §58 If anyone steals a stallion—if it is a weanling, it is not a "stallion"; if it is a yearling, it is not a "stallion"; if it is a two-year- old, that is a "stallion." Formerly they used to give 30 horses. But now he shall give 15 horses: 5 two-year olds, 5 yearlings, and 5 weanlings, and he shall look to his house for it.

> §59 If anyone steals a ram, they used to give 30 sheep. Now he shall give [15] sheep: he shall give 5 ewes, 5 wethers, and 5 lambs. And he shall look to his house for it.

In §59, the penalty consisted of female sheep that could be bred, five males that might develop into breeders, and five lambs; it may be that a group of fifteen rams was not readily available, perhaps due to herding management patterns. As noted in the text of these laws, newer legislation eased the more severe penalty of former times, which required a thirty-fold restitution. The expression "he shall look to his house for it" has been interpreted as a claim on all assets of the offender and his family.

The second most "valuable group" consists of plow oxen, draft horses, and specially trained wild animals, apparently used as decoys in hunting. The laws also preserve memory of a time when penalties for such thefts were even more severe than presently required. These animals appear in Hittite Laws §§63–65:

> If anyone steals a plow ox, formerly they gave 15 cattle, but now he shall give 10 cattle: 3 two-year olds, 3 yearlings, and 4 weanlings, and he shall look to his house for it. If anyone steals a draft horse, its disposition is the same. If anyone

---

59. FLP 1287 iii, 10-15; see Roth, "Scholastic Tradition and Mseopotamian Law," 36; and Roth, *Law Collections*, 49.

steals a trained he-goat or a trained deer or trained mountain goat, their disposition is the same as of the theft of a plow ox.

A third group, less "expensive" than the previous two, addresses theft of female animals; these are dealt with in Hittite Laws §§67–69:

If anyone steals a cow, they used to give 12 oxen. Now he shall give 6 oxen: 2 two-year olds, 2 yearling oxen, and 2 weanlings, and he shall look to his house for it. If anyone steals a mare, its disposition is the same. If anyone steals a ewe or whether, they used to give 12 sheep, but now he shall give 6 sheep: he shall give 2 ewes, 2 wethers, and 2 (sexually) immature sheep; and he shall look to his house for it.

One can see that the Hittite Laws for animal theft impose multiple payments varying from six to fifteen times. The severity of these penalties may reflect the fact that the stolen animals were "slaughtered or sold" as in Exod 21:37. While this is not expressly stated in the laws, one may seriously consider the possibility of this interpretation, because in Hittite Laws §70, we find that if the animals were recovered intact, then the penalty was only two-fold as in Exod 22:3. Hittite Laws §70 states the following:

If anyone steals an ox, a horse, a mule, or an ass, (when) its owner identifies it, he shall take it (back) in full value. In addition, he (the thief) shall give him twice/double; and he shall look to his house for it.

Here, the owner gets his animal back and the thief pays him an additional two animals as compensation. This paragraph, and perhaps also the Sumerian law cited

previously, invites us to look again at how the penalty in Exod 22:3 was calculated in relation to the stolen animal. Was the returned animal, i.e., the principal, included in the multiple penalty? Or was it, in the fashion of Hittite Laws §70, separate from the penalty or compensation, which was two animals in addition to the returned animal? Rabbinic law, perhaps influenced by Roman law, understood the returned property to be included as part of the double payment; in other words, the thief paid back twice what he had stolen. We remain uncertain, however, as to how this was originally understood and applied in Exod 22:3.[60]

There are still other Hittite Laws dealing with the stealing pigs; the penalty for thefts involving pigs, however, are monetary, unlike the multiple payments we have been thus far considering. Thus, for example, Hittite Laws §81:

If anyone steals a fattened pig, they used to pay one mina silver. But now he shall pay 12 shekels of silver. He shall look to his house for it.[61]

It is apparent that pigs were seen as having a lower economic value. But then it is puzzling why one was not required to pay a two-fold multiple penalty, as in the Sumerian law dealing with theft of a pig cited above.[62]

60. Cf. *m. Ter.* 6:4, *m. B. Qam.* 7:3, Maimonides, *Mishnah Torah, Hilkhot Genevah* 1:4. For Roman Law, cf. Thomas, *Textbook of Roman Law,* 358 citing Gaius, *Inst.* 3.90, who refers to *XII Tab.* 8.16, where the thief was not caught during the act of committing the theft.

61. Translation omitted in Hoffner, *Laws of the Hittite,* 85–86; the translation given here follows Friedrich, *Die Hethitischen Gesetze,* 43.

62. Additional cases dealing with theft of pigs— non-fattened, pregnant sow, and piglets—are taken

5.6 THEFT OF PROPERTY OTHER THAN LIVESTOCK

The Bible has no general law on theft of property. What we have are two statements added to other laws: one is appended to a discussion of animal theft (sec. 5.5); and a second is inserted between the laws on deposit and herding of animals (sec. 5.6.2).

5.6.1 The Thief Caught "in the Act"

The first statement is Exod 22:1–2a, which was mentioned above (sec. 5.5):

> Exod 22:1 If the thief is found tunneling in, and is beaten to death, there is no bloodguilt for him; Exod 21:2a but if the sun shone upon him, there is bloodguilt for him.

This passage "interrupts" a sequence of statements dealing with animal theft: Exod 21:37 and Exod 22:2b–3. Because of this proximity, it may likewise concern stolen animals, e.g., by breaking into a barn. But its wording, taken out of its context, also permits application to other thefts, e.g., burglary of a residence. So we are not informed about what manner of property was being sought by this thief. "Tunneling" might suggest a limit on the physical dimensions of the looted goods, unless it was only to describe the means whereby the thief gained entrance. Because of its non-specific language, most interpreters, ancient and modern, have viewed this insertion as an attempt to parenthetically state a general rule, applicable to any type of theft. I believe they are correct.

There has also been discussion and argument over what exactly is the legal difference between "tunneling" and "the sun shining." One understanding— perhaps the likeliest—is that a contrast between nighttime and daytime activity is intended, as evidenced in Job 24:14–17 where murder, theft, and tunneling (along with adultery) occur at night:

> The murderer rises at dusk to kill the poor and needy, and in the night is like a thief. The eye of the adulterer also waits for the twilight, saying, 'No eye will see me'; and he disguises his face. In the dark they dig [i.e., tunnel] through houses; by day they shut themselves up; they do not know the light. For deep darkness is morning to all of them; for they are friends with the terrors of deep darkness. (NRSV)

These images suggest the terror of the house owner who discovers someone breaking in at night; and the association here between theft and murder offers a basis upon which to "justify" the slaying of the intruder by the homeowner in Exod 22:1. Following this reasoning, the Talmud (*b. Sanh.* 72b) states that the homeowner's response is considered as self-defense against the night intruder, who is considered as one who is intent or ready to kill him. This is also the view, e.g., of the medieval scholar Rabad, who argues that a thief who comes in the night must realize that the house owner may be at home and thus he must be prepared to kill him or be killed by him, unlike the daytime thief who comes when the owner is likely to be out, engaged in his business or work.[63]

---

up in Hittite Laws §§82–83, 85. Here, again, the penalties are monetary. (These laws are not cited in the body of this book.)

63. Rabad (Rabbi Abrahm ben David of Posquières) in his gloss on Maimonides, *Mishnah Torah, Hilkhot Genevah* 9:8, argues that night and day

One finds this same line of reasoning expressed earlier by Philo:

> [The thief may] if caught in the act before sunrise, be slain by the householder in the very place where he has broken in. Though actually engaged on the primary but minor crime of theft he is intending the major though secondary crime of murder, since he is prepared if prevented by anyone to defend himself with the iron burglar's tools, which he carries and other weapons.

Philo goes on to argue that the situation is different once the sun has risen since, during the day, the owner can arrest him and bring him to the authorities.[64]

But there was, anciently, another line of interpretation that did not seem to limit the homeowner's right to defend his property even in daytime. Josephus, in his presentation of this biblical law, does not mention the time of day and simply assumes an owner's right of self-defense:

> He that killeth another while engaged in burglary shall be innocent, even though the thief were yet but breaking through his wall.[65]

A similar path of interpretation is behind the reasoning in the Mishnah (*m. Sanh.* 8:6) "One (i.e., a thief) who is (discovered) tunneling is judged according to (what he may do in) the end". The Talmud (*b. Sanh.* 72b) explains this further as "we may assume that one (i.e., the homeowner) will not restrain himself in protecting

his own property." Maimonides supports this view in a very explicit statement, ruling that a thief breaking into one's house or barn is subject to be slain at any time—night or day; as he sees it, the text in Exod 22:1 mentions the tunnel only as one typical example of entry.[66]

There is however evidence of hesitation about slaying the thief found in the Mekhilta (*Mekhilta Mishpatim* 13) to Exod 22:1–2a, which seeks to limit the right of the homeowner to use lethal force. The Mekhilta, was apparently not comfortable using the "arbitrary" determination of night or day. Instead it seeks to explain the contrast as being between uncertainty and certainty about the thief's purpose. In other words, if it is clear that the thief was intending only to rob and not to murder, then it would not be right to slay him. This thinking is reflected in *Targum Onqelos*, which expands the translation of "sunlight" to say: "If the eye of witnesses fell upon him. " In other words, if it needed to be a situation where it was very evident to anyone that the thief did not pose a mortal danger. This is, in fact, the formulation given in *Targum Pseudo-Jonathan*: "If the matter was as clear like sunlight that he (i.e., the thief) had not entered to kill anyone."

It is interesting to note that, according to Josephus, Herod, on his own, imposed an unjustly severe punishment upon housebreakers who were apprehended and not slain by the homeowner; Herod decreed that they be sold into exile as slaves. Josephus found this to be unjust for two reasons; the first point was that, according to the Bible, Jewish debtors were to be taken as temporary slaves

must be understood in literal fashion and cannot be re-interpreted in some figurative way. (Rabad's glosses appear in most editions of Maimonides, *Mishnah Torah*.)

64. Philo, *Spec. Laws* 4.7–10, Colson.
65. Josephus, *Ant.* 4.271, Thackeray.
66. Maimonides, *Mishnah Torah, Hilkhot Genevah*, 9:8.

by their creditors and served only to pay off their debt. The second point was that Jewish debt slaves should not have been sold abroad into gentile hands. (The biblical laws are discussed above in sec. 2.1.)[67]

The ancient Near Eastern sources, however, reveal that the distinction between a daytime and nighttime thief was anciently understood in literal fashion; and that tunneling was known to be an activity of thieves breaking into a field or a residence. Eshnunna Laws §§12–13 deal with property belonging to a tenant occupying royal land:

> A man (i.e., a thief) who has been seized in the field of a commoner among the sheaves at midday—he shall pay ten shekels silver. One who has been seized at night in the sheaves shall die; he shall not live. A man who was seized in the house of a commoner in midday—he shall pay ten shekels silver. One who has been seized at night in the house shall die; he shall not live.

On the other hand, Hammurapi Laws §21 makes no distinction between night and day entry and writes only about burglary of a residence:

> If a man bores a hole into a house, they shall kill that man and impale him in front of that very hole.

Is it possible that the different treatments of the thief in these two Mesopotamian sources are evidence of older debate on the proper social policies relating to the defense of property, similar to what we have found in connection with Exod 22:1–2a? Did Hammurapi Laws §21 deliberately omit the day-night distinction, or was this paragraph excerpted from a large series of ancient law statements in which the day-night distinction was also present? I do not believe that we have enough evidence to answer these questions based upon the present evidence.

The distinction between daytime and nighttime theft was a widespread concept and, interestingly, appears also in the oldest Roman law, in the *XII Tables* 8.12–13:

> If theft has been done by night, if owner kills [the] thief, [the] thief shall be held to be lawfully killed. [It is unlawful for a thief to] be killed by day . . . unless he defend himself with weapon; even though he has come with weapon, unless he shall use [the] weapon and fight back, you shall not kill him. And even if he resists, first call out, that is, raise a shout, so that some persons may hear and come up.[68]

Later Roman lawgivers and jurists, over the centuries, found it repeatedly necessary to revisit this right of the homeowner to defend his property. Some sought to limit the right by amendments requiring that he first try to apprehend even the nocturnal thief without killing him or that the homeowner was required to limit the application of force. But others affirmed his right to kill a thief who showed resistance and extended this right

---

67. Josephus, *Ant.* 16.1. Josephus states that the apprehended thief should have been sentenced to pay four times the value of the stolen property; this penalty is not stated in the Bible. A four-fold penalty for such "manifest theft" is found in Roman law in Gaius *Inst.* 3.189–90, who says that this monetary penalty replaced earlier punishment of scourging and being sold as a slave as stipulated in *XII Tab.* 8.14. Gaius wrote about a century after the death of Herod.

68. *XII Tab.* 8.12–13, Warmington, reconstructed with additions from ancient sources, ibid., 482–85.

also to daytime. This ongoing debate in Roman law may in fact have stimulated the rabbis, who lived under Roman rule, to think about how they should interpret the biblical text of Exod 22:1–2a. The discussion and debate over the nature of a homeowner's right to defend his property has never been settled; and continued into the Middle Ages, into Canon Law, and even into modern times.[69]

There is a law similar to Exod 22:1–2a found in the Hittite Laws; but there is no distinction made between night and day; and the penalty for theft is monetary. Hittite Laws §93 states:

> If they seize a free man [i.e., a would-be thief] at the outset, (that is) before he enters the house, he shall pay 12 shekels of silver. If they seize a slave at the outset, before he enters the house, he shall pay 6 shekels of silver.

The thieves are apprehended during their attempted burglary. The Hittite Laws, as we already have shall see further in other cases, do not consider imposing capital punishment for theft or even for homicide. This is an important cultural divide with the rest of the ancient Near East; and I have discussed this difference further in our treatment of homicide in sec. 4.8. The present law shows us, interestingly, that the Hittites here held fast to monetary penalties despite the association that we have seen between burglary and the possibility that the thief, while breaking in, might do violence against the house owner. The difference between free and slave is also of interest; and we look

at this—and at additional Hittite Laws on theft—in the discussion of the second biblical statement on theft in sec. 5.6.2.

5.6.2 Reclaiming Stolen Property

The second biblical statement on theft appears in Exod 22:8 and deals with the recovery of missing property:

> In any case of wrongdoing involving ox, donkey, sheep, an article of clothing, or (involving) any lost item, about which one (party) states, "This is it (i.e., my stolen or lost item,)" the claims (lit. matter) of both parties shall come before God; the one whom God shall find in the wrong shall pay double to the other.[70]

Exodus 22:8 is a parenthetical comment placed between the law of deposit in Exod 22:6–7 (sec. 5.1) and the herding laws of Exod 22:9–12 (sec. 5.2). Exodus 22:8 reiterates the double payment penalty for theft, already stated in Exod 22:3 in connection with theft of livestock (sec. 5.5). It also presents a general procedure that must be followed to claim and recover all types of movable property, small or large, animate or inanimate, whether stolen or lost.

Exodus 22:8 looks like an "editorial" addition because it begins with stolen livestock, which was the subject of

---

69. For history of this debate, cf. Lührmann, *Tötungsrecht zur Eigentumsverteidigung?*, 7–15; and Sullivan, *Killing in Defense of Private Propery*, 85–144.

70. *Targum Onqelos* translates: "the dispute shall go before the judges; the one whom the judges find guilty will pay two for one to his neighbor." The reason for translating "judges" is the plural form of the verb "find in the wrong." The verb is used with *elohim*, which, although a plural form, is normally translated "God" rather than "gods." The literal translation is in fact "and whom the gods find in the wrong," which would of course in later time be viewed as an unacceptable polytheistic image. The translation "judges" is sometimes also used for "God" in Exod 22:7 (sec. 5.1).

the "larger story" dealing with domestic animals seen in Exod 21:37—22:3—and again in Exod 22:9–12. Exodus 22:8 first lists animals but then mentions clothing, which seems to "continue" the deposit case of Exod 22:6–7; and finally also mentions a lost item, which is a new category not previously discussed in any of the laws before or following this verse.[71] The situation described in Exod 22:8 appears to be one where the original owner claims to have discovered his goods in possession of another person. The owner claims that the animal or property item was still his property; and that he had not sold it or given it away. How then did the present holder come to have it in his possession? Resolution of the owner's claim requires the two parties to come to court in order to establish the truth of ownership. Oaths may have to be sworn by the two parties or by bringing forward witnesses who could confirm the ownership history of the property in question as we see in Hammurapi Laws §124 cited below.[72] Exod 22:8 is written as a general rule that, with the addition of lost items, goes beyond the prior case of the deposit, involving small or inanimate objects, which is the likeliest scenario for Exod 22:6–7.[73] But the inclusion of domestic animals also

allows Exod 22:8 to serve as a transition to Exod 22:9–12, dealing with the safeguarding of animals, that are, of course, both larger and animate, capable of wandering off on their own.[74] The noun *pesha'*, which I have translated as "wrongdoing," is a broad term, which has also been translated "transgression." It encompasses not only the act of theft but also the possibility of negligence on the part of a custodian who may have allowed theft to occur.[75]

It has been argued that biblical law was exemplary in not punishing crimes against property—like theft—with capital punishment but rather only punishing them with monetary penalties.[76] This conclusion may be only partly true because in the biblical narratives we see that the penalty for theft could at times be more than monetary. When confronted by Joseph's steward about the theft of his silver goblet, the brothers propose penalties of death and enslavement. This is recounted in Gen 44:9–10:

---

71. Lost articles are mentioned in Lev 5:22 (sec. 5.1) and Deut 22:3 (sec. 5.9).

72. As mentioned earlier in connection with Exod 22:7 (sec. 5.1), a number of scholars believe that Exod 22:8 requires an ordeal or oracle rather than oath. Cf. Fishbane, *Biblical Interpretation in Early Israel,* 237, who also cites contrary opinions), and some of the other scholars cited in my earlier discussion on deposit (sec. 5.1).

73. Rashbam states that this verse is indeed a general statement, and not necessarily a continuation of the events described in Exod 22:6–7, which is the way it is read by the rabbis in *b. B. Qam.* 62b and elsewhere.

74. This contrast is seen by Philo, *Spec. Laws* 4.35. Paul, *Studies in the Book of the Covenant,* 93 n. 2, cites Rashbam and others who agree that difference between the cases is indeed one of small, inanimate objects, which one can hold in his house with his own possessions and which others might steal, in contrast to animals which can wander away; and that this distinction is in fact the underlying *peshat* or plain meaning of the text.

75. Westbrook, "The Deposit Laws of Exodus 22, 6–12," 394–95, argues that the "wrongdoing" in Exod 22:8 describes "wrongs against another person . . . committed *ex delicto* or *ex contractu.*" In rabbinic contexts, the verb *pasha'* or the noun *peshiya'* frequently refers to the negligence of the house owner or of the herder; cf. for example *b. B. Metz.* 34a, 36b, 58a, 94a-b. See also Maimonides, *Mishnah Torah, Hilkhot She'elah Upiqadon,* 8:2. See further the discussion in connection with deposit in sec. 5.1 above.

76. Cf. Paul, *Studies in the Book of the Covenant,* 89, 90; Houtman, *Exodus,* 3:91–92.

"Whichever of your servants it is found with shall die; the rest of us, moreover, shall become slaves to my lord." He [the steward] replied, "Although what you are proposing is right, only the one with whom it is found shall be my slave; but the rest of you shall go free" (NJPS).

Joseph's steward proposes to act more leniently than the law demands. The penalty of enslavement was, in fact, the penalty anticipated by the brothers in a previous episode, in Gen 43:18, when they found their money returned to them in their sacks of grain:

But the men were frightened at being brought into Joseph's house. "It must be," they thought, "because of the money replaced in our bags the first time that we have been brought inside, as a pretext to attack us and seize us as slaves, with our pack animals"(NJPS)

The medieval scholar Hazzequni, who saw the relationship between these passages, explains that enslavement must in fact have been the customary penalty for theft prior to the legislation of the Torah in Exod 22:2b–3, which imposes a two-fold monetary penalty. In other words, the ancient penalty for theft could demand more than payment of compensation. I would argue that modes of more severe punishment of theft lived on in ancient Israel, and may also be seen in the outburst of King David in response to the story told to him by Nathan in 2 Sam 12:5–6, pronouncing the death penalty upon the man who stole the poor man's sheep (as previously discussed in sec. 5.5).

A similarly severe punishment for theft is pronounced in Gen 31:32, in the statement made by Jacob to Laban, who is seeking recovery of his stolen idols, Jacob, of course, did not know that Rachel had stolen them when he uttered:

The person with whom you find your gods shall not live. In the presence of our brethren, identify what I have of yours and take it.

The stealing of sacred property may have been considered to be a more serious kind of theft and thereby merited a more severe penalty; we shall see this severity again when we look at theft of temple property (in sec. 5.7). Nevertheless, what is clear here is that the concept of a death penalty for theft came naturally to Jacob when he spoke. The issue is clearly theft and not the fact that the stolen objects were symbols of foreign gods, as claimed e.g., by Sforno in his commentary on the verses. This is refuted by what we read much later on, in Gen 35:4:

They (i.e., his family) gave to Jacob all the foreign gods that they had in their possession, and the rings that were in their ears, and Jacob buried them under the terebinth that was near Shechem.

In other words, Jacob's family had not previously considered such objects as sinful. The later rabbinic position on theft is that its penalty should be strictly monetary, in conformity with the two-fold payment mentioned in Exod 22:2b–3 and Exod 22:8.[77] However, it is not possible to prove that this rabbinic view already emerged in biblical times.

---

77. This is repeatedly stated; cf. e.g., *m. B. Qam.* 7:1, *m. B. Metz.* 3:1. See also *Mekhilta Mishpatim* 13 on Exod 22:8, which adds "and they do not die (i.e., they will not suffer death as a penalty).

As in Exod 22:8, the recovery of stolen property is the focus of Hammurapi Laws §§9–13:

> If a man whose property has been missing has seized his missing property in the hands of another person (and) that man in whose hands the missing property has been seized has stated: "A seller has sold it to me before witnesses" and the owner of the missing property has stated: "Let me bring witnesses who know my missing property," (then) the (person claiming to have been a) buyer has brought the seller who sold him and witnesses before whom he purchased it and the owner of the missing property has brought witnesses who know his property . . .

Hammurapi Laws at this point continues with a series of possible outcomes which can be summarized as follows: if the judges confirm that both the owner and the buyer are telling the truth, then the seller is left as the thief and he will be punished by death, unless he, of course, could further carry back the chain of ownership relating to this missing property. The owner will recover his property and the buyer has a claim for what he paid against the seller (who has been declared to be a thief). If the seller had died earlier, then the buyer may claim up to five times the claim value from the estate previously left by that seller. However, if the buyer is unable to show a seller or the witnesses before whom he bought the property now in his possession, then the buyer is adjudged to be the thief and shall die. The laws provide a grace period of up to six months, allowing time for the parties to bring their witnesses forward.

The stated death penalty for theft, while severe, was apparently not always imposed. In Hammurapi Laws §124, we read of a two-fold monetary penalty for the custodian who is convicted of denying that he received an item deposited with him:

> If a man has gave to another man silver, gold, or whatever for safekeeping before witnesses and (subsequently) he (the custodian) has denied it, they (i.e., the authorities) shall convict that man and whatever he has denied he must (now) double it and pay (that amount).

The penalty here is identical to that of Exod 22:7–8; this suggests that the death penalty in Hammurapi Laws §§9–13 may have been more of an "ultimate" threat and that the death penalty was not always imposed for theft. There is, moreover, evidence from trial records dating from the Old Babylonian period that convicted thieves were given monetary penalties, although the death penalty might be meted out if the thief could not pay his penalty.[78] So in Babylonia it appears that there was latitude given to the court on how severely a thief would be punished.

---

78. TIM 4 33 (a theft of flax); UCP 10/1 107 (housebreaking); *AbB* 1 47 (an offer of compensation for housebreaking); YOS 14 40 (unspecified property). These are treated in Fortner, "Adjudicating Entities and Levels of Authority in Lawsuit Records of the Old Babylonian Era," 792–95, 815–17, 892–93. The verdict in the latter case has been restored by some scholars to state that the thief to death would be killed if he could not pay the penalty. However, in UCP 10/1 107 the thief, apparently unable to pay, was given over as a debt slave to the house owner. Similarly, a slave who committed burglary in UCP 10/1 91; for the UCP 10/1 documents see Greengus, *Studies in Ishchali Documents*, 157–59, 171–73.

The Middle Assyrian Laws adds corporal—but not capital—punishment to the financial penalties for theft. Middle Assyrian Laws §C 8, although partly missing and with lines missing, reveals this clearly:

> [If a man has stolen] either [. . .] or an animal, or any other thing, they shall bring evidence (and) convict him; he must pay back the stole[n item] (and) they shall smite him 50 blows with rods (and) he shall do [the king's labor for . . .] days. This judgment shall the judges impose [. . .] should reach, then he shall [return] as much as he sto[le, to the full val]ue, be it little or much and the king shall impose [upon him] as he sees fit.

The statement in Middle Assyrian Laws §C 8, like Exod 22:8, considers all manner of loot including animals and inanimate objects. The king is given latitude in setting the penalties.

Monetary penalties for theft are given in Hittite Laws §92, which deals with theft of swarms of bees and hives:

> If anyone steals [2] or 3 beehives, formerly (the offender) would have been exposed to bee sting. But now he shall pay 6 shekels of silver. If anyone steals a beehive, if there are no bees in the hive, he shall pay 3 shekels of silver.

We have no law in the Bible dealing with bees; however the selling of bee hives is mentioned in the Mishna hand Tosefta.[79] What is interesting in the Hittite Laws is the historical recollection of an earlier time in Hatti when a thief would be subjected to corporal punishment by stinging.

Another situation where corporal—perhaps capital— punishment in former time was eliminated, is Hittite Laws §121, where a thief stole a plow:

> If some free man steals a plow, and its owner finds it, (the owner) shall put [the offender's neck] upon the . . . (a part of the plow?), and [he shall be trampled?] by the oxen. This is how they proceeded formerly. But now he shall pay 6 shekels of silver, and he shall look to his house for it. If it is a slave, [he shall pay] 3 shekels of silver.

There are a number of other Hittite Laws dealing with theft of various items of property: wagon, fowl, plants, bricks, and other implements, where the penalties are payments ranging from one to 12 shekels.[80]

Hittite Laws §§94–97 deal with house burglary and also demonstrate the different levels of responsibility assigned to free persons and slaves:

> §94 If a free man burglarizes a house, he shall give (back the stolen items) precisely in full. Formerly they paid 40 shekels of silver (as fine) for the theft, but now [he shall pay] 12 shekels of silver. If he steals much, they will impose much upon him; if he steals little, they shall impose little upon him, and he shall look to his house for it.

> §95 If a slave burglarizes a house, he shall give (back the stolen items) precisely in full value. He shall pay 6 shekels of silver for the theft. He shall cut off the nose and ears of the slave, and they will give him back to his owner. If he steals much, they will impose much on him; if

---

79. Cf. *m. B. Bat.* 5:3, *t. B. Bat.* 4:7, Lieberman.

80. Hittite Laws §§119–120, 122–125, 128–129. These are not quoted here.

he steals little, they shall impose little upon him. [If] his owner says: "I will make compensation for him," then he shall make it. But [if] he refuses, he shall lose that slave.

§96 If a free man burglarizes a grain storage pit and finds grain in the storage pit, he shall fill the storage pit with grain and pay 12 shekels silver. [He shall look to his house for it].

§97 If a slave burglarizes a grain storage pit and finds grain in the storage pit, he shall fill the storage pit with grain and pay 6 shekels of silver, and he shall look to his house for it.

The basic penalties for theft were 1:1, and could be either increased or reduced in proportion to the value of what was stolen. The fixed amounts stated—12 or 6 shekel—seem to be minimum penalties levied in addition to the replacement of the stolen items. A slave's action was not held to the same penalty standard as that committed by a free person, presumably because there was recognition that a slave was capable of stealing on his own, in disobedience to his owner. Also, possibly, because slaves were not held to the same moral standard as free persons (see presently below).

Burglary of a house, nevertheless, was viewed as more serious than burglary of a granary; but not necessarily because of the value of goods stolen since the monetary penalties are the same. §94 tells us that the penalty was once much higher; and the greater seriousness of the housebreaking offense is also manifested in the corporal punishment given to the slave in §95. The imposition of corporal punishment in Hittite Laws §95, as in Middle

Assyrian Laws §C 8, appears to be a form of chastisement, marking the slave in a permanent fashion as an example and visible warning to himself and to others. It is possible that this more serious view of housebreaking is based upon the threat of bodily harm that is posed by an intruder, as was discussed above in connection with Exod 22:1–2a. In Hittite Laws §95 we see that slave's owner is given the option of paying the monetary penalty incurred by his slave. But if the owner refused to pay for the theft, then the slave was forfeit to the house owner in lieu of the unpaid loss and monetary penalty.

The Bible gives no law on theft by a slave; however, rabbinic law recognized that slaves did steal; indeed in one place, this kind of behavior is said to be typical. A slave could not be held to the same standard of social responsibility as a free individual; his servile status and demeaned condition was associated with moral laxity. We find this sentiment in the Tosefta, *t. B. Bat.* 4:7, (cited earlier in sec. 3.1 and repeated here):

> If one sells a slave to another and he (the slave) is found out to be a thief or a gambler, he (nevertheless) becomes his (the buyer's) property.

In other words, the sale is binding because such behavior was assumed to be sufficiently typical for slaves and thus not considered as a reason to void the sale. This is explicitly argued in a Talmudic comment on this passage, which debates whether most or all slaves are assumed to be suspected of theft"

> Is not (the sale valid) because most (slaves) are (of) such [a character]? . . . No; all of them are such."[81]

81. This comment appears in *b. B. Bat.* 93a.

The Mishnah (*m. Yad.* 4:7) looks at the question whether liability for wrongdoing can be transferred from a slave to his owner; the situation of a slave is seen as different from that of animals owned by the master:

> The Sadducees say: "We cry out against you O Pharisees, that you declare: my ox or ass that caused damage, (the owners) are liable; but my male or female slave who caused damage, (the owners) are not liable. Now, if (in) the case of my ox and ass for whom I am not required to perform commandments, I am nevertheless liable for their damages, then it should follow that for my male or female slave for whom I am required to perform commandments, I should certainly be liable for their damages."[82] They (the Pharisees) said to them (the Sadducees): "No, if you argue from my ox or ass, that they have no understanding, can you say (likewise) about my male or female slave who possess understanding? Because if I provoke him he will go out and set fire to a stack of grain belonging to another and I will be liable to pay for it."

The position of the Sadducees is that full liability for the actions of a slave should be transferred to his owner. But the Pharisees argued that liability rested only upon the slave who caused the damage.

The issue of liability for damages committed by slaves is discussed again in the Mishnah, *m. B. Qam.* 8:4; they are there compared also with women, deaf mutes, idiots, and children:

> A deaf mute, an idiot, and a child—an encounter with them is troubling (because) one who injures them is liable yet if they injure others they are free from liability (since they do not control assets).[83] A slave and a woman—an encounter with them is troubling (because) one who injures them is liable yet when they injure others they are free from liability (since they also do not control assets). Yet they could afterwards pay (on their own) if the woman was divorced (or) the slave set free; (then) they (themselves) become liable to pay.

Some have seen in *m. Yad.* 4:7 and in *m. B. Qam.* 8:4 as a new social policy, introduced by the Pharisees, designed to totally remove liability from the owner of the slave and to leave the full burden of liability only upon the slave.[84] The policy of the Sadducees, on the other hand, clearly mirrors what we find to be widely practiced elsewhere, e.g., in Babylonian,[85] Hittite and Roman law. According to Hittite Laws §95 (cited above), there was also a

---

82. This refers to commandments such as circumcision (Gen 17:12), paschal sacrifice (Exod 12:44). However, Sabbath observance was commanded for slaves and beasts (Exod 20:10; Deut 5:14)!

83. We encounter this same ruling again, in sec. 6.5, which deals with damages caused by fire.

84. The Mishnah (*m. Yad.* 4:7 and other passages relating to disputes between Pharisees and Sadducees) have been subject to discussion and varying interpretations. Baron, *A Social and Religious History of the Jews*, 269, argued that the Pharisees, interested in social reforms, were intent on limiting the legal powers of owners with respect to their slaves; and that this was beneficial to the slaves. But see, with less certainty, Falk, *Introduction to Jewish Law of the Second Commonwealth*, 169, 172.

85. For Babylonian law over the centuries cf. UCP 10/1 91, mentioned earlier and treated in Greengus, *Studies in Ishchali Documents*, 157–59. For later periods see Dandamaev, *Slavery in Babylonia*, 420–22.

public interest when a slave committed a theft, which was "satisfied" by mutilating the slave. Actual liability for damages fell upon the slave directly but an obligation to pay for the damages committed by his slave rested upon his owner. Otherwise the slave was forfeit to the party who suffered the damage or loss. A similar set of principles was followed in Roman law. Responsibility for damages rested upon the perpetrator; however, if he were a slave and living under the legal power of his master, then the master was answerable for the damages before the law. However, the master could escape liability by surrendering his offending slave to the injured party or directly to the authorities.[86]

Our Mishnah sources—clearly representing the Pharisaic view—accept the principle that the slave was responsible for his actions in creating damages; and also that the slave was under the legal power of his master. However, short of manumission, the rabbis fail to describe any circumstances that could give any recourse to the victim who suffered an injury or loss at the hands of an impecunious slave. That slave, if manumitted, would be answerable to pay for damages caused by his own actions. This is stated in *m. B. Qam.* 8:4, which seems likewise to imply that the claim for damages could be raised against the manumitted slave even after an interval of time had passed.[87] The

independent will of the slave—and perhaps also the assumption about his having lower moral standards as mentioned above—could also have been used as an argument for a reduction in liability for his theft, like we see in the Hittite Laws. There is no mention of this here in our rabbinic sources. Nevertheless, it does not seem possible that an injured party would contentedly sit quiet without pursuing any recourse at all. The Gemara's discussion of the Mishnah in *b. B. Qam.* 89a–89b tries to identify a situation where a married woman might be able to pay for her damages out of her dowry; but there is nothing said there about how a slave under the legal power of his master might be able to pay his damages, without the cooperation of the master. Allowing the victim to take possession of the thieving slave would certainly have been a remedy available in a court operating under Roman law. Could one imagine that the Pharisees—in an oblique fashion—were actually recommending manumission rather than see a Jew being forced to surrender his slave for damages, which would certainly have been the result if the victim undertook to sue for his damages in a Roman rather than rabbinic court? Is it perhaps possible that the rabbinic position was in some way linked to their view that a chattel slave, while living in the house of his Jewish master, had already become a quasi-Jew through observing the commandments—as also noted by the Sadducees? According to the rabbis, manumission would confer full Jewish status on the freed slave; and this might indeed be preferable to surrendering the chattel slave to a new master, who might not support his

86. Thomas, *A Textbook of Roman Law,* 381–82, 396, citing *Gaius, Inst.* 4.75–76; *D.*9.4.1–2, 6, 20–21, 33.

87. This point is clearly said by Maimonides in his restatement of the Mishnah passages in *Hilkhot Hovel Umaziq* 4.20–21. Jacob ben Asher, a later medieval commentator, in *Arba'a Turim, Hoshen Mishpat* 424, 9 goes so far as to suggest that the court issue the victim a document establishing a lien on possible future assets owned by the slave.

observance of the commandments.[88] Following this line of reasoning, one could suggest that the Mishnah's position was, in effect, an injunction in favor of treating slaves humanely and not encouraging them to act out in a criminal fashion in order to achieve a better situation with a new master. Its legal power otherwise appears to be limited, being subject to overturn if the victim chose to seek judgment in the Roman courts.

5.7 THEFT OF PROPERTY BELONGING TO TEMPLE OR PALACE

In biblical times it was considered a great sacrilege to steal property regarded as belonging to or dedicated to God. This is told in vivid detail in Joshua 7; a description of the crime and punishment of Achan is described in Josh 7:20–26:

> And Achan answered Joshua, "It is true, I have sinned against the Lord, the God of Israel. And this is what I did: I saw among the spoil a goodly Shinar mantle; and two hundred shekels of silver; and a gold bar weighing fifty shekels; and I coveted them and took them. And they are here buried in the ground inside my tent, with the silver below it." And Joshua sent messengers, and they ran to the tent; and there it was, buried in his tent, with the silver underneath. And they took them from inside the tent and brought them to Joshua and all the Israelites, and laid them out before the Lord. Then Joshua, and all Israel with him, took Achan son of

> Zerah and the silver, the mantle, and the bar of gold, his sons and daughters, and his ox, and his ass, and his flock, and his tent, and all his possessions, and brought them up to the Valley of Achor. And Joshua said, "How you have troubled us! The Lord will this day bring trouble upon you." And all Israel stoned him with stones, and they burnt them, and they cast (more) stones over them. And (so) they raised over him a great heap of stones, which is (there) to this day. Then the Lord turned away from his burning wrath; therefore one calls this place Valley of "Trouble" (i.e., Achor) unto this day.

All of the stolen items had been promised to God as dedicatory offerings out of the spoils of victory; according to this story, Achan's theft had brought divine wrath upon the entire nation; and, as punishment, they were defeated in battle. I leave aside for now discussion of the concept of large-scale vicarious punishment, inflicted upon masses of people for a sin committed by one member of the group, except to note that it was recognized as a form of divine justice within certain early traditions recorded in the Bible; more has been said about this is sec. 4.8.2.[89] The peril of taking property set aside for God had been stated in a warning to the people in Josh 6:18–19:

88. According to the rabbis, sale or legal transfer of a chattel slave was tantamount to setting him free and to live as a Jew according to the commandments. See *m. Git.* 4:4, 6 and our discussion at the end of sec. 2.1.

89. I also not here discuss the larger history of the biblical practice of dedication or proscription. For this, see Greenberg, "Ḥerem." I would, however, note that in the battle against Ai, the people were allowed to take some booty for themselves. Joshua 8:26–27 relates that the inhabitants were slaughtered; and "Only the livestock and the spoil of that city Israel took as their booty, according to the word of the LORD that he had issued to Joshua" (NRSV).

As for you, keep away from the things devoted to destruction, so as not to covet and take any of the devoted things and make the camp of Israel an object for destruction, bringing trouble upon it. But all silver and gold, and vessels of bronze and iron, are sacred to the LORD; they shall go into the treasury of the LORD." (NRSV)

The custom of offering valuable items of booty to deities was widespread in ancient times; temples were places of safety and permanence; and the gifts of booty can be seen as enduring tokens of thanks for divine favors as well as symbolic reminders of divine power. This was probably the reason why the sword of Goliath had been deposited in the shrine at Nob, as told in 1 Sam 21:10:

The priest said, "The sword of Goliath the Philistine whom you slew in the valley of Elah; it is here, wrapped in a cloth, behind the ephod. If you want to take that, take it, for there is none here except that one." David replied, "There is none like it; give it to me."

David took the sword, which may or may not have been formally dedicated; the removal is not described as a sin. However, this act did have fatal consequences for the priests at Nob and their community; Saul, in his wrath, destroyed them all as punishment, we are told, for assisting David in his flight.[90]

The wrongful use of sacred temple vessels is given as a key reason for the

90. Cf. 1 Sam 22:9–20. See also Roberts, "The Legal Basis for Saul's Slaughter of the Priests of Nob (1 Samuel 21–22)." The dedication of war booty—human captives, animals, textiles, wooden utensils, and jewelry—figures prominently in the narrative concerning the war with the Midianites described in Numbers 31.

downfall and death of Belshazzar, as told by the writing on the wall; in Dan 5:23–24 the prophet Daniel declares to Belshazzar:

And against the Lord of Heaven you exalted yourself, and had the vessels of his temple brought before you; and you and your nobles, your royal wives, and your concubines drank wine from them and praised the gods of silver and gold, bronze and iron, wood and stone, which cannot see, hear, or understand; but the God in whose hand is your very breath and who controls your life breath and all your ways— him you did not give praise. So then was sent from him the hand and this writing was inscribed.

Belshazzar was killed on that same night when he used the sacred vessels for his profane purposes. The Talmud, *b. Ned.* 62a, notes the linkage succinctly:

Belshazzar, who used the holy vessels, which thereby became profaned, was uprooted from the world, as it is written (Dan 5:30), "On that very night was Belshazzar slain."

According to the Book of Ezra, these temple vessels were eventually properly restored to the Jews, apparently because they were recognized as property sacred to their God; Ezra 1:7-8 recounts:

King Cyrus (of Persia) brought forth the vessels of the Lord's house, which Nebuchadnezzar had taken away from Jerusalem and had delivered them into the house of his god. And (so) King Cyrus of Persia had them brought forth by the hand Mithredath, the treasurer; and he counted them out to Sheshbazzar the prince of Judah.

The sacredness of temple property, especially of items used in divine worship, was universally recognized. This quality may have also figured in Jacob's readiness to condemn to death any thief who stole the idols of Laban, as he declared in Gen 31:32, discussed above (sec. 5.6.2). The death penalty for stealing divine property continued as a desideratum into rabbinic times as we read in the Mishnah, *m. Sanh.* 9:6:

> One who steals a sacred vessel or who curses by Kosem (i.e., using a forbidden divine name) or who made an Aramean woman his paramour—zealots may fall upon him (and kill him).

This vision of zealots "taking the law into their own hands" is modeled on the act of Phineas in Num 25:7–8 which was mentioned earlier in our discussion of similar responses by a husband who discovered his wife engaged in an adulterous liaison (sec. 1.3.2). The exact nature of the cursing described in the Mishnah is obscure (see further sec. 7.1); but the case of theft is clearer.[91] The Mishnah here seems to preserve memory of older laws in which theft of divine property—as well as blasphemy and certain acts of (public?) sexual impropriety—deserved punishment by death.[92]

Theft of sacred property was subject to the death penalty in Mesopotamian laws. Hammurapi Laws §6 gives the death penalty as punishment for the theft

of palace property, as well as for theft of temple, i.e., divine property:

> If a man stole (valuable) property belonging to a god or to the palace, that man shall be killed; and (likewise) anyone who receives these stolen goods from his hands shall be killed.

But here, again, as we have noted in connection with ordinary theft, the death penalty may have been more an ultimate threat than a requirement. An early Old Babylonian document from Uruk, for example, contains a list of entries, recording penalties collected for various crimes. Among them is listed:

> 1 mina (silver from) Zikir-ilishu, the vizier, because he took food offerings— fish belonging to the regular offerings (supplied by) the king.
>
> 1/3 mina (silver from) Iddin-Nanaya, the chief temple administrator of the goddess Nanaya (and) 1/3 mina (silver) from the sons of Ur-Shubula, his brother, because they stripped off a bronze fitting from the door of the Temple of Nanaya.[93]

Lesser penalties are also found within the laws in Hammurapi Laws §8, which seeks to protect the property—animals or boat—belonging to a temple or to the king or to a commoner who is a tenant farmer on the king's lands The ultimate penalty of death remains as a possibility; but monetary compensation in a hefty amount will be accepted if the thief is able to pay:

91. Cf. the discussion of this Mishnah in *b. Sanh.* 81b–82b.

92. Lerner, *Torath ha-Mischna,* 3, explains that the death penalty was deserved for this theft but not actionable through formal law in Jewish courts, where only two-fold compensation would *normally* be imposed.

93. W 20472,125:5–10, published in Falkenstein, "Zu den Inschriftfunden der Grabung in Uruk-Warka," 48–49. In this entry, HE2.AN definitely describes a fitting that was part of the door made of bronze; but the specific function of this fitting is unclear.

If a man stole an ox, sheep, donkey, pig or boat—if it belongs to a god or to the palace, he shall pay thirty-fold; if it belongs to a commoner, he shall pay tenfold. If the thief lacks the means to pay, he shall be killed.

There is a great deal of evidence for a centuries-long tradition in the thirty-fold penalty for those who were caught stealing livestock or other animals belonging to a god or temple. In temple archives from the late Neo-Babylonian and early Persian periods there are more than a few records of court cases involving theft of sheep, donkeys, fowl, and fish belonging to temples; in each one of these cases, the thieves are sentenced to pay back what they stole thirty-fold.[94] In one document, a thief's mother and sister are given as slaves to the temple to pay off the penalty (which is not stated) for his stealing goats.[95] But I do not know of any case, where the death penalty was actually meted out for theft of livestock belonging to a temple.

From Assyria, Middle Assyrian Laws §N 1–2 discusses theft of temple property juxtaposed with the sin of blasphemy, in the fashion of *m. Sanh.* 9:6, but does not give the death penalty for these acts.[96] The

text of these laws is damaged but sufficient context exists to give us a fair idea of the contents:

> [If] a man in a quarrel [accuses] another man, saying: "You have spoken blasphemy [. . .] and have pilfered a temple" [. . .] they shall smite him forty times with canes [and he shall do the king's labor for . . . days]. If a man in a quarrel [has accused another man] saying: "[You have spoken] blasphemy and pilfered a temple [. . .] but is not [able] to prove it, that man [— they shall smite him . . . times with canes and he shall do the king's labor for] one month.

We do, however, know of cases where the death penalty was given to someone who stole sacred objects or cult related materials; such theft apparently involved entering and "violating" the most sacred precincts of the temple and thus came nearer to the "person" of the deity. Then, too, there may also have been a difference made between livestock, which might wander off on their/its own—or a boat, which might become un-tethered and float off—and objects, which would require someone to move them from their places. There is a case involving the death penalty in an early second millennium BCE document of the Ur III period, recording the trial of a high temple official accused by his son of violating a cultic taboo by taking for himself foodstuffs provided by the king and intended as offerings to the goddess Inanna in Nippur. These accusations were not substantiated and so the accuser was sentenced to death—the very penalty that apparently would have been given to the accused if the charges against him had been substantiated. The accuser was evidently put

---

94. For these cases see San Nicolò, "Parerga Babyloniaca," 327–44; and Figulla, "Lawsuit Concerning a Sacrilegious Theft at Erech." These court cases come from the reigns of Nabonidus, Cyrus, and Cambyses.

95. Jursa, "Neu- und spätbabylonische Texte, 99–100,152, text no. 1 (Birmingham 1982. A.1798); this document is dated to Nabopolassar 11.

96. Middle Assyrian Laws §A 1, unfortunately poorly preserved, has been restored as describing a theft from a temple committed by a man's wife or daughter. What is taken is not mentioned. Their apprehension and conviction apparently results in a divinatory oracle to determine their punishment. For discussion, see Lafont, *Femmes, Droit et Justice*, 434–45.

to death because the remainder of this legal document deals with the disposition of his estate; and this was the reason for the document having been written.[97] It is interesting to note that the stolen foodstuffs were not only sacred property but may also have been considered royal property since they were an offering intended by the king for the goddess. This case can be compared with *m. Sanh.* 9:6 (above) where the death penalty is seen as appropriate for one who steals a cult object, i.e., a vessel used in the worship service within the shrine itself. The two-fold monetary penalty for theft that would be given for ordinary theft was here deemed insufficient.[98] One must, however, also note the monetary penalty given instead of the death penalty in the early Old Babylonian case from Uruk cited above. Were those foodstuffs perhaps stolen before they were actually received in the temple? Or, did the severity of penalty depend on other, mitigating factors, not revealed in the documents, such as the attitude of the judges or the social position and rank of the offender?

The serious consequences for offenses relating to temple property are also attested in an Old Babylonian omen, which states: "an high priestess (var. wife of the chief temple administrator) will steal a sacred object and they will seize and burn her." The application of this form of punishment for sacred theft is mentioned in late Babylonian court records from the end of the Persian period and the early

Seleucid era.[99] The practice of imposing capital punishment for stealing from a temple is still to be found in second century CE "laws" inscribed on stone steles in the northern Iraq city of Hatra. The laws threaten that any person, who stole tools from the temple building site or other possessions from within its precinct, would be punished by stoning.[100]

The Hittites, as we have seen, generally punished theft of property with compensation; but theft of certain property belonging to the palace was viewed in a more serious fashion. Hittite Law §126 lists a series of items; one of which required the death penalty:

> If anyone steals a wooden chair (?) in the gate of the palace, he shall pay 6 shekels of silver. If anyone steals a bronze spear in the gate of the palace, he shall be put to death. If anyone steals a copper pin, he shall pay 25 liters of barley. If anyone steals the threads (or strands of wool) of one bolt of cloth, he shall give one bolt of woolen cloth.

The theft of a weapon belonging to the king was apparently considered to be serious enough to merit capital punishment. We may perhaps assume, on the basis of what we have seen elsewhere, that theft of divine property would have been similarly punished; but a law stating this has not yet been found.

97. See Roth, "Appendix A: A Reassessment of RA 71 (1977) 125ff.," and previous literature cited there. I discuss this document again in sec. 8.1.

98. For further discussion, including evidence for capital punishment for sacrilege in other ancient societies, cf. Jackson, *Theft in Early Jewish Law*, 164–70.

99. Joannès, "Une chronique judicaire d'époque hellénistique"; the omen is cited in *CAD* A/2, 327.

100. Kaizer, "Capital Punishment at Hatra"; see especially inscription H. 281; death by other methods was an "alternative" in some of the laws.

5.8 LOSS OF DOMESTIC ANIMALS CAUSED BY OTHER DOMESTIC ANIMALS

In Exod 21:35–36 we read:

> If a man's ox gores[101] the ox of his neighbor and it dies, then they shall sell the live ox and divide its price; and the dead animal they shall also divide. Otherwise (if) it was known that the ox was accustomed to gore in the past, and its owner did not guard it, he shall restore ox for ox, but he may keep the dead (animal).

The rabbis, however, were not satisfied that the solution of equally dividing the assets, as provided in the first biblical case, could be universally applied. This resolution would work if the two oxen were of equal value; but what would happen, for example, if the dead ox was worth more than the live ox? If there was equal division, then the owner of the live ox could emerge with more money than his own goring ox was originally worth. This would be unjust. Therefore, argue the rabbis, one had to consider the relative values of the two animals, a step which is not stated in Exod 21:35; but which the Mishnah, *m. B. Qam.* 3:9, seeks to clarify further:

---

101. The verbal root used here is NGP "to smite or strike" instead of NGḤ, the verb that is used in the other goring ox cases in Exod 21:28–31, 36. In the Bible, the verb NGḤ is in fact used regularly to describe butting or goring in animal combat. The use of NGP is rare and unexpected; however, the verb is cognate to Akkadian NKP, which is used in the Mesopotamian goring ox laws. Malul, *The Comparative Method in Ancient Near Eastern and Biblical Studies*, 106–7, 129, has argued that the exceptional use of verb NKP in our passage represents a direct borrowing from the ancient Akkadian language laws depicting goring oxen (these laws are cited below and earlier in sec. 4.10).

> (In a case of) an ox worth one mina (i.e., 100 zuz) that gored an ox worth two hundred (zuz) and the carcass was no (longer) worth anything: he (the owner of the dead ox) takes (for his half-damages) the (live) ox (that is worth one hundred zuz).

In this case, the owner of the dead ox is permitted to recover half of his loss but this leaves nothing for the owner of the live ox that caused the mishap. Still, this result, according to the rabbis, would be more just than having both owners take fifty zuz each from the sale of the surviving ox; if this were done, the owner of the gored ox will fail to receive half of what his now dead ox was originally worth.

The rabbis therefore try to imagine a case that would more closely match the biblical laws; the Mishnah continues:

> (In the case of) an ox worth two hundred (zuz) that gored an ox worth two hundred (zuz) and the carcass was not worth anything— Rabbi Meir said "This is (the case) that was depicted (in Exod 21:35 when it said): 'they shall sell the live ox and divide its price.'" Rabbi Judah said to him: "And this is indeed the law (as stated in the biblical case). But (in your example) you have not (shown how one) accomplishes "and the dead animal they shall also divide" (because it had no residual value in your example). So what (then) is the (appropriate) case (that corresponds to Exod 21:35)? This is (a case where) an ox worth two hundred (zuz) gored an ox worth two hundred (zuz) and the carcass was worth fifty zuz— that (here) one (party) takes half of the value of the surviving ox and half (the value) of the dead ox; and the (other likewise) takes half of

the value of the surviving ox and half the value of the dead ox."

In R. Judah's case, each party would emerge with one hundred and twenty-five zuz; the injured party recovers an amount a bit in excess of half his loss; but the owner of the goring ox will not be getting more than his ox was initially worth.[102]

It is my view that the ancient law collections are not complete; and so it is possible that the law we have before us in the Bible is only one illustration of a potentially infinite variety of problem situations. But, at the same time, one suspects that rabbinic exegesis has gone beyond what is written in the biblical text before us. Indeed, Rashbam, in his commentary to Exod 21:35 recognizes that the rabbis have in fact re-interpreted the text: whereas the biblical text speaks of two divisions, the rabbis put them together in order to make certain that the owner of the dead ox will recover at least one-half of his loss. Comparison with the ancient near Eastern laws confirms that the ancient policy was simply for both parties to share the loss equally. It was a form of "no fault" resolution; this kind of accident was prone to happen and no one party was more to blame than the other. This is what we find in Eshnunna Laws §53:

> If an ox gores another ox and causes it to die, the owners of the oxen both shall share the price of the live ox plus the carcass of the dead ox.

The resolution of the case is clearly that the owners are equally to share the loss that has been sustained and that each owner will recover half of what can be salvaged.

Interestingly, the Eshnunna Laws collection omits the second biblical case in Exod 21:36, where the owner of an ox that had previously gored is liable if he fails to curb his dangerous animal. This second case is in fact not preserved in any other ancient Near Eastern law collection, including the Hammurapi Laws. One can easily imagine, however, that the second case of the habitual gorer could very well have been considered in the Babylonian laws, since the resolution is straightforward and this contrast between "first time and repeated offense," appears in the laws, where oxen gore and kill human beings: Eshnunna Laws §54, Hammurapi Laws §§250–252 (sec. 4.10). The biblical law collection thus seems here to contain a more "complete" presentation.[103]

5.9 RETURNING A LOST ANIMAL TO OWNER

A law on returning lost animals appears in Exod 23:4:

> If you encounter your enemy's ox or donkey wandering astray, you must indeed take it back to him.

A more expanded version of this law, applying to animals—and by extension to other lost articles—appears in Deut 22:1–3:

> Do not look upon your fellow citizen's (lit. your brother's) ox or sheep gone astray and ignore them; you

102. In commenting on this Mishnah, the Talmud in *b. B. Qam.* 34a goes on to consider still other permutations of the ox goring ox cases, e.g., where the value of the carcass decreased further after death. The substance of the Mishnah is also found in *t. B. Qam.* 3:3, Lieberman. This problem of "inequitable resolution" is also addressed in Jackson, *Wisdom Laws*, 276–79.

103. See the discussion in Yaron, *Laws of Eshnunna*, 291–97, and our earlier discussion in sec. 4.10 on the "habitual gorer."

must indeed return them to your fellow citizen. If your fellow citizen is not close by to you or you do not know who he is, then you shall bring it into your home and it shall remain with you until your fellow citizen seeks it; then you shall give it back to him. And so shall you do with his donkey; and so you shall do with his garment; and so too shall you do with anything that is lost by your fellow citizen and you find it: you must not ignore (your obligation to help him).

Neither law contains any penalty; and the formulation in Deuteronomy answers questions that might have arisen in response to the shorter statement of Exod 23:4, such as: what if the animal has strayed far from home? What if the finder doesn't know the owner? These are similar to circumstances taken up in the laws dealing with runaway slaves that we have considered above (in sec. 3.2). These biblical laws on lost animals are formulated in the style of moral directives or motivational promptings, namely, one who sees lost property has an ethical obligation to become involved in facilitating its recovery and should not walk away without taking remedial action. But there is no legal duty here in the sense that one could be punished by the authorities if he looked the other way and chose not to help. As such, these are laws "without teeth."

The rabbis, in their exegesis, strongly underscore the moral obligation to restore lost items, inasmuch as a law on lost animals is found twice in the Pentateuch. Moreover, they note that in the Deuteronomy passage, the injunction not to "ignore" is repeated two times. Nevertheless, they also recognize that there may be limitations. Thus, the *Sifre D* 222 on Deut

22:1 states that the obligation is not open-ended; circumstances might prevent one from becoming involved. Thus, for example, a priest is not required to defile himself by entering a cemetery to retrieve the lost item; or an elderly person might not be expected to undertake the physical exertion needed to recover a wandering animal. Other circumstances are not given, but are left to reasonable understanding.[104] *Sifre D* 224 on Deut 22:3 also adds that the finder is entitled to use the lost property while he holds it, as long as he does not damage it.

When we turn to the ancient Near Eastern sources, we see similar provisions; but the duty to restore begins after the finder takes physical possession of the lost property. He must then report it to the authorities. Hittite Laws §71 thus states:

> If anyone finds a (stray) ox, a horse, a mule, (or) a donkey, he shall drive it to the king's gate. If he finds it in the country, they present it to the elders. (The finder) shall harness it (i.e., use it while it is in his custody). When its owner finds it, he shall take it back in full value, but shall not have him (sc. the finder) arrested as a thief. But if (the finder) does not present it to the elders, he shall be considered a thief.

Hittite Laws §45 is a law dealing with lost property other than animals:

> If anyone finds implements [and gives] them back to their owner, he (the owner) will reward him. But if (the finder) does not give them (back), he shall be considered a thief.

---

104. The two examples mentioned are repeated elsewhere as "parade" examples; cf. *b. Ber.* 19b; *b. B. Metz.* 30a; *b. Sanh.* 18b.

§45 is not as detailed as §71 but it is very different in tone; why is there a reward there and none in §71? Was the finder able to return the lost implements because he knew to whom they belonged? Was a reward given here because the implements were otherwise not distinctive enough to be easily identified and reclaimed? We are not told what should happen if the finder did not know the identity of the owner or if these items had been lost far from home. Was he then required to notify the authorities as in §71? Could the finder make personal use of these items while they were in his possession? Or is such use limited to the case of animals, whose care and feeding required financial outlay? Deuteronomy 22:1–3 applies the same rules to lost objects as for animals; can one make the same assumption for the implements in Hittite Laws §45? Such questions seem reasonable if one assumes that the laws within a collection are coherent with one another.

On the other hand, it is curious that the biblical laws say nothing about having the finder contact the civil authorities; the finder and the owner are the only actors mentioned. However, the Jewish *Targum Pseudo-Jonathan* to Deut 22:3 adds this provision to its translation of the biblical text: "you (the finder) shall have (the herald) announce it (as being found) and you shall return it to him." This additional comment would bring Deut 22:1–3 more in line with the practice depicted in Hittite Laws §71, by requiring the finder who took possession to contact the authorities or at least advertise in the community about the lost property. This targumic gloss is based upon rabbinic laws, which require a finder to notify others in the community. We find this requirement

more fully discussed in the Tosefta, *t. B. Metz.* 2:16–17, Lieberman, along with a need for the owner to identify his lost property:

> Formerly, when a person first came and gave identifying features, he would take it (from the finder). But (more recently) since deceivers have multiplied, they (the rabbis) decreed that this person gives (its) identifying features but (must also) brings evidence (e.g., personal references) that he is not a deceiver. Formerly they (the finders) would have public announcement (repeatedly) made at the time of three (consecutive) pilgrimage festivals, and after the (last) festival seven more days. But since the temple was destroyed, they (the rabbis) decreed that one should make public announcement for thirty days. And (most recently,) since the "time of danger" (i.e., the persecutions of Hadrian c. 135 CE) and until the present (time), they decreed that he (the finder) shall make the find known to his neighbors, relatives, acquaintances, and to the men of his city—and that is sufficient.[105]

The next paragraph of the Tosefta, *t. B. Metz.* 2:18–19, Lieberman, addresses the issues of the finder making use of the lost object until reclaimed:

> If one finds an item, if there is in it sufficient (value) to (eventually) return (even) a "penny's worth" to its owner and (at the same time for the finder) to receive a benefit from its use, then he (the finder) should take care of it. But if this is not the case, he may leave it where

105. This Tosefta passage incorporates and expands upon the shorter discussion in the Mishnah, *m. B. Metz.* 2:6.

it lies (without taking further action). (To) what kinds of lost object (does this law apply)? If (e.g.,) he found a spade lying on the road, a garment on the road, a cow grazing among plantings—such an item is a lost object. (However,) a garment resting on the side of a fence, a jar lying between fence posts, a donkey grazing in grass, such is not a lost object. (Nevertheless,) if he (repeatedly) finds them over three consecutive days, this item is lost.[106]

It is interesting that this law introduces the principle of ultimate value—both to the owner and to the finder—as a limiting feature in one's duty to help recover lost property. The use of the lost item by the finder is again addressed in the Mishnah, *m. B. Metz.* 2:7:

> Any (animal or item), which can do work and "eats" (i.e., requires maintenance)—he (the finder) may work with it and it will "eat" (i.e., earn its maintenance). But (any animal) which can do no work but "eats" may be sold (by the finder who will return the money or its value to the owner if he reclaims it).

It seems reasonable to imagine that considerations for publicity and use, like those mentioned both in the rabbinic and Near Eastern laws, might well also have been pertinent during biblical times. The biblical laws, as formulated, appear to address the gap in time between seeing the lost item and taking possession of it. For the Bible, one is obliged to take possession and follow-up with action, unlike the Hittite Laws, where an obligation to restore begins after taking possession. The Bible appears to be urging an expanded level of social responsibility. The Tosefta, however, removes this obligation if the object is of limited value; and also allows the finder to sell an animal that is expensive to maintain. We have no way of knowing if such distinctions were known and practiced earlier. Interestingly, neither the Bible nor the rabbinic sources mention a reward, which is mentioned only with the finding of implements in Hittite Laws §45 but not in connection with lost animals in Hittite Laws §71.

One may get a sharper insight into the biblical law by comparing the biblical injunction to return a lost animal with the law urging non-return with respect to runaway slaves (sec. 3.2). In the case of the runaway slave, the Bible urges the onlooker not to become involved and not to apprehend the slave. In the case of the lost animal, the Bible urges the onlooker to become involved and take responsibility. Otherwise, as we see in the ancient Near Eastern laws, legal responsibility would not begin without the act of physically apprehending the lost animal or runaway slave.

---

106. Similar content discussing a variety of lost objects appears in *m. B. Metz.* 2:1–11.

6

Laws Relating to Immovable Property

6.1 THEFT OF LAND

THE BIBLE ADDRESSES THE theft of land in a number of passages but does so only in the form of prohibitions, i.e., moral exhortations without stating any penalties. The reason for lack of penalties here is not certain. A variety of factors may apply. One may be the form of the law itself: a second person "apodictic" admonition, intent upon forbidding the act without regard to circumstances or degree. The lack of penalty may be linked to a lack of power to adjudicate according to appropriate moral principles. This situation might have been true during periods of foreign rule or when the Israelite authorities imposed penalties different from those advocated by religious lawgivers. Or perhaps the rulers, Israelite or foreign, were viewed as corrupt or unreliable to mete out justice as suggested in Hos 5:10: "The officers of Judah have been like those who remove field boundaries; on them I will pour out my wrath like water."

Alternatively, as many scholars have argued, the theft of land is often a hidden or secret act, difficult to discover and therefore not as often subject to legal punishment.[1] The lawgivers thus rely upon the moral discipline of the faithful rather than upon the coercive powers of the government. Moral discipline is also an important feature of wisdom pronouncement and proverbs; and, as we shall presently see, the prohibition against land theft is a theme present in that literature.

The prohibition against land theft takes the form of admonishments against moving the boundary stones that were evidently put in place to help separate one property from another. The repeated formulations, in the laws, in the prophets as seen above, and in wisdom literature, express both respect for set markers and the prohibition against encroaching upon another's property. The law and wisdom formulations are as follows:

> Deut 19:14 You must not remove your neighbor's boundary marker, which the first owners set on the property that you will possess in the land that the Lord your God is giving you to possess.

---

1. This is suggested by the phrase "in secret," which is used in Deut 27:15, 24 with other misdeeds in the list with Deut 27:17 (see below); thus a resorting to curses. Cf. Ibn Ezra on Deut 27:14 and Hazzequni on Deut 27:15; they argue that these were crimes, which were not likely to be brought before a human tribunal for justice; cf. Driver, *Commentary of Deuteronomy,* 299–300.

Deut 27:17 "Cursed be he who removes his neighbor's boundary marker"; and all the people shall say, "Amen!"

Prov 22:28 Do not remove the ancient boundary marker that your forefathers set up.

Prov 23:10–11 Do not remove an ancient boundary marker or encroach on the fields of orphans, for their title defender [lit. redeemer] is strong; he will plead their case against you.

Job 24:2–3 They remove boundary markers; they rob a flock and put them to pasture (as if their own). They lead away the donkey of orphans; they take the widow's ox for a pledge.

Respect for "the ancient boundary marker," as stated in Proverbs, was connected by rabbinic readers with the phrase "which the first owners set up," found in Deut 19:14. For some, this suggested the tribal division of Joshua's time; for others, this included even markers erected by the Canaanites who inhabited the land previously.[2] The relationship between encroachment of boundaries and theft of property is clearly stated in Prov 23:10–11 and in Job 24:2–3; these offenses are, of course, the reason for the curse in Deut 27:17 and for God's wrath in Hos 5:10.

Admonition against theft of land is also found in Egyptian wisdom literature, in the "Instruction of Amen-em-opet," which is preserved in a text that has been dated between the tenth and sixth century BCE and that exhibits many other

parallels in themes with Proverbs 22–24. The passage on boundary violation is as follows:

> Do not carry off the landmark at the boundary of the arable land,
>
> Nor disturb the position of the measuring cord;
>
> Be not greedy after a cubit of land,
>
> Nor encroach upon the boundaries of the widow.[3]

Just as in the curse of Deut 27:17 and in the condemnation of Hos 5:10, we find a visible religious dimension in the prohibitions against violating boundaries in Hittite Laws §§168–169, where religious rites are required after a violation has occurred:

> §168 If anyone violates the boundary of a field and removes one *akkala-*,[4] the owner of the field shall cut one *gipeššar* (0.25 square meters) of field (from the other's field) and take it for himself. He who violated the boundary shall give one sheep, 10 loaves, and one jug of KA.GAG beer and re-consecrate the field.
>
> §169 If anyone buys a field and violates the boundary, he shall take a thick loaf and break it to the Sungod [and] say: "You . . . ed my scales into the ground." And he shall speak thus: "Sungod, Storm god. No quarrel (was intended).'"

---

2. The tribal idea is expressed, e.g., in *Sifre D* 188 and Nahmanides on Deut 19:14. The Canaanite view is given in *b. Shabb.* 85a: "sons of Seir and Hivites." So, too, Rashi there "Amorites and Hivites."

3. *ANET*, 422–24. Weinfeld, *Deuteronomy and the Deuteronomic School*, 265–67 discusses the relationship between the larger, ancient wisdom traditions and Deuteronomy and argues for the primacy of the former.

4. Hoffner, *Laws of the Hittites*, 216, suggests that this removal represents the result of one who either "deducts a furrow from his neighbor's field" or "in plowing he 'drives' the plow one furrow beyond where he is entitled to and thus encroaches upon his neighbor's field."

Hoffner and Friedrich suggest that §169 may likely be a case of unintentional boundary violation. The verb in the declaration "You . . . ed my scales into the ground" is unclear; perhaps he means to say that his claim to his own purchased field is an honest one, i.e., originating or supported by the balance or scales of just commerce and that his violation was unintentional.[5] This activity evidently falls under the purview of the sun-god, because he was the traditional god of justice. The added appeal to the storm-god could be intended to ward off punishment from that senior god of the Hittite pantheon.[6] The offender has trespassed but has then apparently also recognized the incursion and has retreated, having no wish to retain what isn't his own. The offender in §168 on the other hand, appears to have trespassed and retained a portion of his neighbor's field. He must pay compensation by giving up a part of his own field; and because the violated field is to be reconsecrated, Hoffner sees the additional items as expiatory, i.e., a cultic offering intended for the domestic cult of the rightful owner; he notes that the offerings given are similar in kind to what is given at temples.[7]

5. Cf. Hoffner, *Laws of the Hittites,* 216–17, where he states his basic agreement with Friedrich, *Die Hethitischen Gesetze*, 119.

6. For the primacy of the storm-god and the sun-god, see McMahon, "Theology, Priests and Worship in Hittite Anatolia," 1985–89. Gurney, *The Hittites,* 139 describes the sun-god as "the god of right and justice, a natural conception, since the sun in his daily course surveys from an impartial height all deeds of men." Gurney cites supporting passages from Hittite prayers. Hoffner, *Laws of the Hittites,* 216, cites a literary passage, which affirms that "violating boundaries or roads constituted an attack upon the person of the Stormgod himself."

7. Hoffner, *Laws of the Hittites,* 214; these same items are given for ritual violation of a home in Hittite Laws §164.

Violation of property boundaries is found in religious texts from Babylonia, occurring in lists of hidden or perhaps forgotten sins, especially those involving false oaths, which may have provoked divine wrath against an individual. The religious dimension of these offenses is demonstrated by the fact that those persons afflicted by the gods must now seek release or healing through rites of expiation and absolution. Offenses against property are among the sins included in *Shurpu,* a collection of incantations to be recited in conjunction with expiatory rituals, edited in several versions dating from the middle of the second millennium to the middle of the first millennium BCE. I cite here some of the pertinent lines from the "standard version, " tablet ii, lines 1–3, 31–32, 45–46, 185, 192:

> Incantation. Be it released, great gods, god and goddess of absolution. So and So (To be named by the priest reciting the incantation), son of So and So, whose god is So and So, whose goddess is So and So . . . He does not know what is (his) crime against the god; he does not know what is (his) sin against the goddess. . . He set up an untrue boundary marker, (but) did not set up the true boundary marker, he removed the sign, border, or boundary marker . . . May god and goddesses, as many as there are invoked … may they lift this oath (bringing curses from upon him).

Another passage mentioning the sin of stealing of property and requiring expiation appears in tablet iii, lines 1–2, 53–54:

> Incantation. The effect (i.e., the curse) of any oath this man, son of this god is under, Asalluhi, exorcist among the gods, will undo . . . the

oath of sprinkling (water upon) his hands and going up (to erase?) a boundary line—Asalluhi, exorcist among the gods, will undo; the oath of a boundary marker and having changed it—Asalluhi, exorcist among the gods, will undo . . .[8]

The oaths mentioned were presumably false and were sworn in connection with the many sins and offenses listed in *Shurpu*; the persons who swore them are to be released and given expiation.

But there is no mention of any requirement for restitution to those adversely affected by the false testimony, as is required in Lev 5:20–26 (cited above in connection with laws of deposit, sec. 5.1), where expiation is accompanied by repayment of the loss, plus one-fifth of its value in addition. Perhaps a long interval of time or distance separated the original event and the seeking of an expiatory ritual. Many passages suggest that these incantations were prayers recited for the seriously ill, who now repent and seek absolution from the divine powers, which have now sorely afflicted them.

Yet there is no question that violations of boundaries would be punished if the perpetrators were caught doing so. The Middle Assyrian Laws §B 8–9 include provisions on the theft of land; and the punishments are severe for those who perpetrate such offenses and are caught:

B §8 If a man has incorporated a large border area belonging to his neighbor (and) they have proven and convicted him, he shall give back one third (more) than he incorporated; they shall cut off one of his fingers; they shall smite him

100 blows with rods; he shall do the king's labor for a month of days.

B §9 If a man has encroached upon a small border area allotted to him through lots (and) they have proven and convicted him, he shall pay one talent of lead; he shall give back one third (more) than he incorporated; they shall smite him 50 blows with rods; he shall do the king's labor for a month of days.

The centuries of cuneiform writing yield further evidence that boundary violations were indeed prosecuted and punished. In the Nuzi archives, from the last half of the second millennium, we have a record wherein a man confesses that he indeed did steal an area of his neighbor's field lying next to the boundary of his own and that he did destroy the existing boundary line between their properties. He was sentenced to repay an area twice what he stole plus amounts of grain and straw equal to what would be expected as yield from the area taken, multiplied by the number of years (three) that he held illegal possession of that area.[9]

In rabbinic literature, the law in Deut 19:14 is given only a minor role; it is regarded as an "extra verse," supplementary to what is already implicit in Exod 20:15 "You shall not steal." *Sifre D* 188 on Deut 19:14 thus explains it as adding an additional "spiritual" penalty, but then only for "on the property that you will possess in

---

8. Reiner, *Šurpu*, 13–14, 19–20. For partial citations of these passages) see *CAD* K, 31 and M/2, 114a.

9. JEN 653. This document was published in copy only; significant lines are translated in *CAD* M/2, 114a, Š/1, 81. *CAD* M/2 mentions also JEN 656 (cited as JENu 766), where the guilty party was likewise required to repay the lost harvest, but paid a heavy monetary fine instead of a penalty in land. The fine was stipulated in an earlier agreement between the defendant and the plaintiff's father, whose title was confirmed by the proceedings recorded in JEN 656.

the land that the Lord your God is giving you to possess." i.e., in the land of Israel but not beyond her borders. For the rabbis, the penalty for land theft was basically to be determined in accordance with the basic laws of theft. According to biblical laws, as we have noted above, thieves were normally required to pay twice what they stole; and the penalty paid at Nuzi contains that same feature. We have no information on whether the biblical or rabbinic penalty would require collecting, in addition to the two-fold compensation, the value of lost harvests from the stolen land, as we have it at Nuzi.[10]

6.2 NEGLIGENCE IN AN AGRICULTURAL LEASE

These laws are found both in ancient Near Eastern and rabbinic sources but are lacking in the Bible. They represent legal areas, which did exist and were probably in force during biblical times, but the biblical editors omitted them. These omissions may simply have been accidental. I have already noted, for example (in sec. 5.3) how a law involving hiring of animals was anticipated by the rabbis, although it is barely present, if at all, in the biblical text. So, too, the hiring or lease of parcels of land might also have been expected, for it was certainly practiced in these ancient agricultural societies. The law describes a situation, where a man has contracted with another person to cultivate his field;

but then, through negligence, that person fails to carry out his contractual obligation. The law deals with how to calculate the loss sustained sustained by the owner (lessor) due to the action of his non-performing tenant (lessee).

A law on negligence in an agricultural lease is found in the Mishnah, *m. B. Metz.* 9:3:

> (If) a man leased a field from his neighbor (as a share-cropper) and then let it lie fallow, they (the judges) should estimate how much it was likely to yield, and he (the negligent lessee) must give to him (i.e., the owner according to that calculation), because (in a lease likes this one) the lessee customarily stipulated: "If I let (the field) lie fallow and do not work it, I will pay (compensation) according to its best (yield)."

The Mishnah here takes its language from customary agreements of the day, which incorporated a provision setting compensation in case of default according to the best historic yield of the field in question. Of course, if the lessee performed his contract as he had promised, then he would deliver the agreed-upon share based upon that year's actual yield. The historic yield would only be invoked in case of negligence.

We find an expanded version of this law in the Tosefta, *t. B. Metz.* 9:12, Lieberman:

> (If) a man leased a field (as a share-cropper) from his neighbor (and) after taking it over, let it lie fallow, they (the judges) should estimate how much it was likely to yield and he (the lessee) shall pay (that value) to him (the owner). They should not, however, estimate the

---

10. According to the Talmud, a two-fold payment was no longer exacted for theft in Roman times and never applied in Babylonia; cf. *b. Sanh.* 13b–14a, 31b, *b. Avod. Zar.* 8b. Later rabbinic law did not require one who stole land to recompense the owner for loss of use; however, the thief was required to pay for consuming the existing crops on the stolen land; see Gulak, *Foundations of Jewish Law*, 2:223–24 §100, citing medieval authorities.

field according to (the yield of) the fields next to it; perhaps one was thoroughly plowed and the other was not; or one was manured and the other not; one's (soil) was exceptionally improved by tilling and the other's not. Rather, they should estimate according to what the field itself was likely to yield and compensate him accordingly since (in such leases as this) the lessee customarily stipulated: 'If I let (the field) lie fallow and do not work it, I will pay (compensation) according to its best (yield).

The Tosefta here affirms the practice—in case of default by the lessee—of looking to the historic yield of the field and states that it represents a better method of calculation than looking at the yields in neighboring fields. They argue that it was possible for a neighbor to have enhanced the yield of his field by putting in extra effort and expense. In order to avoid a distorted result, the historic range of yields coming from the field itself over time was seen as more fair. One can therefore assume that farmers would have a good recollection of the yields of their own and neighboring fields during past years; and it was therefore possible to establish "the best yield."

When we look at the ancient Near Eastern laws, we also find laws dealing with negligence in agricultural leases and we see that the method of calculation rejected by the Tosefta was in fact one of the penalty calculations used in Hammurapi Laws §§43–44:

§43 If he (the share-cropping tenant) did not cultivate the field and has left it fallow, he shall pay grain to the owner of the field corresponding to (the yields) of his

neighbors, and he shall (also) plow [var. plow, hoe] (and) harrow the field that he left fallow and (so) return it to the owner of the field.

§44 If a man leased a parcel of (previously) untilled land for three years in order to open it (for cultivation) but has been slack and has not opened the field, in the fourth year he must plow, hoe, and harrow the field and return it to the owner of the field (in this condition) and measure out 10 kors grain per *bur*.

These laws treat previously worked land differently from new land, which is being put into cultivation for the first time. The latter situation was a special type of lease, where the lessee cultivator was not expected to produce any crops for the owner until after a period of years, when the field could become established and its productivity more predictable. That is why the lessee, although negligent throughout the time, has only to pay for the fourth year, when a properly worked new field was expected to become productive. Henceforth, it would be considered like any other previously cultivated field.

This same distinction and similar terms were applied in lease agreements for date orchards in Hammurapi Laws §§62–63:

§62 If he (the share-cropping lessee) did not plant the field which was given to him as a date orchard—if it is cultivated land, the gardener shall measure out to the owner of the field the yield of the field for the years he left it fallow (in amounts) corresponding to that of his neighbors (yields); moreover he shall do the (necessary) work on that field and he shall (thus) return it to the owner of the field.

§63 If it is (a previously) untilled parcel of land, he (i.e., the gardener) shall do the necessary work on that field and return it to the owner of the field and he shall measure out for each year 10 kors per *bur*.

We therefore see two methods used to calculate the penalty for negligence: neighbors' yields for cultivated fields but a fixed payment in produce for land not yet cultivated.

The two methods of calculating the penalty for negligence found in Hammurapi Laws are also found in the in Old Babylonian lease agreements. Moreover, a method similar to the one used in the Mishnah and Tosefta—looking at the crop history of the field in question— also occurs. For example: "(If) he (the sharecropping lessee) leaves the field fallow, he shall measure out the yield of that field." Or, "(If) he (the lessee) leaves the field fallow, he will measure out (grain) according to the yield of a furrowed field."[11]

In Hammurapi Laws, the tenant is obligated to pay compensation as well as to prepare the field for the next year's planting. The obligation of the tenant to plow and harrow the field should not be seen as an additional penalty. This obligation is in fact often expressly stated in actual Old Babylonian lease agreements; it is part of the labors expected from the lessee at the conclusion of a lease.[12] These "extra duties"—along with some extra benefits— are also recognized in the Mishnah, *m. B. Metz.* 9:1:

(If) one leased a field from his fellow—in a place where it was customary (for the lessee) to reap the harvest, he should reap; to uproot (the roots), he should uproot; to plow after him, he should plow. All of these (measures) should follow the custom of the region. (In addition) just as they (the owner and his lessee) share the yield (in the proportions as agreed), they similarly share in the straw and the stubble. Just as (in a vineyard) they share the wine, so they share in the prunings and in the props (supporting the vines); but both must (then also share in) supplying (the props).

The various Old Babylonian negligence penalties emerge out of the different ways in which the lease agreements could be structured. Leases could be arranged for a proportional share— e.g., a third or a half—in the harvest, for a fixed payment of grain or commodities per unit of land, or, for a sum of money or commodities, although that type of lease was much less common. There also are some lease agreements where the payment of the lessee—e.g., a third or half share—would be calculated according to the yields of neighboring fields.[13] This calculation corresponds to the negligence penalty in Hammurapi Laws §43 and §62, which seems to have functioned as the default penalty for previously cultivated land, if no other penalty was stipulated in advance. The fixed penalty of 10 kors per *bur*

11. For Old Babylonian examples, see Mauer, "Das Formular der altbabylonischen Bodenpachtverträge," 138–39; and discussion in Greengus, "Filling Gaps," 156–59.

12. See the discussion and passages collected by in Mauer, "Das Formular der altbabylonischen Bodenpachtverträge," 122–28.

13. The various types are discussed in Mauer, "Das Formular der altbabylonischen Bodenpachtverträge," 105–13. Cf. also the earlier discussion of Driver and Miles, *The Babylonian Laws,* 1:127–136. Sharecropping contracts for one-half or one-third of the harvest appear to be fairly typical arrangements according to Hammurapi Laws §§45–46, which are discussed in sec. 6.3.

in Hammurapi Laws §44 and §63 emerges out of lease agreement for fixed payments of grain, and appears to have been the default penalty for neglect in a lease for previously untilled land. The penalty of 10 kors per *bur*, in modern terms, equals approximately 463 liters per hectare or 5.35 bushels per acre.[14] But this amount did not represent the full, expected yield of such fields; it too represents a "share", which, at least for the gardener in one of the Hammurapi Laws, was estimated at one-half the yield.[15] In Old Babylonian field lease agreements for grain, we find varying payment arrangements, ranging from 6 to 18 kors per *bur*; this would represent a range from approximately 3.3 to 10 bushels per acre.[16] But we are not informed about the share to be retained by the lessee cultivator; such payments, if representing, e.g., one-third to one-half of the harvest, would suggest a total harvest in the range of 10 to 30 bushels per acre (see further below). The expectation of a total harvest yield of 60 kors per *bur* for the region is specifically stated in two Old Babylonian letters; this would translate to as much as 32 bushels per acre.[17] This

could only be an optimal figure, for actual yield would also depend upon the quality of the soil, water supply, as well upon expenses and other variables and events.[18]

When one looks deeper into rabbinic sources, one likewise finds evidence for a variety of lease arrangements, which are similar to what we see the Old Babylonian period leases. A passage in the Jerusalem Talmud, *j. Demai* 25a, enumerates the variety: "one who leases for (a fixed quantity of) commodities, one who rents for (a fixed payment of) money, one who leases for a half, a third, or a fourth (share of the harvest yield) . . ." Moreover, in the (Babylonian) Talmud, *b. B. Metz.* 104a, R. Papa specifically says that the law in the Mishnah cited above (*m. B. Metz.* 9:3) applies for lease agreements for a share of the harvest yield but not for lease agreements made for fixed amounts or commodities or money.[19] In such instances, the penalty for negligence should be for a fixed amount; that is similar to the view taken by R. Judah in the Mishnah, *m. B. Metz.* 9:6, which is cited in sec. 6.3 below. Some of the rabbis living later in Babylonia, however, looked for ways to ease the severity of fixed payment penalties. The Talmud, *b. B. Metz.* 104b, relates a case where a lessee had stipulated: "If I let (the field) fallow, I will pay you one thousand *zuz*." A group of scholars from the academy of Nehardea said that he must pay, in accordance with R. Judah's rule. But Raba argued that this sum was so exorbitant that

---

14. For these units, cf. Powell, " Masse und Gewichte," 480, 497 and further below.

15. This is the arrangement according to Hammurapi Laws §60, which is the first of the series of laws dealing with date orchards. The law is not cited in our text. For a new date orchard, the preparatory period was four years, with produce being divided equally in year five, In the orchard laws, §§62–63, the gardener must pay for every year during which he was negligent, unlike the farmer in §§43–44, who pays only for the final year of his lease.

16. For specific examples, see Driver and Miles, *Babylonia Laws,* 1:132–33; Mauer, "Das Formular der altbabylonischen Bodenpachtverträge," 108–12.

17. *AbB* 3 38:23, 81:20. This same ratio also appears in Hammurapi Laws §58 (sec. 6.4) and §255

(not cited in this study) and appears to represent the total crop.

18. Cf. Powell, "Salt, Seed, and Yields in Sumerian Agriculture," 25–36.

19. Cf. Rashi *ad. loc.* See further *t. Demai* 6:2, Lieberman, and Maimonides, *Mishnah Torah, Hilkhot Skhirut* 8:1.

one could doubt its serious intent; and one might therefore more readily invoke in its place the penalty of "best yield" expressed in the Mishnah, which, in this situation, would be a lesser amount.[20] In Raba's view, the penalty of "best yield" could be invoked as a default measure, in a manner similar to how "neighbors' yields" seems to have functioned as a default penalty in Hammurapi Laws §43 and §62.

Our earliest ancient Near Eastern law on negligence in a lease agreement mandates a fixed penalty of grain; that is what we see in Urnamma Laws §32:

> If a man gave to (another) man an arable field[21] for cultivation (and) he (the tenant) did not cultivate it (and) made it a wasteland he shall measure out (for the owner) 3 kors of barley for each *iku* of field.

The quantity of grain paid by the tenant appears to exceed what might normally have been the share of the yield expected by the owner in a lease agreement. Because, according to data collected and analyzed by a number of scholars, yields of barley in the century long Ur III period ranged from .87 to 2.8 kors per *iku*. From earlier periods, there is evidence of even higher yields, in the range of 3–4 kors per *iku*.[22] The payment of 3 kors per *iku* is the equivalent of approximately 28 bushel per acre.[23] This payment therefore would fall

at the high end of the 10 to 30 bushels per acre total harvests that we estimated in the Old Babylonian period documents. The tenant in Urnamma Laws §32 is thus apparently being held responsible for the loss of the entire harvest, because the amount of his fixed amount penalty leans toward the higher end of harvest expectations. Why was he so severely penalized? Perhaps because he not only failed to cultivate the field as in Hammurapi Laws §44, but also somehow damaged the land and left it in a desolate and ruined condition that would necessitate more than the usual amount of work to repair and restore for future cultivation.[24] In a curious fashion, this fixed amount penalty—and perhaps also the "higher end" 30 bushels of the Old Babylonian period— could be viewed as supplying a conceptual foundation for the "best yield" metric that we find in the later Mishnah and Tosefta. We will encounter the metric of "best yield"

20. Cf. Maimonides, *Mishnah Torah, Hilkhot Skhirut* 8:13; he accepts the position taken by Raba in this case.

21. For translation of this term see Greengus, "Filling Gaps: Laws Found in Babylonia and in the Mishna But Absent in the Hebrew Bible," 156 n. 15.

22. See Jacobsen, *Salinity and Irrigation in Antiquity*, 40–42 and the critique of Powell, "Salt, Seed, and Yields in Sumerian Agriculture."

23. The *iku* is estimated at .36 hectare and the kor (gur) at 300 liters according to Powell, " Masse

und Gewichte," 480. The payment here thus corresponds to approximately 900 liters per *iku*, which comes to about 28 bushels per acre. This would be considered a decent yield for wheat or barley—the two main cereal crops grown in Mesopotamia— even in recent times in North America. According to data from the United States Dept. of Agriculture Economic Research Service, wheat production in the United States from 1900–1950 ranged from 12 to 20 bushels per acre and barley from 18 to 38 bushels per acre. Cf. USDA ERS, "Wheat Data: Yearbook Tables," Table 1 and USDA ERS, "Feed Grains Data: Yearbook Tables, Table 1. (These tables provide historical yields data from 1866 to 2011.) Driver and Miles, *Babylonian Laws*, 1:34–35, report on twentieth-century yields in Iraq, Egypt, and England, ranging from 15 to 33 bushels per acre."

24. Finkelstein, "The Laws of Urnammu," 81 raises this same question and suggests an answer along the lines given here. For the term "wasteland" see lexical passages cited in *CAD* H, 247b sub *hurbū* and *CAD* M/2, 21–22 sub *mērênu*.

again in sec. 6.4, which deal with animal trespass and grazing.

6.3 AGRICULTURAL LEASE AND NATURAL DISASTER

Another recurring problem in agricultural leases was that of unexpected natural disasters, which diminished the expected yield and profit for both the owner and the tenant. These disasters, understandably, were viewed as mitigating factors, requiring adjustment of the original agreement. Laws addressing mitigation are found in the ancient Near East and in rabbinic sources but here, again are "missing" in the Bible.

The Mishnah, *m. B. Metz.* 9:6, addresses cases of natural disaster:

> (In a case where) one leased a field from his neighbor and locusts devoured it(s crop) or if (the crop) were withered (by blight or heat), if the (disaster) was suffered by the entire region, one shall deduct the loss from his agreed rental. If (however) the (disaster) was not suffered by the entire region, one shall not deduct the loss from his agreed rental. Rabbi Judah said: if he had leased for a fixed sum of money, one shall not deduct the loss in either case.

In sec. 6.2 we noted that there were, basically, three modes of lease arrangements: for a share of the harvest; for a fixed amount of produce; or for a fixed sum of money. Mishnah *B. Metz.* 9:6 does not address the situation where the lease agreement was for a share of produce but focuses rather upon lease arrangements for a fixed amount of produce or money. That is because in the situation of leasing for a share of the harvest—e.g., one-half or one-third—the loss would have to be shared both by owner and tenant since both parties hold only a contingent interest. Rashi in his commentary on the discussion of our Mishnah in the Talmud, *b. B. Metz.* 105b, states this clearly: "(This case) can only be one of lease for a fixed amount because if it were for a share, then how can one deduct? They (i.e., the tenant and owner) must share whatever (produce) exists."

In the first statement, the Mishnah makes a distinction between localized or generalized disasters. In the situation, where a disaster was widespread, one cannot blame the cultivator for this loss; and the Mishnah therefore rules that relief should be forthcoming. However, R. Judah, in the second part of the Mishnah, makes a further distinction between a fixed sum of money and a fixed amount of produce. If the rental was for a fixed sum of money, then the obligation should be looked at like any other monetary debt; and the full burden of the disaster should fall solely upon the tenant. This should be true whether the disaster was limited or regional.

Some of the later rabbis, however, wanted to be more lenient. The Talmud in *b. B. Metz.* 106b records the later abandonment of R. Judah's position, which is recounted in a narrative:

> A certain man, to grow garlic, leased land (for a money rental) located on the bank of the "Old Royal Canal" and it became damned up. He came before Raba, and Raba ruled: "It is not usual for the "Old Royal Canal" be become dammed up; this is a widespread disaster; go and deduct for it." The (other) rabbis protested to Raba: "Did we not learn (in the Mishnah) where

Rabbi Judah said 'If he leased it for a fixed sum of money, in either case he cannot deduct for it from his rental'?" He (i.e., Raba) said to them: "No one pays heed to (the ruling of) Rabbi Judah."[25]

A provision dealing with natural disasters[26] and agricultural leases is found in Hammurapi Laws §§45–46:

> If a man has given his field to a cultivator for rent and has already received the rent for that field. Later, Adad (i.e., the storm-god) has inundated the field or a flood has carried away (the crops), the loss belongs only to the cultivator. If he (the owner) has not yet received the rent for his field or if he rented it for a half share (of the crop) or for a third, the owner of the field and the cultivator according to their agreed proportions shall divide whatever grain be available in that field.

This law is interesting in a number of respects. First is the issue of payment received; once been received by the owner, the deal is essentially done or at least "on the way," as far as the owner is concerned. It made no difference whether the fixed amount was of produce or money. Once paid, the risk now belonged to the lessee cultivator.[27] While this type of lease arrangement was less frequently used than those for a share of the produce, it is found in some Old Babylonian contracts, usually with payments of silver, but payments in commodities are also attested. Sometimes there was a partial payment at the time when the contract was made; one may perhaps assume from the wording of the law that any unpaid portion would be subsumed in the post-disaster settlement between the parties. There is, moreover, at least one lease agreement attested where no payment was made; however the owner, who leased the field stipulated: "he will not recognize (for the purposes of this lease agreement losses due to) flood, downpour, costs of irrigation, or (other) expenses (incurred in cultivating) the field."[28] This agreement therefore would not be subject to any later adjustment.

In the Mishnah, there is nothing said about whether the owner, who leased for money, had already received his money in advance. Rabbi Judah's statement seems to imply absolute liability on the part of the lessee cultivator; and it was so understood by the later rabbis, who chose to set aside his ruling. Reasons underlying R. Judah's position are not given; Rashi and other medieval commentators suggest that he would maintain that, since the produce of the field was not yet in existence; produce payments were therefore still subject to the hazards of nature. But a determined sum of money, like the price in a sale, should be a fully settled and stable amount.

25. Maimonides in his commentary on the Mishnah supports Raba's rejection of Rabbi Judah's position and argues against making any distinction between an agreement for produce and one for money.

26. There is difference, of course, in the character of the natural disasters described in the ancient sources. In agriculture dependent upon rainfall, like Palestine, the environmental problems were different from those of the arid but irrigated farms in Babylonia, where uncontrolled waters could wreak havoc. But the legal issue is the same.

27. This is how Hammurapi Laws §§45–46 is understood by Stol, "Pacht. B. Altbabylonisch," 171. For more discussion see Greengus, "Filling Gaps," 159–61.

28. Mauer, "Das Formular der altbabylonischen Bodenpachtverträge," 119–21, 140–41. The document with the disclaimer is UET 5 212, partly cited in *CAD* M/1, 204–5.

6.4 TRESPASS AND GRAZING

The Bible in Exod 22:4 addresses a situation where the owner of an animal has allowed his beast to enter another person's property and graze upon that person's crops. The law is as follows:

> If a man allows (his own) field or vineyard to be grazed over, and (then) lets his beast loose and it grazed in someone else's field, he shall pay the best of his field or vineyard.[29]

We previously encountered a reference to the "best (yield)" of a field in connection with the rabbinic laws dealing with the cultivator who leased a field but then neglected to cultivate it as agreed (sec. 6.2). The focus in our laws is on the loss sustained by the owner of the field and how to give him full value for his loss. The "best of his field" in Exod 22:4 can thus be understood to mean that the amount of compensation is to be computed according to the "best yield" of the damaged field or vineyard. This is in fact how medieval commentators like Rashbam and Hazzequni explain our law.[30]

But for unexplained reasons, some of the rabbis in talmudic times disputed the source of the compensation paid in the verse. Rabbi Ishmael, to be sure, affirmed what seems to be the plain meaning of the verse; he states that compensation is figured according to the best yield of the damaged field. But R. Akiba, took a different direction, as recorded in a *baraita* that is cited and discussed in *b. Git.* 48b–49a (and also in *b. B. Qam.* 6b):

> As it has been taught: "The best of his field and the best of his vineyard he shall pay": [that is to say,] the best of the field of the injured party and the best of the vineyard of the injured party. So (states) Rabbi Ishmael. (However) Rabbi Akiba said: The whole purpose of the text is to allow compensation for damage to be recovered from the best (quality) property [of the animal owner] . . .[31]

Both text readings are then defended in the Gemara that follows:

> What is Rabbi Ishmael's reason? The word "field" occurs both in the first and the second clause (of Exod 22:4); just as in the earlier clause it refers to the field of the claimant (i.e., the injured party), so in the latter it must (also) refer to the field of the claimant. Rabbi Akiba, on the other hand, held that the words, "from the best of his field he shall pay" means, from the best (quality property) belonging to the person who makes restitution.

Rabbi Ishmael's position—looking to the best yield of the damaged field— represents the method of compensation that we know from agricultural leases; it is a method attested in *t. B. Metz.* 9:12 (cited above in sec. 6.2) and in contracts going

---

29. We see a sequence of two actions here: first in the owner's field, second in a neighbor's property; this same sequence occurs in the next verse, Exod 22:5, in his causing a fire (sec. 6.5). Cf. the commentary Sforno on Exod 22:4; see also Houtman, *Exodus*, 3:192–93; Jackson, *Wisdom Laws*, 323.

30. This view is presented also by Bekhor Shor.

31. In *j. Gitt.* 46c one encounters a textual tradition where the positions of R. Ishmael and R. Akiba are reversed. Yet the discussion there then supplies a rationale how damages nevertheless came to be assessed upon the animal owner from his best fields through a rabbinic edict, i.e., independently from Scripture, by R. Akiba! For a discussion of the rabbinic passages see Urbach, *The Halachah: Its Sources and Development*, 111–13.

back to Old Babylonian times. But Rabbi Akiba's position, interestingly, also represents an ancient method of compensation that in fact is found in Hittite Laws. Hittite Laws §106 is a somewhat similar case, when one person caused a fire in his neighbor's field; the party causing the damage replaces the damaged field with crops from his own, best field. Hittite Laws §106 is as follows:

> If anyone carries embers (lit. fire) into his field and lets [it] get away (into his neighbor's field) and ignites a fruit-bearing field, he who ignites it shall himself take the burnt-over field. He shall give a good field to the owner of the (burnt-over field) and he will reap it.

I cite this law here only to illustrate a method of calculation similar to that or R. Abiba's. I will discuss the substance of this law in sec. 6.5, when we look at the wider topic of damage caused by fire. But we must here also note that Hittite Laws §107, which deals with animal trespass and grazing (discussed below in the present section) imposes a fixed penalty of money upon the person causing the damage.

Rabbi Akiba's view of compensation is also supported by a variant textual version of Exod 22:4 found in Greek and Samaritan versions of the Pentateuch and also in an ancient manuscript of Exodus found among the Dead Sea Scrolls. The variant text is an expanded version; what is one case in our "standard" or Masoretic Text of Exod 22:4 is there presented as two cases, differentiated as follows (with the "extra words" in italics):

> [If someone lets his field or vineyard to be grazed over, and then]

> lets [his] beast loose [and it grazes in another man's field, *he shall make compensation from his own field according to its produce, but if the] whole [field is grazed over*, he shall make restitution from the best of his own field and from the best of his own vineyard.][32]

This variant version of Exod 22:4 contains two cases: one of partial loss and one of total loss. In both situations, the basis of calculation appears to be the field of the party who caused the damage. This variant version in fact supports the exegesis of R. Akiba insofar as "the best" focuses upon the party causing the damage, rather than upon the property of the party suffering the loss.

The rabbis of talmudic times—as far as we know—utilized the Masoretic Text and retained no record of the variant text, or of the distinction made between partial and total loss. So one may doubt whether they knew this textual variant. And yet, curiously, they affirmed the position of R. Akiba over R. Ishmael, who follows the plain meaning of the massoretic version of Exod 22:4! But the rabbis fail to explain why they preferred to follow R. Akiba, who restricted the application of Exod 22:4 to a facet of the case, which is not really the focus of that text at all. Rabbi Akiba restricts the purview of the case to a situation where the person responsible for the damage (i.e., the animal owner) had no ready assets and was forced to sell

32. The text and variant follows *The Dead Sea Scrolls Bible: The Oldest Known Bible Translated for the First Time into English*, 54. The text, 4Q22 (paleoExod^m), is not fully preserved; but enough is present to show that it follows LXX and the Samaritan Pentateuch. See Sanderson, *An Exodus Scroll from Qumran*, 76–77. Cf. also for general discussion of issues Jackson, *Wisdom Laws*, 324–27.

some of his land in order to pay the compensation that he owed for the incursion of his beast. If the animal owner's land must to be sold in order to raise funds, then the best of his fields are to be sold first. The talmudic rabbis thus used Exod 22:4 as textual support for *m. Git.* 5:1, which states their ruling: "Those who suffer damages, their compensation must be paid out of land of the best quality."[33]

But the rabbis then further refined R. Akiba's position, maintaining that if the animal owner had assets in addition to his land, then he could first sell these other assets and pay the owner of the field out of them. Money, they say is "best" because it is portable and the field owner is happy to receive this form of payment. In *b. B. Qam.* 7b we read:

> When Rabbi Papa and Rabbi Huna son of Rabbi Joshua arrived from the house of study, they explained (the meaning of Exod 22:4) thusly: "All manner (of movables) are considered 'best' for if they cannot be sold here they could be sold in other town; it is only in the case of land for which payment has to be made from 'the best' so the purchaser will 'jump' at it."

The rabbis thus effectively abandoned the ancient biblical concept of "the best of the field" as a basis for calculating compensation for damages caused by grazing or other trespass. The later rabbinic position is followed and neatly summarized in the medieval code of R. Joseph Karo:

> When the court is required to assist the party suffering damage to collect for damage from the party causing the damage, they collect first from (his) movable property; and if he has no movables or they are insufficient to cover all of the damage, they collect the balance from the best land in the possession of the party causing the damage. Moreover, as long as there are movables available—even bran flour, they do not attach land; and even if (the party causing the damage) possesses money, he can still pay (for his damage) in bran because all movables are described as 'the best.'[34]

Why did the later rabbis so completely reshape the original intent of the biblical case in Exod 22:4? Why did they not retain the principle of "the best of the field" in the calculation of compensation as they do in the case of agricultural lease? I do not know for certain but I can suggest a number of possible reasons. First may be the fact that in the very next verse, Exod 22:5, a case where the crops are damaged by fire (discussed below in sec. 6.5), the party causing the damage pays only for what has been destroyed; there is no mention of "the best of the field." The rabbis may have seen no reason why the owner of the grazing animal should pay more than the neighbor causing the fire. Second, they may have been persuaded by the wisdom of the Roman law of their own time, according to which, redress for all delicts (damage or harm)

---

33. Bekhor Shor reconstructs a possible hermeneutic involving Exod 22:4, based upon the repeated use of particular terms: "pay, give, silver, in place of." These occur in various laws dealing with damages—e.g., here in Exod 22:4 and the ox laws discussed in sec. 4.10. The rabbis could then have extrapolated features from one law to the other—with the result that one may conclude that all damages may be compensated by payment.

34. Joseph Karo, *Shulkan Arukh, Khoshen Mishpat* 419.1.

was monetary.[35] The rabbis seem to have viewed the case of Exod 22:4 as delictal, i.e., an active doing of harm, and therefore to be differently treated from the cases of passive neglect or failure to act, as in the laws of agricultural lease. Third, may have been their desire to keep this monetary compensation fair. There was to be no overtone of penalty; therefore they did not base compensation on the best yield of the property of the animal owner who caused the damage, but rather upon what was actually lost in the field damaged by trespass. Even when requiring the person causing damage to sell "the best of his field or vineyard," the damages were paid in an amount equal to but not exceeding the actual loss. Moreover, if a situation were to arise where penalties were to be added, these were calculated in a way that did need not be symmetrical with the losses sustained. The penalties were punitive in nature and were usually set in a sum fixed by law or else by judges.[36] For the rabbis, Exod 22:4 was to be viewed as a case involving only compensation; and for them, compensation needed to be both monetary and symmetrical with the losses.

Turning now to the ancient Near East, we also find laws on trespass and grazing. Hammurapi Laws §§57–58 deal with a shepherd, who has allowed his animals to graze in a field without permission of its owner:

> §57 If a shepherd has not made an agreement with the owner of a field for grazing on the herbage and has let the sheep graze without (the consent of) the owner, the field owner shall harvest (the plants or fodder remaining in) his field; the shepherd who let the sheep graze without permission shall pay in addition twenty kors grain per *bur* to the owner.

> §58 If after the sheep have left the irrigated cropland at the close of the (open) grazing season (lit. after the "banner of completion" was hung out at the city gate), a shepherd allowed his sheep into a field and to graze, the shepherd who allowed his sheep to graze must (henceforth himself) watch over the field and at harvest must deliver 60 kors of grain per *bur* to the owner.

Both laws involve trespass into fields of still growing plants and allowing sheep or goats to graze without permission of the field owner. After the harvest, it was customary for field owners to invite flocks to graze on the straw and stubble. The animals would leave their droppings on the fields; these would become fertilizer for the next growing season. During the months between harvest and planting, animals were apparently allowed to graze at will on whatever was left or might have grown on its own.

The shepherd in §57 however loosed his flock upon the field without the owner's consent. The damage may have taken place late in the growing season, nearer to or possibly during the harvest time, since

---

35. Thomas, *Textbook of Roman Law,* 349–51. He states there that since earliest times, Roman law had included a case similar to Exod 22:4, "the *actio de pastu pectoris*, which lay against the owner of an animal which grazed on another's land and required him to make good the value or hand over the beast . . ." This ancient law is mentioned in *D.*19.5.14.3. Warmington, *Remains of Old Latin,* 478–79, places it as *XII Tables* 8.6.

36. On the rabbinic categories of damage and penalty, see the discussion of Gulak, *Foundations of Jewish Law,* 2:14–16 (§7). His analysis emerges out of various passages, e.g., *b. B. Qam.* 15a, *b. Ket.* 40b, 46b, *b. Qidd.* 3b.

§57 describes the existence of some residual, harvestable plantings. The penalty paid by the shepherd is twice that of the negligent leaseholder discussed in sec. 6.2 or approximately 10.7 bushels per acre. In sec. 6.2, we also noted a range of harvests from 10 to 30 bushels per acre during the Old Babylonian period. The penalty in §57 thus appears to be moderate.

The damage in §58 appears to be more serious, in view of the higher compensation. The shepherd's penalty there, following the calculations given in sec. 6.2, represents approximately 32 bushels per acre. This is evidently a situation, which threatened total loss of the harvest, since it deals with a field in which grain was recently sown and the community officially closed the "open grazing season". It was the worst time for animals to enter and graze. The shepherd must pay in full and is charged in addition to protect whatever limited amount of grain might yet grow. In the contrast between §57 and §58, we seem to have an "echo" of the distinction between partial and full loss found in the variant biblical text of Exod 22:4 discussed above. The amounts paid by the shepherd in each of the two situations do not appear to be overly punitive in nature.

A law on animal trespass is also found in the Hittite Laws. Hittite Laws §107 states the following:

> If a person lets (his) sheep into a productive vineyard, and ruins it, if it is in fruit, he shall pay 10 shekels silver per *iku* (vars. add: He shall look to his house for it). But if it is bare [i.e., already harvested], he shall pay 3 (var. 5) shekels silver.

The situation is similar to that seen in Hammurapi Laws §§57–58 in that compensation will vary according to what plantings are or are not in the field. But we do not have sufficient data outside of the Hittite laws to know the relative values of the compensation rates, in other words, whether they included penalties, in addition to compensation. One could perhaps interpret the payment of 3 shekels per *iku* for entering a "bare" field as a penalty. On the other hand, the payment there may be for damage done to the vines through trampling. This kind of damage by animals is also considered by the rabbis in their interpretation of the scope of the law in Exod 22:4.[37]

Neo-Babylonian Laws §2 also contain a law on animal trespass but sets compensation according to the yield of neighboring fields rather than by fixed amounts or "the best" of its own yield. The ancient text is badly damaged but enough is present to see the situation:

> [(In the case of) a man who . . .] sheep? [into] a field and [. . .] they grazed [. . .]they grazed [. . .] his testimony [which he will pro]vide [about [. . .] grazing of the field, [grain] according to (the yield) of the neighbors [to] the owner of the field he shall pay [. . . as much as] he grazed [in the f]ield [accord]ing to (the yield) of his neighbors he shall pay grain.

We have already encountered this method of calculating damages in the case of the negligent cultivator (sec. 6.2). It was one of the methods of calculating compensation that were used during the centuries. Since it is based upon actual yields, the compensation here seems to straightforward, without any additional penalty.

37. Cf. Rashi on Exod. 22:4 and *b. B. Qam.* 2b–3a.

6.5 DAMAGE TO FIELD
AND CROPS BY FIRE

Following upon animal trespass in Exod 22:4 is the case of a person who starts a fire on his own property, with the unfortunate result that the fire spreads to his neighbor's property and causes damage to the neighbor's crops. This situation is described in Exod 22:5:

> If fire escapes (into a neighbor's field) and catches upon thorns, and then the sheaves or standing grain or the field (itself) is consumed, the one who started the fire shall surely pay (for the damage).

This case and the case of animal trespass were anciently linked and considered together in pre-biblical times, as we can see if we look at parallel cases in the Hittite laws. The biblical cases are in fact so closely linked that Exod 22:5 omits stating that the damage took place in a field belonging to a neighboring property owner; that information is present in Exod 22:4.

Our parallel case is Hittite Laws §106, which precedes the case of animal trespass and grazing described in Hittite Laws §107 (sec. 6.4). It is interesting to note that Hittite Laws §106 and §107 are in reverse order from that of the cases in Exod 22:4–5, but show the ancient, close linkage of the topics. Hittite Laws §106 deals with damage by fire:

> If anyone carries embers (lit. fire) into his field and lets [it] get away (into his neighbor's field) and ignites a fruit-bearing field, he who ignites it shall himself take the burnt-over field. He shall give a good field to the owner of the (burnt-over field) and he will reap it.

§106 echoes the language of Exod 22:4 in requiring the fire starter to give "a good field," apparently one of his own, to the owner of the damaged field. The method of compensation used in §106 was discussed in sec. 6.4, in connection with R. Akiba's interpretation of Exod 22:4. In conformity with Hittite Laws §106, R. Akiba understood the biblical verse there to mean that the person causing the damage was required to replace the damaged field with one of his own "best fields or vineyards." There is no reference to "best field" in Exod 22:5 but the same legal response would apply.

The biblical case of Exod 22:5 is restated in the Mishnah, *m. B. Qam.* 6:4, in order to give clarification to what might be meant by "or the field (itself) is consumed":

> If he allowed fire to escape and it burnt wood, stones, or (even) earth, he is liable, as it says "If fire escapes (into a neighbor's field) and catches upon thorns, and then the sheaves or standing grain or the field (itself) is consumed, the one who started the fire shall surely pay (for the damage)."

This Mishnah thus explains the "field (itself)" as scorched earth.

The Gemara on this Mishnah (*b. B. Qam.* 60a) suggests, alternatively, that the fire somehow disturbed the furrows or affected the stones in the field, rendering them brittle.[38] In its discussion, the Gemara also brings forward another comment contained in this same Mishnah which is interesting, in that employs an image found in Hittite Laws §106, namely the

---

38. Cf. the comments of Rashi, Rashbam, and Hazzequni to our verse.

carrying of coals or embers into the field. This is stated in Mishnah, *m. B. Qam.* 6:4:

> If a man sent out something burning in the hands of a deaf mute, an idiot, or a minor (and the fire came to damage another's property), he would be exempt from the judgments of man, but liable in the judgments of Heaven.

The transmission of fire by using coals, embers, or a torch was, of course, common and widespread. I cite this passage only to show the persistence of the image in legal tradition and discussions.

But it is also interesting to note that this Mishnah raises the issue of a parent, master, or guardian taking responsibility for actions done by those under his authority or sway, who lacked full legal capacity or mature moral judgment. The Mishnah asserts that the parent or guardian could not be held legally responsible. In some way this is surprising, given the liability of owners for damages committed by their dumb animals. But see my earlier discussion about the positions taken by the Pharisees and Sadducees with respect to damages willfully caused by slaves (sec. 5.6.2). Evidently, the contrast between human levels of human intelligence—even if impaired—and animal intelligence was deemed to be a decisive factor.

6.6 SOWING TWO SPECIES IN THE SAME FIELD

The Bible contains laws prohibiting creating certain mixtures of plants and combinations of animals, as well as the products derived from them; there was a belief that these "mixings" would render the "new" product unfit for normal use. Leviticus 19:19 states:

> You shall observe my statutes. You shall not let your cattle mate with a different kind; you shall not sow your field[39] (with) two kinds of seed; you shall not put on cloth from a mixture of two kinds of material.

No reason is given for these prohibition here; but some additional details are found in the restatement of Deut 22:9–11:

> You shall not sow your vineyard (with) two kinds of seed, lest the total crop—the seed you have sown and the yield of the vineyard—be sanctified (i.e., forbidden for ordinary use).
>
> You shall not plow with an ox and an ass together.
>
> You shall not wear (cloth) combining wool and linen together.

The above laws clearly belong to the sphere of religious practices and—as presented in the Bible—do not involve a social or commercial interaction with other human parties. They affect personal behavior and do not involve a second individual. It is therefore a challenge to discover a rationale behind such rules. Indeed, one rabbinic tradition maintains that these biblical "statutes" defy reason and can only be observed out of respect for the Deity.[40]

But explanations have nevertheless been attempted. Philo explained the prohibition against mating of diverse species as transgressing the ordinances of nature, since the two species are by nature incapable of fruitful union. The prohibition against dual planting will exhaust the

---

39. The Septuagint here reads "vineyard" like in the passage in Deut 22:9.

40. Cf. the comment of Rashi on Lev 19:19, based upon *b. Yoma* 67b.

generative powers of the land by forcing it to yield two crops over a longer season of growth. The prohibition against mixed fibers would result in a weakened fabric that is more ready to tear than to unite. And, finally, the prohibition against yoking different animals together places a cruel burden upon the weaker of the two.[41] The rabbis essentially offer variations on the ideas presented in Philo. They also address these laws in more detail and seek to establish parameters relating to their observance.[42] A modern commentator suggests that, in the biblical view, holiness required that the categories of creation were to be kept distinct from one another and that hybrids were to be avoided.[43]

While the prohibition against planting two species deals with a religious matter, this particular law comes into our focus for the present study, because unexpectedly we find a law on this same subject of mixed planting in Hittite Laws §§166–167:

> If anyone sows (his own) seed on top of (another man's) seed, they shall place his neck on a plow. They shall hitch up [tw]o teams of oxen; they shall turn the face of one in one direction and of the other in the other direction. The man will be put to death, and the oxen will be put to death. The party who first sowed the seed shall reap (var. take) it for himself. This is the way they used to precede. But now they shall substitute one sheep for the man and two sheep for the oxen.

41. Philo, *Spec. Laws* 4.203–13.

42. For the Mishnah, Tosefta, and Palestinian Talumd, see Lauterbach, "Kil'ayim," and Feliks, "Kil'ayim," For medieval commentators, see the discussion in Lokshin, *Rashbam's Commentary on Leviticus and Numbers*, 107–9.

43. Douglas, *Purity and Danger*, 54–55.

He shall give thirty loaves of bread and three jugs of . . . beer, and re-consecrate (the land?). And he who sowed the field first shall reap it.

Scholars have noted the religious aspects in the Hittite Laws. The death penalty for the offender and the subsequent killing of the oxen who performed the execution, along with the need to "re-consecrate (the land?)" are features which suggest that the land and crop were put under some kind of taboo by the sowing of mixed seed.[44] In the first version of the law, putting the offender to death apparently removed the taboo and restored the crop to human use by the owner of the field. In the later revision of the law, the taboo is removed by the sacrifice of sheep in place of the offender and the two oxen. There is also a rite of re-consecration, accompanied by what appears to be a ritual meal; after these, the owner is free to harvest and use the crop.

In the Hittite Laws, it is not revealed whether the offense involved the second person planting a second planting or a second variety of seed, as in the Bible. The Bible, moreover, does not mention any ritual for removing the taboo on the crop. Deuteronomy 22:9 only states that the creation of the mixture "sanctified" the entire crop. In that case, only God and temple priests could use the crop. This is certainly the plain meaning of "sanctification," as noted by Rashbam. The rabbis, however, had further ruled that the produce must be destroyed by being burnt, based upon a fanciful re-reading of the Hebrew letters in the word "be sanctified" as if it could

44. Hoffner, *Laws of the Hittites,* 215. The killing of the oxen is also discussed in sec. 4.10 in connection with the stoning of the ox that gored a human being.

also be read "burnt (in) fire."[45] I believe that this reinterpretation was introduced in order to maintain symmetry with the observance of the other two prohibitions against "mixing" in Deut 22:10–11, where there is no mention of "sanctification." This re-reading provided a way for Jews to observe this commandment after the destruction of the Jerusalem temple in 70 CE and the cessation of formal duties for the priesthood.

Unlike in the Hittite laws, which mention "re-consecration," there is no indication in Deut 22:9 that the field itself might be permanently banned from future use by its owner after its sanctified crop was removed. But even if this were so in the Bible, we know that owners were given a way to remove their property from sanctified status by paying its value to the temple. We see a process for redeeming intentionally consecrated fields described Lev 27:16–21:

> And if a man consecrates to the Lord a field from his holding, then your valuation (for redemption) shall be in accordance with its seed requirements: fifty shekels of silver to a homer of barley seed . . . And if indeed the one who consecrated it wishes to redeem the field, then he shall add one-fifth to your valuation in sliver to it, and it shall (again) be his. But if he did not

redeem the field . . . it shall be holy to the Lord like a (permanently) devoted field; his holding will belong to the priest.[46]

The Hittite laws do not explain why the mixed seeded field needed to be re-consecrated; so one is left here with questions. But the Hittite Laws do inform us that the offense of mixed seeding was once considered so serious as to warrant the death penalty. The later Hittite Laws §167—and perhaps also the biblical laws, as we have them now—represent easing of an earlier, more severe, view.

The biblical law focuses upon an individual and his field; we are not told what would happen if this individual acted upon his neighbor's field rather than upon his own property as was the situation in the Hittite Laws. The question is, however, addressed in rabbinic sources; but there is also disagreement. In the Sifre, *Sifre D* 230 on Deut 22:9, one finds:

> One only notes here (in the verse) "your vineyard"; how does one know (that the prohibition applies as well to) a vineyard belonging to others? The text teaches: "You shall not sow your vineyard (with) two kinds of seed"—this implies two kinds of seed anywhere.

The Sifre argues from the fact that our biblical text can also be read; "You shall not sow two kinds of seed (in) your vineyard." This reading places primary emphasis on "two kinds of seed," which then becomes the most important idea. Support for this opinion but also opposing views are found in the Mishnah, *m. Kil.* 7:4, which

45. This re-reading, which adds an additional letter (aleph), is presented in *b. Hul.* 115a and is restated by Rashi in his commentary to *b. Yebam.* 81a and in Tosafot to *b. Naz.* 37a. The formal halakhic ruling is given in *m. Tem.* 7:5 and *m. Kil.* 8:1. The latter Mishnah, however, makes a distinction between the vineyard in Deut 22:9 and with what was sown in Lev 19:19 where, if not involving a vineyard, there was to be no restriction against the owner eating or using his mixed crop, since the interpolated reference to "burnt (in) fire" is not present in Lev 19:19.

46. See further Milgrom, *Leviticus,* 2383–85, on the problems and interpretations suggested for the phrases in Lev 27:18–20, which are omitted here in our citation of the passage above.

interposes the issue of legal possession of the affected property. The Mishnah is as follows:

> (In the case of) one who allows his vine to intertwine upon the produce of his neighbor: he has indeed sanctified (the neighbor's crop and render it unfit for normal use), and is (therefore) liable for replacing it. Rabbi Jose and R. Simeon say: "One person cannot sanctify something that doesn't belong to him."

The first, anonymous opinion affirms the position taken in the Sifre and sees the sacral threat as the paramount issue. But R. Jose and R. Simeon argue that lack of legal title would "render invalid" any sowing or growing together of mixed plantings. The anonymous view of the Sifre appears again in the Palestinian Talmud, *j. Kil.* 30d:

> It is written: "do not sow your vineyard (with) two kinds of seed." (From this verse) one only knows "your vineyard"; how does one know if it pertains to another's (vineyard)? The text teaches (the answer): (for later in this same verse one find the word) "vineyard" (occurring alone) without (the attached term) "two kinds of seed"; (the prohibition is thus meant to apply to any vineyard).

The argument extending the prohibition seems to rest upon the repetition of the word "vineyard" within Deut 22:9, which is used the second time without the pronoun "your." I have the impression that this must in fact be the older view, i.e., requiring a response to the sacral threat—as in the Hittite Laws; and that the issue of legal title was secondarily raised, perhaps in order to limit the law's wider application.[47]

---

47. Maimonides, in his commentary on the Mishnah passage, supports the view of Rabbi Jose and Rabbi Simeon. He does so, again, in *Mishnah Torah, Hilkhot Kil'ayim* 5:8. Similarly, Joseph Karo, *Shulhan Oruch, Yore Deah* 296, 4. But other authorities disagree, e.g., Obadiah of Bertinoro in his commentary on the Mishnah; and Radbaz (Rabbi David ben Solomon Ibn Abi Zimra) in his commentary on Maimonides, *Mishnah Torah, Hilkhot Kil'ayim* 5:8.

7

Unlawful Address of Supernatural Powers

I N THIS SECTION WE are looking at laws dealing with cursing, blasphemy, and sorcery. For there was widespread belief, both in ancient Israel and among her neighbors, that tangible harm could result from rituals and other practices, which invoked supernatural powers in order to aid or accomplish aggressive acts against others. There was a fear that the unleashing of such forces was in itself a dangerous activity, which might cause unintended harm to others in the community. The laws on these subjects do not include many specific details. These were categories of behavior that were kept vague, either because they were sufficiently well-known, so that further elaboration was considered unnecessary, or else too dangerous to reveal in detail.

7.1 CURSING AND BLASPHEMY

According to Exod 22:27, it is forbidden to curse God as well as one's earthly sovereign:

> You shall not curse God, or make imprecation against a leader of your people.[1]

1. *Targum Onqelos* and the Talmud, *b. Sanh.* 66a, take "God" in this verse, written in the otherwise normal plural form, to indicate the judges, who preside in God' name, being thus in a parallel class with the "leader of your people." Ibn Ezra and

No penalty is stated here; this is another one of the "apodictic laws" or moral admonitions, such as we have discussed before. However, in narrative sources, we find that this offense could be punished by death. This is related in a narrative concerning the Israelite Naboth, who committed no sin but he fell victim, because King Ahab coveted his field. Naboth was unwilling to sell his property and so Jezebel, Ahab's wife, conspired with two villains to falsely accuse Naboth. In 1 Kgs 21:12–13, we read:

> They (the judges) proclaimed a fast and seated Naboth at the head of the (assembled) people. The two villains came in and sat opposite him; and the villains bore (false) witness against Naboth, in the presence of the people, saying, "Naboth cursed God and king." And so they took him outside the city, and stoned him with stones and he died.[2]

Hazzequni link this verse to the preceding verse, Exod 22:6, which ends with the abused poor man crying out to God. (This verse is discussed in sec. 2.5.1.) They suggest that in Exod 22:27 the poor man, out of desperation, may even curse God or the judge, who unjustly ruled in support of the creditor.

2. In this passage, as in the plotting beforehand (1 Kgs 21:10), the Bible euphemistically replaces the verb "curse" with "bless" out of respect for

The ritual of fasting was proclaimed because the name of God was allegedly profaned; this endangered the entire community. The fast was evidently a ritual, seeking forgiveness and forestalling divine wrath until the offender was put to death. We are not told about how the lying villains explained that Naboth allegedly came to curse God as well as his king—only that he did so.

We find God being the direct object of a potential curse in Job 2:9–10, which depicts events after his body was sorely afflicted:

> Then his wife said to him, "Are you still holding on to your (claim of) integrity? Curse God, and die." But he said to her, "You speak as a foolish woman. Even (as) we receive the good from God, do we not also receive the bad?" In all of this, Job did not sin with his lips.

One can see in this passage that there was a difference to be made between mere thought and spoken word.[3] When we read that Job "did not sin with his lips," it seems to confirm that cursing would not be punished with death unless there was audible utterance. However, God might notice and mark in a negative fashion what was not uttered. We see this in Job 1:4–5:

> His (Job's) sons would go and hold feasts, each one on his (appointed) day at his house. And they would send and invite their three sisters to eat and drink with them. And when a cycle of feast days was done, Job sent (for them) and he sanctified them, and then he rose

up early in the morning and offered burnt offerings, according to their total number; for Job said, "Perhaps my children have sinned and cursed God in their hearts." Thus would Job do all of the time.

A second biblical law on cursing is Lev 24:10–16, where we have a narrative followed by a law statement:

> Lev 24:10–12—And the son of an Israelite woman—and he was the son of an Egyptian man—came out among the people of Israel; and the son of the Israelite woman quarreled in the camp with an Israelite man. The son of the Israelite woman uttered the Name (of God) and cursed. And they brought him to Moses—and his mother's name was Shelomith, daughter of Dibri, of the tribe of Dan— and they put him in custody, until a decision might be decided for them according to the word (lit. mouth) of the LORD.

> Lev 24:13–14—The Lord said to Moses, saying: "Bring forth the one who cursed outside the camp; and let all who heard shall lay their hands on his head; then the whole congregation shall stone him.

> Lev 24:15—And to the Children of Israel, say as follows: 'Any person who curses his God shall bear his sin.

> Lev 24:16—And anyone who utters the name of the Lord (in this fashion) shall certainly die; the entire congregation shall stone him—sojourners as well as citizens; when he (so) utters the Name, he shall die.'"

These passages have been subject to scrutiny since there is a subtle change in the description of the offense, from the

---

deity. The same is true for Job 2:9–10 cited below. The actual verb "curse" is used in other passages cited.

3. This distinction is noted by the rabbis, e.g., *b. B. Bat.* 16a, *Bereshit Rabbah* 19,12.

narrative in Lev 24:10–12 to the law statement in Lev 24:13–16. In the narrative, the offense is described by two apparently simultaneous actions: uttering the divine name and cursing. But in the law statement of Lev 24:15–16, the two actions are taken up separately: cursing God and uttering the name of the Lord; and there are different penalties for each action. So one may ask: how did the son of the Israelite woman come to pronounce his curse in the course of the quarrel; did he curse God, or his adversary?

We find an instance of cursing an adversary and uttering the name of God elsewhere in the Bible in 2 Kgs 2:23–24; the story relates to a group of boys who were taunting the prophet Elisha:

> He (Elisha) went up from there to Bethel; and he was going up on the way and some small boys came out of the city and made fun of him, and said: "Go on, baldhead! Go on, baldhead!" And he turned behind him and saw them, and he cursed them in the name of the Lord. Then two she-bears came out of the woods and tore into forty-two of the boys.

In related fashion, we have many passages where, conversely, speakers "bless in the name of the Lord." In all of these cases, the Lord's blessing is being put upon other persons, who are friends rather than adversaries.[4] The name of God was presumably likewise uttered when pronouncing the blessings. Elisha was not punished or reprimanded for his cursing. It seems therefore that one could in fact either curse or bless another person "in the name of Lord." Moreover, if the offender in Lev 24 had cursed another person *using* the

name of the Lord, why did the text there then not simply say "curse *in* the name of God," as in the story of Elisha?

The contrast between the situation of Elisha and that of the man in Leviticus 24 probably helped persuade the ancient commentators that the offense in Lev 24:11 involved the man cursing God rather than his adversary. Thus, in the narrative, the statement that the son of the Israelite woman "uttered the Name (of God) and cursed" was taken as a single action. This interpretation brought the narrative into conformity with what is expressed in the first part of the law in Lev 24:15, namely, "Any person who curses his God shall bear his sin."

But what of the second part of the law in Lev 24:16: "And anyone who utters the name of the Lord (in this fashion) shall certainly die?" For Philo and Josephus, the phrase "his God" which appears in Lev 24:15 was understood to be that any god—even those worshipped by gentiles—should be treated respectfully by Jews, even if they were not to be worshipped.[5] This would be an offense but left to the heavenly courts. However, if a Jew cursed his own God, the earthly court would impose the punishment of death.

Later rabbinic sources likewise kept the two offenses separate—although they did not follow Philo and Josephus in offering respect to pagan gods. They understood the first offense in Lev 24:15 to say that cursing God, although a sin punished by Heaven, was not punished by the courts, since the curser here must have used an epithet but not the explicit divine

---

4. Cf., e.g., Deut 21:5; Ps 129:8; 1 Chr 23:13.

5. Philo, *Spec. Laws* 1.53; *Life of* Moses 2.205–206; Josephus, *Ant.* 4.207; *Against Apion* 2.237. The Septuagint in similar fashion translates with a plural form in Exod 22:27 "You shall not revile gods."

name of God. More serious, however, was Lev 24:16, where one cursed God and used the actual divine name i.e., the Tetragrammaton, namely, YHWH (Yahweh), which is usually translated "(the) Lord" out of reverence, in pronouncing his curse. This distinction is clearly made in the Mishnah, *m. Sanh.* 7:5:

> One who reviles (God) is not culpable unless he explicitly uttered the Name.[6]

In their discussion of this Mishnah in the Talmud, *b. Sanh.* 55b, the rabbis noted that when the son of the Israelite woman is brought out to suffer his punishment, the text in Lev 24:14 states: "Bring forth the one who cursed outside the camp," not the "one who uttered the name." Therefore, say the rabbis, this man's offense combined the acts of cursing God and uttering the explicit Name.

Another rabbinic interpretation suggests that Lev 24:15 refers to cursing using the actual divine name but that it was not audible to witnesses and therefore could not be prosecuted.[7] We see the importance of aural witnesses in Lev 24:13–14 "let all who heard shall lay their hands on his head; then the whole congregation shall stone him." The ritual action of "laying hands" is similar to that requested of one who brings a sacrifice of expiation before slaughtering takes place.[8] The pub-

lic utterance of the curse was a community calamity that required atonement, prefaced by the fasting, which was proclaimed when the alleged sin of Naboth was "discovered."

From the ancient Near East comes a law that, like the narrative case in Lev 24:10–16, likewise deals with a curse uttered in the context of a quarrel. The law is one of a series of Middle Assyrian palace regulations promulgated by the overseers of the king's harem, c. 1185 BCE. This law states:

> Either wives of the king or the many other women [of the palace, who . . .] fight with one other (and) in their quarrel they utter the name of a god for (the purpose of) defamation [. . . he shall e]nter (and) they shall cut the throat of anyone who has [. . .] (the god) Ashur. In their quarrel [. . .] according to [. . .] she shall not pay.

This regulation is followed by a second one, promulgated by the same overseer; it is very fragmentarily preserved but the following lines are clear; like in Exod 22:27, we see the juxtaposition of god and king:

> [. . .]"by]my life" for untruth [. . . the na]me of the king in a quarrel shall not [utter and the n]ame of a god he shall not utter. [A woman of the palace who utters] the name of a god for untruth [or] uttered [the name of the king . . .] they shall not let her live.[9]

6. This point is made is *Targum Pseudo-Jonathan* on Lev 24:15–16 and is taken up by Rashi, Rashbam, and Ibn Ezra in their commentaries on these verses.

7. So Bekhor Shor and Ibn Ezra (in passing). This interpretation seems to be favored by Milgrom, *Leviticus*, 2116–18, who in his discussion reviews a range of opinions regarding these verses.

8. Cf. Lev 1:4, 4:15; Num 8:22 to mention only a few out of many examples. Cf. Milgrom, *Leviticus*, 2113.

9. These regulations are nos. 10–11 in Roth, *Law Collections*, 202, based upon Weidner, "Hof- und Harems-Erlasse assyrischer Könige." The importance of the Middle Assyrian cases for biblical law was discussed in Paul, "Biblical Analogues to Middle Assyrian Law," 346–50.

We see in the first regulation that the death penalty was meted out to anyone uttering the name of a god, especially Ashur, for the purpose of cursing, although, like in Leviticus 24:11, it is not clear who was being cursed—an adversary, a god, or a king. In the second regulation, the death penalty was given to one who used the name of a god or the king in support of a false oath statement, and possibly also in a curse.

In another regulation, it is made clear that it was considered a serious offense to curse a member of the royal family or officer of the royal household on any basis, presumably, even without explicitly using the name of a deity:

> [If a[woman] of the palace [. . .] cursed either the son of Tukulti-Ninurta (the king) or [. . . an official] of the king's house, of the bedchamber [. . .] of the stool (i.e., of seated rank) [. . .] who is below her (in station?) she malevolently curses, [. . .] carrying [. . .], they shall pierce the nose of that woman of [the palace] and smite her [. . .] blows with rods.[10]

The Assyrian regulations reveal that in the ancient Near Eastern societies there existed strong feelings on preventing profanation of both royal and divine names. This is the same concern that we have seen in the Bible, in the tale of Naboth and in Exod 22:27, where royal names are juxtaposed with divine names. In later biblical times, the need to protect royal names disappeared with the loss of native kingship. But protective and reverential feelings continued to exist with respect to the use of divine names. There is evidence both from late biblical and rabbinic times, which shows that these sentiments extended beyond the context of cursing God, which is the background of Leviticus 24 and Job 2.

Ben Sira (23:9–10), writing in Ptolemaic times, reflected upon the potential hazards of uttering the divine name even for reasonable purposes like taking an oath:

> Do not accustom your mouth to oaths, nor habitually utter the name of the Holy One; for, as a servant who is constantly under scrutiny will not lack bruises, so also the person who always swears and utters the Name will never be cleansed from sin. (NRSV)

Philo augments such notions, when he argues, on the basis of Lev 24:15, that anyone who uttered the divine name for a disrespectful reason deserves be punished by death. He compares humans to children who, out of respect, do not call their parents by name but, rather, by titles indicating relationship; in like fashion those "can we still think worthy of pardon those, who with a reckless tongue, make unreasonable use of the most holy name of the Deity and treat it as a mere expletive?"[11] The Essene community also shared this view to the extent that a member would be permanently expelled for saying the "Name" aloud:

> Anyone who speaks aloud the M[ost] Holy Name of God, [whether in . . .] or in cursing or as a blurt in time of trial or for any other reason, or while he is reading a book or praying, is to be expelled, never again to return to the party of the

---

10. No. 17 in Roth, *Law Collections,* 203; this passage is cited in *CAD* A/2, 236, Š/1, 464.

11. Philo, *Life of Moses* 2.207–8, Colson.

Yahad [i.e., the sectarian fellowship and community].[12]

The rabbis later taught that the recitation of the explicit name of God should be uttered only within the Temple and not outside of its boundaries.[13] In consonance with this same mode of thinking, the Talmud states that a person who used the name of God in a curse directed against another person deserved to be punished by the community, even if not with the death penalty. We find this statement in the Talmud, *b. Tem.* 3a:

> R. Iddi son of R. Abin reported in the name of R. Amram, R. Isaac and R. Johanan: (var. R. Judah reported in the name of R. Jose the Galilean:) "In respect of every negative command laid down in the Torah, if one actually does some action (in transgressing it), he is punishable by flogging; but if he does not actually do anything (in transgressing it) he is not punishable, except in the cases of one who takes a (false) oath, exchanges (an unconsecrated animal for a consecrated animal), and curses his fellow using the Name, in which cases, though he did no (real) action, he is (nevertheless to be) punished (with flogging).[14]

This is a widely stated rule within the rabbinic writings; but there was question as to whether this rule applied to epithets as well as to the explicit name of God. Some were of the opinion that this penalty should be extended to the use of epithets.[15]

Thinking along similar lines, the rabbis looked to find some retribution for the deed of Elisha, who had caused the death of the small boys through his curses, which invoked the divine Name as recorded in 2 Kgs 2:23–24. Surely he should not have gone totally unpunished. In the Talmud, *b. Sanh.* 107b, a *baraita* is cited, that tells of Elisha's punishment by God:

> Our Rabbis taught: Elisha was ill on three occasions: once when he incited the bears against the children, once when he repulsed Gehazi (2 Kgs 5:23–27) with both hands, and the third (was the illness) of which he died; as it is written (2 Kgs 13:14), "Now Elisha was fallen sick of his sickness where of he died."

Rashi explains the exegesis of the verse, 2 Kgs 13:14, as follows: the word "sick" represents one; the word "sickness" is two; and "of which he died" makes three.

A severe form of punishment for cursing is described in the Mishnah, *m. Sanh.* 9:6 (another part of this law is discussed in sec. 5.7): "One who curses by *Qosem* may be killed by zealots," i.e., by mob action, without legal process. It is not clear what exactly is meant "by *Qosem*" — whether he cursed another person, using the name of God or whether he publicly uttered a curse against God invoking a

---

12. 1QS 6:27—7:2. See Wise, Abegg, and Cook, *Dead Sea Scrolls,* 126 and the discussion in Schiffman, *Sectarian Law in the Dead Sea Scrolls,* 132–54.

13. Cf. *Sifre N* 39 on Num 6:23; *b. Yoma* 69b; *Bamidbar Rabba* 11,4; Rashi on Exod 20:20.

14. The rabbis are speaking here of divine epithets rather than the Tetragrammaton. This passage also appears in *b. Makk.* 16a *and b. Shevu.* 21a.

15. Abbreviated formulations of this rule are cited, e.g., in *t. Makk.* 5:10, Zuckermandel, *j. Shevu.* 35a. Maimonides, *Hilkhot Sanh.* 26:3 says this rule includes epithets; but Rabad in his comment there argues for the straightforward meaning of the text and restricts its scope to the explicit Name of God. Cf. also *m. Sanh.* 7:8, for a similar argument in the case of one who curses his mother or father.

pagan deity or charm.[16] But what is clear is that cursing and mentioning the name of God was still deemed to be a serious offense of blasphemy. It was worthy of capital punishment, even if it could not be formally addressed and punished under the current law systems—Roman or Jewish—of the time.

7.2 SORCERY

In pre-modern contexts, a "sorcerer" or "witch" is a person who seeks to influence human affairs, usually in a negative way, by inflicting serious harm upon a targeted individual. The sorcerer typically "attacks" his or her target from a distance, through the concoction of a magical spell or ritual exercise, although sometimes also coming closer through stealth or stratagem. The sorcerer's attack is thus not physical but rather symbolic or psychological. In this sense, it is a somewhat like cursing another person. The biblical writers—or at least the ancient Israelites to whom their words were addressed—believed in the power and efficacy of sorcery. They believed that it was somehow possible to invoke supernatural forces and direct them against other persons and thereby to bring them illness and death. For this reason, in Exod 22:17, the Bible commands that a female practitioner of sorcery—and probably the unmentioned male sorcerer as well—must be put to death: "You shall not permit a witch to live" (NRSV). This is the only biblical law that focuses solely upon sorcerers and witches. Although we are given no description of their practices, these were, presumably, sufficiently well known and did not need to be rehearsed.

It is also possible that discussion of the particulars relating to witchcraft was avoided, either for "protective" concealment or because of taboos.[17]

In Deuteronomy, sorcerers appear within a larger list of condemned practitioners and practices of cult and folk religion. Deuteronomy 18:10–12 states:

> No one shall be found among you who makes a son or daughter pass through fire, or who practices divination, or is a soothsayer, or an augur, or a sorcerer, or one who casts spells, or who consults ghosts or spirits, or who seeks oracles from the dead. For whoever does these things is abhorrent to the LORD; it is because of such abhorrent practices that the LORD your God is driving them out before you. (NRSV)

I see this list as reflecting the religious reform, which began in late monarchal times under prophetic influence. This reform had a number of major goals, including exclusive loyalty to the Lord, i.e., Yahweh, and mandating access to "divine powers" solely through the priests of the Jerusalem temple. Child sacrifice, i.e., passing a son or daughter through fire, was totally rejected as a religious rite, even if it was intended for the worship of Yahweh. The remainder of this list sought to discredit popular belief in a variety of practices that claimed to establish and utilize "contact" with supernatural powers.

---

16. Cf. *b. Sanh.* 81b. For other conjectures, see Jastrow, *Dictionary*, s.v. *Qasam*.

17. Philo, *Spec. Laws* 3.94 somewhat fancifully suggests that the witch in this passage is also plotting to do harm by poisoning; capital punishment is therefore justified, indeed even in summary fashion without a trial. The Septuagint rendering of the word "witch" with a Greek word that can also denote "poisoner" apparently influenced Philo's interpretation. The Septuagint also translates "witches," in the plural.

All such practices were looked upon with reprehension if they fell outside of the approved religious framework, which was supported and controlled by the Jerusalem priests. Methods of divination are prominent in this list and include the activities of the "augur, soothsayer, one who casts spells, or one who consults ghosts or sprits, or one who seeks oracles from the dead." These specific practices had to be singled out and enumerated, because the concept of divination itself could not be totally condemned. For there were approved forms of divination, that were practiced by the official priesthood, using lots, or the Urim and Thummim—not to speak of prophets, who foretold the future through dreams and visions. But the claims of lay or unapproved practitioners, or those who appealed to supernatural powers other than the Lord were discredited.[18]

In keeping with these ideas of religious reform, one finds other statements elsewhere in the Bible attacking private divination, especially necromancy or seeking out the spirits of the dead.[19] These practices were the subject of repeated attacks. Thus, for example, we find what reads like a variation on Deut 18:10–12 in an account concerning King Manasseh of Judah in 2 Kgs 21:6:

He consigned his son to the fire; he practiced soothsaying and divination, and consulted ghosts and familiar spirits; he did much that was displeasing to the LORD, to vex Him. (NJPS)[20]

In conformity with the Deuteronomic teaching, Josiah, the grandson of Manasseh, is praised for eliminating these same practices. In 2 Kgs 23:24 we read:

And Josiah also swept away the mediums, the necromancers, and the *teraphim*, the idols, and all the abominations that were seen in the land of Judah and in Jerusalem in order to fulfill the words of the teaching that were written in the book that Hilkiah the priest had found in the house of the Lord.

Necromancy as a form of divination had of course previously been practiced among the Israelites. We see this in the story of Saul in 1 Sam 28:7:

Then Saul said to his courtiers, "Find me a woman who consults ghosts, so that I can go to her and inquire through her." And his courtiers told him that there was a woman in En-dor who consulted ghosts. (NJPS)[21]

The deeply rooted belief in necromancy and its persisting popular acceptance was the object of later prophetic attack, in Isa 8:19–20:

Now if people say to you, "Consult the ghosts and the familiar spirits that chirp and mutter; should not a people consult their gods, the dead on behalf of the living, for teaching and for instruction?" Surely, those

---

18. For lots cf. e.g., Prov 16:33; and for Urim and Thummim, cf. 1 Sam 23:9–12; 30:7-8. On the rejection of methods appealing to powers other than those of the Lord, cf. Deut 13:1-6 and Ricks, "The Magician as Outsider: The Evidence of the Hebrew Bible." The polemical aspect of the biblical prohibitions is repeatedly noted in Janowitz, *Magic in the Roman World, Pagans, Jews, and Christians*, 2–3, 16, 20–21.

19. Divination, especially outside of the priestly cult setting, is repeatedly condemned, e.g., in Lev 19:26, 31; 20:6, 27.

20. A parallel passage occurs in 2 Chr 33:6.

21. In 1 Sam 28:9, a ban on necromancy is attributed to Saul himself.

who speak like this will have no
dawn! (NRSV)

God here tells Isaiah not to doubt that
necromancers would fail to deliver the
truth.

But in the meantime, for those Judeans evidently still not persuaded, a further legal assault against necromancy was
needed. We see this in Lev 20:6:

> And the person [lit. soul] who will
> turn to mediums and necroman-
> cers, to go astray after them—and
> I will set my face against that per-
> son and I will cut him off from the
> midst of his people.

And against the practitioner of necromancy, Lev 20:27 states:

> And a man or a woman—if there
> should be among them a medi-
> um or necromancer—shall be put
> to death; (the people) shall stone
> them with stones; their blood is
> upon them (i.e., the practitioners).

If we look back now on Deut 18:10–
12, one can readily see its intention to
discredit sorcerers by putting them into
a group with diviners, mediums, and
devotees of child sacrifice. There was,
moreover, no attempt made to distinguish between "positive" and "negative"
uses of magical arts. For not every act of
"sorcery" was intended to do harm. On
the one hand, the description of sorcerers
as agents of malevolence continues to be
seen, as in Mal 3:5, where they are associated with perpetrators of moral crimes:

> Then I will draw near to you for
> judgment; I will be swift to bear wit-
> ness against the sorcerers, against
> the adulterers, against those who
> swear falsely, against those who
> oppress the hired workers in their

wages, the widow and the orphan,
against those who thrust aside the
alien, and do not fear me, says the
LORD of hosts. (NRSV)

Yet a less negative view of "sorcerers" is found in Jer 27:9, where they are
grouped with other practitioners who,
like diviners, who were involved in fore-
telling the future. Jeremiah 27:9 states the
following:

> You, therefore, must not listen to
> your prophets, your diviners, your
> dreamers, your soothsayers, or
> your sorcerers, who are saying to
> you, "You shall not serve the king
> of Babylon." (NRSV)

Jeremiah seeks to discredit belief in those
diviners who prophesied and gave predic-
tions contrary to his own more accurate
and true message of doom. Sorcerers are
scorned—but not because they inflicted
harm upon others, like the sorcerer who
is to be put to death in Exod 22:17. Rather,
because sorcerers are associated with the
discredited foretellers of the future, along
with diviners and (false) prophets. Similarly, in Dan 2:2, we again find sorcerers
employed in a more "benign" role alongside of foretellers of the future or interpreters of "prophetic" dreams:

> So the king commanded that the
> magicians, the exorcists, the sor-
> cerers, and the Chaldeans (i.e., as-
> trologers) be summoned to tell the
> king his dreams. When they came
> in and stood before the king, and
> the king said to them, "I have had
> a dream and I am full of anxiety
> to know what I have dreamed."
> (NRSV)

Such passages make it evident that
the Hebrew term for "sorcerer" was
broadly used, covering both "positive"

and "negative" purposes. The biblical writers, of course, were not interested in this distinction, since it was their goal to discredit all lay practitioners of magical arts, even including those who were ostensibly there to help or heal persons who believed themselves afflicted by evil forces. The biblical writers may therefore have suppressed other Hebrew terms that were used to describe "positive" practitioners. They seem to have labeled them all as "sorcerers," a term which typically referred to "negative" or "hostile" magic. Yet there is some evidence of "positive" magical arts preserved in the Bible, e.g., in Isa 3:3, which mentions, in a favorable light, the "expert enchanter"—literally, "the one who is wise in incantation":

> . . . captain of fifty and dignitary, counselor and skillful magician and expert enchanter.

There is further mention of charms or incantations, that, at least in popular superstition, were expected to ward off snake-bites in Jer 8:17 and Eccl 10:11:

> Jer 8:17 See, I am letting snakes loose among you, adders that cannot be charmed, and they shall bite you, says the LORD. (NRSV)

> Eccl 10:11 If the snake bites before it is charmed, there is no advantage in a charmer. (NRSV)

The tradition and use of magical arts survived, despite biblical condemnations; and so we find it still well attested into the rabbinic period, in rabbinic literature, and even into medieval times, where reference is made to "positive" "magical" remedies.[22] The important role of "positive" magical arts and exorcism becomes more evident as we now look at post-biblical Jewish and our ancient Near Eastern sources. There, we can see that, in popular belief, magical arts continued to "play" a helpful role, deflecting evil "sent against" or "falling upon" a victim. People felt a need for spells and rituals to counteract "negative" sorcery as well as threatening omens or evil dreams. We also encounter examples where both "positive" and "negative" actions were believed to come from the same magical practitioner.

The Bible, as I noted earlier, does not tell us a great deal about the means or techniques used by the sorcerers to perform their craft. But in the apocryphal writings of late biblical times, in the Book of Tobit, one can find some descriptive material, as well support for the belief that magical arts could be used for positive ends (so-called "white magic") as well as for negative purposes ("black" magic). To harm innocent persons was sorcery; but Jews could not believe that it was forbidden, or a violation of God's law to use magical arts for defensive purposes. The story of Tobit demonstrates the link that was believed to exist between magic and supernatural powers. The "power" in magic drew upon such powers. In the Book of Tobit, the angel Raphael disguised as a human being, Azariah, instructs Tobias son of Tobit in magical arts. In Tobit 6:3–9 we read:

> Then the young man [i.e., Tobias son of Tobit] went down to wash his feet in the Tigris river. Suddenly a large fish leaped up from the water and tried to swallow the young man's foot, and he cried out. But the angel said to the young man,

22. Cf. e.g., *t. Sanh.* 11:5 and *t. Shabb.* 6–7, Lieberman. For Talmudic passages, cf. Jacobs and Blau, "Incantation." For possible additional terms used to describe magical acts in the Bible and for further discussion of rabbinic and medieval practices, see Dan, "Magic."

"Catch hold of the fish and hang on to it!" So the young man grasped the fish and drew it up on the land. Then the angel said to him, "Cut open the fish and take out its gall, heart, and liver. Keep them with you, but throw away the intestines. For its gall, heart, and liver are useful as medicine." So after cutting open the fish the young man gathered together the gall, heart, and liver; then he roasted and ate some of the fish, and kept some to be salted. The two continued on their way together until they were near Media. Then the young man questioned the angel and said to him, "Brother Azariah, what medicinal value is there in the fish's heart and liver, and in the gall?" He replied, "As for the fish's heart and liver, you must burn them to make a smoke in the presence of a man or woman afflicted by a demon or evil spirit, and every affliction will flee away and never remain with that person any longer. And as for the gall, anoint a person's eyes where white films have appeared on them; blow upon them, upon the white films, and the eyes will be healed." (NRSV)

Later in the story, Tobias finds opportunity to use this magic. In Tob 8:2–3 he defeats the demon, who intends to slay him and part him from Sarah, his bride:

Then Tobias remembered the words of Raphael [i.e., Azariah], and he took the fish's liver and heart out of the bag where he had them and put them on the embers of the incense. The odor of the fish so repelled the demon that he fled to the remotest parts of Egypt. But Raphael followed him, and at once bound him there hand and foot. (NRSV)

And later, when Tobias comes home, he is able to heal his blind father, Tobit as we read in Tob 11:10–15:

Then Tobit got up and came stumbling out through the courtyard door. Tobias went up to him, with the gall of the fish in his hand, and holding him firmly, he blew into his eyes, saying, "Take courage, father." With this he applied the medicine on his eyes, and it made them smart. Next, with both his hands he peeled off the white films from the corners of his eyes. Then Tobit saw his son and threw his arms around him, and he wept and said to him, "I see you, my son, the light of my eyes!" Then he said, "Blessed be God, and blessed be his great name, and blessed be all his holy angels. May his holy name be blessed throughout all the ages. Though he afflicted me, he has had mercy upon me. Now I see my son Tobias!" (NRSV)

The exorcizing of demons was a familiar theme in Judaism of the late biblical period. For example, Josephus relates a story about which he says he was eyewitness:

. . . I have seen a certain Eleazar, a countryman of mine, in the presence of Vespasian, his sons, tribunes and a number of other soldiers, free men possessed by demons, and this was the manner of the cure: he put to the nose of the possessed man a ring which had under its seal one of the roots prescribed by Solomon, and then, as the man smelled it, drew out the demon through his nostrils, and, when the man at once fell down, adjured the demon never to come back into him, speaking Solomon's name and reciting the incantations which he had composed. Then, wishing to convince the bystanders and prove to them that he had this power, Eleazar placed a cup or foot-basin full of water a little way off and commanded the demon, as it went out of the man, to overturn it and make known to the spectators that he had left the man. And when this was done, the understanding and wisdom of Solomon were clearly revealed . . .[23]

The harnessing of supernatural powers to accomplish healing is of course also an important theme in the New Testament, where Jesus, who, with the power of Heaven on his side, is described as able to heal many sicknesses and cast out demons.[24]

The abiding fear of harmful magic and the punishment of sorcery is depicted in a story told in the Mishnah *m. Sanh.* 6:4, about witchcraft in Hasmonean times:

> The sages say: "A man is hanged, but not a woman." Whereupon Rabbi Eliezer said to them: "But did not Simeon ben Shetah hang women (for witchcraft) at Ashkelon?" They retorted: "(Indeed on that singular occasion) he hanged eighty women (but otherwise) one does not (hang women nor) judge two offenders (charged with the same crime) on the same day."[25]

A misogynic view about witchcraft and women occurs in the Talmud, *b. Sanh.* 67a, where, in commenting on Exod 22:17, the rabbis state:

> (This verse) applies to both man and woman. If so, why is a female witch stated?—Because mostly women engage in witchcraft.[26]

The Talmud, in *b. Sanh.* 100b, attests to an association of witchcraft with elderly women; in a discussion comparing the wisdom of Ben Sira with their own popular sayings, it is stated:

> (Ben Sira says:) "A daughter is a vain treasure to her father: through anxiety on her account, he cannot sleep at night. As a minor, lest she be seduced; in her majority, lest she play the harlot; as an adult, lest she be not married; if she marries, lest she bear no children; if she grows old, lest she engage in witchcraft!" And the Rabbis have said the same: "The world cannot exist without males and females; happy is he whose children are males, and woe to him whose children are females."[27]

The rabbis also distinguished benign magic from forbidden magic or sorcery;

---

power to the Pharisees, as described by Josephus, *Antiquities* 16.405–30. This tale about Simeon is told in more detail in *j. Sanh.* 23c; cf. Lauterbach," Simeon ben Shetah."

26. This idea is widely shared in antiquity. Cf. Sefati and Klein, "The Role of Women in Mesopotamian Witchcraft."

27. Ben Sira 42:9–10; but the part of the citation dealing with witchcraft in old age is missing in the Greek version. It also is not found in the extant Hebrew mss. The Talmudic passage may be a variant or else a midrashic elaboration of the Rabbis. (This is an oral suggestion by Richard Sarason.) On the "demonization" of women as witches, see also Janowitz, *Magic in the Roman World*, 86–100, and literature cited there.

23. Josephus, *Ant.* 8.46-49, Thackeray.

24. Cf., e.g., Matt 4:23–24; 8:28–34; 12:22–45; for other passages see the discussions in Reese, "Demons. New Testament," and in Garrett, "Light on a Dark Subject and Vice Versa: Magic and Magicians in the New Testament." (1989). The Talmud in *b. Meʿil.* 17b relates a tale of how Rabbi Simeon bar Yohai exorcised a demon from the emperor's daughter.

25. Simeon was said to have gained this unusual authority during the reign of Salome Alexandra, who, during her period of regency, gave great

they also attempt to distinguish "real" sorcerers from theatrical magicians. Thus, for example, we read in the Mishnah, *m. Sanh.* 7:11 "(As for) as sorcerer—one who actually does the deed, he is liable (for the death penalty) but not one performs an illusion." The Talmud, in *b. Sanh.* 67b, comments further:

> Abaye said: (The sorcerer) who is particular about (using specific) paraphernalia, (works through) a demon; he who does not, works by (the skill of) sorceries.

> Abaye said: The laws on sorcerers are like those of the Sabbath: certain actions are punished by stoning; some are exempt from punishment, yet forbidden; others are entirely permitted. Thus if one actually performs magic, he is stoned; if he merely creates an illusion, he is exempt, yet it is forbidden. What is entirely permitted?—Such as was performed by R. Hanina and R. Oshaya, who every Sabbath eve were occupied in studying the Laws of Creation, by means of which they created a three year old calf and ate it.[28]

The above passages are only a few of the many illustrative sources attesting to popular Jewish belief in magical arts, which continued, among some communities, even to the present day.

The ancient Near Eastern literature, especially that of Mesopotamia, attest to examples of "positive" as well as "negative"

magical arts. The terms for "sorcerer," are generally used for the "negative" practitioner.[29] "Positive" practitioners are described by other terms, notably *ashipu*, translated "exorcist, incantation priest, conjurer, magician" and even "physician."[30] The variety of translations is a reflection of the many diverse situations where the "exorcist" was called upon to help. Easing the mind from "evil" dreams is one of these and we have seen his presence, attending the king, in Dan 2:2 cited above. While it is true that passage in Daniel describes a scene in the Babylonian court of Belshazzar, where the accessibility of an exorcist is expected, the easing of troubling dreams is addressed also in the Talmud, along with rites and rituals for other maladies, etc.[31]

The legal sources from the ancient Near East are concerned with persons, who were suspected of performing negative or hostile magical arts, i.e., "sorcerers." They were viewed as both harmful and dangerous. Accusations concerning such negative activities were taken most seriously. Thus in Hammurapi Laws §2:

28. This passage is discussed in Geller, "Deconstructing Talmudic Magic." Geller also reviews the scholarly literature on magic in the Talmud and its relationship to the ancient pre- and post-classical world. Rabbinic deliberations on "beneficial magic" and the reception of this distinction in early Christianity are discussed in Janowitz, *Magic in the Roman World*, 20–26.

29. Abusch, *Mesopotamian Witchcraft*, 9–10, 28, 66, suggests that the Akkadian terms for male and female sorcerers in an earlier time may originally have been more neutrally applied, i.e., to persons doing both "positive" as well as "negative" magic, but that, over time, the negative association became dominant.

30. Scurlock, "Physician, Exorcist, Conjurer, Magician." In this work, I have favored the translation "exorcist." One should also mention the learned term *mashmashshu*, which is formed from the older Sumerian term for "exorcist." See *CAD* M/1, 381.

31. A prayer dealing with dreams is given in *b. Ber.* 55b. On the subject of prayers and rituals addressing dreams cf. Oppenheim, *The Interpretation of Dreams in the Ancient Near East,* especially 299–307. For relieving other maladies and afflictions, see references collected in Geller, "Deconstructing Talmudic Magic."

If a man brings (lit. flings) (a charge of) sorceries upon another man and is unable to convict him, the one upon whom (the charge of) sorceries was brought shall go to the river-god. (If) the river-god has overwhelmed him, his accuser may carry off his estate. If the river-god has cleared that man and he has come through (the ordeal) safely, the person who brought (the charge of) sorceries upon him shall be killed. The one who came through (the ordeal of) the river-god safely shall carry off the estate of his accuser.

We have previously encountered the river ordeal in connection with accusations of adultery (sec. 1.3.2) In this case as well, because of the seriousness of the matter, the accused rather than the accuser bears the burden of proof and must submit to the ordeal in order to clear himself.[32] The stakes are high in the present case. The accuser must be ready to suffer death and financial ruination if he brings a false charge, while one accused and "convicted" by the river-god will also lose both life and fortune. Frivolous charges are thus discouraged.

An ordeal following upon an accusation of sorcery is reported in a diplomatic letter sent to the king of Mari, which was written during the time of Hammurapi. A young girl, Marat-Ishtar, was accused of bewitching a young boy. The girl's mother, apparently because of her daughter's young age, stood in for her and underwent the ordeal in her place. The letter reports as follows:

Thus they had her speak: "(I swear) that my daughter Marat-Ishtar did not perform sorcery against Hammi-epuh son of Dadiya. This girl, neither at door or anywhere else, did not give him bewitched wood nor give him to eat bread, beer or anything (else)." After they had her speak thus, she fell into the midst of the River god and perished; she did not release (herself) at all (through her oath and plunge); (however) the young boy—he was (thereby) released from (his) bewitchment.[33]

The reference to "bewitched wood" is obscure; it has been suggested that it may relate to food cooked over such wood.

In another Mari letter, there is a report of an ordeal imposed upon a lady-in-waiting upon the queen (unnamed) of a local ruler, Yarkab-Addu. Although she was highborn and a kinswoman of the great king Shamshi-Addu, the lady-in-waiting was required to answer to a triple accusations of sorcery, treason, and adultery, which hovered over the queen and to which she, her attendant, may have acted as accomplice. The letter relates as follows:

The chief priest and Ashtamrum, the governor of Hit [the location of the rapids where the ordeal took place] came here and reported as follows concerning Amat-Sakkanim, the kinswoman of Shamshi-Addu, whom the River god overcame. Thus they reported: "we put her to the ordeal as follows: "(You swear) that your mistress (the queen) did not perform sorcery against Yarkab-Addu, her lord, that she (the queen) did not reveal a (confidential) matter of the palace, and that another man did

32. A parallel to Hammurapi Laws §2 may be present in Ur-Namma Laws §13; but the context is not certain; the discredited accuser in that case only pays a fine of 3 shekels.

33. The report (A. 4187) is cited in Durand, "L'ordalie," 532–33, no. 253: rev. 3'–14'.

not 'open the thigh(s) of your mistress,' and that your mistress did not sin against her lord." These are what we made her swear; the River god overcame her; she did not resurface.[34]

The triple accusations suggest an "all out attack" upon the queen, who for whatever reasons was put under a general cloud of suspicion. Her highborn attendant faced the ordeal on her behalf. We do not know the queen's subsequent fate after her attendant drowned. If she herself was not executed, then the "trial and conviction" of her female attendant should no doubt have provided grounds for divorce.

Middle Assyrian Laws §A 47 brings forward a situation where there appears to be more concrete evidence of wrongdoing:

> If a man or a woman performs sorcery and these (i.e., magical preparations) are seized in their hands, (and) they (i.e., the judges) have thoroughly investigated them and proven them guilty, then they shall execute the practitioner of sorcery. (In the case of) a man who saw sorcery being performed—he who heard about it from the mouth of the eyewitness to the sorcery, who told to him "I saw (it)," he—the hearsay witness—shall go to the king (and) tell. If the eyewitness (subsequently) denies what he (the hearsay witness) told the king, then he (the hearsay witness) must declare (in an oath) before the Divine Bull, son of the Sun god: "he surely told me" and then he is clear (of blame). (As for the alleged) eyewitness who told but then denied—he king shall keep interrogating him

as he is able and do so thoroughly (lit. look at his "back"). (In addition) an exorcist shall (endeavor to) make the man speak out when (lit. on the day) he performs a purification ritual and he (thus) shall say (to him as follows): "No one shall release you (from) the dread oath that you uttered by the king and his son; you are under oath according to the (words on the) written tablet by which you swore by the king and his son."

Every measure must be taken to ferret out sorcerers; the interrogation of a potential eyewitness must therefore be thorough and leave no stone unturned. We are not told whether there was any reward for the hearsay witness in the event that his report turned to be true.

An edict issued by the Hittite king Telepinu (c. 1500 BCE) proclaims a similar concern for disclosure of sorcery that extended even to the palace; in §50 of his edict, he stated:

> Regarding cases of sorcery in Hattusha [i.e., in the Hittite homeland]: keep cleaning up instances [of such practices]. Whoever in the royal family practices sorcery, seize him and deliver him to the king's court. But it will go badly for that man (var. add: and for his household) who does not delivery him.[35]

The (later) Hittite Laws contain a number of cases, which add details concerning the practices involved sorcery. In Hittite Laws §111 we read:

> [If] anyone forms (?) clay for [an ima]ge(?) (for magical purposes), it is sorcery (and) a case for the king's court.

---

34. This report (A. 457) is cited in ibid., 527–28, no. 249:31–44. Excerpts from this and the previously cited document are also cited in Lafont, "The Ordeal."

35. Translation follows H. Hoffner, which appears in Roth, *Law Collections,* 237–38.

The forming of clay images is well known in Mesopotamian rituals dealing with healing and exorcism. Thus, for example, an "afflicted" person is instructed to recite a "healing" incantation stating: "You have buried figurines of me with a dead man, you have placed figurines of me in the lap of a dead man."[36] Images could also be burned as a counter-measure against unknown sorcerers or witches, who are blamed for afflictions, suffered or intended. One example of such burning is accompanied by an incantation to the sun-god:

> O Shamash, these are the images of my sorcerer, these are the images of my sorceress . . . You, Shamash the (divine) judge know them, but I do not know them . . . Since they are not present, I lift up their images . . . Judge my case, render my verdict! Burn the warlock and the witch![37]

Whereas Hittite Laws §111 (above) deals with the preparation of figurines, which could be used in negative magical rites, Hittite Laws §170 describes a different mode of incipient witchcraft:

> If a free man kills a snake, and speaks another's name, he shall pay one mina (i.e., 40 shekels) of silver. If it is a slave [i.e., who did so], he himself shall be put to death.

There was evidently a belief that magical powers could be drawn from killing a snake. Here again, one can look to Mesopotamia, where, in a hemerology from the more or less contemporary Middle Babylonian period, it is stated: "(On the)

twentieth day of the month (of Ayaru)—let him kill a snake and he will go forth pre-eminent."[38]

The products used in magical arts, even when positively intended, were seen as "dangerous." Hittite Laws §44b addresses a situation where a rite of purification was performed, e.g., the burning of effigies as described above; what should happen to the "radioactive" ashes? The case is as follows:

> If anyone performs a purification ritual on a person, he shall dispose of the remnants (of the ritual) in the incineration dumps. If he disposes of them in someone's land or house, it is sorcery (and) a case for the king.

Another text, related or perhaps a later version of §44b, resolves an apparently similar situation as follows:

> . . . and he shall make it ritually pure again. And if in the house anything goes wrong, he shall make it ritually pure again as before. And he shall make compensation for whatever else is lost.

Cleanup of magical residues is addressed also in Neo-Babylonian Laws §7:

> A woman who performs a magical procedure or a purification ritual in a man's field or in a boat or in an oven or in any place whatever, (if in a field, then as for) the trees (among which) she performed the purification ritual, she shall pay to the owner of the field threefold its yield. If she performed the purification ritual in a boat, in an oven,

---

36. These passages are cited in *CAD* Ṣ, 206.

37. These lines are taken from *Maqlû* I 73–121, and discussed in Abusch, *Mesopotamian Witchcraft*, 125–26.

38. This passage (5R 48 ii 23) is cited in *CAD* Ṣ, 148. Killing a snake is also "recommended" for the 24th day of Ayaru (5R 48:34). For the total composition and other months' activities, see Labat, "Un Almanac Babylonien."

or in any other place, she shall pay (for) the losses that she caused in the property [lit. field] three(fold). Should she be caught . . . in the doorway of a man's [house], she shall be killed.[39]

The last part of this law is broken away and missing from the ancient tablet; perhaps it referred to her coming "too close" to the domicile when she performed the ritual. It is not clear for whom or against whom the ritual that she performed was intended. It is clear that residue from purification rituals was clearly seen as "contaminating" and "dangerous." The careless "dumping" of residue created a presumption of hostile intent.

Our ancient Near Eastern laws place a great deal of focus upon unspecified acts of sorcery, as well as upon specific activities, which were component rituals of magical practices. However, even "benign" magical ritual activities, could create products that might become potentially threatening and "dangerous."

I assume that this is because, in the ancient understanding, there was danger in all such rituals that created "contact" with powerful supernatural forces. Much of this still remains obscure. There in fact existed a whole range of magical activities that were performed by a variety of practitioners. Akkadian literature provides us with many such practitioners, with names that as yet cannot all be translated. Some of these practitioners performed both "positive" and "negative" magic and could be either male or female. At present we lack the knowledge necessary to know the fine points of their magical activities with certainty or how they may relate to our extant legal cases.[40] In this regard, there is also need to remember that in the ancient Near East, unlike the Bible, divination performed outside of the Temples was not linked with sorcery and was usually viewed in a positive light.

39. The reading follows Roth, *Law Collections*, 146. For traces of the missing lines, see Driver and Miles, *Babylonian Laws*, 2:338–41.

40. One must be here content to list them briefly: *mušlaḫḫu/mušlaḫḫatu*, "snake charmer" *CAD* M/2, 276–77; *eššebû/eššebûtu*, "ecstatic," *CAD* E, 371. Others, as yet without translation, are: *naršindu/naršindatu*, *CAD* N/1, 362; *agugillu/agugillatu*, *CAD* A/1, 159. There is also a female "exorcist," *ašiptu*, about which at present little is known, *CAD* A/2, 431.

8

The Courts and the Justice System

8.1 FALSE WITNESS

COURTS TODAY REQUIRE THE testimony of eyewitnesses and the oaths that they may be asked to swear in support of the truthfulness of their statements. But the ancient courts were even more heavily dependent upon oath statements, because the possibility of obtaining alternative, forensic evidence was so limited. Their justice systems would be fatally compromised when witnesses, who did not fear or respect the gods by whose name they swore, committed perjury and gave false testimony. It was assumed that a god whose name was linked with falsehood would punish a lying witness; but earthly rulers would also mete out penalty when they became aware of false testimony. This is the situation described in Deut 19:16–21:

> If a malicious witness comes forward against another man to accuse him falsely, then both parties having the dispute shall stand before the Lord, before the priests or the judges who will be (in authority) in those days, and the judges shall investigate thoroughly. (If) then the witness is a false witness, in that he testified falsely against his brother, then you shall do him just as he had meant to do to his fellow [lit. brother] and you shall purge the evil from your midst. Those remaining shall hear and be afraid, and let them not ever (consider) doing something this evil again in your midst. And show no pity: life for life, eye for eye, tooth for tooth, hand for hand, foot for foot.

The principle in this law is that a false witness must himself bear the consequences that would have befallen the person against whom he testified. One may see this law as an extension of more general statements against false testimony such as those found in the Ten Commandments, Exod 20:16: "You shall not bear false witness against your neighbor" and, again, in Deut 5:20: "You shall not bear deceitful witness against your neighbor."

The talionic formula at the end of Deut 19:16–21 focuses on physical retaliation; but what if the case involved monetary loss only? The monetary case is more explicitly set out in the Mishnah, *m. Makk.* 1:2, where talionic retribution is explained as requiring the false witness to compensate his victim by paying him the amount in question; but there is disagreement on whether physical punishment is also required:

(If witnesses stated) "We testify that this person owes his friend two hundred zuz" and it is found out that they were (intentionally) false, they are flogged and (must also) pay compensation because the verse (lit. name) that brings one to flogging (Exod 20:16 or Deut 5:20) is not the same verse that brings one to compensation (Deut 19:16–21). This is the position of Rabbi Meir; but the Sages say that one who pays is not to be flogged.[1]

The rabbis build upon the principles stated in Deut 19:16–21 and consider the kinds of testimony that, if contradicted, could lead to an actionable charge of falsity, as well as distribution of responsibility when multiple witnesses are involved. These kinds of determinations were doubtlessly important; but, as far as our evidence goes, they find no correspondence in the known ancient Near Eastern laws. I will therefore not pursue them here.[2]

The Mishnah, however, in *m. Makk.* 1:6, brings forward an interesting historical anecdote on the disagreement between Sadducees and Pharisees on the question: at what stage in the legal proceedings would the courts mete out punishment for falsity? The Mishnah recounts as follows:

> Witnesses who have been shown to be intentionally false witnesses (in a capital case) are not executed until after the verdict (in the case) has been given (by the judges). (It is important to note this) because the "Sadducees" maintain (that

the false witnesses are not executed) unless the defendant (against whom they falsely testified) was (in fact) put to death, since Scripture states (in Deut 19:20) "life for life." But the Sages responded to them: "Does not the passage also state (in Deut 19:19) 'You shall do him just as he had meant to do to his fellow?' So this fellow must still be alive!" But if so, then why does (Scripture) then say: "life for life?" (The answer is that) one might assume that (punishment was meted out) at the time when (the judges heard) their testimony (falsified). So this verse comes to teach that they are indeed not to be executed until (after) the verdict.[3]

Although the exegesis of the Sages seems a bit forced, it does make us aware of the various stages involved in a trial. One can readily imagine a sequence: initial declaration of the issue to be resolved; the coming forward of witnesses to testify for or against the person or persons involved; the taking of oaths in support of testimony; and finally the verdict and its resulting judgment.

The Mishnah in *m. Makk.* 1:1 also adds a curious case, where, although there is falsified testimony affecting the status of a priest, the judges cannot in fully symmetrical fashion apply the talionic consequences of Deut 19:16–21 to the false witnesses:

> How are witnesses punished for falsification (as in Deuteronomy 19)? (If they say): "we bear witness against So and So that he is the child of a divorced woman or one rejected (by her husband's brother) for a levirate marriage," (the

---

1. These two groups of verses are also linked in the exposition of the rabbis in *Sifre D* 190, relying on Deut 19:19, "You shall do him just as he had meant to do to his fellow."

2. See, e.g., *m. Makk.* 1:1–6; *b. Makk.* 5a–b; *t. Makk.* 1:1–6, Zuckermandel.

3. A similar statement appears in *t. Sanh.* 6:6, Zuckermandel.

judges) cannot declare that they (i.e., the witnesses are to be punished) by being legally declared in his place as son of a divorced woman or of a woman rejected for levirate marriage. So, rather, they are to be flogged (with) forty (lashes).

The defamed individual, if he were a priest and the charges were true, would suffer degraded status according to the rule of Lev 21:7, which forbids marriage between a priest and a divorcee. But the punishment meted out to the false witnesses cannot in this situation mirror the consequences that would have been suffered by that priest. The natal status of the witnesses cannot be changed; therefore these witnesses must be penalized in a different fashion—flogging.

We turn now to the ancient Near Eastern sources. The perspectives coming from the Mishnah, *m. Makk.* 1:1, may perhaps help us imagine what may be happening in Urnamma Laws §28–29:

> If a man came forward to be a witness but is shown to be a liar,[4] then he shall pay 15 shekels silver. If a man came forward to be a witness (but) turned away from (taking) an oath, he must compensate (for) whatever (sum) is involved (in that case).

The second law seems straightforward, applying the principal of proportionality that we have already seen in Deut 19:16–21. The witness "incriminates himself" by his refusal to swear an oath in support of his testimony. He must therefore suffer a penalty equal in amount to what the

judges would have required his victim to pay. We can surmise that the witness had already given his testimony and that it was provisionally accepted. But before a final verdict was handed down, he was then sent to a temple to confirm his testimony under oath. After this was done and reported, the judges were prepared to render final judgment. This would explain why it was necessary to wait for the announcing of the "final verdict," as described in *m. Makk.* 1:6. By failing to swear, the now "false" witness would then be sentenced to bear the penalty his victim would otherwise have suffered.

The first law is a bit more puzzling. The witness is confirmed as false; but his penalty is a fixed sum of silver rather than a penalty in proportion to what his victim would have to pay. Why was this so? One might explain the first law in the light of what we see in *m. Makk.* 1:1, namely, a fixed payment will apply to a situation where the punishment cannot be in proportion to the offense. But while the rabbis imposed flogging, Urnamma imposes monetary compensation. Another possibility may be that the witness was disqualified from testifying, on the grounds that he was previously, i.e., in another case, shown to be a liar. Being therefore identified as having been a false witness, he is barred from giving any credible testimony here. One may find an echo of this type of situation in the Mishnah, *m. Sanh.* 3:3, where persons who engage in unseemly activities are disqualified from serving as witnesses or judges.[5] But this determination was not always a straightforward

4. The translation, "liar" is supported by a number of references discussed by Falkenstein, *NSG* 1:74 n. 6 and *NSG* 2 no. 84:16. The term denotes a person of untrustworthy character, also one who is a thief.

5. Various other disqualifications are discussed in the Gemara to this Mishnah in *b. Sanh.* 24a–27a, including the issues raised in the Tosefta cited here.

matter. The Tosefta (*t. Makk.* 1:11, Zuck-ermandel) brings a different perspective:

> A perjured witness is (subsequent-ly) disqualified from all testimo-nies mentioned in the Torah; so says Rabbi Judah. Rabbi Meir said to him: "This rule only applies for one who perjured in a capital case; but if he was perjured in a case in-volving payment of money, he will not be disqualified except for that single case.

One may conjecture that Urnamma Laws §28 may have imposed a fine on a person, who came forward to testify but who, in the course of the legal proceedings, was shown to be untrustworthy on the basis of his past record.

The principle of talionic punishment that we find in Deuteronomy 19 is suc-cinctly stated in Lipit-Ishtar Laws §17:

> If a man accuses (another) man out of malice about a matter of which he had no knowledge (and) that man cannot prove it, he must bear the penalty of the matter regarding which he brought the accusation.[6]

We are not told why the accuser could not convict the accused person. Was it for lack of evidence or was it because the accuser was unwilling to take the oath in support of his testimony, as in Urnamma §29?

A similar situation is described in Hammurapi Laws §§3–4, which, like we have seen in the Bible, extends the prin-ciple of talion to capital cases; and like we have seen in the Tosefta, brings in a dis-tinction between cases involving money and those which could result in capital punishment. The laws are as follows:

> If a man came forward in a case with false testimony but has not confirmed the word(s) he spoke, if that case is a case of a life (and death), that man shall be killed. If he came forth in testimony (in-volving) grain or silver, he shall bear the penalty for that case (var. he shall pay the claims relating (to that case).

The consequences are talionic, regardless of whether the cases involved capital pun-ishment or monetary compensation. This part is clear. But again, we are not told how the witness had failed to "confirm" his testimony. Was this witness required to bolster his testimony by bringing other evidence, as some have suggested? Im-posing this extra "burden of proof" upon, e.g., an eyewitness to a crime, would cer-tainly make a witness wary of reporting it and testifying to it in court. On the other hand, all witnesses could reasonably be expected to swear an oath in support of their testimony. And, after such an oath, the burden of refutation would fall upon the accused person. This may very well be what is meant by the failure of the accuser to "confirm" his statement.[7]

The serious consequences of lying in capital cases, together with the principle of talionic retribution, are reiterated in Hammurapi Laws §§1–2. We have already considered Hammurapi Laws §2 above (sec. 7.2), which deals with a charge of sorcery. Hammurapi Laws §1 deals with a charge of murder:

> If a man accuses (another) man and brings (lit. hurls) a charge of murder against him but has not

6. A collated reading and translation of this law is given in PSD A/2, 61.

7. This line of reasoning follows Westbrook, "Evidentiary Procedure," who sees a distinction between plausible assertions made in court and those resulting in "confirmation" by a formal oath.

confirmed it, his accuser shall be killed (instead of him).

Although the earlier Sumerian laws do not formally invoke the principle of talion in connection with accusations of capital crimes, we know that the principle was indeed recognized in Sumer. We have a legal record from Nippur, which begins by recalling that some years earlier, the son of the prefect of the Inanna temple accused his father of an unspecified serious crime for which he was sentenced to death. But the prefect was somehow able to satisfy the mind of the king and so the king spared his life. More than several years later, in the reign of a later king, the son now accused his father of violating a cultic taboo and of diverting ingredients intended for divine offerings to his personal use. But the son failed to confirm the accusations and so the king sentenced him to death, apparently the same punishment that would have befallen his father had the father been found guilty of these desecrations. The king in his judgment allowed the exonerated father to designate a younger son as heir-successor to his prefecture in place of the older brother who was executed. The rest of the elder brother's estate was divided between the younger son and two other sons of the exonerated prefect.[8]

Another situation similar to the Mishnah, *m. Makk.* 1:1, is found in the later Middle Assyrian Laws §A 19 (discussed above in sec. 1.7). A man has gone around accusing another man of being a sodomite and claims that he can prove the

charge. But when the matter came before the court, he was unable to offer convincing proof. The man who made the accusation was punished by caning, forced labor, and monetary penalty. There is similarity with *m. Makk.* 1:1 in that "the punishment cannot fit the crime" in a case of slander and defamation, because the court could not punish the defamer by declaring him to be a sodomite. So, like in the Mishnah, he was punished by flogging and with other penalties.

8.2 CORRUPTION OF JUDGES

The Bible in many places condemns dishonest judges who take bribes and subvert justice. The legal formulations do not appear in narrative or case form but, rather, are stated as exhortations accompanied by supporting arguments. Exodus 23:8: declares:

> Do not accept a bribe, for a bribe blinds those who (otherwise) see clearly and overturns the words of the just.

Deuteronomy 16:18–20 likewise declares:

> You shall appoint judges and officials in all your (city) gates which the Lord your God is giving to you, according to your tribes, and they shall judge the people (in) righteous judgment. You shall not thwart justice; show no partiality; you shall not accept a bribe, for a bribe can blind the eyes of the wise and overturn the words of the just. Justice, justice shall you pursue, that you may live on and inherit the land that the Lord your God is giving you.

This same sentiment is again stated in Exod 18:21–22, where Jethro advises an overburdened Moses as follows:

---

8. The document is dated to the second year of Ibbi-Sin of the Ur III dynasty (c. 2027 BCE) and has been most recently treated in Roth, "Appendix A: A Reassessment of RA 71 (1977) 125ff." I also discuss this document in sec. 5.7.

You should also look for able men among all the people, men who fear God, are trustworthy, and hate dishonest gain; set such men over them as officers over thousands, hundreds, fifties and tens. Let them sit as judges for the people at all times; let them bring every important case to you, but decide every minor case themselves. So it will be easier for you, and they will bear the burden with you. (NRSV)

The perversion of justice by persons seeking bribes is repeatedly condemned by the prophets, e.g., Isa 1:23:

> Your rulers are rogues And cronies of thieves, Every one avid for presents And greedy for gifts; They do not judge the case of the orphan, And the widow's cause never reaches them. (NJPS)[9]

The Temple Scroll 51:11–18 offers an expanded version of the law given in Deut 16:18–20, which I cited above:

> You shall appoint judges and officials, in all your towns, who will judge the people righteously. They must be impartial in judgment. They are not to take bribes or pervert justice. Most certainly bribery perverts justice, subverts the testimony of the righteous man, blinds the eyes of the wise, causes great guilt, and defile the courthouse with iniquitous sin. You shall pursue justice and justice alone, so that you may live, entering and inheriting the land that I am about to give you as an inheritance forever. Any man who does accept a bribe and perverts righteous judgment must

be put to death. You shall not fear him; put him to death.[10]

An important addition in the Temple Scroll is the imposing capital punishment upon a judge, who is convicted of having taken a bribe and delivering a false judgment. This is surprising in view of what we find elsewhere in the Hebrew Bible. One may compare the speech of Samuel to the people in which he asks them to justify why they no longer have confidence in prophetic leadership but prefer a king. In 1 Sam 12:3 the prophet declares:

> Here I am; testify against me before the LORD and before his anointed. Whose ox have I taken? Or whose donkey have I taken? Or whom have I defrauded? Whom have I oppressed? Or from whose hand have I taken a bribe to blind my eyes with it? Testify against me and I will restore it to you." (NRSV)

We see here that the expected punishment for taking a bribe would normally be compensation, not the death penalty. Other, divine punishment might of course also follow. We see this in Deut 27:19, which invokes a public curse upon a judge, who fails to give fair judgment to the poor and powerless:

> "Cursed be anyone who deprives the alien, the orphan, and the widow of justice." All the people shall say, "Amen!" (NRSV)

Although this is not overtly stated here, it is likely that the injustice was the result of the judge taking a bribe or favoring a rich person, who could bestow other benefits. The point to be taken from this curse is that any punishment beyond

---

9. Cf. also Jer 6:13; Ezek 22:27; Prov 15:27; 17:23.

10. Wise, Abegg, and Cook, *Dead Sea Scrolls: A New Translation*, 619–20.

compensation—if it could indeed be collected even here—was left to Heaven.

In the ancient Near Eastern law collections, we encounter a law involving a judge who is punished and disbarred for changing his verdict. This is described in Hammurapi Laws §5:

> If a judge has judged a case, delivered a verdict, (and) had (a scribe) record (it in) a sealed document but afterwards has changed his judgment, then they shall convict that judge for having changed his judgment and whatever claims there are in that case he shall pay twelve-fold. And in the assembly they shall remove him from his seat of judgeship and he may never return and may not (ever) sit with (other) judges in judgment.

We are not told why the judge changed his mind; evidently the reason why was not as important as the fact that the judge did so. A judge was not expected to recant after delivering his verdict. Bribery is of course a possible cause, but there could also have been a genuine change of heart on the part of the judge. The law does not describe all of the consequences that might follow from the judge changing his verdict. For example, was the verdict now to be overturned? If not, then the heavy penalty could have been a way to compensate the party, who lost the suit under that first decision.

Babylonian judges usually presided over cases as part of a group, assisted by other colleagues, officials, and respected community leaders. Nevertheless, we know that a single false judge was capable of corrupting the process of justice. We see this depicted in a hymn to the sun-god, the patron of justice:

You show the unscrupulous judge (to his) fetters, one who accepts a bribe (and) does not judge rightly you make him bear his punishment. As for him who declines a bribe, who takes the part of the weak, this is pleasing to Shamash, and he will prolong his life.[11]

In these Babylonian contexts a dishonest judge was not executed. Hammurapi Laws §5 penalizes the suspect judge with a heavy monetary payment; and the hymn leaves it to the sun-god to mete out divine punishment, in the manner of the curse in Deut 27:19. The sun-god hymn mentions fetters; these were typically put on persons who were at risk of being sold as slaves because they were unable to pay their debts. This would fit with the heavy monetary punishment described in Hammurapi Laws §5. The guilty judge would either pay or he himself would be sold into slavery.

The situation of the recanting judge may be compared to a law later found in rabbinic sources, dealing with witnesses who are not allowed to recant after giving formal testimony. The Tosefta (*t. Sanh.* 6:4–5, Zuckermandel) states:

> Witnesses may revise their testimony up to the time that their testimony is (formally) examined in court; after their testimony is examined, they cannot recant. For this is the rule in this matter: Witnesses who testified—in matters relating to rendering impure or pure, to expel or to reinstate, to forbid or to permit, to acquit or to find guilty—up to the time that their testimony has not been formally

11. These lines are from the "great hymn" to Shamash, ll. 97–100, published in Lambert, *Babylonian Wisdom Literature,* 132–33.

examined (by the court) and they say "We are mistaken," they are believed. However, after (they have testified and) their testimony has been formally examined, and they declare: "We are mistaken," they are not believed.[12]

The testimony of the witnesses must stand and the judgment could only be reversed if new evidence, which was not available at the trial, is brought to the attention of the court in a timely fashion, before the verdict was handed down.[13]

From all the evidence we have at present, it would appear that the death penalty prescribed in the Temple Scroll represents a departure from the customary remedy of requiring a false judge to pay financial compensation. We also find the practice of compensation in Roman law, which required a judge who was "guilty of partiality, enmity, or even corruption" to pay "a just assessment of the damages."[14] Later rabbinic law, in similar fashion, required a judge who took a bribe to compensate the party who was unjustly treated.[15] One must therefore seek to find a reason for the severity of the Temple Scroll. Perhaps it was an angry form of criticism and protest against the current government, whose policies and actions were condemned by the sect and served to motivate them to withdraw and live apart from the larger society of their day.

---

12. A parallel citation is found in *t. Ket.* 2:1, Lieberman.

13. This is stated in *t. Sanh.* 6:4, Zuckermandel.

14. Thomas, *Textbook of Roman Law,* 377, who cites a number of sources, including *D.5.1.15.1,* from which the passage given above is taken.

15. Maimonides, *Mishah Torah, Hilkhot Teshuva* 4:5. Additional, heavenly punishments were also thought possible; cf. *b. Ket.* 105a.

9

Final Thoughts and Perspectives

IN THIS STUDY WE have examined the early history of Jewish law through the lens of the ancient Near Eastern legal traditions. Based upon what we have found, I can identify four major categories within the early Jewish laws:

1. Ancient Near Eastern law statements, although absent in the Bible, that lived on virtually unchanged over many centuries of time into rabbinic times.

2. Biblical laws that are essentially identical with ancient Near Eastern laws and that continued with little change over further centuries into rabbinic times.

3. Biblical laws that contain noteworthy departures from ancient Near Eastern practice.

4. Biblical laws that were subject to later reinterpretation by the rabbis.

1. The first category consists of laws attested in the ancient Near Eastern collections going back as far as the second millennium BCE. We find them still preserved and "re-emerging" in the later, rabbinic collections of the second and third centuries CE, and sometimes even later. It is most striking to note that the laws in this group do *not* appear in the Bible, nor are they preserved in any extra-biblical Jewish materials of the first millennium BCE period. Laws belonging to this first category deal with marriage cancellation (sec. 1.2.2); dissolution of marriage because of illness (sec. 1.2.3); the "rebellious wife" (sec. 1.2.4); sale of chattel slaves (sec. 3.1); injuries to chattel slaves (sec. 4.2); assault on dignity (sec. 4.4); hiring of boats and loss through negligence (sec. 5.4); negligence in an agricultural lease (sec. 6.2); and agricultural lease and natural disaster (sec. 6.3). These are all in areas that were integral to the social order and economy of ancient times. It is therefore reasonable to assume that laws governing legal practices of such similar or identical character would have been operative during the biblical period, even though they are not preserved in the biblical law collections.

This long trail of continuity supports the postbiblical Jewish claim concerning the existence of ancient "oral laws" that had been "handed down" alongside of the written laws of the Pentateuch. Josephus reports this claim being made by the Pharisees; and it was similarly invoked by the later rabbis who wrote the Mishnah and Tosefta, which incorporate many Jewish laws that are not found in the biblical law collections.[1] Josephus records that the Sadducees rejected the oral laws presented by the Pharisees; and we find further description of discord recorded in the New Testament, e.g. Mark 7:5, where the Pharisees are said to be following "the tradition of the elders." But I suspect that the heart of their controversy was with respect to laws relating to theological doctrines and with particular ritual and cultic observances rather than about the "practical" laws that we list here in our first category. These laws after all pertain to the fabric of everyday life and did not affect theology. The Sadducees moreover also recognized practices and procedures that were not recorded in the written Torah.[2] The conflict between Pharisees and Sadducees may have turned upon the binding authority of oral traditions not contained in the written Scriptures, with the Pharisees arguing that both categories should be viewed as possessing the same degree of divine authority.[3] Later rabbis, as I have noted (Introduction), went so far as to assign divine authority even to oral laws shared by Jews with gentiles, explaining them as oral commandments originally given by God to Noah after the Flood.

1. Cf. the famous passages in Josephus, *Ant.* 13.297–98; and in *m. Avot* 1:1. The term "Oral Torah" appears in the *baraita* cited in *b. Shabb.* 31a, in *b. Yoma* 28b, *b. Qidd.* 66a. It is also found in the "halakhic midrashim": *Sifra Behuqotai* 2:8 on Lev 26:46 and *Sifre D* 351 on Deut 33:10. For more detailed discussion see Rivkin, *A Hidden Revolution.*

2. See *m. Yad.* 2:7 on an owner's liability for theft committed by his slave (sec. 5.6.2). There both Pharisees and Sadducees are arguing about oral laws not written in Scripture.

3. For this point cf. Rivkin, *A Hidden Revolution,* 246–47; and Mansoor, Sadducees." For the early rabbis, see the *baraita* cited in *b. Shabb.* 31a and other references cited above in connection with "oral laws."

2. The second category consists of biblical laws that are essentially identical with earlier ancient Near Eastern laws, and that subsequently were continued with little change over later centuries down to rabbinic times. This group of laws includes "foundational" incest prohibitions prohibiting sexual relations between members of the natal family: father, mother, brother, and maternal sister (sec. 1.1.1). For the family expanded by marriage, we find prohibitions affecting a man's stepdaughter (sec. 1.1.4) and closely similar laws relating to accusations of adultery (sec. 1.3.2), rape and seduction (secs. 1.4.1–1.4.3). Additional similarities in the areas of family and sexual behavior can be found in laws on homosexuality and bestiality (secs. 1.7–1.8); and rights of redemption (sec. 2.5.2).

There are similar laws relating to personal injury and homicide: striking a parent (sec. 4.5); injury to male genitals (sec. 4.6); striking a pregnant woman (sec. 4.7); injury and homicide through negligence on property (sec. 4.9); unsolved homicide (sec. 4.11); kidnapping (sec.4.12). Similar laws dealing with property include: deposit of goods for safekeeping (sec. 5.1); animal keepers and their responsibilities (sec. 5.2); borrowed or hired animals or tools (sec. 5.3); theft of livestock (sec. 5.5); loss of domestic animals caused by other domestic animals (sec. 5.8); theft of land (sec. 6.1); trespass and grazing (sec. 6.4); damage to field and crops by fire (sec. 6.5). Also belonging to this category are laws on sowing two species in the same field (sec. 6.6); cursing and blasphemy (sec. 7.1); false witness (sec. 8.1); and corruption of judges (sec. 8.2). To this list one could also add adoption, for which we have seen limited biblical evidence in poetic passages but no law statement (sec. 1.6).

The laws in this category reflect the presence of shared moral values between Israelites and their neighbors, and similar responses to problems within the social and economic order. The laws in this category, like those in the previous group, continue, essentially unchanged, in the later development and history of Jewish law.

3. In the third category of laws, on the other hand, one encounters biblical laws containing noteworthy departures from ancient Near Eastern practice. These represent changes that were almost certainly generated from within the Israelite community rather than imposed from without. There are a number of significant changes in the structure of the family. For example, in the restriction affecting a man's paternal sister (i.e., father's daughter by a different mother); biblical narratives tell us that such unions took place during the time of the monarchy and earlier, yet this union became forbidden in the formal biblical laws (sec. 1.1.1). We also find changes when the natal family is expanded through marriage. Levirate marriages between a man and the widow of his son, brother, or father became more restrictive than formerly. The earlier practices, more in line with ancient Near Eastern laws, are preserved in biblical narratives (sec. 1.1.2). Similar disparities between narrative and law are found in the ban against a man marrying his wife's sister or his father's sister (sec. 1.1.3), remarriage with a divorced wife (sec. 1.2.1), proven adultery (sec. 1.3.1), the return of a lost or runaway slave (sec. 3.2), and with the rejection of

compensation by the families of homicide victims (sec. 4.8.2).

The earlier practices depicted in the narratives may be taken to reflect "Israelite" law during the monarchy period or even earlier; these may be viewed as the oldest legal practices of the Israelite people and nation. The same can be said for the biblical law statements that I have cited above in the first and second categories, which did not much change from what we find in the ancient Near Eastern law collections. These "unchanged, older" biblical law statements can even be viewed as going back to a time before the Pentateuch itself was composed. They are the "stuff" that some scholars have associated with Canaanite or Amorite law practices that might have been followed before the settlement of the land by the Israelites. I would affirm that they are part of the "customary law" traditions that were widely known and followed within the ancient Near Eastern world. The Bible itself treats older and newer laws alike; and changed laws are rarely identified as such. But even for those so identified, the reasons for change are not usually given except, e.g., in general statements condemning the older laws as practices of non-Israelite neighbors worthy of rejection (as in sec. 1.1.5).[4]

The biblical innovations or variances, on the other hand, define an inflection point in the development of biblical law. The biblical law statements that depart from the ancient Near Eastern traditions may be viewed as the fruits of a great religious "awakening," that I believe was

4. A specific reason for changing inheritance law for women is given in Num 36:6–9, in connection with the daughters of Zelophehad (sec. 1.5.2). This is quite exceptional.

ignited by the prophets and fueled by the foreign conquests of Samaria and Jerusalem. It is widely believed by many modern scholars that the Pentateuch, which contains all of our formal biblical laws, took its present shape during the restoration that was fostered by the Persian king Cyrus and his successors. It is during this era that a religiously centered approach to law crystallized and consciously separated from earlier "Israelite" practices from the time of the monarchies, that were more in line with common ancient Near Eastern practices. Important factors behind this transformation were the acceptance of universal monotheism and the concept of the people living as a sacred community living under God's rules and ultimate sovereignty. These beliefs created an increased sense of social separation from their polytheist neighbors. The Judeans, living with weakened political self-determination eroded through conquest, embraced voluntary self-determination under religious auspices, which allowed them to structure more aspects of their lives under their own community rules. This community life was led by the temple priests, to whom was given authority to teach and interpret the rules in the Pentateuch, subject of course, to the pleasure of their temporal, non-Jewish rulers.[5] This pattern of communal governance continued into Roman times. Even the Samaritans, while breaking with Judeans and championing Shechem over Jerusalem, still maintained the concept of priestly leadership along with the Pentateuch.

The newer laws, like those relating to marriage rules and incest (sec. 1.1), promoted exogamy over close endogamy. Exogamy was a way to create bonds within the community of the faithful, while at the same time creating new marriage boundaries against non-Judean polytheists.[6] The revised, more limiting marriage rule for Zelophehad's daughters and its evident reception as recounted in the book of Tobit (sec. 1.5.2) may also be seen as a check on "free" exogamy, favoring closer inheritance of property within the patriarchal family framework that was the norm. The book of Tobit shows that Judeans living in diaspora communities maintained a degree of solidarity with norms and patterns established in the Judean "homeland." The tracking of lineage becomes important for identity and may have contributed to the disuse of adoption (sec. 1.6). Members living within the Judean "covenant community" were required to treat others with fairness and justice; and as stated in many laws, to extend these standards to the "sojourner, stranger, and God-fearers" who lived within the Judean community and respected its religious values. I believe that the incorporation of ritual calendar and sacrificial regulations into the written body of the Pentateuch was a byproduct of the formation of the new religious order and the increased powers of the priesthood.

This uniting of religious observance rules with laws of secular governance was a novel development, unlike what had long been the situation in the ancient Near East, as well as in ancient Israel under the monarchies. Law collections written under royal patronage deal

5. For discussion of the interaction between the Persian kings and their subject peoples with respect to local autonomy see Watts, *Persia and Torah,* and MacGinnis, "A Judgment of King Darius."

6. See, e.g., Deut 7:1–4; Ezra 9:1–2; Neh 10:29–31. See further Kohler, "Intermarriage."

with civil laws, e.g., related to personal status, marriage rules, and property. Ritual and religious laws and practices are also found in ancient written collections; but these belong to the circle of priests and temple. Combining these ritual laws with "civil" or secular laws served to enhance a religious commitment to internal community solidarity. The power of the community belief system rather than the courts was used to support the expanded range of incest prohibitions that were seen as protecting the holiness of the community (sec. 1.1.5). We see a late "echo" of this solidarity concept in 1 Cor 6:1–6, where Paul enjoins members of the emerging Christian community to settle their disputes internally rather than going before magistrates who are unbelievers. For there was, to be sure, a long tradition for the practice of private "arbitration" in the ancient world; one could always turn to mutually respected persons to settle disputes outside of any state-controlled framework. This practice was known in ancient Babylonia; it is found in the Hebrew Bible, and it continued to exist alongside of the regular Roman courts, as well, of course, in rabbinic law.[7]

We also find, moreover, departures from ancient Near Eastern practice that are not explicitly revealed within the biblical narratives; but it is clear from the law statements themselves that they were intended either to reject or change earlier existing norms. For example, situations

7. Cohen, "Arbitration in Jewish and Roman Law"; this arrangement is well-stated in the *Theodosian Code* 2.2.10 (decree dated to 398 CE) where in civil suits only, Jews were enabled to seek internal arbitration of their disputes. For earlier, Babylonian examples see also *CAD* M/1, 41 sub *mitguru*.

of debtors and debt slavery are addressed in a number of law statements. Whereas ancient Near Eastern laws attempted to regulate interest, the Bible prohibits the practice entirely between members of the Judean community (sec. 2.5.1). The Bible takes up the ancient Near Eastern idea of setting debt slaves free after a period of time; but then also tries to prevent sexual exploitation of female debt slaves as well as give her offspring legitimate status within the religious community (sec. 2.1). Biblical society was familiar with the ancient Near Eastern practice of periodically giving relief to debtors as a group by canceling their debts. But this required royal sponsorship, which evidently was infrequently given under the monarchies of Judea and Samaria; and such relief, of course, was not to be expected after the foreign conquest of the lands. The concept of royal releases was then transferred to God, who, it was hoped, would one day manifest his rule over the nations (sec. 2.3).

During this period of religious redefinition, when the remedies depicted from the ancient Near Eastern laws were no longer applicable, the Judean community proposed new legal processes to alleviate the condition of debtors who fell into slavery. One method was to institute a general release after a set period of years but we have no record of its actual application (sec. 2.4). The narratives do, however, relate episodes where the populace undertook voluntary release of fellow citizens who were held as debt slaves; this took place just prior to the Babylonian conquest and under later Persian rule. I believe that this method may have been the most successful one and could have been renewed from time to time (sec.

2.2); calendar-based releases may also have been attempted during this period (sec. 2.4).

The stamp of religiously motivated changes can also be seen in the biblical laws dealing with sexual offenses against slaves (sec. 1.4.4), injury and homicide caused by domestic animals (sec. 4.10), returning a lost animal to owner (sec. 5.9), and sorcery, which was condemned along with other, originally non-related and permitted practices (sec. 7.2). We also encounter biblical changes in the ancient Near Eastern practices dealing with the mistreatment of debt slaves and debt hostages; this widespread social problem was, however, apparently also being addressed in other, non-Jewish societies as well (sec. 4.1).

This study has not deeply looked at changes within ancient Near Eastern legal traditions to the extent that it has explored changes within biblical and later Jewish law. We have noted, for example changes in Hittite Laws, favoring compensation over capital punishment in homicide and other cases. Surprisingly, despite a much larger quantity of ancient Near Eastern legal materials, we seem to know less about their putative causes of change. This remains an important desideratum, but it is one that falls beyond the scope of the present endeavor.[8]

4. In this fourth category are biblical laws that were subject to later reinterpretation by the rabbis, sometimes entirely changing the ancient parameters. Examples of such changes are seen in connection with levirate marriage (sec. 1.1.2); the institution

of a required written divorce record (sec. 1.2.1); protecting a bride from accusations of previous infidelity (sec. 1.3.2); sexual relations with a slave (sec. 1.4.4); the inheritance of a wife's dowry by her husband (sec. 1.5.2); restricted definition of homosexual activities (sec. 1.7); giving only monetary damages as compensation for personal injuries (sec. 4.3); redirecting liability for accidental homicide of a pregnant woman and for her foetuses (sec. 4.7); "leveling" the punishment for theft of non-livestock property (sec. 5.6) as well as for theft of land (sec. 6.1); recalculating the losses for injuries caused by one domestic animal to another (sec. 4.10); liability of kidnapper (sec. 4.12); redefining the prohibitions against mixed seeding (sec. 6.6); and modifying the calculation of damages for trespass and grazing (sec. 6.4). To this list one may consider adding the measure allowing the father to reject the suit of the man who raped his unmarried daughter (sec. 1.4.2), although this right is already anciently attested in Assyrian Laws §A 55, as noted in our discussion.

The existence of this fourth category shows the need for additional study on rabbinic attitudes. To begin with, their departures from biblical laws should receive more attention, in contrast to what has more commonly occurred, namely, trying to re-interpret earlier biblical laws, so as to bring them into conformity with later rabbinic interpretations. Secondly, while there has been study of rabbinic hermeneutical methods, more attention needs to be paid to the categories of laws to which rabbinic hermeneutical interpretations were applied. In various places within this work I have put forth the suggestion that some changes came from

8. Jackson, *Comparison of Ancient Near Eastern Law Collections,* endeavors to address this need.

rabbinic contact with Roman laws and legal theory that penetrated throughout the empire, I believe that this relationship has not yet been fully probed.[9] In similar fashion, I have explained other rabbinic revisions as adjustments to the moral standards of their own times; but this was not always so, as we can see in the fact that the rabbis, e.g., maintained the possibility of marriage between a man and his niece, which was earlier condemned by Philo and the Essenes, and was not practiced by the Romans (sec. 1.1.3).

It is noteworthy that within all four categories, we have identified important legal details that could well have been included had the law statements been more completely formulated. Thus, for example, ancient Near Eastern laws explain the circumstances surrounding the requirement for a keeper of deposited goods taking an oath, while rabbinic laws add details on how negligence in deposit might have been determined (sec. 5.1). Both rabbinic and ancient Near Eastern laws tell us about the role of community authorities, which are unmentioned in the biblical law formulation on injury and homicide through negligence (sec. 4.9). Another example may be the manner in which the community established an ox as a habitual gorer, as well as the wider application of this same law to vicious dogs (sec. 4.10). In the hiring of boats and in cases of loss through negligence, we have seen that the rabbinic laws add significant details on defining negligent behavior (sec. 5.4). To this list one can perhaps add Exod 21:20–21, which supplies a time factor in determining cause for a severely chastised debt

slave who subsequently died (sec. 4.1) and insight on the physical punishment of false witnesses (sec. 8.1).

Such "omissions" again remind us that the laws contained in the Hebrew Bible only represent a selection out of a larger body of customary laws or legal traditions that were recognized but not included in our extant written collections. This is clearly evident for laws dealing with the hiring of work animals, for which the rabbis seek to create an "anchor" in Scripture (sec. 5.3). We find another illustration of this ancient "selective process" in laws dealing with theft of property belonging to temple or palace (sec. 5.7). These laws are included in the ancient Near Eastern and rabbinic law collections; and although a similar view is reflected in the biblical narratives, the subject was not addressed in the formal biblical law statements. Another illustration of incompleteness is the incest prohibition on a man having sexual relations with his own daughter; it is a universal taboo, attested in the ancient Near East as in rabbinic law yet it was omitted in the Bible. However, it was certainly operative as evidenced from the prohibition between grandfather and granddaughter, which is preserved among the biblical laws. (sec. 1.1.1).

I see the extant written law statements emerging out of a dynamic, mainly orally transmitted "customary law" tradition, that was present in the ancient Near East, that continued over centuries of time. From time to time, laws were written down, producing the various law collections—both formal and informal—that are the subject of our study. The incomplete nature of our written law collections—ancient Near Eastern as well as biblical—also explains why we encounter

---

9. For an overview of scholarly literature exploring the relationship between rabbinic and Roman law see Hezser, "Introduction."

poorly formulated law statements within the Bible as in the laws on hired animals (sec. 5.3), theft of livestock (sec. 5.5) or trespass and grazing (sec. 6.4), and damage to field and crops by fire (sec. 6.5). Such statements apparently assumed pre-existing awareness outside of the law statement that would "compensate for" or could "excuse" incomplete or hasty written formulations. The biblical laws and law collections are "secondary additions" that were inserted into the Pentateuch, which was primarily a narrative account. Only in the later Mishnah and Tosefta do we encounter comprehensive legal compilations that were topically arranged and that focused solely on laws.[10]

It is my belief that exploring the relationship of ancient Near Eastern law with biblical and rabbinic laws enables us to achieve a perspective on their fundamental levels of meaning, closest to what the ancient peoples themselves may have understood these laws to say in their own time and setting. It is therefore my hope that this present study will serve to motivate more historically based analyses of Jewish law, that are sensitive to the real debt owed by Jewish law to its ancient Near Eastern roots. At the very least, I hope that scholars will come to recognize that the similarities between biblical and ancient Near Eastern laws represent more than curiosities of history. They are to be seen as part of a shared cultural tradition and must therefore be part of any scholarly analysis of biblical and early rabbinic legal texts. Finally, I offer this study as one way to illustrate how the biblical writers and later rabbis worked to bring the ancient and traditional laws governing human social behavior into greater conformity with values and principles that emerged from their evolving understanding of divine truth and justice.

---

10. These rabbinic collections represent a clear and innovative departure from earlier compositions, as is pointed out by Neusner, *Vitality*, vii–xv.

Historical Timeline

	Periods/Events	Laws and Literature
2100 BCE	Neo-Sumerian Period (Ur III)	Laws of Urnamma
	Kingdoms of Isin and Larsa	Lipit-Ishtar Laws
1900 BCE	Old Babylonian Period	Eshnunna Laws
1800 BCE		Hammurapi Laws
1400 BCE	Middle Babylonian Period	
	Middle Assyrian Period	Middle Assyrian Laws
	Hittite Empire in Anatolia	Hittite Laws
	Kings of Judah and Israel	Emar Texts
850 BCE	Neo Assyrian Empire	
625 BCE	Neo-Babylonian Empire	Neo-Babylonian Laws
		Literary Prophets
539 BCE	Persian Empire	Pentateuch
		Psalms
333 BCE	Alexander the Great	
	Ptolemies	Proverbs
	Seleucids	
100 BCE	Hasmoneans, Herodians	
	Romans	Dead Sea Scrolls
	Early Rabbis	Philo, Josephus
100 CE	Emergence of Christianity	New Testament
200 CE		Mishnah, Tosefta. Baraitot
		Mekhilta, Sifra, Sifre
	Byzantine Empire	
600 CE		Palestinian and Babylonian Talmuds
	Emergence of Islam	
	Gaons of Babylonian Jewry	
1000 CE		Maimonides
		Medieval Jewish Commentators

Appendix

Salient Features in the History and Culture
of Ancient Israel and Her Neighbors

THE FOLLOWING HISTORICAL NOTES relate to the various collections of ancient laws that are the focus of this book. I also have added key facts relating to post-biblical times that pertain to the development of rabbinic and later Jewish law. This discussion may be helpful to readers of this book and can be used along with the Historical Timeline.

It is useful to remember that we derive most of our knowledge about the history of ancient Israel from the Hebrew Bible itself. But important additional data also comes to us from a great body of nonbiblical records and artifacts. These materials include ancient religious and historical writings, which, like the Hebrew Bible, were also preserved from antiquity, like the writings of Josephus, Philo, the New Testament, and the law books of the rabbis (Mishnah, Tosefta, Talmud). During the past 150 years, our data has been vastly augmented by remarkable new findings recovered through archaeology, e.g. the Dead Sea Scrolls and the ancient Near Eastern law collections, which are dealt with in this book. Historians and other scholars have endeavored to merge this enormous body of data into a coherent scheme; but the task is far from complete; for there remain gaps to be filled, contradictions to be explained, and complexities yet to be integrated into a larger framework.

The use of writing in the ancient Near East goes back to the late fourth millennium BCE, and private legal contracts appear not long afterwards; political treaty documents are known from the third millennium BCE. However, only at the end of the third millennium do we begin to find abstract formulations of laws being assembled in collections. In the present study, the earliest law collection that is pertinent to our investigation is the Laws of Urnamma, from c. 2100 BCE, which is written in Sumerian. Urnamma (or Urnammu) was a Sumerian ruler who established a regional empire that included most of modern Iraq and Syria—the geographic area between the Euphrates and the Tigris Rivers, which is known as Mesopotamia. He was the founder of what historians call the Third Dynasty of Ur (abbreviated Ur III). This dynasty lasted for about a century; and after the empire crumbled, other formerly subordinate local rulers took control of parts of the former empire.

One of these was Lipit-Ishtar, king of Isin c. 1930 BCE, from whom we have a collection of laws, which are referred to as the Laws of Lipit-Ishtar. Although this king—as did most of the Ur III kings—bears an Akkadian, i.e., a Semitic name, his laws are written in Sumerian, presumably because of a desire to wear the prestigious mantle of the previous Ur III empire and the long established, historic use of Sumerian in the writing of important cultural documents. (The Sumerians appear to have invented the cuneiform writing system that was used to write Sumerian, Akkadian [i.e., Babylonian and Assyrian], Eblaite, and, later, Hittite.) Sumerian continued to be a favored language long after it ceased to be spoken; it was retained in religious liturgies and used by scribes in various literary compositions, into the first millennium BCE. By the end of the Ur III period, Akkadian became the more common everyday spoken language even in Sumer; and one finds increasing use of Akkadian written documents, especially in the northern regions of Mesopotamia, where the majority of inhabitants were non-Sumerians.

A major shift in political power began around 1850 BCE, with the establishment of a series of kingdoms controlled by the Amorites, who were originally Semitic tribesman from the Syrian Desert. The Amorites spoke a West Semitic language related to Hebrew but chose to conduct their affairs in Akkadian, which was the language used by their Mesopotamian subjects. Rulers from two of these Amorite kingdoms have left us law compositions, which are the earliest written in Akkadian. The largest and most famous collection is that of Hammurapi (often written as Hammurabi) of Babylon, who

died c. 1750 BCE. A second, smaller collection is the Eshnunna Laws, which date from about fifty years earlier; it is thought that the king for whom these were written down was Dadusha, king of Eshnunna; but a key line in the text, where his name might have appeared, is damaged. Babylon eventually controlled the southern region between the Tigris and Euphrates rivers, which became known as Babylonia. Eshnunna, in its heyday, controlled the neighboring areas to the east of the Tigris.

Because of the prominence of the dynasty of Hammurapi, the era from c. 1900–1600 BCE, has become known among modern scholars as the Old Babylonian period. During this period the cities of this region produced a rich variety of documents. While the principal language was Akkadian, we also find a number of important, smaller law collections from this period still being written in Sumerian. These were assembled by scribes, apparently for the teaching and training of other scribes.

Other groups of Amorites penetrated into Syria and Palestine; and they were a constituent group among the Hyksos, who conquered and ruled Egypt from c. 1800–1550 BCE. These Amorites also adopted the use of Akkadian in writing their documents and thus made it into an international language of communication. We therefore find cuneiform tablets discovered at sites at scattered sites throughout the areas of their penetration and influence, e.g., at Mari in Syria and at Hazor, Megiddo, Gezer, and Hebron in Palestine.

After 1600 BCE the Amorite kingdoms fell into eclipse with the rise of new empires in the North of Mesopotamia and Anatolia (modern Turkey): the Hurrians and the Hittites. Important compositions recording the Hittite Laws were found in their ancient capital city, Hattusas in northwest Anatolia. They were apparently collected at the behest of the Hittite kings; but none of the tablets reveal the names of the kings involved. The Hittite Laws date to c. 1250 BCE. The number of Hurrian documents is very small and no law compositions are known.

In the last centuries of the second millennium, we see the rising power of Assyria in northern Mesopotamia. The Assyrian kings inaugurated a growing militarism that, over time, led to the growth of an empire, gradually expanding its scope at the expense of the Hurrians, Babylonians, and the Hittite holdings in Syria. From this period we have compositions called the Middle Assyrian Laws and the Harem Edicts. The laws do not preserve the name(s) of their patrons; but the Edicts are dated to kings ruling c. 1000 BCE. Assyrian power reached its zenith during the Neo-Assyrian period, from c. 900–600 BCE. Their western expansion eventually brought Assyria into conflict with the Israelite kings of Samaria and Judea. Samaria (the capital of the northern kingdom of the Israel) was conquered in 722 BCE and absorbed into the Assyrian empire; Judea (to the south) survived, although in a much reduced state.

The Assyrian empire collapsed after the fall of Nineveh in 612 BCE. Its place was quickly filled by a century of Neo-Babylonian rulers, notably Nebuchadnezzar (also called Nebuchadrezzar), who conquered Judea in 596 BCE. After a rebellion led by his regent Zedekiah, Nebuchadnezzar destroyed Jerusalem in 586 BCE, deporting a large number of Judean political and religious leaders to exile in Babylonia. This deportation and earlier deportations of Israelites out of Samaria by the Assyrian kings, together with the flight of refugees into Egypt, mark the beginning of important diaspora communities that became additional centers for Judean religion and culture despite the disappearance of political autonomy in Judea. Archaeologists have recovered a fragmentary collection of laws from Babylonia, which are referred to as the Neo-Babylonian Laws; here again we have no ruler's name preserved. The Neo-Babylonian Empire came to an end when Babylon was conquered by the Persians in 539 BCE.

Shortly thereafter the Persian king Cyrus allowed groups of Judean exiles to return to their homeland and to rebuild the historic temple in Jerusalem, which had originally been founded by King Solomon many centuries earlier. About a century later, the Persian king Artaxerxes, allowed Nehemiah, a Judean exile who rose to become a high Persian official, to rebuild the walls of Jerusalem. These restorations inaugurated an era that historians refer to as the period of the Second Temple. The Persians ruled over most of the ancient Near Eastern "heartlands" including Anatolia and Egypt until the conquest of Alexander the Great in 333 BCE. No law collections have survived from the Persian rulers; many therefore believe that the Persian rulers tended to maintain existing laws in the conquered regions; but this is not known for certain.

The Israelites emerge into general ancient Near Eastern history already during the second half of the second millennium BCE. The Egyptian king Merneptah (c. 1200 BCE) claims to have defeated the people Israel in battle during one of his military campaigns in Syria-Palestine. The Bible mentions Amorites, Hittites and Hurrians (Horites) as well as first millennium rulers of Assyria, Babylonia, Persia by name. There are, moreover, important archaeological findings relating to the royal dynasties of Judea and Samaria. But our most extensive external evidence comes from sources of the first millennium BCE, from the time of the Neo-Assyrian kings and later. Egypt, a close geographical neighbor, figures importantly in the Bible and certain Egyptian kings of the first millennium BCE are mentioned by name. It is therefore unfortunate that we possess so little information about Egyptian laws, despite the use of writing in Egypt that goes back to the beginning of the third millennium BCE. This is a lacuna that archaeology has not yet been able to fill. I have included Egyptian evidence where it exists and is pertinent; most of this is later material from the end of the first millennium BCE.

According to the Bible, the Israelites were originally a tribal society under the leadership of clan leaders, elders, and war chieftains. This is in keeping with the reference by Merneptah and is in the background of the stories told about Abraham and the other patriarchs; and this is essentially the same setting for the accounts in Joshua and Judges—and to some extent also for Moses (about which more will be said below). According to the Bible, the people, in settling the land, had become sedentary farmers rather than roaming herders. Fixity of their residence and key assets left the people vulnerable to raids and pillaging by outsiders. This could take the form of temporary incursions, abated either by the invaders capturing goods and persons or receiving payments of tribute.

The continuing state of hazard and loss led to the establishment of monarchy. Under this system, kings undertook the permanent job of war-leaders, supported by a standing corps of mercenaries and levies of citizen labor to build fortifications and other infrastructure. According to the Bible, there was first an attempt to establish a united monarchy under Saul, David, and Solomon; but c. 900 BCE, the land was permanently divided into two rival political units: the larger kingdom of Israel in the north and a much smaller kingdom of Judea (Judah) in the south. Rivalry between tribal groups clearly played a role in this division, although by the end of the monarchy period, the tribes had lost their earlier political importance.

Whereas in a tribal society, law and legal process is typically based on custom and tradition, monarchy, with its centralized authority, has greater power to make changes in the law. In this study I demonstrate both customary laws that are preserved relatively unchanged over time as well laws that departed from the older norms. But, as I also indicate in this study, it is difficult to firmly connect these changes with individual monarchs. During the Second Temple period, the Persian kings supported the exercise of religious freedoms that did not conflict with royal interests and state controls. The priests of the Jerusalem temple functioned under this royal patronage and they were thus able to serve as representatives both of the state and of the Judean community. As I see it, the reshaping of older, customary norms seems to have reached a climax during the Second Temple period in a process that culminated in the writing of the Pentateuch as we have it now. The prophets, especially those who flourished during the period from 750–500 BCE, clearly played an important inspirational role in motivating the people to change their values relating to polytheism, idolatry, and moral conduct. Prophets, however, disappeared from the scene and had no visible public role after the rebuilding of the temple in Jerusalem. Their place seems to have been adequately filled by the temple priests and the written Pentateuch.

During the Second Temple period, there developed a religious and cultural schism between the returned Judeans and the Samaritans. The Samaritans were those Israelites who either remained in the land after the destruction of Samaria and the deportations by Assyria in 722 BCE or who may have later returned to their homeland. The Judeans believed Jerusalem to be the "place chosen by the Lord to set his name," whereas the Samaritans affirmed Shechem to be this most sacred place. The Bible refers to a "place where God chose to establish his name" in a number of places in Deuteronomy (e.g., Deut 12:5; 14:23; 16:2; 26:2) but does not explicitly name the location. This omission may reflect a time when multiple shrines existed; one may here note a similar reference to Shiloh in Jer 7:12. The account given in 2 Kings 17 alleges that the Samaritans established a flawed religious practice; but the schism can also be seen as a continuation of the historic rivalry that existed earlier between the southern and northern kingdoms. Both communities adopted nearly identical versions of the Pentateuch; but the Samaritans did not subsequently add any of the additional books now in the Hebrew Bible to their sacred canon.

The Pentateuch contains the earlier histories of the patriarchs, the story of Egyptian bondage, the exodus and wilderness accounts. The figure of Moses is very important in these last sections; he is credited with bringing the Ten Commandments and other laws to the people, which are important elements in the covenant, i.e., the relationship that is understood to exist between God and his chosen people of Israel. The Pentateuch appears to speak "in advance" about later events: the institution of monarchy, the conquest and deportation of the people into exile, and the institution and duties of the priestly establishment. To my mind, therefore, the Pentateuch can be viewed as a summary view of the history of Israel from earliest times until after the exile. It inserts previous events into a framework that offered meaning to the past as well as guidance for the future. The Pentateuch thus served as the constitution for the Judeans (and Samaritans) living under the secular rule of Persia but ultimately under the divine rule of God.

This system and its stable state of affairs maintained itself after Alexander conquered the Persian Empire in 333 BCE and for some time thereafter while Judea came under the sway of the Ptolemies in the division of Alexander's empire. But the situation changed after the Seleucids in Syria wrested control of Judea from the Ptolemies in 198 BCE. The financial demands of the Seleucid kings, their divisive hellenizing policies, and the poor leadership of the Judean high priests led to a Judean revolt under the Maccabees in 166 BCE. This led to increasing independence from Syria and to the establishment of the new priestly dynasty led by the descendents of the Maccabees, i.e., the Hasmonean family line that stayed in power until 63 BCE. At that time, under the Roman general Pompey, Judea became a protectorate of Rome, first under Antipater the Idumean, and then under his son Herod, a non-priest, who was made king in 40 BCE. Herod established a dynasty that continued to rule parts of Judea until 44 CE; after that date only Roman governors ruled.

The success of the Maccabees and the rule of the Hasmoneans had not put an end to the internal controversies among the Judean people. The historian Josephus records that a civil war soon broke out between two religious factions: the Sadducees supported by the Jerusalem Temple and the Hasmonean ruler against the Pharisees, a "separatist" group which enjoyed widespread allegiance among the common people. An uneasy peace was established but was disrupted by further civil war between the last Hasmonean heirs, who took opposing sides with each faction. The Pharisees undertook to interpret the religious laws in new ways and to expand their scope through their own teachings or "Oral Law." In this way, they created a new "lay" leadership class that was non-hereditary and functioned apart from the Jerusalem Temple. The Sadducees, on the other hand, seem to have drawn their authority from the priesthood and the established Second Temple system that was put into place by the Pentateuch. But this is only part of a larger picture; the introduction and spread of Hellenistic culture introduced new ideas and ways of thinking; and the consolidations of Roman political power brought formerly isolated cultures into everyday contact with one another. It was clearly a time of religious ferment and new challenges to Judaism. We can see further evidence of this in the sectarian literature

of the Dead Sea Scrolls and in the development and growth of Christianity as recorded in the New Testament.

The destruction of Jerusalem and the Temple by Rome, following the Judean revolts in 66–70 CE and in 132–135 CE, were cataclysmic events. Jerusalem was rebuilt as a pagan city; Jews were not allowed to live there; and the province of Judea was "erased from the map" and renamed Syria Palestina. It was then that the term "Judean" in Hebrew as well as in Greek translation became dissociated from geography and could only be used as a term describing religious and ethnic identity. One here (at least in English translation) may begin to speak of "Jews" rather than of "Judeans." In the absence of the Temple and its worship, the Jews developed new rites under new religious and communal leadership. The new leaders were called "rabbis" i.e., "teachers" and they taught, preached, and prayed in local communal centers called synagogues. The introduction of synagogues began much earlier in diaspora communities, where Jews had settled during the centuries, first in the lands of their deportations instituted by Assyria and Babylonia, and later in other lands through voluntary migrations. Synagogues appear in Judea even before the destruction of the Jerusalem Temple and were apparently used by the Pharisees and other groups as places where prayer and especially learning and discussion of the Pentateuch and other sacred writings could take place.

The foundation of rabbinic authority was their role as teachers and interpreters of Jewish law and practice. The rabbis determined which writings were "canonical" i.e., to be included in the Bible and which ones were considered non-sacred. We still retain some of these excluded works in the Apocrypha and the Pseudepigrapha. The next project of the rabbis was to write down their own teachings, i.e., the "Oral Law" and create a framework of reference. The first of these efforts was the Mishnah, which was redacted c. 250 CE. This was a major "law book" but other legal compositions also emerged. These include the Tosefta, which added material not included in the Mishnah, and the exegetical midrashim. These midrashim present legal discussion as part of a larger, verse by verse commentary on the Pentateuch; these include the Mekhilta, Sifra, and Sifre, which I also cite in my discussions.

The rabbis then began a new phase of work: the collection, organization, discussion, and analysis of all the Jewish laws, carried on now in their everyday language of Aramaic. They used the Mishnah as their starting point; but the their discussion and analysis is wide ranging, often adding additional legal material not in the Mishnah or Tosefta but of equal antiquity. These additional legal materials are called *baraitot* (sg. *baraita*). The discussion by the rabbis on the Mishnah is called the Gemara.

This monumental effort, encompassing the Mishnah and Gemara, resulted in the Talmud of Babylonia and the Jerusalem Talmud of Palestine, which were redacted into written form during the centuries between 500 and 700 CE. These Talmuds in turn were similarly subject to continuing commentary, refinements, and adjustments in the studies of the gaonic period in Babylonia down to c. 1000

CE. By that time, the overwhelming, expanding volume of legal literature and the degraded conditions for Jews living in the older Jewish centers of learning in Babylonia and Palestine fostered a need for more portable legal compendia or codes for the larger diasporas. The first code, entitled *Mishnah Torah*, was written and published in Egypt by Maimonides c. 1180 CE. Although other codes were written in subsequent centuries in Europe, the work of Maimonides continued to be studied and remained authoritative for Jews living in the ancient Near Eastern lands.

The last body of Jewish legal literature of importance to my study consists of commentaries on the Pentateuch and other biblical books written by noted rabbis living in France and Spain during the Middle Ages. These medieval commentators introduced a new trend in the interpretation of the Hebrew Bible; they focused upon language and original content beyond the limitations of theologically conditioned interpretations. They looked at grammar and at word usage in the same fashion that modern scholars follow today. However, because these rabbinic scholars also were deeply learned in Jewish law, they were able to relate their biblical text study to the wide range of rabbinic legal studies over the centuries, from the time of the Mishnah up to their own day. I frequently mention their contributions in my discussions, e.g., Rashi, Abraham Ibn Ezra, Rashbam, Nahmanides, Hazzequni, David Qimhi, etc. They are listed in the List of Abbreviations and in the Bibliography.

Bibliography

Abrabanel, Isaac. *Commentary on the Torah.* Edited by Meshullam Heller. Czernowitz: Eckhardt, 1860. [Hebrew]

Abraham, Kathleen. "The Middle Assyrian Period." In *Security for Debt in Ancient Near Eastern Law*, edited by Raymond Westbrook and Richard Jasnow, 161–221. Culture and History of the Ancient Near East 9. Leiden: Brill, 2001.

Abraham, son of Maimonides. *Perush Hatorah Lerabenu Avraham ben HaRambam Z"L al Bereshit u Shemot*, edited and translated [from Arabic] by E. J. Wiesenberg. London: Sassoon, 1959. [Hebrew]

Abusch, Tzvi. *Mesopotamian Witchcraft: Toward a History and Understanding of Babylonian Witchcraft Beliefs and Literature.* Ancient Magic and Divination 5. Leiden: Brill, 2002.

Alster, Bendt. *The Instruction of Šuruppak: A Sumerian Proverb Collection.* Mesopotamia 2. Copenhagen: Akademisk Forlag, 1974.

Altman, Amnon. "On Some Basic Concepts in the Law of People Seeking Refuge and Sustenance in the Ancient Near East." *ZAR* 8 (2002) 323–42.

Arnaud, Daniel. *Recherches au Pays d'Aštata: Emar vi.3: Textes sumériens et accadiens.* Paris: Recherche sur les Civliisations,1986.

Baines, John. "Literacy (ANE)." In *ABD* 4:334–37.

Barmash, Pamela. *Homicide in the Biblical World.* Cambridge: Cambridge University Press, 2005.

Baron, Salo Wittmayer. *A Social and Religious History of the Jews: Ancient Times.* Rev. ed. 2 vols. New York: Columbia University Press, 1952.

Barton, George A. and Louis Ginzberg. "Caleb." In *JE* 3:497–98.

Becking, Robert. "The Two Neo-Assyrian Documents from Gezer in Their Historical Context." *JEOL* 27 (1981–82) 76–89.

Beckman, Gary. *Hittite Diplomatic Texts.* SBL-WAWS 7. Atlanta: Scholars, 1996.

Berlin, Adele. "Sex and the Single Girl in Deuteronomy 22." In *Mishneh Todah: Studies in Deuteronomy and Its Cultural Environment in Honor of Jeffrey H. Tigay.* edited by Nili Sacher Fox, David A. Glatt-Gilad, and Michael J. Williams, 95–112. Winona Lake, IN: Eisenbrauns, 2009.

Ben Zeev, Miriam Pucci. *Jewish Rights in the Roman World: The Greek and Roman Documents Quoted by Josephus Flavius.* Texts and Studies in Ancient Judaism 74. Tübingen: Mohr/Siebeck, 1998.

Black, Henry C. *Black's Law Dictionary.* 8th ed. Edited by Bryan A. Garner. St. Paul, MN: Thomson West, 2004.

Blenkinsopp, Joseph. "Was the Pentateuch the Civic and Religious Constitution of the Jewish Ethnos in the Persian Period?" In *Persia and Torah: The Theory of Imperial Authorization of the Pentateuch*, edited by James W. Watts, 41–62. Atlanta: Society of Biblical Literature, 2001.

Bottéro, Jean and Petschow, Herbert. "Homosexualität." In *RlA* 4:459–68.

Breneman, J. Mervin. "Nuzi Marriage Tablets." PhD diss., Brandeis University, 1971.

Brewer, David Instone. "Deuteronomy 24:1–4 and the Origin of the Jewish Divorce Certificate." *JJS* 49 (1998) 230–43.

Brichto, Herbert Chanan. "The Case of the *Śōṭā* and a Reconsideration of Biblical Law." *HUCA* 46 (1975) 55–70.

Cardascia, Guillaume. "L'Adoption matrimoniale a Babylone et a Nuzi." *Revue Historique de Droit Français et Étranger* 1 (1959) 1–16.

———. "Adoption matrimoniale et lévirat dans le droit d'Ugarit." *RA* 64 (1970) 119–126.

———. *Les Lois assyriennes.* Paris: Cerf, 1969.

Bibliography

Charpin, Dominique. "Les Décrets royaux à l'époque Paléo-Babylonienne, à propos d'un Ouvrage récent." *AfO* 34 (1987) 36-43.

———. Charpin, Dominique. "Les Représantants de Mari à Ilânṣûrâ." *Archives épistolaires de Mari I/2*, 31-202. Archives royales de Mari 26. Paris: Recherche sur les Civilisations, 1988.

Chavalas, Mark. "Nazbum in the Khana Contracts from Terqa." In *Crossing Boundaries and Linking Horizons: Studies in Honor of Michael C. Astour on his 80th Birthday*, edited by Gordon D. Young, Mark W. Chavalas, Richard E. Averbeck, 179-88. Bethesda, MD: CDL, 1997.

Chirichigno, Gregory C. *Debt Slavery in Israel and the Ancient Near East*. JSOTSup 141. Sheffield: Sheffield Academic, 1993.

Civil, Miguel. "New Sumerian Law Fragments." In *Studies in Honor of Benno Landsberger on His Seventy-Fifth Birthday, April 21, 1965*, edited by Hans G. Güterbock and Thorkild Jacobsen, 1-10. AS 16. Chicago: University of Chicago Press, 1965.

———. "On Mesopotamian Jails and Their Lady Warden." In *The Tablet and the Scroll: Studies in Honor of William W. Hallo*, edited by Mark E. Cohen, Daniel C. Snell, and David B. Weisberg, 72-78. Bethesda MD: CDL, 1993.

———. *Materials for the Sumerian Lexicon 14: Ea A = nâqu, Aa A = nâqu, with their Forerunners and Related Texts*. Rome: Pontificium Institutm Biblicum, 2007.

Cohen, Boaz. "Arbitration in Jewish and Roman Law." *RIDA* 3e Serie 5 (1958) 165-223. Republished in Boaz Cohen, *Jewish and Roman Law: A Comparative Study*. 2 vols. 2:651-709. New York: Jewish Theological Seminary, 1966.

Cohen, Chaim. "Exodus 21:22-25 and the Current Debate on Abortion." In *Mishneh Todah: Studies in Deiteronomy and Its Cultural Environment in Honor of Jeffrey H. Tigay*. edited by Nili Sacher Fox, David A. Glatt-Gilad, and Michael J. Williams, 437-58. Winona Lake, Indiana: Eisenbrauns, 2009.

Cross, Frank M. "A Report on the Samaria Papyri." In *Congress Volume, Jerusalem 1986*, edited by J. A. Emerton, 7-26. VTSup 40. Leiden: Brill, 1988.

———. "Samaria Papyrus 1: An Aramaic Conveyance of 335 B.C.E. Found in the Wâdī Ed-Dâliyeh." In *ErIsr* 18: *Nahman Avigad Volume*, edited by Yigal Yadin, Benjamin Mazar et al., 7-17. Jerusalem: Israel Exploration Society, 1985.

Crüsemann, Frank. *The Torah: Theology and Social History of Old Testament Law*. Translated by Allan W. Mahnke. Minneapolis: Fortress, 1996.

Dan, Joseph. "Magic." In *EncJud* 11:703-15.

Dandamaev, Muhammad A. *Slavery in Babylonia*. Translated by Victoria A. Powell. Edited by Marvin A. Powell and David B. Weisberg. DeKalb: Northern Illinois University Press, 1984.

Daube, David. *Studies in Biblical Law*. 1947. Reprint, New York: Ktav, 1969.

The Dead Sea Scrolls Bible: The Oldest Known Bible Translated for the First Time into English. Translated and with Commentary by Martin Abegg Jr., Peter Flint, and Eugene Ulrich. San Francisco: HarperSanFrancisco, 1999.

De Zulueta, Frances. *The Institutes of Gaius. Part II Commentary*. Oxford: Oxford University Press, 1953.

Diamond, A. S. *Primitive Law, Past and Present*. London: Metheun, 1971.

Douglas, Mary. *Purity and Danger: An Analysis of the Concepts of Pollution and Taboo*. 1966. Reprint, London: Routledge & Kegan Paul, 1996.

Driver, G. R. and John C. Miles. *The Assyrian Laws*. 1935. Reprinted with Supplementary Additions and Corrections, Darmstadt: Scienta Verlag Aalen, 1975.

———. *The Babylonian Laws*. 2 vols. Ancient Texts and Translations. 1952-55. Reprint, Eugene, OR: Wipf & Stock, 2007.

Driver, S. R. *A Critical and Exegetical Commentary on Deuteronomy*. 3rd ed. ICC. 1901. Reprint, Edinburgh: T. & T. Clark, 1986.

Durand, Jean-Marie. "L'ordalie." In *Archives épistolaires de Mari I/1*, 507-32. ARM 26. Paris: Recherche sur les Civilisations, 1988.

———. "Trois études sur Mari." *MARI* 3 (1984) 162-80.

———. "La vengeance à l'époque amorrite." In *Recueil d'études à la mémoire d'André Parrot*, 39-50. Florilegium marianum 6. Mémoires de *NABU* 7. Paris: Societé pour l'étude du Proche-Orient ancien, 2002.

Eichler, Barry L. "Examples of Restatement in the Laws of Hammurabi." In *Mishneh Todah: Studies in Deuteronomy and Its Cultural Environment in Honor of Jeffrey H. Tigay*, edited by, Nili Sacher Fox et al., 365-400. Winona Lake, IN: Eisenbrauns, 2009.

Falk, Ze'ev. *Introduction to Jewish Law of the Second Commonwealth*. Arbeiten zur Geschichte des Antiken Judentum und des Urchristentums 11. Leiden: Brill, 1978.

Falkenstein, Adam. *Die neusumerischen Gerichtsurkunden*. 2 vols. Bayerische Akademie der Wissenschaften, Phil.-Hist. Klasse, Abh. n.f. Heft 39–40. Munich: Beck, 1956.

———. "Zu den Inschriftfunden der Grabung in Uruk-Warka 1960–1961." *BaghM* 2 (1963) 1–82.

Feliks, Jehuda. "Kilayim." In *EncJud* 10:999–1000.

Figulla, H. H. "Lawsuit Concerning a Sacrilegious Theft at Erech." *Iraq* 13 (1951) 95–101.

Finet, Andre. *Le Code de Hammurapi*. Paris: Cerf, 1983.

Finkelstein, Jacob J. "The Laws of Urnammu." *JCS* 22 (1969) 66–82.

———. "An Old Babylonian Herding Contract and Genesis 31:38f." *JAOS* 88 (1968) 30–36.

———. *The Ox That Gored*. Transactions of the American Philosophical Society 71/2. Philadelphia: American Philosophical Society, 1981.

———. "Sex Offenses in Sumerian Laws." *JAOS* 86 (1966) 355–72.

Fishbane, Michael. *Biblical Interpretation in Early Israel*. 2nd ed. Oxford: Oxford University Press, 1988.

Fortner, John D. "Adjudicating Entities and Levels of Authority in Lawsuit Records of the Old Babylonian Era." PhD diss., Hebrew Union College-Jewish Institute of Religion, 1996.

Friedberg, Maurice. "Hagar." In *EncJud* 7:1075–76.

Friedrich, Johannes. *Die Hethitischen Gesetze*. 2nd ed. Documenta et Monumenta Orientis Antiqui 7. Leiden: Brill, 1971.

Garrett, Susan R. "Light on a Dark Subject and Vice Versa: Magic and Magicians in the New Testament." In *Religion, Science, and Magic: In Concert and in Conflict*, edited by Jacob Neusner, Ernest S. Frerichs, and Paul V. M. Flesher, 142–65. Oxford: Oxford University Press, 1989.

Gaster, Theodor H. *Myth, Legend, and Custom in the Old Testament*. 2 vols. 1969. Reprint, New York: Harper Torchbooks, 1975.

Geller, Markham J. "Deconstructing Talumdic Magic." In *Magic and the Classical Tradition*, edited by Charles Burnett and W. F. Ryan, 1–18. Warburg Institute Colloquia 7. London: Warburg Institute, 2006.

———. *Evil Demons: Canonical Utukku-Lemnutu Incantations*. Studies in Ancient Assyrian Cuneiform Texts 5. Helskinki: Neo-Assyrian Text Corpus Project, 2007.

George, Andrew. *The Epic of Gilgamesh: A New Translation*. London: Penguin, 1999.

Gogel, Sandra Landis. *A Grammar of Epigraphic Hebrew*. SBLRBS 23. Atlanta: Scholars, 1998.

Gray, L. H., O. Schrader et al. 1918. "Blood Feud." In *ERE* 2:720–35.

Greenberg, Moshe. "Herem." In *EncJud* 8:344–50.

———. "Some Postulates of Biblical Criminal Law." In *Yehezkel Kaufmann Jubilee Volume*, edited by M. Haran, 5–28. Jerusalem: Magnes, 1960.

Greenfield, Jonas. "Asylum at Aleppo: A note on Sfire III, 4-7." In *Ah, Assyria . . . Studies in Assyrian History and Ancient Near Eastern Historiography Presented to Hayim Tadmor*, edited by Mordecai Cogan and Israel Eph'al, 272–78. Scripta Hierosolymitana 33. Jerusalem: Magnes, 1991.

Greengus, Samuel. "Bridewealth in Sumerian Sources." *HUCA* 61 (1990) 25–88.

———. "Filling Gaps: Laws Found in Babylonia and in the Mishna but Absent in the Hebrew Bible." *Maarav* 7 (1991) 149–71.

———. "Law: Biblical and ANE Law." In *ABD* 4:242–52.

———. "Legal and Social Institutions of Ancient Mesopotamia." In *CANE* 1:469–84.

———. "New Evidence on the Old Babylonian Calendar and Real Estate Documents from Sippar." *JAOS* 121 (2001) 257–67.

———. "The Old Babylonian Marriage Contract." *JAOS* 89 (1969) 505–32.

———. *Old Babylonian Tablets from Ishchali and Vicinity*. Uitgaven van het Nederlands Historisch-Archaeologisch Instituut te Istanbul 44. Leiden: Nederlands Instituut voor het Nanije Oosten, 1979.

———. "The Quarrel between Ishboshet and Abner in 2 Sam 3:7-11." Paper presented at the Fourteenth World Congress of Jewish Studies. Jerusalem, Israel, July 31, 2005.

———. "Redefining 'Inchoate Marriage.'" In Old Babylonian Contexts." In *Riches Hidden in Secret Places: Ancient Near Eastern Studies in Memory of Thorkild Jacobsen*, edited by Tzvi Abusch, 123–39. Winona Lake, IN: Eisenbrauns, 2002.

———. "The Selling of Slaves: Laws Missing from the Hebrew Bible?" *ZAR* 3 (1997) 1–11.

———. "Sisterhood Adoption at Nuzi and the 'Wife-Sister' in Genesis." *HUCA* 46 (1975) 5–31.

———. "Some Issues Relating to the Comparability of Laws and the Coherence of the Legal Tradition." In *Theory and Method in Biblical and Cuneiform Law*, edited by Bernard M. Levinson, 60–87. JSOTSup 181. Sheffield: Sheffield Academic, 1994.

———. *Studies in Ishchali Documents*. Bibliotheca Mesopotamica 19. Malibu, CA: Undena, 1986.

———. "A Textbook Case of Adultery in Ancient Mesopotamia." *HUCA* 40–41 (1969–70) 33–44.

Gropp, Douglas M. "The Samaria Papyri from Wâdī ed Dâliyah: The Slave Sales." PhD diss., Harvard University, 1989.

Gulak, Asher. *Foundations of Jewish Law*. 4 vols. 1922. Reprint, Tel Aviv: Devir, 1967. [Hebrew]

———. *Legal Documents in the Talmud in Light of Greek Papyri and Greek and Roman Law*. Translated, revised and supplemented by R. Katzoff. Jerusalem: Magnes, 1994. [Hebrew]

———. *Otzar Hashṭarot Hanehugot Beyisrael*. Jerusalem: Defus Hapoalim, 1926. [Hebrew]

Gurney, O. R. *The Hittites*. Harmondworth, UK: Penguin, 1954.

Halevy, Elimelech Epstein. "Hagar In the Aggadah." In *EncJud* 7:1075.

Hallo, William W. "Compare and Contrast: The Contextual Approach to Biblical Literature." In *The Bible in the Light of Cuneiform Literature*, edited by William W. Hallo et. al., 1–30. Ancient Near Eastern Studies 8. New York: Mellen, 1990.

———. "Love and Marriage at Ashtata." In *Sex and Gender in the Ancient Near East,* Proceedings of the 47th Rencontre Assyriologique Internationale, Helsinki, July 2–6, 2001, edited by Simo Parpola and R. M. Whiting, 1:203–16. 2 vols. Helsinki: Neo-Assyrian Text Corpus Project, 2002.

Harris, Rivkah. "Hierodulen." *RlA* 4:391–93.

Hezser, Catherine. "Introduction." In *Roman Law in Its Roman and Near Eastern Context*, edited by Catherine Hezser, 1–15. Texts and Studies in Ancient Judaism 97. Tübingen: Mohr/Siebeck, 2003.

———. "Slaves and Slavery in Rabbinic and Roman Law." In *Roman Law in its Roman and Near Eastern Context,* edited by Catherine Hezser, 133–76. Texts and Studies in Ancient Judaism 97. Tübingen: Mohr/Siebeck, 2003.

Hoffner, Harry A. Jr. "Incest, Sodomy, and Bestiality in the Ancient Near East." In *Orient and Occident. Essays Presented to Cyrus H. Gordon on the Occasion of his Sixty-fifth Birthday,* edited by Harry A. Hoffner, Jr. 81–90. AOAT 22. Neukirchen-Vluyn: Butzon & Becker Kevelaer, 1973.

———. *The Laws of the Hittites: A Critical Edition*. Documenta et Monumenta Orientis Antiqui 23. Leiden: Brill, 1997.

———. "On Homicide in Hittite Law." In *Crossing Boundaries and Linking Horizons: Studies in Honor of Michael C. Astour on his 80th Birthday*, edited by Gordon D. Young, Mark W. Chavalas, Richard E. Averbeck, 293–314. Bethesda, MD: CDL, 1997.

Horbury, W. and D. Noy. *Jewish Inscriptions of Graeco-Roman Egypt*. Cambridge: Cambridge University Press, 1992.

Horowitz, Victor (Avigdor). "'His Master Shall Pierce his Ear with an Awl' (Exodus 21.6)—Marking Slaves in the Bible in Light of Akkadian Sources." *PAAJR* 58 (1992) 48–77.

"Hospitals Are Asked to Maim Man in Punishment." (Associated Press) *New York Times*, August 20, 2010, A9. Online: http://www.nytimes.com/2010/08/20/world/middleeast/20saudi.html.

Houtman, Cornelius. *Exodus*. Historical Commentary on the Old Testament. Translated by Sierd Woudstra. 3 vols. Leuven: Peeters, 2000.

Jackson, Bernard S. "Modelling Biblical Law: The Covenant Code. Part I." *Chicago-Kent Law Review* 70 (1995) 1745–827.

———. "Reflections on Biblical Law." In *Essays in Jewish and Comparative Legal History by Bernard S. Jackson*, 25–63. Studies in Judaism in Late Antiquity 10. Leiden: Brill, 1975.

———. *Theft in Early Jewish Law*. Oxford: Clarendon, 1972.

———. *Wisdom Laws: A Study of the Mishpatim of Exodus 21:1—22:16*. Oxford: Oxford University Press, 2006.

Jackson, Samuel. *A Comparison of Ancient Near Eastern Law Collections Prior to the First Millennium BC*. Gorgias Dissertations 35. Near Eastern Studies 10. Piscataway, NJ: Gorgias, 2008.

Jacobs, Joseph and Ludwig Blau, "Incantation." In *JE* 6:568.

Jacobsen, Thorkild. "An Ancient Mesopotamian Trial for Homicide." *Studia Biblica et Orientalia 3: Oriens Antiquus*. Analecta Biblica et Orientalia 12. Rome: Pontificio Istituto Biblico (1959) 130–50

———. *Salinity and Irrigation in Antiquity*. Bibliotheca Mesopotamica 14. Malibu, CA: Undena, 1982

Janowitz, Naomi. *Magic in the Roman World. Pagans, Jews, and Christians.* London: Routledge, 2001.

Jas, Remko. *Neo-Assyrian Judicial Procedures.* SAAS 5. Helsinki: University of Helsinki, 1996.

Jasnow, Richard. "Egypt: New Kingdom." In *A History of Ancient Near Eastern Law*, edited by Raymond Westbrook, 1:289–359. Handbook of Oriental Studies 72. Leiden: Brill, 2003.

Joannès, Francis. "L'absence d'Atamrum: l'expédition de Himdiya contre la ville d' Amaz." *Archives épistolaires de Mari I/2*, 327–55. ARM 26. Paris: Recherche sur les Civilisations, 1988.

———. "Une chronique judicaire d'époque hellénistique et le châtiment des sacrileges à Babylone." In *Assyriologica et Semitica: Festschrift für Joachim Oelsner*, edited by Joachim Marzahn and Hans Neuman with assistance of Andreas Fuchs, 193–211. AOAT 272. Münster: Ugarit-Verlag, 2000.

Josephus, Flavius. *Josephus.* Translated by H. St. J. Thackeray et al. LCL. Cambridge: Harvard University Press, 1950–1967.

Jursa, Michael. "Neu- und spätbabylonische Texte aus den Sammlung der Birmingham Museums and Art Gallery." *Iraq* 59 (1997) 97–174.

Juynboll, Th. W. "Crimes and Punishments (Muhammadan)." In *ERE* 4:290–94.

Kaizer, Ted. "Capital Punishment at Hatra: Gods, Magistrates and Laws in the Roman-Parthian Period." *Iraq* 68 (2006) 139–53.

Kee, H. C. *Testaments of the Twelve Prophets.* In *The Old Testament Pseudepigrapha*, edited by James H. Charlesworth, 1:775–828. New York: Doubleday, 1983.

Kohler, Kaufmann. "Intermarriage." In *JE* 6:610–12.

Koschaker, Paul. *Rechtsvergleichende Studien zur Gesetzgebung Hammurapis Königs von Babylon.* Leipzig: von Veit, 1917.

Kraus, F. R. *Königliche Verfügungen in altbabylonischer Zeit.* Studia et Documenta ad Iura Orientis Antiqui Pertinentia 11. Leiden: Brill, 1984.

Labat, René. "Un Almanac Babylonien." *RA* 38 (1941) 13–40.

———. *Traité Akkadien de Diagnostics et Pronostics Médicaux.* 2 vols. Paris: Academie Internationale d'Histoire des Sciences, 1951.

Lackenbacher, Sylve. "Les Lettres de Buqâqum." *Archives épistolaires de Mari I/2.* Archives royales de Mari 26. Paris: Recherche sur les Civilisations, (1988) 401–39.

Lafont, Bertrand. "The Ordeal." In *Everyday Life in Ancient Mesopotamia*, by Jean Bottéro, with Contributions from A. Finet, et al., translated by Antonia Nevill, 199–209. Baltimore: Johns Hopkins University Press, 2001.

Lafont, Bertrand and Westbrook, Raymond. "Mesopotamia: Neo-Sumerian Period (Ur III)." In *A History of Ancient Near Eastern Law*, edited by Raymond Westbrook, 1:183–226. Handbook of Oriental Studies 72. Leiden: Brill, 2003.

Lafont, Sophie. *Femmes, Droit et Justice dans l'Antiquité orientale: Contribution à l'étude du droit penal au Proche-Orient ancien.* Orbis Biblicus et Orientalis 165. Göttingen: Vandenhoeck & Ruprecht, 1999.

Lambert, Wilfred G. *Babylonian Wisdom Literature.* 2nd ed. Oxford: Oxford University Press, 1967.

———. "The Laws of Hammurabi." In *Reflets de deux fleuves. Volume de mélanges offerts à Andre Finet*, edited by M. Lebeau and P. Talon, 95–98. Akkadica Suppl. 6. Leuven: Peeters, 1989.

———. "Nebuchadnezzar, King of Justice." *Iraq* 27 (1965) 1–11.

Landsberger, Benno. *Die Serie ana ittišu.* Materialien zum sumerischen Lexikon 1; Rome: Pontifical Biblical Institute, 1937.

Lauterbach, Jacob Z. "Kil'ayim." In *JE* 8:492.

———." Simeon ben Sheṭaḥ." In *JE* 11: 357–58.

Lerner, Meir. *Torath ha-Mischna.* Heft I. Berlin: H. Itzkowski, 1914. [Hebrew]

Levenson, Jon D. "Genesis, Introduction and Annotations." In *The Jewish Study Bible: Jewish Publication Society Tanakh Translation*, edited by Adele Berlin and Marc Zvi Brettler, 8–101. Oxford: Oxford University Press, 2004.

Levine, Étan. *Marital Relations in Ancient Judaism.* Beihefte zur Zeitschrift für Altorientalische und Biblische Rechtsgeschichte 10. Wiesbaden: Harrassowitz, 2009.

Levinson, Bernard M. "A Lost Chapter in Rabbinic Legal History: The Wall Topos of the Edubba." Paper presented at the 208th Meeting of the American Oriental Society, New Orleans, Louisiana, April 5–8, 1998.

———. "Textual Criticism, Assyriology, and the History of Interpretation: Deuteronomy 13:7a as a Test Case in Method." *JBL* 120 (2001) 211–43.

Llewelyn, K. N. and Hoebel, E. Adamson. *The Cheyenne Way: Conflict and Case Law in*

Primitive Jurisprudence. Norman: University of Oklahoma Press, 1941.

Linder, Amnon. *The Jews in Roman Imperial Legislation,* Detroit: Wayne State Press; Jerusalem: Israel Academy of Sciences and Humanities, 1987.

Liptzin, Sol. "Princess Hagar." *The Jewish Bible Quarterly: Dor le Dor* 7 (1980) 114–26.

Lockshin, Martin L., translator and editor. *Rabbi Samuel b. Meir's Commentary on Genesis: An Annotated Translation.* Jewish Studies 5. Lewiston, NY: Mellen, 1989.

———, translator and editor. *Rashbam's Commentary on Exodus: An Annotated Translation.* Brown Judaica Studies 310. Atlanta: Scholars, 1997.

———, translator and editor. *Rashbam's Commentary on Leviticus and Numbers: An Annotated Translation.* Brown Judaica Studies 330. Providence, RI: Brown University, 1991.

Lührmann, Olivia. *Tötungsrecht zur Eigentumsverteidigung? Eine Untersuchung des Notwehrrechts unter verfassungsrechtlichen, menschenrechtlichen und rechtsvergleichenden Gesichtspunkten.* Frankfurt: Lang, 1999.

Lutz, Henry Frederick. *The Verdict of a Trial Judge in a Case of Assault and Battery.* University of California Publications in Semitic Philology 9/6. 379–81. Berkeley: University of California Press, 1930.

MacGinnis, John. "A Judgment of King Darius." *JCS* 60 (2008) 87–99.

Malul, Meir. "Adoption of Foundlings in the Bible and Mesopotamian Documents: A Study of Some Legal Metaphors in Ezekiel 16:1–7." *JSOT* 46 (1990) 97–126.

———. *The Comparative Method in Ancient Near Eastern and Biblical Studies.* AOAT 227. Neukirchen-Vluyn: Butzon & Becker Kevelaer, 1990.

Manning, Joseph G. "Egypt: Demotic Law." In *A History of Ancient Near Eastern Law,* edited by Raymond Westbrook, 2:819–62. Handbook of Oriental Studies 72. Leiden: Brill, 2003.

Mansoor, Menahem. "Sadducees." In *EncJud* 14:620–22.

Mauer, Gerlinde. "Das Formular der altbabylonischen Bodenpachtverträge." PhD diss., Ludwig-Maximillian Universität zu München, 1980.

McMahon, Gregory. "Theology, Priests and Worship in Hittite Anatolia." In *CANE* 4:1981–95.

Middleton, Russell. "Brother–Sister and Father–Daughter Marriage in Ancient Egypt." *American Sociological Review* 27 (1962) 599–611.

Milgrom, Jacob. *Numbers.* JPS Torah Commentary. Philadelphia: Jewish Publication Society, 1990.

———. *Leviticus.* AB 3. 3 vols. New York: Doubleday, 1991–2001.

Morgenstern, Julian. "The Book of the Covenant, Part II." *HUCA* 7 (1930) 19–240.

Müller, David H. *Die Gesetze Hammurabis und ihr Verhältnis zur mosaischen Gesetzgebung sowie zu den XII Tafeln.* Vienna: Holder, 1903.

Neusner, Jacob. *The Vitality of Rabbinic Imagination: The Mishnah against the Bible and Qumran.* Studies in Judaism. Lanham, MD: University Press of America, 2005.

A New English Translation of the Septuagint and Other Greek Translations Traditionally Included under That Title, edited by Albert Pietersma and Benjamin G. Wright. Oxford: Oxford University Press, 2007.

Nissinen, Martti. "Are There Homosexuals in Mesopotamian Literature?" *JAOS* 130 (2010) 73–77.

Obermark, Peter. "Adoption in the Old Babylonian Period." PhD diss., Hebrew Union College-Institute of Religion, Cincinnati, 1992.

Oppenheim, A. Leo. "A New Prayer to the 'Gods of the Night." *Studia Biblica et Orientalia 3. Oriens Antiquus. Analaecta Biblica 12.* Rome: Pontificio Istituto Biblico, (1959) 282–301.

———. *The Interpretation of Dreams in the Ancient Near East with a Translation of an Assyrian Dream Book.* Transactions of the American Philosophical Society n.s. 46 pt. 3. Philadelphia: American Philosophical Society, 1956.

Otto, Eckart. "Die rechtshistorische Entwicklung des Depositenrechts in altorientalischen und altisraelitischen Rechtskorpora." *Zeitschrift der Savigny Stiftung für Rechtsgeschichte.* Rom. Abt., 105 (1988) 1–31.

Paul, Shalom M. "Adoption Formulae: A Study of Cuneiform and Biblical Legal Clauses." *Maarav* 2:2 (1980) 173–85.

———. "Biblical Analogues to Middle Assyrian Law." In *Religion and Law: Biblical-Judaic and Islamic Perspectives,* edited by Edwin B. Firmage, Bernard G. Weiss, and John W. Welch, 333–50. Winona Lake, IN: Eisenbrauns, 1990.

———. "Leshonot 'imutz." In *H. L. Ginsberg Volume*, edited by Menahem Haran et al., 31–36. *ErIsr* 14. Jerusalem: Israel Exploration Society/New York: Jewish Theological Seminary of America, 1978. [Hebrew]

———. *Studies in the Book of the Covenant in the Light of Cuneiform and Biblical Law.* VTSup 18. 1970. Reprint, Eugene, OR: Wipf & Stock, 2006.

Petschow, H. P. H. "Inzest." In *RlA* 5:144–50.

Philo. *Works: English and Greek.* 12 vols. Translated by F. H. Colson and G. H. Whitaker. LCL. Cambridge: Harvard University Press, 1929–1970.

Porten, Bezalel. *Archives from Elephantine: The Life of an Ancient Jewish Military Colony.* Berkeley: University of California Press, 1968.

Porten, Bezalel and Ada Yardeni, editors. *Textbook of Aramaic Documents from Ancient Egypt Newly Copied, Edited, and Translated.* Vol. 2, *Contracts.* Jerusalem: Hebrew University Press, 1989.

Postgate, J. N. "Some Old Babylonian Shepherds and Their Flocks. With a contribution by S. Payne." *JSS* 20 (1975) 1–21.

———. *Fifty Neo-Assyrian Legal Documents.* Warminster: Aris & Phillips, 1976.

———. "On Some Assyrian Ladies." *Iraq* 41 (1979) 89–103.

Powell, Marvin A. "Masse und Gewichte." In *RlA* 7:457–517.

———. "Salt, Seed, and Yields in Sumerian Agriculture: A Critique of the Theory of Progressive Salinization." *ZA* 75 (1985) 1–38.

Rabinowitz, J. J. "Neo-Babylonian Legal Documents and Jewish Law," *JJP* 12 (1961) 131–75.

Rabinowitz, Louis I. "Levirate Marriage and Halitzah." *EJ* 9:122–31.

Radner, Karen. "The Neo-Assyrian Period." In *Security for Debt in Ancient Near Eastern Law*, edited by Raymone Westrook and Richard Jasnow, 265–88. Culture and History of the Ancient Near East 9. Leiden: Brill, 2001.

———. *Die Neuassyrischen Privaturkunden als Quelle für Mensch und Umwelt.* State Archives of Assyria Studies 6. Helsinki: University of Helsinki, 1997.

Reece, David George. "Demons. New Testament." In *ABD* 2:140–42.

Reiner, Erica. "Runaway—Seize Him." In *Assyria and Beyond: Studies Presented to Mogens Trolle Larsen*, edited by J. G. Dercksen, 475–82. Leiden: Nederlands Institut Voor Het Nabije Oosten, 2004.

———. *Šurpu: A Collection of Sumerian and Akkadian Incantations.* AfO Beiheft 11. Graz, 1958.

Ricks, Stephen D. "The Magician as Outsider: The Evidence of the Hebrew Bible." In *New Perspectives on Ancient Judaism*, edited by Paul V. M. Flesher, Studies in Judaism 5, 125–34. Lanham, MD: University Press of America, 1987.

Ries, G. "Lösegeld." In *RlA* 7:77–80.

Riskin, Shlomo. *Women and Jewish Divorce: The Rebellious Wife, the Agunah and the Rights of Women to Initiate Divorce in Jewish law: A Halachic Solution.* Hoboken, New Jersey: Ktav, 1989.

Rivkin, Ellis. *A Hidden Revolution: The Pharisees' Search for the Kingdom Within.* Nashville: Abingdon, 1976.

Roberts, Jim. "The Legal Basis for Saul's Slaughter of the Priests of Nob (1 Samuel 21–22)." *JNSL* 25 (1999) 21–29.

Rofé, Alexander. "The History of the Cities of Refuge in Biblical Law." In *Studies in Bible*, edited by Sara Japhet, 205–39. Scripta Hierosolymitana 31. Jerusalem: Magnes, 1986.

Roth, Martha. "Appendix A: A Reassessment of RA 71 (1977) 125ff. *AfO* 31:9–14." (This article is an Appendix to Richard L. Zettler, The Genealogy of the Hours of Ur-Me-me: A Second Look. *AfO* 31 (1984) 1–8.)

———. "Homicide in the Neo-Assyrian Period." In *Language, Literature, and History: Studies Presented to Erica Reiner*, edited by Francesca Rochberg-Halton, 351–65. AOS 67. New Haven, CT, 1987.

———. *Law Collections from Mesopotamia and Asia Minor.* SBLWAWS 6; Atlanta: Scholars, 1997.

———. "The Scholastic Exercise Laws About Rented Oxen." *JCS* 32 (1980) 127–46.

———. "Scholastic Tradition and Mesopotamian Law: A Study of FLP 1287, A Prism in the Collection of the Free Library of Philadelphia." PhD diss., University of Pennsylvania, 1979.

———. "'She Will Die by the Iron Dagger' Adultery and Neo-Babylonian Marriage." *JESHO* 31 (1988) 186–206.

Salonen, Armas. *Nautica Babyloniaca.* Studia Orientalia 11/1. Societas Orientalis Fennica: Helsinki, 1942.

———. *Die Wasserfahrzeuge in Babylonien.* Studia Orientalia 8/4 Societas Orientalis Fennica: Helsinki, 1939.

Sanderson, Judith. *An Exodus Scroll from Qumran: 4QPaleoExod^m and the Samaritan Tradition.* Harvard Semitic Studies 30. Atlanta: Scholars, 1986.

San Nicolò. "Parerga Babyloniaca." *ArOr* 4 (1932) 34–40 (Parts I–II); 179–92 (Parts III–V); 325–48 (Parts VI–VIII).

Sarna, Nahum M. *Genesis.* JPS Torah Commentary. Philadelphia: Jewish Publication Society, 1996.

Sasson, Jack M. "Biographical Notes on Some Royal Ladies from Mari." *JCS* 25 (1973) 68–71.

"Saudi Arabian Justice: Cruel, or Just Unusual?" *The Economist* vol. 259 no. 8226, June 14, 2001, 46. Online: https://www.economist.com/node/656147.

Schacht, J. "Ḳiṣāṣ." In *The Encyclopaedia of Islam*, edited by H. A. R. Gibb, J. H. Kramers, E. Lèvi-Provençal, J. Schacht, 5:177–88. Leiden: Brill, 1979.

Schiffman, Lawrence H. *Sectarian Law in the Dead Sea Scrolls. Courts, Testimony, and the Penal Code.* Brown Judaic Studies 33. Chico CA: Scholars, 1983.

Scherechewsky, Ben Zion. "Adoption: Later Jewish Law." In *EncJud* 2:302.

Schorr, M. *Urkunden des altbabylonischen Zivil- und Prozessrechts.* VAB 5. 1913. Reprint, Hildesheim: Georg Olms, 1971.

Scurlock, JoAnn. "Physician, Exorcist, Conjurer, Magician: A Tale of Two Healing Professions." In *Mesopotamian Magic: Textual, Historical, and Interpretative Perspectives*, edited by Tzvi Abusch and Karel van der Toorn, 69–80. Ancient Magic and Divination 1. Groningen: Styx, 1999.

Sefati, Yitschak, and Jacob Klein. "The Role of Women in Mesopotamian Witchcraft." In *Sex and Gender in the Ancient Near East: Proceedings of the 47th Rencontre Assyriologique Internationale.* Helsinki, July 2–6, 2001, edited by S. Parpola and R. M. Whiting. 2 vols. 2:569–85. CRAI 47. Helsinki: Neo-Assyrian Text Corpus Project, 2002.

Shaffer, Aaron. "Gilgamesh and Huwawa." *JAOS* 103 (1983) 307–13.

Shearing, Linda S. "Abigail." In *ABD* 1:15–16.

Shemesh, Aharon. "4Q271.3: A Key to Sectarian Matrimonial Law." *JJS* 49 (1998) 244–63.

Shilo, Samuel. "Wills." In *EncJud* 16:519–30.

Smith, Morton. "East Mediterranean Law Codes of the Early Iron Age." In *ErIsr* 14: *H. L. Ginsberg Volume*, edited by Menahem Haran

et al., 38*–43*. Jerusalem: Israel Exploration Society, 1978.

Sperber, Daniel. *Nautica Talmudica.* Bar-Ilan Studies in Near Eastern Language and Culture. Ramat Gan: Bar-Ilan University Press, 1986.

Sperling, S. David. "Dinah, 'Innah, and Related Matters." In *Mishneh Todah: Studies in Deiteronomy and Its Cultural Environment in Honor of Jeffrey H. Tigay.* edited by Nili Sacher Fox, David A. Glatt-Gilad, and Michael J. Williams, 73–93. Winona Lake, IN: Eisenbrauns, 2009.

Sprinkle, Joe M. "Theft and Deprivation of Property." In *Dictionary of the Old Testament: Pentateuch*, edited by David Baker and T. Desmond Alexander, 841–42. Downers Grove, IL: InterVarsity, 2003.

Steele, Francis Rue. "An Additional Fragment of the Lipit-Ishtar Code Tablet from Nippur." AnOr 18 (1950) 489–93 (with plates vii–viii).

Steinsaltz, Adin. *The Talmud. The Steinsaltz Edition. A Reference Guide.* New York: Random House, 1989.

Stol, Marten. *Birth in Babylonia and the Bible—Its Mediterranean Setting (With a chapter by F.A. M. Wiggerman).* Groningen: Styx, 2000.

———. *Epilepsy in Babylonia.* Cuneiform Monographs 2. Groningen: Styx Publications, 1993.

———. "Fragment of a Herding Contract." In *Miscellanea Babylonica: mélanges offerts a Maurice Birot*, edited by J.-M. Durand and J.-R. Kupper, 273–75. Paris: Éditions Recherche sur les Civilizations, 1985.

———. "Muškēnu." In *RlA* 8:492–93.

———. "Miete. B.I. Altbabylonisch." In *RlA* 8:162–74.

———. "Pacht. B. Altbabylonisch." In *RlA* 10:170–72.

Strack, H. L., and G. Stemberger. *Introduction to the Talmud and Midrash.* Translated by Markus Bockmuhl. Edinburgh: T. & T. Clark, 1991.

Sullivan, Shaun J. *Killing in Defense of Private Property: The Development of a Roman Catholic Moral Teaching, Thirteenth to Eighteenth Centuries.* Missoula, MT: Scholars, 1976.

Thomas, J. A. C. *Textbook of Roman Law.* Amsterdam: North Holland, 1976.

Tigay, Jeffrey H. "Adoption." In *EncJud* 2:298–302.

———. *Deuteronomy.* JPS Torah Commentary. Philadelphia: Jewish Publication Society, 1996.

Todd, S.C. *The Shape of Athenian Law.* 2nd ed. Oxford: Clarendon, 1995.

Toorn, Karel van der. "The Domestic Cult at Emar." *JCS* 47 (1995) 35–49.

Treggiari, Susan. *Roman Marriage: Iusti Coniuges From the Time of Cicero to the Time of Ulpian.* Oxford: Clarendon, 1991.

Tsevat, Matitiahu. "Marriage and Monarchical Legitimacy in Ugarit and Israel." *JSS* 3 (1958) 237–43.

Tyan, E. "Diya." In *The Encyclopaedia of Islam,* edited by H. A. R. Gibb et al., 2:340b–343a. New ed. Leiden: Brill, 1970.

Van Seters, John. *A Law Book for the Diaspora: Revision in the Study of the Covenant Code.* Oxford: Oxford University Press, 2006.

Urbach, Ephraim. *The Halachah: Its Sources and Development.* Jerusalem: Yad La-Talmud, 1986.

USDA ERS. "Feed Grains Data: Yearbook Tables." http://www.ers.usda.gov/Data/FeedGrains/FeedYearbook.aspx (accessed July 20, 2011).

———. "Wheat Data: Yearbook Tables." http://www.ers.usda.gov/Data/Wheat/WheatYearbook.aspx (accessed July 20, 2011).

Van Praag, A. *Droit matrimonial Assyro-Babylonien.* Allard Pierson Stichtung, Archaeologisch-Historische Bydragen 12. Amsterdam: N.V Noord-Hollandische Uitgevers Maatschappij, 1945.

Veenhof, K. R. *Letters in the Louvre. AbB* 14. Leiden: Brill, 2005.

VerSteeg, Russ. *Early Mesopotamian Law.* Durham, NC: Carolina Academic, 2000.

Wacholder, Ben Zion. "The Calendar of Sabbatical Cycles During the Second Temple and the Early Rabbinic Period." *HUCA* 44 (1973) 153–96.

Warmington, E. H. *Remains of Old Latin III. Lucilius, The Twelve Tables. LCL.* 1938. Repr., Cambridge: Harvard University Press, 2004.

Watts, Jame W. editor. *Persia and Torah. The Theory of Imperial Authorization.* SBL Symposium Series 17. Atlanta: Society of Biblical Literature, 2001

Weidner, Ernst. "Hof- und Harems- Erlasse assyrischer Könige aus dem 2. Jahrtausend v. Chr." *AfO* 17 (1954–56) 257–93 and plates vii–xii.

Weippert, Manfred. "Die Petition eines Entarbeiters aus Meṣad Ḥašāvāhū und die Syntax althebräischer erzälender Prosa." In *Die Hebräische Bibel und ihre zweifache Nachgeschichte: Festschrift für Rolf Rendtorff zum 65. Geburtstag,* edited by Erhard Blum et al., 449–66. Neukirchen-Vluyn: Neukirchener, 1990.

Weinfeld, Moshe. *Deuteronomy and the Deuteronomic School.* 1972. Reprint, Winona Lake, IN: Eisenbrauns, 1992.

———. *Social Justice in Ancient Israel and in the Ancient Near East.* Jerusalem: Magnes, 1995.

Weisberg, Dvora. *Levirate Marriage and the Family in Ancient Judaism.* Waltham, MA: Brandeis University Press, 2009.

Weiss Halivni, David. *Peshat and Derash: Plain and Applied Meaning in Rabbinic Exegesis.* Oxford: Oxford University Press, 1991.

Westermarck, Edward. "Asylum." In *ERE* 2:161–64.

———. *The History of Human Marriage.* 3 vols. 5th ed. London: Macmillan, 1925.

Westbrook, Raymond. "Anatolia and the Levant: Emar and Vicinity." In *A History of Ancient Near Eastern Law,* edited by Raymond Westbrook, 1:657–791. Handbook of Oriental Studies 72. Leiden: Brill, 2003.

———. "Codification and Canonization." In *Law from the Tigris to the Tiber: The Writings of Raymond Westbrook,* edited by Bruce Wells and Rachel Magdalene, 1:119–31. Winona Lake, IN: Eisenbrauns, 2009. Reprint from *La codification des lois dans l'antiquité: Actes due Colloque de Strasbourg, 27–29 November 1997,* edited by E. Lévy, 33–47. Travaux du Centre Recherche sur le Proche-Orient et la Grèce antiques 16. Paris: De Boccard, 2000.

———. "The Character of Ancient Near Eastern Law." In *A History of Ancient Near Eastern Law,* edited by Raymond Westbrook, 1:1–90. Handbook of Oriental Studies 72. Leiden: Brill, 2003.

———. "Conclusions." In *Security for Debt in Ancient Near Eastern Law,* edited by Raymond Westbrook and Richard Jasnow, 327–40. Culture and History of the Ancient Near East 9. Leiden: Brill, 2001.

———. "The Deposit Laws of Exodus 22, 6–12." In *Law from the Tigris to the Tiber: The Writings of Raymond Westbrook,* edited by Bruce Wells and Rachel Magdalene, 2:361–77. Winona Lake, IN: Eisenbrauns, 2009. Reprint from *ZAW* 106 (1994) 390–403.

———. "Evidentiary Procedure in the Middle Assyrian Laws." In *Law from the Tigris to the Tiber: The Writings of Raymond Westbrook,* edited by Bruce Wells and Rachel Magdalene, 2:211–29. Winona Lake, IN: Eisenbrauns, 2009. Reprint from *JCS* 55 (2003) 87–97.

———. "Lex Talionis and Exodus 21, 22–25." In *Law from the Tigris to the Tiber: The Writings of Raymond Westbrook,* edited by Bruce Wells and Rachel Magdalene, 2:341–60. Winona Lake, IN: Eisenbrauns, 2009. Reprint from *RB* 93 (1986) 52–69.

———. "Nature and Origin of the XII Tables." In *Law from the Tigris to the Tiber: The Writings of Raymond Westbrook*, edited by Bruce Wells and Rachel Magdalene, 1:21–71. Winona Lake, IN: Eisenbrauns, 2009. Reprint from *Zeitschrift der Savigny-Stiftung für Rechtsgeschichte* 105 (1988) 74–121.

———. *Old Babylonian Marriage Law.* Archiv für Orientforschung Beiheft 23. Horn, Austria: Berger, 1988.

———. *Property and the Family in Biblical Law,* JSOTSup 113. Sheffield: Sheffield Academic, 1991.

———. "Reflections on the Law of Homicide in the Ancient World." *Maarav* 13.2:145–74, 2006.

———. "Social Justice in the Ancient Near East." In *Law from the Tigris to the Tiber: The Writings of Raymond Westbrook*, edited by Bruce Wells and Rachel Magdalene, 1:143–60. Winona Lake, IN: Eisenbrauns, 2009. Reprint from *Social Justice in the Ancient World*, edited by K. D. Irani and Morris Silver, 149–63. Westport, CN: Greenwood, 1993.

———. "The Trial Scene in the *Iliad*," In *Law from the Tigris to the Tiber: The Writings of Raymond Westbrook*, edited by Bruce Wells and Rachel Magdalene, 1:303–27. Winona Lake, IN: Eisenbrauns, 2009. Reprint from *HSCP* 94 (1992) 55–76.

Whitelam, Keith W. *The Just King: Monarchical Judicial Authority in Ancient Israel.* JSOTSup 12; Sheffield: JSOT Press, 1979.

Wilcke, Claus. *Early Ancient Near Eastern Law. A History of its Beginnings. The Early Dynastic and Sargonic Periods.* SBAW 2005.2, Munich: Beck, 2003.

———. "*CT* 45 119: Ein Fall legaler Bigamie mit *nadītum* und *šugītum*." *ZA* 74 (1984) 170–80.

———. "Der Kodex Urnamma (CU): Versuch einer Rekonstruktion." In *Riches Hidden in Secret Places: Ancient Near Eastern Studies in Memory of Thorkild Jacobsen*, edited by Tzvi Abusch, 291–333. Winona Lake, IN: Eisenbrauns, 2002.

Willetts, Ronald F. *The Law Code of Gortyn.* Kadmos Suppl. 1. Berlin: de Gruyter, 1967

Wise, Michael, Martin Abegg Jr., and Edward Cook. *Dead Sea Scrolls: A New Translation.* 2nd ed. New York: HarperCollins, 2005.

Wiseman, Donald J. *The Alalakh Tablets.* Occasional Publications of the British Institute of Archaeology at Anakara 2. London: British School of Archaeology at Anakara, 1953.

Wright, Christopher J. H. "Jubilee, Year of." In *ABD* 3:1025—30

Wright, David P. *Inventing God's Law: How the Covenant Code of the Bible Used and Revised the Laws of Hammurabi.* Oxford: Oxford University Press, 2009.

Wunsch, Cornelia. "Findelkinder und Adoption nach neubabylonischen Quellen." *AfO* 50 (2003–2004) 174–244.

Yaron, Reuven. *The Laws of Eshnunna.* 2nd ed. rev. Jerusalem: Magnes, 1988.

Yoffee, Norman. *The Economic Role of the Crown in the Old Babylonian Period.* Malibu, CA: Undena, 1977.

Younger, K. L., Jr. "The Contextual Method." In *The Context of Scripture: Archival Documents*, edited by W. W. Hallo and K. L. Younger Jr., xxxv–xlii. Leiden: Brill, 2000.

Yuhong, Wu. "Rabies and Rabid Dogs in Sumerian and Akkadian Literature." *JAOS* 121 (2001) 32–43.

Zaccagnini, Carlo. "Mesopotamia. Nuzi." In *A History of Ancient Near Eastern Law*, edited by Raymond Westbrook, 1:565–617. Handbook of Oriental Studies 72. Leiden: Brill, 2003.

Index of Hebrew Bible

Index of Ancient Near Eastern Documents

Index of the Apocrypha, Pseudepigrapha, Dead Sea Scrolls, New Testament, Philo, and Josephus

Mark

6:17–18	28
7:5	283
10:11–12	37
12:18–25	17

Luke

3:19	28
6:27–29	137
20:27–35	17

John

18:23	157

Acts

18:14	157

1 Corinthians

5:1	33
6:1–6	286

2 Corinthians

6:15	20

~

PHILO

Allegorical Interpretation

3.32	211

Every Good Man Is Free

19	86

Life of Moses

2.205–6	259
2.207–8	261

On the Virtues

84	103–4

Special Laws

1.53	259
3.20	20, 27
3.22–24	32
3.26	20, 27
3.27	28
3.30–31	36
3.62	54
3.94	263
3.108	142
3.144	177
3.145	173
3.181–82	131
4.7–10	216
4.34	188
4.35	219
4.203–13	254

~

JOSEPHUS

Against Apion

2.202	145
2.237	259

Antiquities of the Jews

4.196	9
4.207	259
4.271	216
4.277	162
4.278	142
4.280	130
4.287	188
8.46–49	267, 268
13.56	156
13.297–98	283
15.259	37
16.1	217
16.405–30	268
18.109–19	28

Index of Greco-Roman Writings

Index of Rabbinic Works

~

TOSEFTA

~

BABYLONIAN TALMUD

~

JERUSALEM TALMUD

~